D1453451

FANNY DUNBAR CORBUSIER

FANNY DUNBAR CORBUSIER

Recollections of Her Army Life, 1869–1908

Edited by PATRICIA Y. STALLARD

UNIVERSITY OF OKLAHOMA PRESS • NORMAN

ALSO BY PATRICIA Y. STALLARD

Glittering Misery: Dependents of the Indian Fighting Army (San Rafael, Calif., 1978; Norman, 1992)

This book is published with the generous assistance of The McCasland Foundation, Duncan, Oklahoma.

Library of Congress Cataloging-in-Publication Data

Corbusier, Fanny Dunbar, 1838–1918.
   Fanny Dunbar Corbusier : recollections of her Army life, 1869–1908 / edited by Patricia Y. Stallard.
      p.   cm.
   Includes bibliographical references and index.
   ISBN 0-8061-3531-X (hc : alk. paper)
   1. Corbusier, Fanny Dunbar, 1838–1918.   2. Corbusier, William Henry, 1844–1930.   3. Women pioneers—West (U.S.)—Biography.   4. Officers' spouses—West (U.S.)—Biography.   5. Pioneers—West (U.S.)—Biography.   6. Frontier and pioneer life—West (U.S.)   7. United States. Army—Military life—History—19th century.   8. West (U.S.)—Social life and customs—19th century.   9. West (U.S.)—Description and travel.   10. Southern States—Description and travel.   11. West (U.S.)—Biography.   I. Stallard, Patricia Y.   II. Title.

F594.C94 2003
355.1'2'092—dc21
[B]

2003044752

CONTENTS

ILLUSTRATIONS

MAP

PHOTOGRAPHS

Unless otherwise noted, photographs are courtesy of the Corbusier Family Collection.

THE CORBUSIERS' CONTINENTAL UNITED STATES

INTRODUCTION

Fanny Dunbar Corbusier never intended her "Recollections" for the world at large. In her humility, she thought that her memories of army life might be "of more than ordinary interest" only to members of her family. Her writings were intended for her private sphere, wherein her descendants might learn more of their parents' and grandparents' lives with the U.S. Army. Yet she succeeded in describing far more than a personal life. Born in Baltimore in 1838 at the beginning of the railroad era, she crossed the continent many times, and her "Recollections" depict a period of intense development in the United States, which was growing into both a continental and world power.

When Fanny Dunbar married the young Yankee contract surgeon William Henry Corbusier, little did she realize that their future would be played out against a world panorama—that she would accompany him from the burning deserts of Arizona, Nevada, and New Mexico to the tropical jungles of the Philippines as the U.S. Army attempted to control Native peoples at home and abroad. She had begun her travels as a six-week-old infant when her mother, Caroline Robinson Dunbar, sailed with her from Baltimore to the cosmopolitan city of New Orleans, where her father had finally settled after following the nascent railroad industry from Maryland southward. Young Fanny was educated at home and then at female academies until her father's death and the loss of most of his estate. In 1855, Mrs. Dunbar took Fanny and her three siblings, May, George, and Henry, back to Baltimore, where Fanny grew to young womanhood among an extended family that was prominent in local society. With war clouds looming in 1860, her mother chose to return to Louisiana with her children to salvage the remnant of her husband's property there.

Only sketchily did Fanny Corbusier describe her family's experiences during the Civil War. After briefly operating a hospital at their home in Amite, Louisiana, Mrs. Dunbar and her two daughters joined family members in Mobile, Alabama, for the remainder of the war. During federal occupation after the war, Fanny Dunbar met the contract surgeon with the U.S. First Infantry who became her husband after a year's courtship. Although there is no record of her family's reaction to her betrothal to a Yankee, relatives in Baltimore did receive them during their wedding trip, and so it can be assumed that the family was given to reconciliation.

Fanny's marriage, at age thirty, was considerably later than average for Southern women of her class—a delay that may be partially explained by the societal dislocations of the war. Another factor may be that in her upbringing, Fanny was somewhat different from other members of her class. Her ideals were influenced by the Northern values that her father had cultivated during his lifetime. Although landed, her family possessed few slaves and these were freed prior to the war, and she and her sister were reared not on the plantation but in the cities of New Orleans and Baltimore. Her choice of a member of an occupying army as spouse could not have been popular locally but can be explained by the obvious lack of other available suitors. Her mother's unexpected death on the eve of her wedding freed her from filial responsibility and allowed her to join the doctor in his move to the Pacific Coast.

Dr. William Henry Corbusier descended from some of the first Dutch settlers in New York and from early colonists in Bermuda. His father, William Morrison Corbusier, had joined other Argonauts in California in 1849, leaving his young son and wife behind in New York. At the time of his marriage to Fanny in 1869, Dr. Corbusier had journeyed across the country to California at least three times. In him Fanny found a companion with a kindred spirit. He enjoyed traveling and observing natural phenomena with the same enthusiasm she expressed. Their marriage evolved from companionate to patriarchal after the children were born, and back to companionate during their later years.

More than any other paradigm explaining the behavior of nineteenth-century women, the Cult of True Womanhood as articulated by Barbara Welter best explains Mrs. Corbusier's experiences as a wife and mother. A true woman possessed four cardinal virtues: piety, purity, domesticity, and submissiveness.[1] Throughout her life, Mrs. Corbusier was known for her upright character, her kindness, her devotion to church, family, and home, and her loyalty to her husband. During her forty-nine-year marriage, she most often deferred to her husband's wishes, opposing him only when her great concern for the health and happiness of their children caused her to choose another course. As an officer's wife, she could not wholly separate her private domestic sphere from her institutional environment, but she performed her official duties with as much grace and style as frontier conditions allowed.

After the Civil War, Mrs. Corbusier remained loyal, at least in spirit, to the Southern cause, but because she was always on guard against offending her husband's associates and superiors, she focused her "Recollections" on her family rather than on political issues. Realizing that the "bloody shirt" could be waved on the domestic scene as well as in the political arena, she quietly excused herself from the room and conversation when the topic turned to the Civil War. Although her feelings were hurt when Southern women refused to associate with her and other army spouses when the Corbusiers were stationed in the South, she submerged her divided loyalties under a pleasant façade.

Several years older than her peers among army officers' wives and more experienced in domestic economy, Mrs. Corbusier enthusiastically entered army society. At their first duty station, Camp McDermit, Nevada, she found herself at a remote post, living a life of straited circumstances much like those she had left behind in the South. And since she had been reared in a society characterized by both class and caste, she joined the hierarchal organization that was the Old Army with relative ease.[2] As the wife of an army doctor, she gained a position of prestige and personal responsibility in the military community. From her writings, one can discern that she readily accepted her dual roles as a doctor's spouse and an officer's wife. She and her husband found their closest friends among the most conservative members of the army community, who carefully observed the distance between officers and all other members of the garrison.

From her "Recollections," it is clear that Mrs. Corbusier expected to be in charge of her domestic sphere but not to be burdened by the most taxing household chores. She required a servant for the cooking and laundry and a nurse for the birth and care of an infant. She employed soldier-strikers, Indian and Chinese servants, and even an Indian wet nurse for her first child—an unheard of thing back home. These circumstances were imposed by frontier life, but they also demonstrate the Corbusiers' willingness to find novel solutions to age-old problems.

With an innate curiosity and experience as a teacher, Mrs. Corbusier joined her husband in his ethnological pursuits and took much comfort and joy in the natural world. Her world was filled with physical wonders, from ball lightning to moonbows. Always teaching her sons by word and deed, she sought to give them the broadest Christian education she and her husband could provide and often ignored her personal needs in order to be of service to others. When her second son was born, she also nursed the child of a company laundress who assisted her in her recovery from childbirth. And as she lay dying, her thoughts were in France with her three sons who were serving in World War I.

Since her husband often moved between eastern and western assignments, the reader of the "Recollections" can discern the differences among various army posts and the improvements in transportation with each change of duty station. When located in the East, Mrs. Corbusier explored the surroundings and participated more fully in society than she could in the West, but only Forts Wayne and Monroe offered the complete social experience that both Corbusiers craved.

As her children grew up, Mrs. Corbusier's focus changed from the daily demands of a life at a remote location to concerns about the family's distance from good schools and polite society where her sons could reach social maturity. The educational needs of her children forced her to choose between their welfare and that of her husband, who was ordered to Fort Supply in Indian Territory in 1893. Whatever she wrote in her "Recollections," she revealed her true feelings in her diary during the next seven years, when she spent a considerable amount of time apart from her husband and in charge of five spirited sons. Without her husband's presence she proved less self-confident and more prone to negative feelings and minor illnesses. Maintaining a separate household in civilian society strained the family budget and added to her stress and unhappiness. It is significant that she stopped keeping a diary when they were reunited in 1900.

Though in declining health from 1908 to 1918, Mrs. Corbusier enjoyed the companionship of her husband as they traveled at home and abroad, doing genealogical research and visiting their children and eight grandchildren. Throughout the last ten years, she and her husband searched out their combined family history. She died on February 8, 1918, and was buried in Arlington National Cemetery.

Fanny Dunbar Corbusier's "Recollections" are an important contribution to the fields of western military history as well as to women's and family history. They also add to the emerging field of gender studies since they demonstrate that both Dr. and Mrs. Corbusier functioned in areas defined not by sex but by necessity. Her husband's thirty-nine-year career and her long life allow the reader a rare opportunity to experience the period between the Civil War and World War I in totality, including her exceptional memories of the Spanish-American War and the Philippine Insurrection.

Mrs. Corbusier was a product of her times and as such merits being judged by the standards of her day. Her ideals compare favorably with the tenets of "true womanhood." Reared in the South, she lived most of her life in a patriarchy, and as a military wife she subordinated her individual needs to those of her spouse and of the U.S. Army. Her life as an army officer's wife, constrained by the military hierarchy, kept her from occupying Nancy Cott's "separate sphere," since her home life could never be separate from her husband's world of work.[3] Despite these constraints, she wore her husband's rank as a cloak, not as a straightjacket.

Dr. Corbusier's status as a military officer and surgeon gave them both entrée into the highest levels of civil and military society, as her attempts in gaining an audience with President William McKinley aptly demonstrate. She realized that although merit had its place, sometimes political influence counted more. In her effort to use the military system to secure an officer's billet for her son, she moved into both the political arena and into her husband's sphere of influence, thereby violating the Cult of True Womanhood. By refusing to submit to the dictates of "good military order" in seeking an officer's commission for Philip, she followed a higher code: Do whatever is necessary for the good of your children.

I have examined Mrs. Corbusier's life and experiences relative to those of her peers among other officers' wives. For the most part, Mrs. Corbusier compares favorably with her counterparts in her adaptation to the military environment. During the early years, her writing emphasized the novel aspects of their duty stations and described in great detail her inventiveness and creativity in establishing the proper officer's home. Surmounting hardships became an everyday accomplishment.

Later, as her family grew and her children's individual needs became manifest, she became more absorbed in shaping their lives and preparing them to be good citizens. Four out of her five sons volunteered for military service, and two came back from war with injuries, resulting in the death of one and a life of delayed achievement for the other.

Regardless of the sacrifices Mrs. Corbusier and her family made during their years of service to our country, one comes away from reading her "Recollections" with the feeling that she surmounted the heartaches and hardships and achieved her goals of providing an appropriate and nurturing home for her husband and sons. Everywhere they were stationed, they planted flowers and trees, adding to the natural beauty of each place. More than "true women," she and the other women associated with the Old Army improved their military world just by being there.

EDITORIAL NOTE

Mrs. Corbusier wrote her "Recollections" after her husband's retirement in 1908, and he had them typed for the first time in 1914. From then until her death in 1918 she amended them, and Dr. Corbusier retyped them in 1918. He gave copies, along with his own memoirs, to each of their five sons. Throughout the years between his death in 1930 and William T. Corbusier's use of them in his *Verde to San Carlos* in 1968, both memoirs remained in the family's hands. From that time until the present, copies of both have made their way to various depositories throughout the country. Only Mrs. Corbusier's diary from 1892 to 1900 still exists in its original form, and it is in the custody of a granddaughter, Nancy Corbusier Knox. Many other family papers perished in the great San Francisco earthquake and fire of April 1906. Other personal information has been obtained from descendants of both the Corbusier and Myers families and from genealogical research on the Internet.

In editing the present work, I have tried to keep faith with both history and Mrs. Corbusier by intruding upon the text as little as possible, saving most corrections and amendatory materials for the footnotes. Minor changes were made to the text, such as shortening paragraphs, updating punctuation, and rearranging some misplaced clauses and modifiers. Chapter titles come from within the text and give the reader a sense of their contents. Subtitles with location and date help keep the reader oriented in time and place.

Mrs. Corbusier's use of the passive voice and her flowing style remain intact, contrary to the dictates of today's more direct and concise constructions. She wrote well and painted word pictures that will remain with the reader long after her final page is read.

In editing the work, I used ellipses to indicate that either a word has been deleted or a paragraph has been shortened. Mrs. Corbusier's capitalization and hyphenation have for the most part been retained. So has her spelling, which is characterized by her use of British spelling in the word *centre* and the French in *syndic*. Her obvious misspellings have been noted initially in brackets and thereafter silently corrected. On those occasions in the text when Mrs. Corbusier was not able to remember a name or recall a specific fact, she indicated that lapse with either a blank or brackets. Wherever I could provide the appropriate information, the correct information has been given inside brackets. She also was not consistent in her use of numbers, and I have left them as they occurred in the text, either spelled out or written in Arabic form. Names and ranks of military officers have been spelled out in the text as an aid to those descendants who will search for mention of their ancestors in Mrs. Corbusier's "Recollections."

ACKNOWLEDGMENTS

Thirty-one years ago when I began reading about army dependents on the frontier, little did I know that the pursuit of their history would inform the rest of my life. In researching them, I learned more about my family and myself, and I soon realized that their stories deserved to be told to the world at large. Fanny Dunbar Corbusier and her family, whom I discovered a few years ago, have now joined that parade of military personages who have marched through my life, forming part of the pageantry we call American history. She and her family have spent over a century in the service of our country, and in these trying days, their experiences may provide some insights into our present dilemma.

As with any work of history, this project required that I depend on the kindness of friends and a few strangers who soon became cheerful providers of family history and obscure historical facts. In the list of usual suspects are my colleagues in the field of western military history, some of whom have been friends from the beginning. Elaine Everly, late of the National Archives, and Mary Williams of the Fort Davis National Historic

Site, performed their usual magic, bringing sources and information to my attention. Douglas McChristian, Bruce Dinges, and Gordon Chappell answered questions in their areas of expertise with alacrity and finesse. Darlis Miller and Bill and Shirley Leckie, through their many scholarly contributions, have become preeminent in the field of western military history as well as boon companions and dear friends.

My mother and my sister-in-law, Florence and Sherry Yeary, accompanied me on a trip through Arizona and New Mexico that rivaled the Corbusiers' sojourn in 1884. Dr. Wayne Kime, editor of Richard Irving Dodge's *Journals*, answered my questions about one of Dodge's itineraries through that same territory. Willa Reister and Kevin Mallory of the Knox County, Tennessee, Public Library Interlibrary Loan Department responded to all my requests with alacrity and obvious enthusiasm. Sue Ginter Watson, director of the University of Wisconsin–River Falls Area Research Center and University Archives, and her two eager young assistants, Cate Dodson and Daniel Wendorf, provided an excellent environment in which to explore the lives of William B. Cairns and his siblings. Janette Prescod, reference and government document librarian of the John C. Hodges Library at the University of Tennessee, helped me locate government documents useful in my research. Sheila Edmunds, Village of Aurora historian, scoured local sources for information about Cayuga Lake Military Academy.

Since this is a work of family history, I employed some of the resources and techniques involved in genealogical research and utilized the Internet to gather information that was otherwise unavailable to me. Family, friends, and new colleagues volunteered: Arlene M. Goff, Linda Foflygen, Carol Willis, Bill Smith, Ginger Scott-Johnson, Minna Sellers, Phil Porter, Mary Godwin, Jyl Pannell Walker, and Gwendolyn Yeary-Brooks responded to my e-mail pleas for assistance and found answers in the ether. Nancy Corbusier Knox welcomed me into her home and shared her grandmother's life with me, as did her cousin Dorothy Pierson Kerig, who located a picture of Mahala Myers Corbusier, Dr. Corbusier's mother. Judy Baber, my counterpart from Navy Recruiting District Richmond, braved February weather and found Dr. and Mrs. Corbusier's gravesites at Arlington.

Ann Woodward, Eleanor Thomsen, and Nancy Gammon, friends since graduate school, accompanied me on research trips, tempered my enthusiasms, told me when I was wrong, and provided aid and comfort throughout these years. Diana Clark Estes, the "Vampire Lady" of 1830

White Avenue and mother of two of the eight most wonderful godchildren in the world, has been a steadfast friend through all the navy years. Donna and Brian Dippie have been co-conspirators since Minneapolis 1984 and were there to bail me out in case I was arrested by the Secret Service. In addition to Mary and Jerry Lambert, my brother Dennis and sister-in-law Emma Yeary helped me when, as Mrs. Corbusier described it, the "years of anxiety broke me down." The three Willard Lee Stallards, as well as the three Claude Swanson Yearys, have left greater imprints on my life than they will ever know, and so have all the Rainwaters—Pam and her progeny—who also provide me with food for body and soul.

Additionally, there are five others I must thank for their contributions to western military history and to me personally: Michael Harrison, fellow Civil Service retiree and love, the late Sara D. Jackson, Don Rickey Jr., Dan L. Thrapp, and Constance Wynn Altshuler. Sara and Don I never thanked enough, and I was never able to tell Dan or Constance how much I appreciate their excellent Arizona reference books, which saved me from many mistakes in the current work.

Every book needs an editor, and this one has been blessed with two: Jean Hurtado, my editor at the University of Oklahoma Press, and Patricia L. Heinicke Jr. of WordShine. For their advice and careful copyediting I owe them both an enduring debt of gratitude. All these, but most especially Meleta and Mary Amanda Jane Stallard, navy wife and navy daughter, "lift me up on eagle wings."

Patricia Stallard

Knoxville, Tennessee

FANNY DUNBAR CORBUSIER

Recollections of Her Army Life, 1869–1908

CHAPTER ONE

"Of More than Ordinary Interest"

THE EARLY LIFE OF FANNY DUNBAR, MARYLAND, LOUISIANA, MISSISSIPPI, AND ALABAMA, 1838–1869

O N RELATING TO OUR CHILDREN incidents in my past life, they have so often requested me to write all that I can remember that I have undertaken to comply with their wishes. For many years after my marriage I kept a diary, the first part of which was destroyed in the great fire of San Francisco, April 18, 1906.[1] It recorded the occurrences and happenings that made up our daily life and the events of more than ordinary interest, the sayings and doings of our children, and their height and weight, which were taken and recorded every month. All of these cannot be remembered, but perhaps with Father's assistance and a few old letters I may be able to recall enough to give such a sketch of our life at that time as will interest them and their children.[2] I began a second book in 1892 and kept it until after Father returned from the Philippines in 1900. It is not so full as the first one was, but it brings those years vividly before me.

I was born on May 15, 1838, at the home of my grandfather, Joseph Robinson, in Waterloo Row, now 622 Calvert Street, Baltimore, Maryland.[3] Going on the sailing vessel *Alabama*, which was becalmed and took six weeks to make the voyage, my mother joined my father in New

Orleans, where he was Engineer of the Board of Public Works of the state of Louisiana when I was six weeks old.[4] At one time the mosquitoes were so numerous that an American flag was thrown over my crib to protect me from their bites. One day a sailor climbed with me nearly to the top of one of the masts, to the terror of my Irish nurse.

My father met us in New Orleans and took us to the farm of Mr. Bankston in the "Piney Woods," where we passed the summer. We lived in New Orleans in winter and usually spent summers across the lake on Lake Pontchartrain and Madisonville, Bay of St. Louis, or Biloxi, Mississippi. Mother, my sister May, who was born June 25, 1840, and I spent the winter of 1842–43 in Baltimore with my grandfather Robinson.[5]

My father was a lover of nature, and his friends and his associates were such men as Audubon. [A]nd when still a lad he made a large collection of insects, birds, and plants of the southern states, and for many years [he] gathered material for a work on Ichthyology, which he did not live to complete. I often sat by him as he caught a fish and watched him note in his field book its colors and other characteristics.

My mother too was a lover of nature, and from both parents I inherited the same love so that I was able to content myself even when at the most isolated frontier posts. I loved flowers and they loved me, responding to my care of them. When we were pretty well grown my mother used to call May and me at night to see some beautiful constellation of stars that she admired, and we would recall the mythology connected with them.

I was educated at home until I was nine years of age and then entered Madame Van Huten's school on Camp Street, New Orleans, where I remained a few months until Miss Sarah Hull, who was the teacher of English there, opened a school of her own on Carondolet Street, opposite Lafayette Square, which I entered and attended until I was seventeen years old. . . .

My father . . . died December 29, 1850, on the steamer *Alabama* at the mouth of the Coatzacoalcos River where he had arrived December 25, one of the engineers of a scientific commission under the direction of Major J. G. Barnard, U.S. Engineer Corps, [employed] to make a survey for a railroad across the Isthmus of Tehuantepec.[6] My mother [thereafter] lost the greater part of his large property through the sharp practices of the Syndic appointed to settle his estate.

Of the two slaves that he bought because they had been badly treated, Mingo was his body servant and was with him in Nicaragua [Mexico] when he died and brought back to New Orleans all of his personal effects. After that he was given his freedom, and Mary, the cook, was also set free by my mother. Dunbar, a town in Pennsylvania on the Baltimore and Ohio Railroad, was named after my father.[7] My mother had to sell her house on Common Street where Hotel-Dieu Hospital now is and buy a smaller house. This was on Magazine Street, where she opened a school for young ladies, which she conducted four years and then in 1855 went to Baltimore.

In a short time she was appointed Principal of the Hannah More Academy, Reisterstown, Baltimore County, Maryland, of which she had charge for five years, and here I finished my school education. The John Tolley Worthington homestead, Montmorenci, was near by and we often spent two weeks at a time with our relatives there.[8] They often drove us to the City in their carriage, or we would go in a stagecoach. In winter there was fine sleighing, and many were the dancing parties that we attended at their home and elsewhere.

We went to New Orleans in 1860 and on the outbreak of the Civil War went to Amite, Louisiana, in 1861. [H]ere my mother owned some land and . . . bought ten acres more, together with a dwelling, separate school rooms, servants' cabins, stables, etc., which had formerly been a school and situated about half-a-mile from the railroad station. She named the place "Dunbarton" and opened a boarding school for young ladies, which on account of the unsettled state of the country she closed in the fall of 1862 to return at the close of the war and reopen and carry on to the time of her decease. I taught some of the English branches, and May, an accomplished pianist, taught music.

On the breaking out of the war, we converted our home into a hospital and with the help of our servants nursed and fed sick and wounded Confederate soldiers. The few luxuries we could procure were given to our patients. Old Aunt Millie, one of our servants, carded the colored border of blankets, which she taught us to spin into yarn and knit into socks for our soldiers. We also spun and knit cotton, and we embroidered with the raveled wool of various colors. We made our blankets and ingrain carpets into overcoats for the soldiers and knit socks for them. For admission to fairs, musicals, and such entertainments, the charge was a pair of socks.

Oil for illuminating purposes was not to be had, and at length we could no longer procure candles. We then burned pine knots in the fireplaces to light our house, keeping one piece of candle in case the Yankees came at night. When they did come, however, it was in the daytime, and when they stopped at our gate the colored guide told them that only a widow and her two daughters lived on the place, so they passed on. But one night we heard a great noise at the gate and the hooting of men, which alarmed us until we learned that they came from some Jews who had been hiding in the woods from the conscripting officers, whom we informed where to find them.

It was not long before we gave out of everything except the very necessities of life. We usually had chickens, eggs, milk, and butter for our men and ourselves, but later these were scarce and there were some days when we only had corn bread and coffee made of sweet potatoes cut into small pieces, dried, parched, and ground. We carded and spun cotton; often raveling the silk in our old gowns to mix with it to get some color and then sent it to a weaver. We bleached and braided palmetto to make into hats and made the uppers of our shoes of homespun material to have soles put on by a shoemaker.[9] After General Butler came to New Orleans, we were able to get tea and a few other articles through the lines for our sick and wounded.[10]

In the fall of 1862 our relatives in Mobile, Alabama, having heard a rumor that the Federal troops were to make a raid in Louisiana, advised us to come to them. We accordingly left our home and drove across the country in a carriage, stopping at night at houses, which we were not always permitted to enter, but granted the favor of sleeping on the gallery. Sometimes we were suspected as spies both by the Federals and the Confederates who were in the country that we traversed. We were in Mobile in August 1864 when Admiral D. G. Farragut entered the bay, and when General E. R. S. Canby's troops marched into the city, we saw them through closed blinds. We witnessed the bombardment of the forts from the roof of the house.[11] One day shortly after August 20, one of my small nieces said to me, "Aunt Fan, I smell a Yankee," and there under one of our windows sat a soldier eating cheese and crackers. How we did long for some too, but we soon had cheese and other necessary food as well as some luxuries.

My brother, George Towers Dunbar, or as we called him, "Buck," born August 22, 1845, served in Fenner's Louisiana Battery of Light Artillery of Hood's Division and was severely wounded through both thighs on May 28, 1864, at New Hope Church, seventeen miles from Atlanta, Georgia, and infected bandages caused [him to develop] hospital gangrene.[12] My mother went to the hospital to nurse him and remained for weeks. Afterward he could do light duty but never became quite strong again.

We returned to Amite in 1865 and here remained until I was married. My mother, May, and I were largely instrumental in the building and maintenance of an Episcopal church. We contributed money and made fancy work to sell, and it was at a supper we had to raise money for the church that I first met Father. Those precious quiet days, passed at home with my darling mother and sweet sister May, far from the gay world, were full of real pleasures with our books, music, and flowers, and rich in our love for one another. They now seem like fair pearls in the setting of the picture of my life, and the sweet memories of them are left to me.

Father and I were engaged to be married September 19, 1868, while he was Surgeon with the Company of First Infantry, stationed at Amite, Louisiana, of which Brevet Major Robert H. Offley was Captain; the First Lieutenant Charles D. Viele for a time, and Allen Smith later; and the Second Lieutenant, John J. O'Connell.[13] Afterward he [Dr. Corbusier] went to New York, intending to go before the Army Medical Board as a candidate for a commission, but the Board had dissolved, so he decided to go to California.

He returned to Amite for our wedding and found my darling mother very low with pneumonia, by which disease she was taken away from us, March 21, 1869, at the age of fifty-eight years, lacking two days. My uncle Charles Miltenburger came up from New Orleans and advised that the wedding take place before my mother's funeral, so Father and I, and my sister May and Henry Sands Addison, [born September 5, 1838 in Louisville, Kentucky] who had served in Fenner's Battery of Light Artillery throughout the Civil War, were married on March 22, in my home Dunbarton, Amite, Louisiana, while our dear mother lay in her coffin in an adjoining room. The ceremony was solemnized by the Reverend John Francis Girault of Saint Peter's Church, New Orleans, who also officiated at my mother's funeral.

Father and I remained a week longer so as to settle my mother's estate. May and Henry remained at our home until he died in 1891, and after that she sold it.

Father has described me as follows: height 62 5/16 inches; weight, 106 pounds; fair complexion, brown hair, blue eyes with a very little brown near the pupil, slightly crooked nose, moderately thin lips, and broad chin.[14]

CHAPTER TWO

ᘒᘓᘔᘕ

"His Pay Was $125.00 a Month and a Ration"

EN ROUTE TO FORT McDERMIT, NEVADA, APRIL–DECEMBER 1869

F ATHER AND I VISITED HIS MOTHER in New York for about ten days and then on April 21, 1869, we sailed for San Francisco, California, at noon from the foot of Canal Street, North River, on the Pacific mail steamer, *Henry Chauncey*, Captain Conner, which carried 800 passengers. Our fare was $225.00 each and we were each allowed one hundred pounds of baggage.[1]

I was seasick most of the time and could eat crackers only. As soon as we set foot on the dock at Aspinwall (now Colon), I felt fine and was ready to eat anything set before me, but the beautiful beach and a lovely little church built of coral rock claimed my attention first. I had dreamed of just such a beautiful sight. We were buying some fruit at a stand on the street when a monkey jumped from his perch on to my shoulder. I screamed of course, and was a source of amusement to everyone standing around, and to the natives in particular. We crossed the Isthmus by rail to Panama, where we visited the cathedral, which the natives entered on their knees. The train that carried us was so slow that the natives ran along side, picking beautiful scarlet hibiscus and other flowers, which they handed in to us. Much of the track was thickly covered with the sensitive plant, and for the first time I saw a vanilla vine with beans on it. We were taken out to our steamer, the *Constitution*, Captain Hudson, on a small one, as the water in the harbor was very shallow close to shore.

There were some very pleasant people among the passengers with whom we became well acquainted before we arrived in San Francisco. Among them [were] Bishop Benjamin Wistar Morris of Oregon, his wife and four children, accompanied by his sister, Miss Mary Morris and the Misses Mary and Clementina Rodney, sisters of Mrs. Morris, who were going to Portland, Oregon, to establish a girls' school. . . .[2] Since then we have met women in many parts of the country who were educated by them. Lieutenant Colonel Charles. H. Tompkins, Quartermaster, United States Army, wife and children, were on their way to take station at Sitka, Alaska.[3] Mrs. Arthur Sloat, wife of a Presbyterian minister who turned out to be a granduncle of Father's in San Francisco, [was] going to join her husband there; [also on board were] Mrs. A. Shedd, from Connecticut; Miss Columbia Whitney from Maine; Mr. C. E. Batchelder, Mr. Ben. Truman, and with us as far as Panama were Mrs. and General Judson Kilpatrick, United States Minister to Chile, on their way to that country.[4]

One day on the Pacific, while I was sitting on deck, I heard one of the second class passengers ask another one, "Where is that lady that used to eat crackers all the time?"

After passing Cape St. Lucas we saw thousands of what looked like blue butterflies, fluttering over the water, but they were the tiny nautilus floating on the water. Whales spouted and porpoises sported, and the sailors caught a beautiful dolphin. We stopped at Acapulco, Mexico, and Father went ashore. The harbor is so enclosed by high mountains that as we lay at anchor we could scarcely tell where we came in. There is a very old church here, chimes of a very old date, and a very old bridge; Father was there once on Palm Sunday, heard the chimes, and saw a procession with waving palm branches enter the church. We bought delicious pineapples, avocados (alligator pears), limes and other fruits, seashells, and coral from the natives, who crowded about the ship in canoes and small boats.

The sea was very calm all the way to San Francisco [and] the nights were gorgeous with stars, but the Southern Cross, which we saw last after we left Panama, was not so brilliant as we supposed it would be. For the first time I saw the sun drop into the ocean and witnessed the wonderful afterglow which lighted the western sky with stripes of red and white, and one evening while the stripes were still visible, stars appeared in the east, making a wonderful representation of our flag. After a very interesting honeymoon voyage of about twenty-three days, we arrived in San Francisco at 10 A.M., May 14, fourteen days and twelve hours from Panama.

A doctor in San Francisco, whom Father had known some years before, had made him what seemed to be a very flattering offer, but the doctor had only a small practice and a little drug store poorly supplied with drugs, for which he was in debt. [So] Father accepted an offer from Colonel Charles McCormick, Medical Director, Department of California, to go to Camp McDermit, Nevada, as Acting Assistant Surgeon, United States Army. His pay was $125.00 per month and a ration.[5] We kept house while in San Francisco and meats, fish, vegetables and fruits were much lower in prices than they are now. . . . [With no hope of] picking up a good practice, we were glad to get away after a stay of about two months.

The Union Pacific Railroad had been finished only a short time before, and we witnessed the celebration of its completion in San Francisco on the Fourth of July, when there was a grand display of fireworks about where the City Hall now stands, on some sand hills, which were pretty well covered with brush.[6]

We left San Francisco on the afternoon of July 22, and reached Sacramento before daylight the next morning, where Father's father came to see us July 23, and at 6 A.M. [we] took the train on the Union Pacific Railroad for Winnemucca, reaching there at 1:45 A.M. of the 24th.[7]

The sail up the Sacramento River was delightful. The beautiful rounded hills were covered with thousands of cattle. There were no fences, and they roamed where they wished. The grass was brown, as it always is at this time of the year in California; still it does not spoil the beauty of the hills.[8] It was very different soon after we took the train, and the country became more rugged. During the day while we were crossing the Sierra Nevada Mountains, the scenery was grand, [and] many of the peaks were capped with snow. Towards night we reached the desert, and the alkali dust rolled in and filled the cars the rest of the way to Winnemucca. In California there was nothing green except the live oak trees. The mountains were covered with pines, but we did not see a tree after we left the mountains and very little grass.

— 11 —

Winnemucca, 325 miles from San Francisco, was only a small collection of houses in the desert, through which runs the Humboldt River. Here we found an ambulance waiting for us and our trunks, and we started on our drive of eighty miles at 3 A.M. For about twelve miles the road was quite sandy, but beyond this [it] was gravelly and good. We drove until late in the afternoon and then stopped at a home station for the stage line, which was the only house on the road for a long distance. It had two rooms, one of which was occupied by the hostler and the other as a stable for the two stage horses. . . . The cook fried us some bacon, made baking powder biscuits and coffee. He served them on a table made of rough boards without any tablecloth, and the dishes were of tin. Flies were in myriads and made eating very difficult.

We made our bed in the ambulance with the cushions and a tick filled with hay. I was not long in going to sleep, in spite of the high wind which was blowing, but was soon awakened by what seemed to me a fearful yell, and as the Indians had only recently been out, I supposed it might be their war cry. But Father reassured me at once by telling me it was only a coyote; however, I was afraid to stay in the ambulance any longer, so we went into the house and slept as well as we could on our blankets and a bed tick on the floor, the hostler going into the stable.

We were up at three the next morning and made a very early start so as to escape the hot sun and reached McDermit about noon. Our road led through high sagebrush over a rolling country on the west side of the Santa Rosa Mountains. About every fifteen miles or so there was a very small house on a small creek which was fed by the melting snow in the mountains and along which small willows grew. One creek that we crossed would run for about twenty minutes and then stop to run again after awhile. . . .

We reached Camp McDermit on Saturday, July 25th, and First Lieutenant James M. Ropes, who was the only officer at the post, and wife welcomed us. Brevet Lieutenant Colonel James N. McElroy, the captain of Troop M, Eighth Cavalry, which numbered about thirty-five men and garrisoned the post, was absent on leave. Father relieved Dr. George Gwyther as Post Surgeon and the latter left the next day.[9] The post was located in the northern part of Humboldt County not far from the southern boundary of Oregon, at the foot of the Santa Rosa Mountains, about 4,700 feet above the sea level, near the mouth of a canyon, through which descended a clear stream known as the east branch of Quinn River. It was built around a parade ground 660 feet by 225 feet. There were three sets of officers' quarters on the north side, one of adobe (sun dried bricks) and two of stone, and two sets of stone quarters for the men on the south side near the creek.

In the middle of the parade ground was a very crooked flagstaff made of three small willow trees spliced and bound together with iron hoops. An officer, visiting at the post, while going to the sutler store asked what ailed the men who erected it, and on returning from the store looking up again, said, "Oh. I see." Old Glory floated serenely from it when the wind did not blow too hard but was often whipped about by the high winds, and many a time I mended his tatters. There were a few dried up bunches of grass on the parade ground, but nothing green to relieve the eye.

We were assigned to quarters in a house having six rooms, four of which were of adobe and two at back of rough boards. The two front rooms were plastered with mud and whitewashed. The ceiling was of boards having cracks between them, through which the dust sifted during the high winds which frequently blew. The plaster was most artistically cracked, and to keep it in place, Father fastened it up with roller bandages, which was only a broader style of decoration. One of these rooms had a large fireplace in which we burned mountain mahogany that cost fifty dollars a cord in [the] winter of 1869, but other years we burned willow that usually cost thirty-five dollars a cord. Father's allowance of hard wood was three and a half cords a month. The adobes of the other two rooms were simply whitewashed. Lieutenant and Mrs. Ropes occupied one side of the house and we messed together, having the dining room and kitchen in common.

We at first had a Chinaman to cook for us who had been a miner, and we had to pay him forty dollars a month [in] gold at the time when our greenbacks were worth only ninety cents. [B]ut we soon found that he did not know how to cook, so we discharged him.[10] Then Mrs. Ropes and I tried to do the cooking, but as she did not know when water was boiling, I had most of the work to do. She did not like to wash the dishes and neither did I, so we trained a Piute Indian boy, whom we named Tom, to do that work for us. We soon found a soldier who was willing to cook for us, and he did so well that after his discharge he opened a restaurant in Santa Fe, New Mexico, and made considerable money. Later I trained one soldier after another and sometimes had one who learned to cook very well. One had been a commissioned officer and had been dismissed from the service.

We employed Indians to bring water from the creek to fill the water barrels in the kitchen, to chop wood, fetch commissaries, scrub floors, etc. The water from the river was very good until all the snow in the mountains melted, and then the river became low and filled with vegetable matter. Casks were then sunk near the river for the water to filter through the gravel into them. There was a heavy growth of willow along the creek above the post, but very few of the trees were as large as eight inches in diameter.

There were some 150 Piute Indians under Chief Winnemucca, who had given the troops a great deal of trouble and were now held here just below the post and fed by the Government.[11] It was from this band that we procured our Indian servants. One boy we had learned to make a fire in the stove, roast coffee, turn the griddle cakes, and keep the stove and cooking utensils clean. He also washed out the towels and scrubbed tables and floors, doing every task very well, until one day I was sick and had to remain in bed, when he left. Father asked Sarah Winnemucca, our interpretress, to learn why he had left.[12] Tom sent word back that he didn't know how to keep house and neither did Father. He would wait until I was well and then would return. Sure enough, the day I was out of my room, Tom peeped into the window and then came in.

He used to amuse himself by putting the kitchen door a little ajar, throw[ing] some grain out, and then stand[ing] with bow and arrow of his own make in his hand to shoot black birds, which he would stick under his belt until he had himself girdled with them, all their heads hanging over his belt. After a time he left me to go out on a hunt, and the Indian who succeeded him told me, as a recommendation of himself, that he was to be trusted, "Me good Injun, me only kill one white squaw. Me no hurt you."

CHAPTER THREE

"Pi-u-je Papoosee"

FORT McDERMIT, NEVADA, JANUARY 1870–DECEMBER 1871

T HE PIUTES SLEPT IN SHELTERS, or wick-ee-ups, made of bushes and branches of trees, stuck in the ground in a circle upon which grass or rabbit skins were thrown.[1] The squaw was the boss in her wick-ee-up, as was told me by a buck, who came one morning without his hat, of which he had been very proud. He said his squaw threw it into the fire and drove him out. He had probably been flirting with another squaw.

They cut rabbit skins into strips, which they fastened together to make wraps for their bodies. When one had anything to sell he would stand near the door perfectly still, with his blanket wrapped about him. If no one spoke to him he would very likely, after a time, walk away; but if asked what he had, he would hold out a string of fish, a bunch of dandelions and garlic, a rabbit, or possibly a basket. The women made no pottery and no beadwork and only one kind of basket. That was cone-shape to be carried on the back, supported by a band passed around the forehead. They gathered various kinds of seeds in it by striking the plants with their hands. They often mashed the seeds by pounding them with stones and made them into balls.[2]

Sarah was a daughter of Chief Winnemucca and paid interpretress of the Government. She rode a fine horse in a sidesaddle, and her habit was a black velvet waist and skirt and a large hat with red plumes.[3] She was our laundress, and she and her Indian women were very industrious. They made buckskin gloves to sell, and trimmed overcoats with furs, etc. She had a little education, which she had acquired in a convent, and occasionally wrote letters in behalf of her people, whose welfare she had at heart. [Her letters] were corrected and revised by an officer or a soldier and then sent to the newspapers to print.[4]

She frequently played a sort of football with the other squaws on the parade.[5] They said she often gambled with the soldiers after payday, but it is doubtful if she won their money. She sometimes drank to excess, poor creature, and caroused with the men. After a time she became troublesome and lost her position as interpretress when she went to Utah and there was married to Edward Bartlett, who had been a lieutenant of cavalry in the army and had been permitted to resign.[6] He had tried to marry her while he was still an officer, but the Roman Catholic priest who was visiting the post at the time declined to marry them, as it was against the Nevada law for a white to marry an Indian.[7]

One night, in the absence of Captain Wagner while young Bartlett was still an officer and temporarily in command of the post, he ordered out all of the men. Ten of them he sent to mount their horses and circle around the hospital and then around the commanding officer's quarters. With the others he brought out a mountain howitzer and, not finding any shot, loaded it with blank cartridges and fired toward the Indian camp upon which he then charged. Natchez, one of the sons of Winnemucca, hearing the noise, came out to meet the men, and Bartlett told him they were looking for hostile Indians. Natchez informed him that there were none there and called out to his people that the soldiers were only drilling. Then a plunge into the river cooled Bartlett off a little and he turned his men back. Father at length enticed him into his quarters and locked him in, as he considered the outburst one of delirium from drink. While the mounted men circled about our quarters firing their revolvers, I sat on the floor in the corner of our bedroom where Father had placed me.[8]

Chief Winnemucca, the father of Sarah, had sons Natchez and Lee. He was a dignified old man and did not approve of all the actions of his daughter. He once said to me, "Truckee Sal no good."[9] This name had been given her when she was on the Truckee Reservation. He used to walk quietly into our quarters when the doors were open and was much entertained with what he saw. I was writing a letter one day when I heard a satisfied grunt behind me, and on looking around I was rather startled to see him looking over my shoulder. He wanted to know what I was doing, and I told him, or rather, showed him, as he could speak only a few English words, that I was writing a letter to my sister, to go far, far away on the train. He wanted to know what I had written and said, "Heap good," when I told him.[10] The Indians used to gather at mealtime about the soldiers' quarters, and he would see them and say, "Heap a hogeedie, heap a Piutee." (Hogeedie means eating or food.)

The post was usually garrisoned by one troop of cavalry, and there were rarely more than two officers with the troop. Camp Winfield Scott, a one-company post, was 35 miles south across the mountains in Paradise Valley. Camp C. F. Smith, which had only a detachment of men and was shortly abandoned, was 50 miles northwest [in Oregon]. Camp Three Forks, Owyhee River, at which there was usually a company of infantry, was 75 miles northeast.[11] A daily stage passed through the Post on its way from Winnemucca to Boise and left us a mail. Letters took from ten to twelve days from New York.

There was a sutler store a little west of the Post, just where the road crossed the creek. Fred Brougham was the sutler, but Charles Bolling ran the store.[12] The latter's wife was with him, and they had a little girl whose dog had just the stump of a tail, which she called his thumb. He made regular trips to the creek to catch fish, of which he was very fond. The fishing in this creek was fine, and one day I caught a splendid trout, weighing three pounds and an ounce, the largest that had been caught up to that time. One day from another creek Father took twenty-five trout in an hour using artificial flies that Grandmother had sent him.[13]

The Post was a lonely, desolate place and so very quiet, as there were very few insects or birds to break the silence. It was a very healthful place, and Father had but little work to do. In the winter very little snow fell, but we often had very high winds. We rarely saw a soldier on the parade ground. The bugler would open the door and blow a call and then disappear until it was time to blow the next one. We would sometimes see the men going to the stables, but rarely at other times. The men had Indians to wait upon them and do nearly all, except their strictly military duty.

There were few desertions from the Eighth Cavalry, but many from the other troops. The life was probably too monotonous a one for the man who enlists in the army.

During the night the sentries on guard would call the hour and "All is well." There were some of them who had fine voices, and the calls sounded musical in the still night. We used to go to the top of the mesa to see the sun set. The afterglow on the mountains when the sun had gone down was beautiful. Then the rocks of the mountains turned purple, and the horizon was all shades of pink and lilac that tinted the snow on the high peaks. We rode horseback a great deal, going up on the mesas and into the mountains. We studied zoology, geology, French, history, etc., and gathered a great variety of beautiful wild flowers which we classified and pressed; so our time was well occupied and we were very happy.

Just before Thanksgiving day we received a box of apples from Sacramento, and on that day, November 21, 1869, we had a fine dinner of chicken pie, baked calves [calf's] head, calf's head soup, rice, potatoes, canned tomatoes and string beans, squash, currant jelly, potato salad, pickles, apple, mince and squash pies, custard with float on it, and fine cheese. We were very successful in raising chickens and had more eggs than we could use, so [we] sent many to the hospital and the laundresses. Mrs. McElroy took dinner with us, and the Colonel would have done so but he had gone after some deserters, which he succeeded in capturing.

Besides chickens, we raised more ducks and pigeons than we could eat. We had splendid beef from the herd which was kept at the Post and fattened on the fine grass in the valley and had cuts from the tenderloin until we were tired of them. Cows were loaned us from the herd, so I made all of our butter and put up some for the winter. The Indians brought us young dandelion greens and wild garlic and onions in the spring. They had a long rod which they ran into the ground alongside of the young dandelion plant and forced it up. It was bleached and looked like endives and made a fine salad. We gathered lamb's quarter that grew in profusion at the corral and bushels of mushrooms, which I broiled, stewed, pickled, and made into catsup. We had prairie hens and plenty of fish, but rarely any except canned fruits and vegetables. Fresh potatoes cost five cents a pound, when we could get them. Once in a great while we were able to buy a little fruit from the freighters that were on the way to Boise City, but it was very dear, a box of one hundred costing eight dollars gold.

There was very little large game in the country, as the Indians had killed most of it. They hunted the numerous jack rabbits by forming a long line, and as it advanced very few escaped them. There were some doves, but one hated to kill them. Prairie and sage chickens, ducks, and blackbirds were plentiful. Coyotes came around nearly every night to feed at the garbage cans and try to steal our chickens. They would often sit on the hills and fill the air with their yelps. There were also some skunks. Father and Colonel McElroy hunted coyotes with two gray hounds and a setter dog, and during the first winter [they] killed fourteen or fifteen, one of them on the parade, when everyone turned out to see the end of the exciting chase.[14]

Second Lieutenant Henry W. Sprole joined [us] in September 1869. The troop left for New Mexico about April 1, 1870, and was relieved by a troop of the Third Cavalry, which was followed by a troop of the First Cavalry under command of Captain Camillo C. C. Carr, who had as a First Lieutenant Alexander Grant.[15] For a while, Second Lieutenant Eugene O. Fechét of the Second Artillery was Quartermaster. Mrs. McElroy was at the Post from the latter part of September 1869 until the latter part of January 1870, and she was a very congenial companion. Her father, Mr. Francis H. Woods, and mother visited her in September and helped to relieve the monotony of the post. I was sorry when they left and more so when she had to go.

For a short time, I think in 1871, after Captain Carr's troop left, two companies of the Twelfth Infantry under Captains May H. Stacey and Erskine A. Camp were at the Post. Second Lieutenant Louis A. Nesmith was with them. Mrs. Stacey, whose first name was also May, was with them, and she entered into our field studies with enthusiasm. I wished that her stay could have been prolonged. She died January 21, 1918. Then came Captain Henry Wagner's troop of the First Cavalry and, for a time, Second Lieutenant Henry A. Reed, Second Artillery, was the Quartermaster. Second Lieutenant Thomas T. Knox joined about September 1871.

At first we had no neighbors, except one man who lived on the road half a mile below the Post, but later three or four other settlers came into the valley, and one of them, after clearing the sagebrush from a piece of land, raised two such fine crops of barley that he went back to his home in Boston with a well-filled purse.

We sometime had a general court martial at the Post and would then meet officers from other stations. Among them were Second Lieutenant Nathaniel Wolfe; Captain George T. Olmsted Jr., of the Second Artillery; First Lieutenant Charles C. Cresson, First Cavalry; Captain Edward Field, Fourth Artillery; and Brevet Lieutenant Colonel Carle Woodruff, Captain, Second Artillery.

On one of their trips from the Presidio of San Francisco, Captains Woodruff and Field and Lieutenants Wolfe and Olmsted had some amusing experiences. While on the cars they played tricks with cards, and the train newsboy, who saw them, informed the new conductor at Sacramento that he had better keep an eye on them. When the conductor boarded the train he recognized them as old acquaintances and had a good laugh at the expense of the thought-to-be-sharpers. On the road from Winnemucca they stopped at a new ranch house, built by an old timer by the name of Snapp, who was newly married and was having a house warming. A cowboy was trying to play a banjo but failed to make pleasing music, so Lieutenant Olmsted played for the company and he and the other officers sang. They entertained the assembled guests so well that Snapp refused to take any money for their meals and lodging, but said, "Come again."

Occasionally officers stopped at the Post on their way to other posts; among them were Brevet Major Joel C. Trimbell [Joel Graham Trimble], Captain, First Cavalry, and his family; Lieutenants William C. Manning and Frederick L. Dodge, Twenty-third Infantry; and Lieutenant Charles F. Roe, Second Cavalry, from Camp Harney, about 200 miles away north of Steins [Steens] Mountains. Colonel Roger Jones, Assistant Inspector General, was with us several times. He was born in the District of Columbia and took a great interest in us because I was from the South.[16] Whenever he left I put him up a lunch of cold roasted squabs or fried chicken and short cake, which upon one occasion he found more than acceptable, as a soldier who was guiding him over the mountains to Camp Scott lost the trail for several hours.

Other visitors whom I remember were Second Lieutenant Thomas T. Thornburg, Second Artillery, who became a paymaster April 26, 1875, and Major, Fourth Infantry, October 20, 1876, [and] was killed in the affair with the [Ute] Indians at Milk Creek, Colorado, on September 29, 1879,[17] and

First Lieutenant Jesse M. Lee, Ninth Infantry, who, with another officer, came to talk with "Old Horse," an Indian Chief, and tried to induce him to go to the Indian reservation. But the Chief, in an eloquent speech, declined to go.[18]

Captain Thomas M. K. Smith, Twenty-third Infantry, and wife and child were with us for some days. Major Thomas H. Halsey, Paymaster, came several times. First Lieutenant Edward H. Theller, Twenty-first Infantry, who was killed June 17, 1877, by Nez Percé Indians, and whose wife was in [the] charge of Father's father on his trip to California in 1854, was on duty at the Post for a time.[19]

We occasionally had visits from the officers of the neighboring posts in 1869 and 1870, and among them were Brevet Colonel John J. Coppinger, Captain, Twenty-third Infantry, and Dr. E. Colmache, from Camp Three Forks.[20] Colonel Coppinger had been an officer in the Pope's army and was one of the "Soldiers of Fortune" who had come to the United States to serve in our army during the Civil War and upon whom the Fenians had built great hopes, expecting them to lead an army into Canada at the close of our war.[21]

Colonel C[oppinger] made an excellent record during our war but was chaffed a good deal about his extreme neatness in dress, etc., and about his dressing case, which he carried into the field when after hostile Indians. In the morning his orderly would stand with three tooth brushes in his hand and the Colonel would say, "Wadley, give me tooth bwush number wun, now, tooth bwush number twoo," and then "tooth bwush number free." He could not pronounce the *wah*, *R*, when speaking English but could trill it when talking French. The Indians at length got the dressing case from him, and he had to do without a toothbrush for a time. On his first trip after Indians, it is said that he inquired of a trapper if he was then on "the woad to the wild Indians." We had many "Soldiers of Fortune" in the army at that time. . . .[22]

We rode or drove nearly every day and once went on a visit, about September 15, 1869, to Fort [Camp] C. F. Smith, 50 miles away. There was a stream thirty miles from us which was full of trout, and here we stayed over night with a settler who was living by himself and raised hundreds of chickens. He could stand at the back door of his house and catch trout from the creek, and those that we had for supper that night were all caught here or near the house, cleaned immediately and dropped into boiling lard to fry. Besides trout, we had coffee, biscuits made with baking powder, and a large milk pan piled up with hard-boiled eggs.

We went around the mountain the next day to C. F. Smith, but on our return came over the mountain, to the top of which we were driven by a team from Smith, and then walked down at least a thousand feet to our own team, which had gone around. Our mules, from the top of the mountain, looked the size of Cinderella's rats. The trail was so steep that we threw a package that we had with us ahead every now and then to roll and bump down, and we squatted on our feet and tobogganed most of the way. Our shoes were somewhat the worse for wear by the time we reached the bottom, but it was fun, and we laughed all the way down.

In March 1870 I was sick and craved the sympathy and society of a woman. The only one within 80 miles was the very nervous wife of an officer; [but then] one day into my room walked a sweet smiling young woman who took my hands into hers and said, "We heard you were ill so my husband and I came from Winnemucca to see you." I felt as if an angel had appeared; I was so happy that I cried. She was the wife of Dr. J. C. Watkins, a former Acting Assistant Surgeon, United States Army.[23]

The second year we were at McDermit an irrigation ditch was dug that ran in front of our quarters, and we took water from it above the Post to irrigate a garden which we planted. [T]his was thriving when we had an invasion of grasshoppers, which flew down in great clouds and ate up everything green. [A]nd another year large crickets ate our garden clean in about an hour. The Indians feasted on both grasshoppers and crickets; they drove them into pits and roasted them to eat at once or mashed them to keep for future use.

Our kitchen was a lean-to at the back of the house, and the boards had shrunken so that there were plenty of wide cracks between them. The crickets could crawl right in, and I gave some of the little Indians permission to come in and catch them. Soon I smelt something I had not smelled for a very long time, that is, the odor of roasting crabs. On going into the kitchen I found the little barelegged boys dancing about the stove, watching the crickets roasting and making a dive every now and again for some to eat. We did not have Kodaks in those days or I would have taken many a picture worth preserving.

Father planted wild roses and wild currants along the ditch that ran in front of our quarters, and years afterwards we were told that there was a beautiful hedge of them in front of all the quarters, as the line had been extended by other officers. We planted something wherever we went and left a Post richer by trees, shrubs, and various other plants.

I did my shopping by mail, and one day eight four-pound packages were brought to me on a wheelbarrow by an orderly who thought it a great joke to tell everyone he passed that it was the doctor's mail. We even had to send away for postage stamps, envelopes, and our letter paper.

Claude was born here August 3, 1871, a dear sweet baby who completed our happiness. What could we have done without him? He grew very fast and was always hungry for his meal, which, fortunately, after the first week or two, I could furnish fresh from the mamma dairy. We had to send to San Francisco for a nurse, but the one we wanted could not come and sent another one, Mrs. Withers, who turned out to be a very stupid elderly woman, as she knew very little about nursing or cooking. She came by rail to Winnemucca, from whence an ambulance brought her to the Post. She delayed on the way, so we had a large hotel bill to pay, which added to her fare both ways. And her twenty-five dollars a week in gold, when our greenbacks were at a discount, made her a dear luxury, but we had to put up with her. We kept her only three weeks and then were glad to be rid of her.

For a week we had an Indian woman as a wet nurse for him. Father examined the woman and her husband to see if they were free from disease. She took a full bath with plenty of soap, shampooed her head, and new clothes were put on her. Each time she came to the house her breasts were carefully bathed and her hair rolled up and tied in a cloth. Claude's nightgown was fastened close around his neck, the sleeves were drawn close to his wrists, and the gown fastened all the way across the bottom; this was to prevent any uninvited guests from crawling on him. The woman nursed him only once a day, and her whole family waited nearby for the "hogeedie" or meal, which they got after Claude had his.[24]

Father made him a nice crib out of pine packing boxes and later a beautiful high chair of lumber from the same yard. His bed had no springs, but a hair mattress was laid on a tick stuffed with fresh barley straw. Our bed was furnished the same way as his. I had plenty of time to look after my baby, as we had a fine cook, a soldier by the name of Varnet from

Maryland.[25] Claude had a gift of a beautiful carriage, so I kept him out in the fresh air at least six hours a day the year round. In the winter he was covered with a lynx robe.

His nurses were two Piute girls. They would push his carriage about and sing and dance to him when he was awake and I usually kept them in sight, but one day they escaped me for a time and went upon the mesa behind our quarters. When I sighted them they were picking sagebrush from his clothes and the carriage, which they had turned over. I was frightened, for I thought he might be hurt, but he was smiling, so I did not scold them but watched that he was not taken so far away again. When the girls got tired they would come to me and say, "Papoose yarowing, heap hungry," but they did not fool me. They were hungry, and some crackers would set them rolling the carriage again. Claude was always well, and he cut his teeth easily and was never anything except sweet-tempered. The Indians called him "Pi-u-je papoosee."[26]

Captain Henry Wagner was in command of the Post in 1871, and his wife and two little girls were with him. The children loved to come over and play with Claude, and Lucy used to ask him for a "Juicy kiss."

We had a Christmas tree for him and the other children of the Post. Varnet was Santa Claus and sat at the head of the table and entertained the wives and children of the enlisted men. We took Claude in to see the tree, which was a very small one, simply some willow branches for which I made leaves out of green paper. It was decorated with cranberries, popcorn, candles, and candy.[27]

A little boy, son of a couple who lived near the Post, came early, about four o'clock, as he did not want to miss seeing Santa Claus. The latter arrived about six-thirty P.M., shaking his bells. The little fellow, who was about nine years old, had never seen Santa Claus or a Christmas tree before. It was sweet to see his enjoyment.

When he was leaving I wrapped up his presents and candy and cake and handed them to him. "Oh," he said, "I don't deserve all that. I have had such a good time." He didn't want to take the things; he had no idea what Christmas meant. He was not poor, as his father had plenty, but they were so far away from all such things, and it may be they had no memories of Christmases past to tell their little son about.

CHAPTER FOUR

"Dry Salted Codfish and a Glass of Champagne"

EN ROUTE TO CAMP DATE CREEK, ARIZONA TERRITORY, NOVEMBER 1872–JANUARY 1873

I N NOVEMBER 1872, FATHER WAS ordered to Prescott, Arizona. We left McDermit on the 16th, a bitter cold day, in a large spring wagon drawn by four horses, a so-called ambulance. It was late when we started, as Captain Wagner at first declined to give us transportation, and we had a long drive before us.[1] By the time we reached the ranch where we were to spend the night, the air had become bitter cold and we were glad to find a rousing big fire of sagebrush in a huge fireplace. It was so hot that we couldn't get within ten feet of it, so we sat halfway across the large room in a semicircle with several frontiersmen.

We were not long in getting warmed through, and then after eating our supper we went to our room. It was also large but had a very small stove, which we found stuffed with old rags and paper. Father tried to light a fire but could not get one to burn. There was discarded underwear in piles on the floor, which I kicked aside, and examining the bed, [I] found a thick feather bed on top of a straw tick. The bedding was clean but the room was so cold that we took off only our outer clothes. When I placed Claude on the bed, he yelled with terror when he found himself going down into the feather bed, so I had to get in quickly and assure him that it was all right. We slept soundly, as we were very tired, having had a drive of sixty-eight miles.

In the morning Claude saw a cat and exclaimed, "Oh dere my Nan." She was just like the kitty we had to leave behind. She used to scratch at the bedroom door in the morning, and when we let her in she would jump into Claude's crib and cuddle up to him, purring.

We made an early start in the morning and at Winnemucca took the train for San Francisco. There we stayed until November 27th, waiting for a steamer to take us to Arizona. We found a very comfortable boarding house, one of the few in the city at that time. It was kept by Madame Rassette, who was a French Canadian from Three Rivers in Canada. She engaged a little French girl to take care of Claude. While here, we had Claude baptized in Trinity Church by the Reverend G. W. Mayer.[2] As we went up the aisle, he [Claude] kept saying, "Bear, bear," much to the amusement of the congregation. We had taken him to Woodward's Garden the day before, and the bright lights in the church probably made him think he was going to see the bears again.[3]

We had a great deal of shopping to do, as we had sold our household effects at McDermit. In those days our baggage allowance was so small and freight rates were so high that when we changed Posts we usually sold all that we could of our furniture, bedding, dishes, etc. When there were settlers around a Post, we could get good prices for everything we wished to sell. We bought matting for the floors of our quarters, china, table linen, bedding, a few folding chairs, etc. and were allowed by the merchants ten percent discount on all of our purchases.

Colonel Roger Jones procured a pass for me on the steamer *Newbern* and we had no freight to pay. Father was the medical officer in charge of about 125 recruits. They were [under the] command of Captain Edward Field and another Artillery officer, and Second Lieutenant Orlando L. Wieting, Twenty-third Infantry. There were two other medical officers on board, Doctors Benjamin and Davis.[4] Mr. Wieting had his wife with him. She was a daughter of Colonel Israel Vogdes, First Artillery. They had been married only a short time and had two trunks with clothes, a couple of barrels of china and silver, but no furniture or bedding to take with them to go to a frontier Post.

There was one other woman on the steamer *Newbern*, the wife of a civilian. We had a very pleasant voyage down the coast of California, around Cape St. Lucas and up the Gulf of California, to Port Isabel at the mouth of the Colorado River. The artillery officers left us here to return to San Francisco. I was very seasick the first day or two, but on Thanksgiving Day I was carried to the upper deck and Captain McDowell, master of the ship, sent me some shredded dry salted codfish and a glass of champagne, which made me feel better. The nausea disappeared and I was ready for my next meal.[5]

A stern-wheel steamboat took us up the river, and we had a very comfortable stateroom. We towed a flatboat, which held the recruits. At night we tied up and the men went ashore to cook their meals and to sleep on the banks of the river.

There were many sandbars in the Colorado, and as we approached one of them, we always listened to the man at the bow of the boat call out the depth of the water after he had measured it with a graduated pole. When he called "mark twain" (two feet) we listened more attentively, as he would then begin to call off the inches.[6] The boat would go on very slowly until there would be eighteen inches of water or less and then would usually run aground. Then the Captain would send some of the deckhands, who were usually Yuma or Mojave Indians, with a hawser to tie to a tree, and the other hands were set at work at the capstan, while the wheel of the boat would be reversed. As the sand was washed from under the flat bottom of the boat we would be dragged over the bar. Sometimes a spar would be set upright in the sand near the bow of the boat and that would be raised while the wheel washed the sand from underneath.[7]

It was said of the Colorado steamboat captains that they could run a boat on the dew if any was on the grass. On account of the quicksand and whirlpools, very few men who fell overboard were recovered. Many recruits had been lost in this way, so our men were advised to be very careful. The Captain, Jack Mellon, was said to be a very profane man and his profanity of a pyrotechnic character.[8] We were told not to go near him whenever he was making a landing, but we found him so quiet like and gentle that we forgot this advice until we reached Fort Yuma, when, on unloading our baggage, one of Mrs. Wieting's trunks dropped into the water, and the Captain broke forth with the most peculiar oaths and we women fled.

We were three days reaching Fort Yuma and had to wait here for about two weeks for the *Cocopah*, Captain Polhemas, to come and take us up to

Ehrenberg.[9] We stayed with Dr. George S. Rose, U.S. Army, and were there on Christmas Day, 1872.[10] I remember that we had watermelon on that day, raised by the Yuma Indians. The Fort was located on a rocky bluff over-looking the river and about 160 miles from its mouth. The officers lived in one-story adobe buildings provided with double roofs and having large rooms with lofty ceilings. Spacious verandas enclosed with lattice work surrounded the quarters and mostly met. The commanding officer was Alexander B. McGowan, Captain, Twelfth Infantry, and among the other officers were First Lieutenant John L. Viven and First Lieutenant David J. Craigie, Brevet Captain.

Arizona City, across the river, was the home of the bad man in those days, and frequently in the morning we would hear that men had been killed the night before. It was impossible to keep the recruits from going over there, and one day when Father and Mr. Wieting went over they met one of them at the landing who had on only a breach clout. He said his clothing had been stolen from him while he was asleep the night before, but he had probably sold or exchanged them for whiskey.

From Yuma to Ehrenberg the navigation of the river was easier. One day we saw a trapper coming down the river in a canoe; the Captain called and asked him if he had any beavers' tails. He had, so the Captain laid on a supply and the next morning the Chinaman cook served them fried, along with buckwheat cakes; they were delicious and somewhat like pigs' feet, only better.

We expected to find an ambulance waiting for us at Ehrenberg, but there was none, so Father and Mr. Wieting bought, through the Goldwater brothers who had a store here, a light spring wagon, two broncho [bronco] ponies and harness from a man who had brought a load of fruit across the desert.[11] Mrs. Wieting, Dr. Benjamin, Claude, and I rode in the wagon with Father, who drove. Mr. Wieting rode horseback most of the way. Wagons hired for the purpose were loaded with our tent, provisions, rations for the soldiers, hospital supplies, trunks, and men's kits. Some water was carried in casks, one on each side of a wagon.

Mr. Wieting had difficulty in getting the men out of the town, as some of them had been drinking and would try to get back for more whiskey. We drove only a few miles the first day and camped at an arroyo where some dry gold mining was done by Mexicans. They pulverized, shook, and stirred the dry earth in large shallow wooden bowls to settle the gold at the bottom and then would gradually throw out the superincumbent earth. In this way they separated only the very coarse gold, which was in paying quantities for the class of people who worked these mines. This was January 1, 1873, and we had our dinner under a large palo verde tree, seated on the ground in the warm sunshine. Father opened a bottle of claret and handed it to Dr. Benjamin, whose nose was quite red and who said he would drink it, as there was nothing stronger.

The next day we drove through a forest of saguaro, or giant cactus, some of them 40 to 60 feet tall, but most of them 20 to 40 feet. The skeletons of these cacti are formed of strong fenestrated rods. Many of these had stiff branches at intervals along their sides, looking like great candelabras. The seeds are gathered from the dried fruit by the Indians, roasted, ground between stones, and made into balls, of which they are very fond. Besides these [saguaro] there were many other varieties.

The second day we camped at Tyson's Well and saw many cochineal bugs breeding on some of the Opuntia.[12] We met an ambulance the second or third day out conveying Second Lieutenant Adolphus Greely, Fifth Cavalry, who was on his way to Washington.[13] At one of our camps there was a very deep well, the water from which was hauled up in a barrel by a mule that walked round and round turning a windlass. When the barrel reached the top it emptied itself, and the mule then turned the other way to let it down into the well to fill again. The contractors lost their mules during the night, and we were obliged to delay there a day. The animals were probably lost knowingly, so that another day's supply of water would have to be paid for by the Government. It was strongly impregnated with sulfur and we drank very little of it.

The fourth day out, just as we were about to make camp, the rain fell in torrents and fires had to be made to dry our tent and the ground on which it was pitched, while we sat in the wagon. Our mattresses were laid on ponchos spread on the ground. We discovered before we left Ehrenberg that the Wietings had no tent or bedding. They said they would sleep at the ranches, but there were no accommodations at the few we passed, [so] they were obliged to sleep in the wagon.

This night they asked to sleep in our tent. We had two single mattresses and I needed one to myself, as I was always very tired after a drive, often having to sit on the floor of the wagon to rest; but we pushed the mattresses close together and gave Mrs. Wieting the side next to the tent.

I lay on the edges of the two, Claude next to me, and Father on the outside. That was bad enough, but when Mr. Wieting and Dr. Benjamin came in we had to huddle together the rest of the night. Claude cried with cramp about midnight, and Mrs. Wieting confessed that she had given him blackberry jam. I shall never forget that dreadful night; it was a wonder that Hal was not born then and there.[14]

We messed together and as there was no one who could cook, I tried to instruct a soldier, which was a very difficult task while the wind was blowing the sand and smoke into one's face and into the food. We generally had coffee, eggs, bacon, bread and butter, condensed milk, and hard bread for breakfast; canned meat, vegetables, bread and butter, coffee, and canned fruit for dinner. The meals were served on a red and white tablecloth spread on the ground, and we sat on boxes. Father, Claude, and I each had a tin plate, cup, knife, fork, spoon, and napkin, but the others managed somehow.

Claude and I often sat on the large anthills and picked up beautiful bits of stone of amethyst, opal, and garnet color and small white crystal looking like little diamonds. I was taken back to my childhood when I used to hunt for hidden treasures in an anthill. Claude would soon be covered with ants, and I had to pick them off when he was ready to have more crawl on him for the fun of seeing me pick them off. He had such a sweet disposition and was always contented. He was the best traveler I ever saw, taking an interest in everything that was going on. He talked a great deal but mostly in his own language, although seventeen months old. He called himself Taudle and Taudla. When asked how many eyes he had, he would point to them and say, "Two," very emphatically; how many hands, nostrils, and feet—"Two," but he couldn't go beyond two.

One of our camps was made at a ranch where there was an American, named Cullin, I think, who had a Mexican wife. She was a very sweet looking woman and her manners were very gentle and kindly, just like the little ringdoves she had as pets in a cage. I can hear them calling as I write and see the desert country where there were hardly any living creatures and not a sound but the mournful notes of these doves. What a life for a woman to lead, no women for companions, but only the sad little doves. I was so sorry for her. They had some burros, and Claude was so pleased with a little one that after playing with him for some time, [he] went to sleep with his head on the little fellow, who had lain down to take his siesta near the house.

When not far from Camp Date Creek we drove ahead of the wagons, telling the drivers we would wait for them at a certain place where we wished to make camp. We drove to the place and waited for the wagons a long time. The sun set, night was coming on, and we were hungry. A house was nearby, and the smell of bread baking made us so ravenous that Father went in and obtained a loaf of hot bread, which we ate with a piece of toasted cheese rind left from our lunch. Then we turned back and drove until we reached the wagons. We found the drivers were settled for the night, asleep or pretending to be. It was very exasperating, but they didn't wish to travel too fast, as they were employed by the day.

CHAPTER FIVE

"Making Soup from a Stone"

CAMP DATE CREEK, ARIZONA TERRITORY, JANUARY–SEPTEMBER 1873

T HE NEXT DAY, JANUARY 4TH OR 5TH, we reached this Post in the evening and drove to the quarters of Captain James B. Henton, Twenty-third Infantry. Mrs. Henton and Mrs. Trout ran out to meet us.[1] Mrs. Henton took a large bundle of wraps that I had in my lap and carefully carried it into the house, where she opened it but did not find what she expected. They had heard at the Post that a baby had been born on the road. Dear little boy, it was a narrow escape.[2] There was a bright fire burning in the parlor and a nice dinner ready for us on a clean table in the dining room. It all seemed so good after camp meals. A real bed was also a treat. Some of the recruits were left here, and the rest went on to Prescott under Mr. Wieting and Dr. Benjamin as Medical Officer.

Our quarters were two rooms, front and back, built of adobe, the roofs of dirt that had recently been shingled over and the ceilings were made of shelter tents sewed together and stretched overhead. The dirt roof harbored scorpions, centipedes, and we don't know what also. Back of these was a jacal, a brush shelter about twelve feet square which separated the two rooms from the kitchen and dining room, which were also of adobe but having old canvas roofs. The canvas leaked badly, and during a rain the water poured down in streams. The floors were pounded earth, and the pools of water in the wet season soon became muddy. We placed bowls on the dining table to catch the water when it rained, and the cook wore his boots, hat, and slicker. The stove would get so wet that it was hard to keep the fire burning. We had a soldier, an ex-French soldier named Blot, to cook for us. He was an indifferent cook and very erratic, so we didn't keep him long. Our next incumbent was a big Swede named Sorensen, who prided himself on having cooked at the sailor's home in San Francisco. He treated us to raisin soup and other strange dishes but was very good natured and willing. Dr. Josephus Williams, Indian Agent, [and] Mr. Vincent, who was his clerk, messed with us.[3]

We had no variety in the way of food, and when we had company, and we often had, it required much thought and planning to get up a nice meal. I made oyster soap with canned oysters and condensed milk, which was the sweetened kind, and it was pronounced fine to make me feel comfortable. No one had any better and perhaps not such good soup, as they had not studied the art of making soup of a stone.[4] When we could get them, we had potatoes, which cost twelve cents per pound. Our commissary was not very well supplied, and freight charges were very high. We paid four dollars a gallon for kerosene oil. Father planted watercress that was brought to him from the Hassayampa [River]. It grew luxuriantly in the creek at the base of the bluff, and in a short time it choked the water and we had more than we or the soldiers could eat.[5] It was a greatful [grateful] addition to our canned fare and often was the only fresh vegetable we had.

The jacal helped to keep some of the heat from the house, and in it we hung our two ollas, which we had brought from Fort Yuma. They were porous earthen jars holding five and ten gallons each, through which the water percolated, and the evaporation was so great from the outside that the water within was cooled to a considerable extent. The Mojave Indian women made them out of red clay and baked them in an open fire. After forming the bottom of a coil of clay, the woman continues the coil until the olla is built up, shaping the vessel with both hands as she works. We hung them by ropes to a beam overhead. The water in the ollas was deliciously cool, and everyone came to ours for a drink in the middle of the day.

I have seen an olla set in a box that contained sand in which barley or oats were sown. The water that percolated the olla made the grain grow and the grass around the jar was very pretty, but hanging the jar up was certainly more sanitary. We kept our butter under the drip. It came in four-pound glass jars and was melted to an oil when we received it. Twice Father bought some oranges from a pedler, who had brought them from California, and paid twenty-five cents each for them. They were delicious, but it seemed like eating gold.

We were obliged to use condensed milk which was sweetened, so we borrowed a cow from the herd and anticipated having plenty of fresh milk. As she had just come off the range our man, as a precaution, tied her to a fence and approached her very cautiously, put a box on the ground and seated himself, keeping an eye on Mrs. Cow. As he began to milk she upset him, his pail and box, tore off a section of the fence and galloped away to freedom. We never saw her again nor did we ever have fresh milk at Date Creek. . . .

We had a large roll of matting to cover the floors of our two rooms. A rough-board frame, hospital bed-springs, and a mattress covered with creton[n]e made a comfortable couch. The Quartermaster furnished us with a bedstead, bureau, and tables, made by the Post carpenter, and a few chairs; we had two black walnut rockers and two folding carpet chairs of our own. On our bed was a tick filled with straw on which was laid a hair mattress. A small table was used as a washstand. For a wardrobe we put up some hooks and hung a cretonne curtain in front. After unpacking our lamps, china, clothing, a few books, etc. we were at home.

I had worked hard to have the quarters in order before Harold was born. The last thing I did was to iron the muslin lining of his basket and put in the clothes, etc. the night before, sitting on the floor. He arrived on time the next morning at eight o'clock, January 14, 1873.[6] Our babies have always had the habit of being on time. Father had taken Claude to breakfast but I had to call him and our second boy made his appearance. The nurse, a laundress, Mrs. Leahy, was there in short order. Mrs. Henton came from next door and took Claude to her house. She came every day for a week and washed and dressed the baby for me. Mrs. Trout was very kind also; so everything went on smoothly.

Claude was perfectly delighted with the baby brother; called him *his* and wanted to hold him. Mrs. Leahy came every morning for two weeks, cooked my breakfast, and often made Father a plate of delicious corn griddle cakes. She also washed and dressed Claude, made the beds, and put me and the rooms in order. I had so much milk that Harold could not take it all, and I was glad to have Mrs. Leahy's baby, who was several months old, have some of it. He was always very hungry and pulled hard. When he was satisfied he looked very happy.[7]

Harold was a sweet, plump baby and very good. One morning I had left him asleep in his crib and Claude in our bed while I went to breakfast. When I came back Claude was seated in the crib with Harold in his lap. "Two boys a bidden (in bed), Mamma," was his greeting. He was very well pleased and Harold perfectly serene. The Indians were very proud of Hal because he was born in their country and claimed him as one of them, calling him "Apache papoose," meaning "a child of our people."

In very warm weather Claude used to wake very early and say, "Taudla din-din—wawa o-ee, Papa," and Father would open the door for him to go out into [the] jacal for it. One morning when Father himself went, he found a large copper-colored rattlesnake coiled at the side of the door. He dispatched it without any loss of time. There were a great many of them among the great piles of rocks near the Post, and one had to be very careful in walking among the rocks and especially in stepping over them, as a snake often lay coiled on the opposite side.

There were also Gila monsters, and Father had one twenty-two inches long, which he put in alcohol. Tarantulas are fierce fighters. One day when we were out among the rocks we watched two of them near one of their holes. They would jump at each other, back, and then come together again. We always examined and shook the children's and our own clothing and shoes before putting them on, as scorpions, tarantulas, and centipedes would often be found hidden in them. I killed many scorpions in one corner of our sitting room. They crawled down the wall above Hal's head as he lay on our improvised lounge. There must have been a nest of them in the dirt roof.

The Post was built on a rocky slope about 700 yards from the creek, which runs through a cañon which was about 150 feet wide and from 50 to 200 feet deep. There was porous lava on top of red sandstone. High rocky hills of decomposing granite half surrounded the Post. On the far side of the creek was an extended mesa of mal pais (porous volcanic rock), thickly covered with *yucca baccata* or date plants, from which the creek received its name. The fruit of this yucca has the appearance and taste of banana and is very good when roasted. Inside the pulp are three stacks of black seeds. The plant has strong stalks three to four feet high on which the pretty white or cream colored flowers grow, which are very fragrant at night. These are fertilized by a kind of insect which is very numerous in them. Three miles east of Date Creek was the divide between the Hassayampa, a tributary of the Gila River, and Williams Fork, a tributary of the Colorado River, of which Date Creek is one of the head waters.

In summer the rocks [were] burning hot and we had to keep our house shut up until sundown, when we opened it and did not close it until near day break. The air outside about noon seemed like a blast from a furnace, and the temperature was often 104°F, but it was so very dry and the evaporation so great that we did not perspire nor suffer as we would in a humid atmosphere.[8] Thunder storms, with terrific lightning, were frequent and the reverberation from the rocks was deafening. We were sitting at our front door one day when a ball of fire about eight inches in diameter rolled across the parade ground. The shock knocked down a woman who was ironing in her house across the parade from us and caused others to scream out.[9]

The parade was all rock, without a spear of grass on it. The Post was garrisoned by one troop of the Fifth Cavalry, Captain George F. Price and [Second] Lieutenant Charles D. Parkhurst, and a company of the Twenty-third Infantry, Captain James B. Henton, who was in command of the Post, and First Lieutenant John F. Trout.[10]

Early in the summer about 500 Apache Yuma Indians under their Chief Ochicama, that had been brought in from the surrounding country, were taken over to Rio Verde Reservation by their Agent and his clerk, guarded by troops.[11] The Post was to be abandoned shortly and the company of Infantry leaving; I lost my laundress. The cavalry laundress's husband was the troop tailor and had a great deal of work, so she would only do Father's washing. I had to try my hand at the clothes so I washed, dried, and starched them as I thought was right, but they were so stiff that I could not get them off the lines, and [since] I was not yet very strong, I could not help crying as I carried water from the barrel in the kitchen to loosen them. Claude stood by me and was so distressed that he cried, too. That stopped me and the little fellow patted my bare arms saying, "My Mamma no washerwoman," repeating it several times. Darling little boy, he was always tender-hearted. I couldn't do that work again, so Father appealed to Captain Price, who ordered the laundress to do my washing also.

The cavalry was then at length ordered away, and only a guard of a few men of the Twenty-third Infantry was left, Lieutenant Trout in command. Mrs. Trout and I were the only ladies left and we had to entertain a great many people, as the Post was on the road to Prescott, Hassayampa, Wickenburg, etc. We divided the large parties between us. Every effort was fatiguing in that torrid climate, but there was no help for it. . . .

Claude would sometimes get away and run to the cavalry corral, where the Sergeant would put him on a horse at the picket line and he contracted epizootic.[12] I can see him running across the parade as fast as he could go, his little legs flying, to reach the corral before he was caught. He had few or no toys but amused himself with empty tin cans which I would make smooth around the tops. He would pile up the sand and fill the cans and run a little way off with them, saying all the time, "Taudle tin tan," over and over again. . . . He would play this way for a long time.

Father had been given some turkey eggs that were the second remove from the wild bird, the feathers of which the Apache made their war caps. He had them set under a hen at the hospital and raised five. They were worth a great deal. One of them was a splendid gobbler whose feathers were a beautiful dark bronze color. He strutted about chasing the chickens and making a great noise. Claude admired him very much and would go close to him until I told him that the turkey might peck his nose. After that, every time he heard the gobbler he would put his finger on his nose, saying, "No-oose." It was very funny. Father took two of them to the Rio Verde Reservation when he went over there.

We had a few chickens and I tried to raise some little ones, but the heat was so great that if the eggs were left in the nest a day they would be hard. I had to sprinkle those that I set twice every day. Some of the chickens must have had malaria or rheumatism, as they walked on their elbows. I gave them quinine and whiskey with their food and it cured them. We learned afterward that the Chief Commissary of the Department, Major M. P. Small, when he set a hen, made a shallow depression in the ground where the eggs were put and dug a little ditch around the nest. The ditch was kept filled with water to keep the eggs from drying up and he was very successful. This was the irrigation method.[13]

Father was to be ordered to the Verde Indian Reservation when Date Creek was abandoned, and as Harold and I were not at all strong and there was epizootic among the Indians, we concluded that the children and I must not go there, but better go to Father's mother in Elmira, New York. We had many dry goods on hand, but there was a great demand for them, and Mrs. Crook kindly told me to send them to her at Whipple to dispose of. . . .[14]

Father, the children, and I left Date Creek for Fort Whipple, August 30, 1873. At one part of the road the rocks were very high and the space on either side narrow. Indians used to conceal themselves behind these rocks and shoot those who were passing, almost touching them with the guns. We made the drive to Whipple in two days and were entertained by Lieutenant Colonel and Mrs. John D. Wilkins and daughter Carrie, Eighth Infantry. Miss Carrie was a very sweet and attractive young woman and is probably the heroine in Captain Charles King's story, "The Colonel's Daughter."[15]

All of the officers and their wives called on us in the evening, and we were very jolly. Captain John G. Bourke, Aide to General Crook, was very witty and kept everyone laughing. General Crook said very little, as was his habit, but his eyes would twinkle with merriment.[16] Most of these officers and their wives had been in the army for years and knew how to make the best of their surroundings. Mrs. Dana had visited us at Date Creek when she, Mrs. Crook, and Mrs. Crook's sister had come through with the Paymaster. She was very much interested in what I told her of our life at Camp McDermit, but especially with the butter making, which she thought wonderful and told everyone about it.[17] She once invited the officers, their wives, and some civilians from Prescott to a strawberry pic-nic. She gave them Arizona strawberries, that is, baked beans, as a joke. . . .

The officers were Brevet Major General George Crook, Lieutenant Colonel, Twenty-third Infantry, in command of the Department of Arizona; Lieutenant John G. Bourke, Third Cavalry, his Aide; Colonel David L. Magruder, Medical Director; Brevet Brigadier General James J. Dana, Major, Quartermaster Department; Brevet Brigadier General Michael P. Small, Major, Subsistence Department; Captain and Assistant Surgeon Henry Lippincott; Lieutenant Colonel John D. Wilkins, Eighth United States Infantry; Captain Charles Porter, Eighth United States Infantry; Captain Azor H. Nickersen [Nickerson], Acting Adjutant General; Major

James H. Nelson, Pay Department; Lieutenant Greenleaf Goodale, Twenty-third Infantry.[18]

Father, having learned that an ambulance was to leave Whipple for Ehrenberg on the Colorado River to meet Captain James Burns and family, decided it would be best for us to go in it. I had bruised my thumb in packing and it was so painful all night that Father opened the felon, which relieved the pain, and [he] told me it must be kept open for a time with my penknife, if he should not be with me. But that made me shiver, so I used sharpened matches instead. Many people in Arizona were affected with felons, especially the soldiers that worked in the kitchens and had their hands in hot water a great deal.[19]

We left Prescott on September 5th or 6th for Ehrenberg on the Colorado River, drove through Skull, Antelope, and Pursland Valleys and reached Ehrenberg about September 9, 1873, where we put up at a so-called hotel kept by a Chinaman. Father had to leave us the next morning to return to Prescott on a buckboard that carried the mail. The weather was very hot, but I was afraid to leave the windows open, as although they were protected with vertical iron rods, they were near the ground and some Mexican and Chinamen outside were making a great noise. A hole in the roof was the only ventilation. I put the children to bed and sat fanning them, too heartsick and terribly lonely to go to bed. As soon as the day began to break, I opened the window and then lay down with my clothes on.

Mr. Tyng, a nephew of the Reverend Doctor Tyng, at one time Rector of Trinity Church in New York, who had charge of William Hooper and Company's business in Ehrenberg, came over to see me in the morning and invited me to come and stay at his house at night if I did not mind sleeping on the gallery on a cot, as his wife and children did.[20] I accepted the invitation gladly. We were very comfortable on the cots. Mr. Tyng was also the Sheriff and he told me not to get excited if I heard a shot in the night, as the Mexicans were always quarreling and shooting pistols. Sure enough, he was called out but soon came back, saying a man had been shot.

CHAPTER SIX

"I Felt Like the Lady in the Circus"

BACK TO ELMIRA, NEW YORK,
SEPTEMBER 1873–SEPTEMBER 1874

WHEN WE DECIDED THAT WE could not go with Father to the Indian Reservation and that the children and I might better go home, we thought I could take the steamer at the mouth of the Colorado River that usually made regular trips to San Francisco. But Colonel Roger Jones telegraphed Father that the boat would not make her usual trip, and it was not certain when she would come. It might be a month or longer, so I was compelled to go to Los Angeles in a buckboard. Father had been promised by the man who ran the stage line that a stage would be sent for us, but he sent a one-seated buckboard, so we were obliged to go in that. Mr. Tyng furnished us with delicious canned meat, potted chicken and turkey, fruit, condensed milk, crackers, preserves, coffee, tea, chocolate, etc.—everything that we could possibly need. We had canteens in which we carried water. There had been several good rains which had cooled the air and laid the dust so that the road was fine.

The children and I left Ehrenberg early in the morning, about September 12th. My large trunk and the box of eatables were put in the back of the buckboard, and two men who were also passengers had to ride there. The driver, whom everyone knew, had been driving a stage for some years. Mr. Tyng said we would be perfectly safe with him, and he would tell him to instruct the next driver to take care of us. I have forgotten his name, but it seems to me it was Robinson. He took his seat and held the reins while the children and I were helped to get seated. Claude was placed between the driver and me; Harold, then nine months old, was on my lap. A wide leather strap, fastened to the side of the seat, was passed in front of me and the children and buckled to the seat back of the driver, to prevent us from falling out in case the bronco horses plunged too much. As soon as all were seated, the driver passed the reins around his wrist and gave the order "All ready." A man on each side then quickly hooked the traces and jumped back.

The horses plunged forward but were soon brought down to a trot. I felt like the lady in the circus, but no one held a hoop for me to jump through. It was well that I was not afraid of a horse, for those broncos certainly sustained their reputation for rearing and plunging. The driver's hands were inflamed and very painful from a fall into some cholla cactus a few days before while [he was] trying to catch a horse. We had not driven far before he took Harold on his lap and passed the reins to me, wrapping the ends around the lower part of his wrists to be safe.

Our first drive was forty miles to the next stage house, and I drove most of the way. He complimented me on my driving and told everyone how much pluck I had. One of the men passengers would have driven, but the children and I could not sit where they were sitting and the reins could not be passed back to one of them. The horses were fast trotters, so [we] made good time. The children, particularly Claude, thought it was fun. It would have been if only dear Father had been with us. There was a buggy top over the seat, but as we were going northwest, the sun was in our eyes during the afternoon.

When about twenty miles out, we stopped to eat our lunch that Mrs. Tyng had put up for us and to take a drink of water from our canteens. The driver washed his hands to cool them off, and I bound them up in some soft rags. The cholla cactus is the worst sort of one to come in contact with. Each thorn is barbed and comes off the plant and pierces the flesh on the slightest pressure, and the small ones are hard to find.

When the sun went down, there was a wonderful change in the desert. The air became soft and clear and the stars were very brilliant. As the night went on, the moon rose and our road was flooded with light. Not a sound was to be heard, except the beating of the horses' hoofs as they trotted steadily along. The children went to sleep, as I think did the men behind. The driver and I talked of Arizona and what it might be in years to come, when there was water with which to irrigate the land, as he knew there would be. He had been with all the Indian tribes in Arizona and knew them well, so his talk was very interesting. When we reached the station where the horses were to be changed, it was not yet really dark. There was still the desert light, or afterglow.

We all descended with stiff legs from the uncomfortable seats. Claude was glad to be on his feet again and began to run about. My lunch box was opened and I took out canned meat, soft bread, hardtack, coffee, sugar, milk, and jam. It was put on a table made of two rough boards. Claude and I were very hungry. I had my own cups, forks, knives, napkins, and plates. The station keeper made the coffee and supplied the others with dishes. He charged us each a dollar for his services. I furnished more than enough food for all, and he had what was left for his dinner the next day.

We changed drivers here and in an hour left with two plunging mustangs as before. Many times in the night we heard rattlesnakes that had been disturbed by us. The rattling was very distinct in the clear, still air. I felt no fear and wondered why I did not, so far from everyone I knew. There were no Indians out, and as we were traveling in a buckboard, we were not so likely to be stopped by bandits as if we were in a stage carrying express matter, but I did not think of that until the night before we reached San Bernardino. The third driver said that the last stage that went over the road had been robbed by Valasquez, a noted road agent, at a place on the road which we would soon reach.[1]

The outlaws had chosen a spot where the bushes were thick on each side, dug a shallow trench across the road, and covered it with brush. We were nearer the spot than he supposed, for as he whipped up his horses that we might pass the place quickly, there was a sudden jolt, which threw us all into the bottom of the backboard and gave us a great fright. The belt caught me under the chin, and Harold, who was asleep on my lap, slid to the floor, as did Claude also. The horses kept right on and we heard shouts behind us, which caused the driver to give his team the whip again. As the shouting continued, the driver looked around and saw that our two passengers were not on the buckboard but were running fast to catch up with us. We then stopped and I was given a little whiskey, the men reseated themselves on my trunk, and we continued on our way.

Early the third morning we stopped at a ranch on the road not far from San Bernardino. Some people from Virginia had settled there and had built a very pretty house and planted a garden, which was full of flowers and fruit. After a good wash to refresh us, we had a delicious breakfast of fried chicken, corn bread, coffee, etc.[2] Hal and I took a nap, but Claude was too much interested in all he saw to sleep. . . .

We left in a couple of hours and reached Los Angeles in the evening. I was worn out with the trip of three days and two nights, nearly 60 hours, and had to be carried into the hotel and upstairs.[3] We just missed the boat running to San Francisco so were obliged to wait nearly a week for the next one, and I was not sorry. Dr. W. F. Edgar, a retired Army Surgeon, was in the hotel, the Bella Union, and came to see me.[4] His wife soon followed him, and she sent for a Mexican girl as a nurse for the children. I stayed in bed for a couple of days to rest, and the doctor and his wife were very kind to me.

They owned an orange grove in the neighborhood. Los Angeles was then only a small Mexican town of adobe houses, but as the route for a railroad had been surveyed, people were looking forward for prosperous times.[5] Dr. Edgar wanted me to buy a ranch of a few acres, which was offered for $800.00. I did not wish to assume responsibility of buying it, as I knew California as a country where money was sometimes made but where more was lost. . . .

We left Los Angeles in the afternoon on a train made up of one passenger coach, a baggage car, and engine, for Wilmington, the seaport of Los Angeles.[6] There was no porter on the train, and I had a number of packages and the two children to take care of. I began to plan how to get off when, just before we stopped, a gentleman came from the other end of the car and asked if he and a young man just opposite might help me. He handed Hal over to the young man, who was much confused and blushed. Then he gathered up all of the packages so that I had nothing to carry. We walked to the end of the very long dock to take a small steamer to get into a larger one which was anchored out in the bay. The sea wall was then in course of construction. It was after sundown when we reached our ocean steamer.

The evening was a beautiful one, and the water was still and blue. We were told that the cooks and waiters were drunk and there was no supper for us, but we went into the dining-room and sat down at a table, hoping something would happen. Something did happen: a waiter came out of the kitchen carrying a tray, and everyone began to hope, as there were several besides ourselves waiting for something to eat. He passed by the others, stopped behind me, and said, "Mrs. Corbusier, I saw you coming on board, and knowing there was no supper cooked, I have prepared something for you." I turned and saw an ex-soldier named White, who had been stationed at Camp McDermit when we were there and whom I had taught to cook many dishes for the officers' mess. There was plenty on the tray for all, and they were profound in their thanks to me and White. You cannot know how happy I felt to be able to repay a little the gentlemen who had so kindly assisted me.

The next morning I was not well enough to eat my breakfast, so White gave Claude his breakfast and after finishing his work, took both boys and kept them amused. The old gentleman who helped me with the children said he liked to travel with such a fortunate person as me. When we reached San Francisco, he went in the carriage with us to Madame Rassette's, on the upper side of Kearny Street a few doors from Market Street, to whom I had written asking her to reserve me a room, and she had engaged a girl to take care of the children. The cooking was delicious. We stayed a week to rest, before taking our long trip to Elmira.

The next morning I took a check to William Hooper & Company that Mr. Tyng had given me, as I carried only money enough with me to pay my expenses this far. No one in the office knew me, so I couldn't get the check cashed and I was very indignant. I then went to Colonel Roger Jones, who cashed the check and said he would look after me and I should have sent for him as soon as I arrived. He arranged for my tickets to Elmira, saw that my baggage was properly checked, etc.

There were no dining cars on the trains in 1873, but at or near meal time the train usually stopped for twenty minutes at a station where there was a dining room. Madame Rassette put me up a big lunch and I didn't have to get out very often. The porter would bring me coffee and milk in two small tin pails that I carried and anything else that I needed. . . .

We left San Francisco on a sleeper, and I think we changed at Ogden to another one, which went as far as Omaha, where we changed again. I think it took us seven days to get to Elmira. Father's mother was at the train to meet us and delightedly gathered us up, as a hen would her chickens. We were all very tired, and what bliss it was to be in a real house again and to eat an eastern home meal. I felt as if I never wanted to move again. Claude was very happy to be able to run about, and it was comical to see Hal, who did not walk yet, fly across the rooms by hitching himself along. Claude had seen so few trees that he didn't know one from a lamp post. He would touch each telegraph pole, lamp post, and tree as he walked along, saying each time, "Tree, tree, tree." Mother found a little Swedish girl whom we engaged as a nurse. She took good care of the children and they became very fond of her.

All of us needed clothes, so Mother engaged a dressmaker and a woman to do plain sewing. Mother and I often sewed until after midnight. We remained with her several months and then went to Amite, Louisiana, to visit my sister May and her husband, Henry S. Addison, who lived at Dunbarton, our old home. After remaining there a couple of months we returned to Elmira.

While we were with her, Mother introduced Samuel L. Clemens, "Mark Twain," to me. We found him very agreeable, but nothing was said or done to draw from him a characteristic remark. She also introduced "Brick" Pomeroy, editor of the *La Cross Democrat*, whom we found very jolly and witty; also the daughter of Henry Ward Beecher.[7]

CHAPTER SEVEN

❦

"Sand and Cedar"

FOLLOWING THE TRAIL OF COLONEL DODGE, NEW MEXICO AND ARIZONA TERRITORIES, SEPTEMBER–OCTOBER 1874

ABOUT THE MIDDLE OF SEPTEMBER 1874 I received a telegram from Father from Camp Verde, Arizona, sent over the new telegraph line built in Arizona by the army. His telegram came the longest distance of any that had up to that time been received in Elmira, and the newspapers noted it.[1] Father said that he would meet us at Las Animas, Colorado, in about a month from that date. Later I received a letter from him, giving me the probable date of his arrival in Las Animas. I fitted out with china, mattresses, pillows, sheets, etc., and bought a melodeon of fine make, the legs of which folded under and which we wrapped in a bed comfort and put into a trunk. I had nearly a thousand pounds of baggage, which was checked through to Las Animas owing to the good offices of a friend of Mother's who had some business connection with the railroads.[2]

We left Elmira on the Erie Railroad, changed at Buffalo for Detroit and from there went to Chicago, changed again for Kansas City, where we took the Kansas Pacific Railroad via Kit Carson to Las Animas, which was the terminus.[3] Mother went with us to Las Animas so as to see Father and then continued her trip and went to Salt Lake City. She was very much interested in everything she saw, and always so cheerful and merry. We had to change at Kit Carson, a town of one store and two or three houses right on the prairie, miles from nowhere. One time we stopped an hour or more and saw many antelope and rabbits. As we walked about picking flowers while waiting for a train to pass us, Mother saw "Hotel" on one of the houses, so she went to explore and came back with a large piece of tough pie in her hand, which she said she had bought to encourage the proprietor, for the reason that he was from some place in New York State.

Father had been ordered to take Captain James Burns, Fifth Cavalry, who was very sick and whose station was Fort Whipple, to Las Animas and there place [him and his family] on a train en route to Washington, D.C., their home. He took charge of them at Camp Verde, Arizona, but Captain Burns died on the road at Dead Man's Creek, about ninety miles west of Fort Wingate, to which Post Father sent his body . . . to be buried.[4] Father followed with the captain's wife and two small children and came on to Las Animas, where he started them by rail for Washington, D.C.

As soon as we arrived at Las Animas we inquired at the hotel if an army officer had recently arrived and were told that some army wagons had just come in from the west. I returned to the station and found Father on the platform. He had my telegram in his hand and was starting to look for us. His beard had grown and he was covered with dust and, not having had time to clean up, looked like a tramp. Mother and I cried about his looks, but we were glad to be with him again.[5] We stayed in the hotel, Mr. Kitchen proprietor, for two or three days. Las Animas is on the south bank of the Arkansas River, which here runs eastward. Fort Lyon, an Infantry Post, was situated on a low sandstone bluff on the north bank of the river a mile or so east from the town.[6] The next day we met Brevet Colonel Joseph R. Smith, Surgeon, who was just leaving, and on driving over to the Post we met some of the officers stationed there, among them Major J. C. J. Happersett, Brevet Colonel, Surgeon.

When Father left Camp Verde he had an escort of nine soldiers, some of which were discharged at Fort Lyon and others deserted. A corporal was the only enlisted man who returned with us. Father brought with him Cobre, his Apache Mojave Indian boy, aged about fifteen, who had come to him nearly a year before and said he wished to work for him. He took care of Father's horse and waited upon him. He was a bright, intelligent boy and we were soon all very fond of him.

Mr. Kitchen recommended to Father a man who was his baker and who wanted to go to Arizona with us. We were glad to have him, as he knew how to cook out of doors. He was one of the many men met in the West who had the wanderlust and had been pretty well over the country. Not long before this he had been out in some portions of New Mexico selling crucifixes, rosaries, highly colored pictures, etc., but as the people had no money his venture was not a successful one.

Father had been a month coming over and it would take that much time for us to get to the [Rio Verde] Agency, so we had to lay in a good supply of provisions. Our cook helped to choose the groceries, etc. that we would need at the commissary, and we laid in a surplus of sugar, as the Mexicans who lived at many of the places where we would camp and where there were no stores wanted sugar and would gladly exchange meat, chickens, eggs, and vegetables for it. They had no other use for money than to make buttons for their clothes and ornaments for their bridles and saddles.

We had a thorough-brace wagon, one with platform springs, and an army escort wagon, each drawn by four mules. There was a wall tent and fly to pitch every night and three cots to sleep on, also a mess chest furnished with all the necessary table-ware. The top turned back, and a bread-board then exposed formed a table. We ate our meals in the shade of rocks, trees, or bushes unless the wind was blowing, and then we had our spread under the tent fly. Every morning after our breakfast, the dishes were all put into the chest and it was shoved into the back of the wagon, the last thing. The dishes were washed when we reached our next camp, which was usually about noon. Our breakfast was ready sharply at sunrise, and by the time we finished the tent had been struck, the bedding rolled up, the cots folded and put into the wagon. We then stepped into our wagons and were on our way.

Our cook always had good meals, and he was neat and intelligent. Father arranged our drives so as to stop at a ranch every night where we could get feed and water for the mules. There were only a few American settlers in the country, and their houses were small. There were no fences, except the corrals for cattle and horses, and no gardens or fruit trees. Our first camp was about twenty-five miles from Las Animas. One day we made Purgatory River, "Picket wire," as the settlers called it.[7] Trinidad, one hundred miles southwest, a town of two short streets and near the mountains, was one of our camps.

After this we traveled more south, and the grade gradually became greater until we reached the top of Raton Pass in the Rocky Mountains.[8] From here the scenery was grand. We stopped to look at the high peaks north and south of us, the great valley to the east, and Trinidad glistening at the base of the mountains. No wonder the Spaniards thought that the towns they found were built of marble.[9] They were of adobe, sun-dried brick, coated with a thick whitewash made of gypsum, burned in the open air. It was put on by hand mostly; just as was done in Trinidad. . . .

The growth on the mountains was luxuriant, and we saw places among the thick ferns where deer had been lying. We descended past Dick Wooten's [Wootton's] in the Raton Pass and made camp at a cattle ranch in the open country at the foot of the mountains.[10] Thence we traveled across Maxwell's ranch, where we saw the first Indians; crossed Turkey Hills, the Vermejo, and the Cimarron.[11] Wild plums were abundant on both of these creeks and we gathered a great quantity of them.

We lay over one day at Fort Union, which is at an altitude of 6,750 feet and 100 miles northeast from Santa Fe in a beautiful valley affording fine grazing and good water. We were entertained by Captain John Lafferty, Eighth United States Cavalry, whose wife was East at the time. Among the officers stationed here was Captain W. R. Shoemaker, Storekeeper, Ordinance Department. Father had left four shave-tail mules here to rest on his way to Las Animas, as they were not acclimated to the altitude. We returned the borrowed mules and took the others.[12]

Our next camp was at Las Vegas [New Mexico], twenty-eight miles west of south from Fort Union, on the Santa Fe route. There are numerous mineral springs near here, which have since become a resort for invalids.[13] Somewhere along here two civilians and ten miners with thirty burros joined us.[14] We stopped on the road to visit the ruins of the Pecos Church, a very old adobe building, fast crumbling. There was no roof, only the sidewalls and some of the rafters, on which we saw crude carving in many places. The wood was very dry and well preserved, owing to the arid air. The building was originally much larger. No one could tell us when it was built, or when it began to fall into decay.[15]

The country began to grow more beautiful and mountainous again. There was good grazing in the valleys, and Union Spring near by the road furnished fine drinking water. There were groves of pine, piñon, scrub oak, and along the creeks cottonwood and willow grew to a good size. From Las Vegas our road ran north of west to Santa Fe, New Mexico. We camped at La Glorieta, or Pigeon's Ranch, where there was a fight, March 26–28, 1862, between the Confederate Texans and Federal Troops. We were shown two large crude pictures in oil, which had been painted to depict the engagement. We also saw some bullet holes in the trees and a few relics in the house. A tree was pointed out from which a sharpshooter had killed some men.[16]

We rested a day in the old Mexican City of Santa Fe. Its altitude is 7,000 feet and is situated about one hundred miles by our road south of west from Fort Union. The abandoned military Post of Fort Marcy was here.[17] The church of San Miguel is the oldest in the town. It was built of adobe, and some of the rafters and the door are rudely carved. An inscription in Spanish tells when and by whom the church was built. It was almost effaced but Father was able to get the date. . . .[18]

The original Cathedral is very old. When we saw it the walls were undergoing repairs. Some of the pictures, we were told, were painted in Spain, but they were very crude and look[ed] like the attempts of a child. The statues of the saints were of wood, clumsy, badly painted, and dressed in tawdry garments but were probably the best the poor people could afford.[19] We were shown some very handsome vestments. The very old bells had a sweet tone.

Near the Cathedral was the Convent, and inside its high fence was a garden beautiful with flowers, fruit trees, and grape vines. One of the nuns in charge of the hospital asked Father to examine a patient and prescribe for him, which he did, and she gave us a basket of delicious grapes, apples, and pears and some lovely roses, a great treat for us at that time. Grapes grew in abundance and the Mexicans and Indians pressed out the juice to drink unfermented.

There was a plaza in the center of the town, which was used as a market place. Any time during the day one could see many burros, each laden with a huge pile of small wood and branches for fires. Only their legs were visible. They had to peep through the branches to find their way about. There were very few trees on the plaza and not many in the gardens, as water is needed to make them grow and water was not plentiful. The shops were very poor ones, patronized mostly by Mexicans, as there were only a few Americans to buy their goods. We saw nothing that we wanted, except a bracelet of filagree [filigree] silver daisies, very pretty, and a pair of ear rings in the shape of a palm leaf of the same, which Father bought. Men who have a piece of charcoal, which they keep red hot with a blowpipe, make them from pesos, the Mexican dollars. They work the silver into the wire or cut it into shape on the charcoal. The ornaments are beautiful when first made, but soon tarnish and must be gold-washed to last well.

Our next drive was to Peña Blanca on the Rio Grande, and the road down to it was very rough, covered with porous volcanic rock, called mal pais. A few patches of ground were under cultivation, and there were some trees along the river. The village was typically Mexican, having adobe houses, not whitewashed, and a small church. In the evening the women went to vespers, wearing a black mantilla or a handkerchief on their heads. The people raised red peppers, squash, corn, and some wheat.

At a small town further on the people were more prosperous and were very busy harvesting their crops. They drove sheep over a well-beaten piece of ground to thrash their wheat and tossed it in the air from a shallow basket to winnow it. Some families were sitting on the ground shucking a pile of corn, others were stringing peppers to hang on the walls to dry, and still others were cutting squashes into strips to lay on the roof to dry. The cattle were driven out in the morning by a herder and brought in at night and kept in corrals, having high adobe walls. We saw very few cattle anywhere. These people keep goats for the milk, meat, and skins, and burros for transportation.

We crossed the river where it broadened out and was shallow and sandy. In the sand hills on the far side we picked up large pieces of obsidian and many pebbles of so-called smoky topaz, which were in reality water-worn pieces of obsidian. We climbed over high sandy hills covered with cedar trees to reach San Ysidro, a village of five or six houses where we stopped next, in the valley of the Santa Anna [Ana] River, along which were some trees and a little grass. When our cook heard the name he said it was well named, "Sand and cedar." The Indians here seemed to be better off than the Mexicans. They sold us grapes and peaches, which they had raised not far back on the right of our road at the Pueblo of Santo Domingo.[20]

The next morning we stopped for a while at the mineral springs in the Santa Anna [Ana] Valley. Some of the water was strongly charged with carbonic-acid gas, making it a delicious table water, and after drinking all that we could, we filled our kegs, demijohns, and canteens. We had not gone far before the corks began to pop out. We always carried drinking water with us for use in case the water should not be good at our next camp. The country shows the effects of great volcanic upheavals that look like piles of ashes, mountains high, bare of all growth, and I shuddered while looking at them. What wonderful moving pictures this scenery would make.

Before we made our next stop the country had improved very much, and at San Mateo, near mountains of that name, in which there were perhaps two hundred Mexicans, we saw many cattle and sheep. Our tent was pitched just beyond the town and at the Baca Ranch, the largest and best one we had seen west of the Rio Grande.[21] There was a large, well-fenced garden, and the walls of the corrals were of adobe. Some wheat was raised and much corn, many squashes, beans, and red peppers. Bins in the house made of adobe held the produce. The Baca's cattle herd was a large one, and there were thousands of sheep.

It rained for the first time on our trip, and the mistress of the house invited us in. Our room was chilly, so Father asked for a fire, but I saw no fireplace and asked him where a fire could be built. He pointed to a narrow nich[e] in one corner, about a foot from the floor and very white from many coats of gypsum or plaster of Paris, which I thought was intended for an image. A peon woman brought in some green wet sticks of wood about eighteen inches long, stood them on end and soon had a good fire burning. The wood would probably not have burned if it had been laid down. Water soon began to run down and streak the whitened adobe walls. Several of the household then turned out to carry dry earth up to stop the holes in the roof.

On getting into the ambulance the next morning we found red peppers, green corn, etc.—a present from our hostess of the night before. Her husband and nearly all of the men were away at the time. There were no Americans in these villages, and the people led a very primitive life. Their customs recalled those of the Israelites as described in the Bible.

In one town we heard laughing, singing, and the notes of a guitar after dark, and on going out [we] found that the people, young and old, were making syrup from the stalks of the Indian corn that they raise, which is much sweeter than the stalks of any other corn. An adobe furnace, twelve feet or so long with holes in the top, held brass kettles into which the stalks, cut into pieces, were boiled in water to extract the sugar.

Afterward the kettles were emptied into a press made of a section of a hollow tree about three feet high [and] a plunger of a solid section of another tree, on the top end of which lay a tree eighteen or twenty feet long, one end of which was secured. Men, women, and children crowded upon this to add to the weight. They moved their bodies up and down to the r[h]ythm of their songs until the cornstalks were pressed dry. The juice that had been caught in the kettles was then boiled to the consistency of syrup. Torches of fat pine stuck in the ground added very much to the picturesqueness of the scene. It was far into the night before the people quieted down and went to their homes.

Our cook always had hot bread of some kind for us, boiled hominy or cracked wheat and eggs and bacon or beefsteak or muttonchops and excellent coffee for breakfast and dinner. After crossing the Little Colorado we had venison instead of beef or mutton.

Cobre loved a joke, as do all Indians. Harold was fast enlarging his vocabulary, and among his new words was "mountain," which he pronounced "Moum." At breakfast when he started to ask for "More hominy," Cobre, who waited upon us, would watch closely and as soon as he uttered the word "more," Cobre would point at a mountain and Harold would end by asking for "moum." Or Cobre would point at a mountain and as the word "big" came from Harold's lips, he would point at the hominy so as to make Harold ask for "Big hom." This went on morning after morning for days.

One of our camps was at Agua Azul, or Blue Water, where we had peaches and grapes again, which we bought of some Pueblo Indians who were peddling them. We passed Bacon's Ranch, where Father made one of his camps when he was coming. We afterward crossed the Continental Divide and arrived at Fort Wingate, New Mexico, having traveled by a shorter road than the one through Albuquerque, one hundred fifty miles back.

Fort Wingate was on the Pacific side of the continent, beautifully situated on gently sloping ground on the south side of an open grassy valley.[22] The hills back of it were well-wooded pines, and at their base is a large, clear spring called Ojo del Orso, "Bear Spring," from which the water supply of the Post was procured. The mountains west and north are mostly red sandstone, and one can readily imagine, when looking across the valley, that the high sharply cut rocks that looked like spires really topped a great cathedral. They were called the "Navajo Church."[23] It is a wonderfully beautiful sight just after sunset, when they and the rocks about them are lighted up by the reflection from the rich afterglow in the sky. Some companies of the Third Infantry garrisoned the Post. We had delicious fresh grape juice, procured from the Pueblo Indians. The quarters were very comfortable ones, and there were some fine trees in front of them. Light rains fell from July to September and a little snow during the winter months and until the end of April. The gardens produced all of the usual fresh vegetables, except potatoes, which had not been planted.

Father used the itinerary of Lieutenant Colonel Richard I. Dodge, Twenty-third Infantry, as a guide from here on and found it very reliable. It told us where he had found wood for his fires, feed for his animals, and water.[24] At Wingate we left all white men and Mexicans behind and made our next camp at the Navajo villages, where there were about 7,500 Indians on their Reservation who had been living there since about 1868.[25] [They] are a very industrious people and raise enough Indian corn for their own use, besides squash, muskmelons, and water melons. They had large flocks of sheep and some cattle, goats, burros, and ponies. Their clothing was made from the wool of the sheep, which they weave into blankets, jackets, skirts, leggings, garters, and bands to hold their hair in place. The weaving is done on crude upright looms, usually set up under a pine tree in front of a "hogan," a kind of house of one small room that they live in. They used the natural black and white wool separately or mixed them to procure gray and dye the white wool with indigo to get different shades of blue. For red they raveled an English material, called "Gayetta" [bayeta], that they bought of the traders and mixed with the white wool.[26]

The ears of the Indian corn, or maize, are small, and the grains are red, purple, and white and very sweet. The women ground their meal on metates, or large stones with raised sides, using an oblong stone to break the grains, giving it a forward rolling motion. When still in the milk they crush it to make a thick cream, which they spread in thin layers on flat heated stones to bake. A pile of these thin cakes make only a mouthful and are very delicious.[27]

We bought some garters and two small blankets from the Navajos. It was a very peaceful scene in the evening to hear the tinkle of the sheep bells and the voices of the Indian boys as they drove in the flocks from pasture. The springs were simply mudholes, as the sheep and other animals were all watered there, but the Indians drank the water. We did not dare to use it, but we had plenty, which we had brought with us from Wingate.

Beyond the villages we met some Zuni Indians and bought several pieces of pottery from them. What they made was very beautiful, ornamented as it was with various designs in red and black on a background, [such] as sunflowers, roadrunners, etc. Both design and ornamentation are artistic. We saw many prayer sticks left by the Navajo and Zuni Indians along the road, which they had traversed on their trading expeditions.[28]

There was a thick growth of sunflowers for miles, and after coming through so much drab coloring, their yellow and black were very pleasant to the eye. We passed a group of mud springs, in and around which were many bones of cattle that had sunken into the mud and died. We crossed Dead Man's Creek [and] Cariso [Carrizo] Creek and made a camp at Lithodendron Creek in the Petrified Forest. It was a wonderful sight, as great trees were lying on the ground completely turned into beautiful agate of all shades of rich red and pink streaked with white, light gray, and even tints of lilac.

We walked among them and picked up a great many beautiful pieces that had broken off. Near our camp Father picked up a petrified plum pit that had probably once been in a can of plums brought here by a camper. There was no water in sight, but after the men dug down and sank a cracker box into the sand of the wash, it ran in as fast as they could dip it out. It was of a reddish color from a fine clay, which we settled with alum to drink but used it as it came out of the box to make our coffee.

A star mail route had been established between Fort Wingate and Prescott, and a buckboard made a weekly trip. It was a dangerous drive for one man to make, and at least one driver had been killed near the little Colorado River by the Apache Indians who were for years a menace to the white prospectors, trappers, and settlers.[29] As we approached the Apache country we drove slower so that the miners with their burros could always keep in sight of us.[30] Our next drive was to the Little Colorado River, which we crossed to make our camp on the far side. We always crossed rivers and creeks before making camp, for in this country they often rise suddenly during the night and are impassable in the morning.

From here to the Mogollon Mountains our road was steeper. One of our camps was at the edge of Quinriñon cañon, where we found good water in large holes, so called tanks, among the rocks in the bed of the creek.[31] Hundreds of antelope were grazing in the side of the hills near by, and Father started out to kill one but soon turned back, as he felt sure that hostile Indians were prowling about. Not long afterward, First Lieutenant Charles King, Fifth Cavalry, in command of a scouting party, sent out from Camp Verde, was wounded in the arm by Indians at this place or near here.[32]

We now passed through large groves of piñon trees full of nuts, and we camped at Snow Lake. The San Francisco Mountains were in sight for several days, and the view as we ascended the Mogollons became more extended and magnificent. At the summit we made our camp close to springs in a beautiful grove of quaking aspens, among thick ferns and breaks, some of which were nearly as high as my head. In places we saw spots where the deer had recently lain, and the next day we saw many deer. We could hear the wild turkeys going to roost after sunset and when leaving early the next morning. The air was crisp and bracing, and we needed a fire in front of our tent to warm us when we went to bed and arose. This was the most enjoyable part of our trip.

The descent of the Mogollons on the other side was more rapid than the ascent on the east, and the road was often over the bare, rough rock or was strewn with pieces of porous volcanic rock. We passed Stoneman's Lake, which was below us in the crater of an extinct volcano, north of the road and not far from our camp. Most of the way down the red rock country was near us, extending north along the Verde River. The rocks are of red sandstone and worn into the semblance of huge forts, castles, turrets, minarets, and other shapes which when the clouds dip behind them and the sun is rising or setting, are brought out in bold relief. We passed close to several precipices and looked down into the chasms, probably two thousand feet or more. At the foot of the mountains we crossed the Verde River and turning upstream, passed the old ruins at Oak Creek.[33]

We drove seven or eight miles and then, turning to the left after a gradual ascent of about two miles, reached our destination, the Indian Agency, which was situated near the foot of the Black Mountains on a small, clear, rapid stream of water that sank into the rocks three miles above and came out hot water below. The Yuma and Mohave Apache called it Aha-ka-roo-ya.[34] It soon cooled off and then deposited lime for some distance along its course.

The last day of our drive was very tiresome, owing to the roughness of the roads, although a very enjoyable one, as every day of our trip had been. We had everything with us to make us comfortable, and the country, even where it was barren, was interesting to me from its very desolateness and newness. It was a journey the like of which very few army women and not many officers have taken, but we are glad that we took it, and we wish that all of our sons could go over the same road.

CHAPTER EIGHT

"John Brown Had a Little Indian"

RIO VERDE INDIAN RESERVATION AND CAMP VERDE, ARIZONA TERRITORY, OCTOBER 1874–MAY 1875

THE RESERVATION EXTENDED forty miles along the Rio Verde and ten miles on each side. The tents and two or three adobe buildings at the Agency overlooked the river, beyond which was the wonderful red rock country. Our quarters at the Agency consisted of a hospital tent in front, framed and floored and provided with a board door and a large fireplace and chimney, a smaller tent at the back, and connecting was surrounded by a bulletproof adobe wall to protect the children and me if there should be any trouble with the Indians. To the left of us was a large tent used as a dining room for our mess. [Second] Lieutenant Walter S. Schuyler, Fifth United States Cavalry, was in command of the detachment of Troop K, Fifth Cavalry, and Oliver Chapman was the Indian Agent. Dr. Josephus Williams [had] left on account of failing health.[1] The man we brought from Las Animas cooked for us, receiving $75.00 per month. The meals were good, as we had fine fresh beef and procured canned goods from the commissary at Camp Verde, sixteen miles down the river.

The opening of our luggage was entertainment for the Indians. After the melodeon was set up and I began to play, they gathered around the tents in a crowd, wondering at the sounds they heard, not knowing how they were made, and didn't want me to stop. When I uncovered my sewing machine and began to sew they covered their mouths with one hand and drew in a sharp breath, they were so astonished. We were very comfortable, and as winter came on, enjoyed the bright fire in our fireplace.

Cobre went to the camp of his people for many nights after our arrival to relate what had occurred day-by-day on the road to Las Animas and back. He had seen big wagons go without horses but had not seen as much as the two Apache Yuma Indians, Washington Charley (Arriwana) and Pakotey, who had been to Washington, the former's name indicating that he had been there. On their return Arriwana gave each [such] an account of the wonderful things he had seen and heard that his people looked upon him as a Monchausen [Munchausen] and said he was the biggest liar they had ever heard talk. Pakotey had very little to say after that, and his veracity was not questioned. The first time I saw Charley, I asked him, "Have you been to Washington?" His reply was, "Twenty minutes for breakfast," in the tone of a brakeman.[2]

Cobre kept the tents clean, polished the shoes, and kept an eye on the children. Claude was a great surprise to the Indians, on account of his fair complexion and beautiful light brown wavy hair. The old squaws would stroke it whenever they could, smiling and talking all the time, but he didn't like their dirty hands and would dodge them. The old ones were hideous and by no means clean. The Indians here were the Apache Yuma from Date Creek, the Apache Mojave from the Mogollons and other mountains, and the Apache Tonto from Tonto Basin. The Tontos spoke an entirely different language from the others.[3]

General Crook whipped a tribe and then would use the men as scouts to subdue the next tribe and that against another, until he brought them all to the reservation. Al Sieber was for a long time at the head of the Indian Scouts; he understood their character very well and soon picked up the different languages.[4] Oliver Chapman, the former clerk, had succeeded Doctor Williams as Agent and had several Americans as employees. One was named Pangborn and another Jenkins, I think.

Father was the surgeon for the Agency and received $1,000.00 a year in addition to his army pay.[5] He studied the Indian languages, of which he already had some knowledge, and young men were often sent by their chiefs to teach him. No whites or Mexicans knew more than a few words

or sentences. The Indians trusted him, as he had inspected the first annuities that had ever been issued to them, condemned a lot of sugar that was
full of sand. . . . When he or Lieutenant Schuyler issued them their rations,
they received all that was due them. Then their medicine men, whom he
treated with respect, looked up to him as the great "Pasemache."[6]

Men and boys brought him rats that had pouches, birds, young coyotes, colored stones, and other gifts. They made bows and arrows for the
children, and one of them took from his neck a perfect quartz crystal that
he had sewed in buckskin and wore as a charm and gave it to me. One
medicine man gave Father a pipe, the shape of our cigar holder, made
from a green translucent stone with a mouthpiece of wild turkey bone, a
kind of pipe that the medicine men prize. They were constantly trying to
do us favors in return for what Father was doing for them. An Indian
whose son [had] been thrown from a horse [and] sustained a very bad
wound of one of his legs, which father had treated until it was well, in
gratitude brought his daughter as a "lowah" wife. And when Father said he
already had a wife, the Indian said, "Have two. One white and one Apache,
good." Father at length got rid of him by saying that the two would not
agree and get along together, and he went away laughing.

Father would gather many boys at night to teach them English and to
pick up Indian words from them. He taught them to count by beginning
with the song "John Brown Had a Little Indian," and the next day one
could hear them singing out to one another and to the employees, "One
little Injun boy," or "ten little Injun boy," etc.[7] He taught them other songs
and used the pictures in illustrated papers, etc., with great success. What
surprised me was to hear them speak English without any foreign accent.

The Indians would divide the last morsel of food they had with anyone
who was hungry. I once saw the workings of the custom. A man divided
a loaf of bread with another one who on meeting him said he was hungry. The one who received the half loaf met another one who said he was
hungry and . . . was referred to number one, who divided his remaining
half-loaf. And if he had met a third man he would have divided his quarter loaf with him, but the one to whom he had given one-half the loaf
retained it.

There were many children, and I took a great interest in them. One
day a squaw came to me with a naked babe and I gave her some clothes
to put on it. Pretty soon another squaw brought a naked babe, which I

also clothed, but when a third one appeared, I suspected it was the same babe and told them so. They ran off laughing at the trick they had played. Some of the women would try to tease me by casting the reflection of the sun from one of their little round mirrors into my face or on my book or sewing. One day a group of girls pushed open the back door so many times in fun that I became tired of closing it, so I filled a dipper with water and when the next girl pushed in the door, I poured the water upon her head. The others shouted with laughter and ran off teasing her. This will give you some idea of what they considered fun. They are all great at puns, and a good one is much appreciated and more especially when it is a combination of Indian and English.

Father, while throwing a stone, accidentally struck an Indian man and to make up, gave him a bag of smoking tobacco. From that time on the man was a frequent visitor at our tents. Before they came in contact with the whites, they were not habitual smokers of tobacco but smoked their wild tobacco only on ceremonial occasions.

They believed that disease and injuries of men were due to the evil influences of spirits which were instigated usually by women. A medicine man would indicate the woman, whom the men would seize [and] tie to a tree by her wrists to await the outcome of the case. If the man died she would be stoned to death. One night we heard someone crying at our front tent door, and opening it, Father found Keniah, a bright, young, intelligent woman, crouching close by. She begged protection, saying that a man was dying and men were searching for her to tie her up. Women not infrequently came to us to escape stoning, and they were usually the smartest of the tribes.

Before I arrived at the Agency, Bwawee Yuma, a Chief, had died from the effects of a kick in the abdomen by a horse, and his wife was stoned to death. The chief's own brother was said to have taken a hand in the stoning, in spite of the fact that he and all the tribe thought much of her and always respected her counsels, but she had lived for some years in a white family and the medicine man selected her as the one that had bewitched the horse to kick her husband.

General Crook was very fond of hunting and frequently came to the Agency to hunt ducks on Peck's Lake, which was in the river bottom a little way up on the far side of the river. He always was very successful, and we had wild ducks and other game when he stayed with us. One morning, after he had gone to the lake, I found the floor of the front tent littered with bits of paper. And he apologized when he returned, saying that he had not worn his hunting boots for some time and when he turned them upside down before putting them on, he found a mouse had made its nest in one of them.[8]

We had snow sometimes, but the little that fell melted in a very few hours. Only one night it was so heavy that Father, fearing that the roof of the tent, which was rather old, would give way, had to shovel it off.

The Indians had been successful at truck farming under the direction of army officers and were contemplating the extension of their patches in the spring. If left where they were, they would soon have been self-supporting, but the Indian Department sent a special Commissioner, Colonel L. E. Dudley, who had been an officer in the Civil War, to remove them to the San Carlos Reservation. They were very happy in their own country and did not wish to go where their enemies were numerous. Colonel Dudley tried to convince them that the change would be for their good and that he came from General Grant in Washington, who said they must go. They did not believe him and came to Father to know why they should leave the country that had always belonged to them and which the Government had promised should be theirs and their children's forever.[9]

Father assured them that General Grant said that they must go. We heard the wails of the women all night, and in the morning the chiefs returned and told Father they would go if he went with them. After he had promised, they had another talk with the Commissioner and consented to move.

In the latter part of February, when the day came for them to start, they gathered what belongings that they could carry. The very young children, old people, and sick were put into their cone-shaped baskets to be carried on the backs of the strong ones. One old man carried his old sick wife on his back in one of these baskets. The recommendations of Father and others to take the Indians around the mountains by wagon road was [were] ignored, and the march across rivers and over high mountains was begun.

They moved along slowly in a long, silent, sad procession. When they reached Camp Verde, sixteen miles down the Verde River, Father had not yet come up and they refused to go on unless he was with them. After he had joined them, they went on, but sullenly. Second Lieutenant George

O. Eaton, Fifth United States Cavalry, was in command of a detachment of men that went along as a guard, and one was needed, as very poor arrangements had been made for feeding the Indians. . . .

Before they reached San Carlos they were fighting hungry. One morning, after the food had all given out, a bullet whizzed over the Commissioner's head as a warning. He left quickly, promising to send back food very soon. When Father left them at San Carlos the women and children cried and the men begged him to stay with them or come back, as they were among their old enemies and they did not know the white man at the Agency.[10]

The children and I stayed at Camp Verde, where quarters were assigned to Father. The Post was about fifty miles by road east of Prescott and ninety miles by trail north of Camp McDowell, on a mesa west of the Rio Verde just below where Beaver Creek emptied into it. The Black Mountains on the west and Mogollons on the east were well covered with trees. Rains fell in March and July and together with the melting snow from the mountains, often caused a sudden rise of many feet in the river, which then was a raging torrent, and Father has seen it carry along great trees and large rocks. The old road was down Grief Hill, on which many a wagon has been wrecked, but it was very rarely traveled now as a fine graded road had just been completed by the troops through Copper Cañon. The river runs south into a cañon, but here its valley broadens and the bottomlands have a very rich soil, which with irrigation, yields abundant crops of all sorts. The Post garden produced beets, onions, corn, cabbages, cucumbers, melons, etc., and most of the officers had chickens.

The garrison was composed of companies from the Fifth Cavalry and Twenty-third Infantry. Brevet Lieutenant Colonel Julius W. Mason, Captain, Fifth Cavalry, had been in command and was followed by Brevet Colonel [J. J.] Coppinger, Twenty-third Infantry. Later, the Twenty-third Infantry was relieved by companies of the Eighth Infantry. At the time we went there Brevet Major George M. Brayton, Eighth Infantry, was the commanding officer. Some of the other officers were Lieutenants Charles Porter, Gordon W. Winslow, John McEwen Hyde, and W. H. Carter, who about this time transferred to the Sixth Cavalry.[11] Captain Henry M. Cronkhite was Post Surgeon, and at different times Doctors [Ira L.] Sanderson, [Richard E.] Lightburne, and [Warren E.] Day, Acting Assistant Surgeons, were there.[12]

Everyone was very kind to us. Captain Brayton came every evening to exercise and play with the boys, as Father always did. He was very jolly and I think enjoyed the play as much as the boys. There were water barrels placed in front of the quarters in case of fire, and Claude liked to stand on tiptoe to look into the water, and Harold would give him stones to drop in. I once caught him when he was handing a large glass jar that butter came in. The Captain would often lift Claude and Hal over to see where the stones, bottles, etc., had gone. Hal liked to prolong the word hound over an empty barrel.

The officers kept a large pack of fox and grey hounds with which they hunted jack rabbits, coyotes, etc., which would frequently start at one end of the long line of quarters and race over the verandas to the other, baying as they went. If they found a door open, in they would go and up stairs to the second story and then down. They were always hungry and once came into our kitchen and took a large steak from the gridiron over the coals, and in another kitchen stole a roast from the oven of a range, the door of which they found open.

All along the Verde River, perched on the bluffs or in the bluffs themselves, are very interesting ruins of buildings and walled-up caves. Some of them [are] in a fair state of preservation, many of them having parts of the walls still standing with piles of stone at the base. On Beaver Creek is a dwelling of several stories, five as I recollect. The lower story was reached by a ladder resting against a ledge of rock, along which one had to pass in order to go in the entrance. The second story we reached through an opening in the ceiling in the first, and so on up. In front of the last story was a balcony protected by a low wall, provided with apertures, through which the dwellers could shoot their arrows at an enemy. The Moqui Indians, according to their traditions which they related to Father, said that their ancestors lived here long ago but abandoned the valley about three hundred years back.[13]

One of the other places of interest is Montezuma Well, a great ampitheatre or pit, in the bottom of which is the water. It seems to have been formed by the gradual erosion of the soft rock, some of the debris of which lies at the base of the walls. The water probably enters by a subterranean passage, but the outlet is visible at the point where we entered. For some years it was said that the water was bottomless, but to decide the question, one of the officers of the Post borrowed an airbed from the hospital, and after paddling on it out to the middle, struck bottom after letting out seventy feet of line.[14]

In the bluffs, high enough up to be protected, are walled up caves, and at one which was down low I saw the imprint of a hand, which had probably been used to lay the mortar between the stones. The people occupying these ruins did not seem to have horses, nor did the Apache Indians have any until they were brought to the reservation, when General Crook encouraged the scouts to buy some with their pay.[15]

CHAPTER NINE

"The Almighty Made It Last"

ARIZONA TERRITORY AND ELMIRA, NEW YORK, MAY 1875–MAY 1876

AFTER FATHER'S RETURN WE remained at Camp Verde until May 2, 1875, on which day the troops of the Fifth Cavalry started eastward to go to another department and we started to go "inside," i.e., to California.[1] Arizona was then out of the world and was thought to be a country fit only for the Apache to live in. The Almighty made it last and didn't have much material left. He placed the creeks and rivers under the ground so that the water wouldn't all evaporate in the extremely dry air. Wood was cut with a spade, hay, grama grass (Boateloua gracilis) with a hoe, and corn planted with a crow bar.

We drove to Prescott to go with a man named Hussey over a new route that had just been opened, and the first stage was coming over. There were two other passengers, one of them Paymaster Johnson's brother and clerk, whom people called "Square" because he always took a square drink, he thought. The same four-horse team had to take us through, and we were to stop every night and camp where there was water. Grain was carried for the horses, and we lay in a supply of canned soups, meats, fruits, jams, hard bread, coffee, milk, etc., so that we could prepare our meals with very little labor, but we had no tents or cots. We passed old Camp Wallapi which, after General Crook had subjugated the tribe with the assistance of the Piutes, was abandoned.[2] The name Wallapi is a corruption of the name of the tribe, "Hualyapaia," the "people of the pines," that occupied this pine covered country.

We went to old Camp Mojave which was located on a gravelly mesa about seventy-five feet above the Colorado River on its east bank. The temperature in summer often reached 118°F and in winter the lowest is 35°F.[3] There are rain showers in July and August, but the river rises in June and is always muddy. The mails from the west came via La Pas from Los Angeles, 250 miles away. The Mojave Indians occupy this country, and their women wear kilts made of strips of bark hung over a belt. The rest of the body has a coating of red clay through which the fingers dig various designs. The men have a clout passed between the legs and hanging a few inches over a belt in front and almost to the feet behind, and they also cover the body with red clay.

That night Father gathered a great pile of twigs of the *larrea Mexicana* as there was nothing but the sand on which to make our bed, but after placing our comforts and blankets on the pile and we lay down to sleep, it sank, stuck together and formed a thin hard mat, no softer than the sand.[4] After this we always found a little hay on which to sleep. The boys would pick up straws and put them in their mouths to "Moke gars," as Harold said.

We crossed the river at Hardyville, and I think our next camp was at Marl Spring, after we had driven forty miles. The water had a ratty odor and was not agreeable to the palate, but every available spring or waterhole along the road had been located, as water was very precious in this country. We had some drinking water with us, so used the water here only to wash our faces and hands in.[5] . . .

While Father was taking some of our canned supplies out of the stage, the man came and invited us to eat dinner with him, but when Father declined he said, "You do not remember me, but you did me a favor three years ago at Camp McDermit, and I have killed and cooked one of my four chickens for you." So we had dinner with him. It was served on a board about six feet long fastened to two stakes driven into the ground and we sat on boxes that contained canned goods.

This was the sort of hospitality we appreciated and which we frequently met in the West. You could go into any house outside the towns and get a meal. If the proprietor was not in, you were at liberty to cook a meal yourself, but not to wash the dishes after eating from them or leave some kindling to build the next fire was a breach of hospitality, not easily excused.

The country was covered with stones of many colors and the road rather rough. Here, as in Arizona, there were many lizards, and the driver was expert with his whip in striking them. When at the Verde Reservation, I used to watch these animals catch the flies in our tents, and one in particular that had lost a part of his tail, and from the stump of which two tails appeared after a time. The air was wonderfully clear and objects in the distance were greatly magnified and seemed near, but at midday everything seemed to quiver. We saw many desert willow, which are also very common in Arizona, in the arroyos or washes.

From the hills on our approach to Soda Lake, which was one of our camps, we saw before us a great body of water on the far side of which was a castle surrounded by large trees and near which cattle were grazing. But when we reached the foot of the hills, the water kept receding from our view and a flat covered with soda appeared which gradually increased in size as we advanced, taking place of the water, which disappeared. . . . [W]e were near the low buildings of a ranch around which were bushes and some cattle. We had seen one of the mirages which are so common in dry countries. We could not wash in the water here, as it was strongly alkaline and would peel the skin from our hands and faces. The soda was washed down from the mountains by the occasional heavy rains, and the water, having no outlet, evaporated and left the deposit.

After this we passed through old abandoned Camp Cady, San Bernardino County, California, near some hills on the far side of the Colorado desert and about three hundred yards from the Mojave River.[6] There were adobe houses around the parade and a few trees, but we saw no people. There were some grass, cottonwood trees, and willows along the river and mesquite farther back. The soil is sandy and alkaline, and sand storms are frequent. The rainfall is small and in summer the temperature reaches 116°F, and 22°F in winter. We made a camp in Cajon Pass, in which the vegetation was different.[7] Father gathered an armful of *yerba santa* to take East with him, as he had seen it used by the Mexicans in California with good results for coughs. Before reaching Los Angeles we stopped at the Cucamonga Ranch and sampled the wines, but did not like any of them.

This was a very hard trip for me, but I was not so exhausted as I was after reaching Los Angeles a year and a half prior. The children, however, enjoyed the moving picture during the day and looked at the glorious stars at night while lying in the small hay piles with straws in their mouth[s], pretending to smoke, while Father was enjoying his cigar. Sometimes burros would come nosing about, and nearly every night coyotes would serenade us with their continuous yelps, which seemed to come from every direction. After resting a few days, we went by rail to Wilmington and there embarked on a steamer which took us to San Francisco, where Madame Rassette had a room ready for us.

Dr. Silas Mouser, an old friend of Father's father who had an extensive practice, thought there was a good opening for a physician in South San Francisco, so we went out there.[8] The only vacant house we could find was a vine-covered cottage on Fourteenth, now Newcomb Avenue, No. 175, between Phelps and Newhall Streets, and we set up housekeeping in it. We had a sitting room, dining room, bedroom, kitchen, and servant's room. There was a small yard in front filled with roses, fuchsias, geraniums, and other flowers. A grass covered lawn at the side and back, besides some flowers, had several fruit trees on it, and a windmill furnished us water from a well for household and irrigating purposes.

A Chinaman, who was a very good cook, did all of our work, but I had to stop him from sprinkling the clothes before ironing them by taking water in his mouth and blowing it over them in a fine spray. I listened for fear he might spray the bread and biscuit in the same manner, as I heard that some of his countrymen did. One day Ling hung a tablecloth near the stove, and a spark from the wood fire burned a hole in it. I pointed to the hole and told him he must be more careful, when he replied, "Me no bunny him, he bunny hisself." Most of our firewood was knotted roots of bushes dug out of the sandhills in the city.

There was only one other house on the block, and we had no neighbors with whom I could affiliate. A horse-car line on Kentucky Avenue, a block and a half away, would take us into the City, but it was a long ride, past slaughter houses and through the Potrero.[9]

. . . On July 4, 1875, at 9:40 o'clock A.M. our third and welcomed son, Philip Worthington Corbusier, was born amid more than the usual noise made to celebrate the day. Some boys had two anvils between which they placed a charge of powder on a playing card and set it off by means of a

long iron rod heated at one end. They kept up the salute from early
morning until late at night, while others were setting off fire crackers, tor-
pedoes, etc.

My nurse was a scrawny woman who knew very little about babies,
and Phil was beginning to turn purple from cold after she bathed him,
when Father took him from her to the fire. We soon sent her away as she
was too stupid and conceited to follow the directions given to her. She
once said, "My, you must be a one when you are about." We replaced her
with a capable German girl named Emma.

Father soon saw that the suburb was not growing and had no immedi-
ate future, and as he had intended when he accepted the position of acting assistant surgeon to enter the service permanently, we left for the East
when Phil was four months old and went to Elmira, New York, where the
children and I lived with Father's mother while he went to New York City.

The boys were delighted to be at their grandmother's, and they were
very sorry when the time came for us to leave. She had a German girl
named Theresa Freeman, whom she had taught to do all sorts of house
work and who had taken care of Claude and Harold when I was home
before. Mother and I did a great deal of sewing on her machine.

She had many warm friends, some of them belonging to a card club
that met oftener at her house than elsewhere, and after the games of
whist, she would have a delicious supper to which the husbands were
invited. I did not play cards, so I would sit working a piece of embroidery
and listening to the merry talk which Mother started.[10] Phil was very
much admired, and I always had to bring him in to let everyone see what
a thriving and handsome baby he was.

CHAPTER TEN

"*Proceed without Delay*"

SOUTHERN SOJOURNS,
MAY 1876–NOVEMBER 1877

FTER FATHER HAD PASSED A successful examination before the medical examining board as a candidate for a commission in the Army, he was ordered to Fort Macon, North Carolina, as an Acting Assistant Surgeon to relieve Captain Charles Styer, Assistant Surgeon.[1] He came after us and took us to his station, where we arrived May 9, and on August 5, 1876, he was commissioned an Assistant Surgeon, United States Army, with the rank of first lieutenant. His pay was $1,600.00 a year, which was less money than he had received at the Rio Verde Indian Agency, where he drew $1,000.00 a year free from the Indian Department in addition to his army pay.[2]

The Fort was at the east end of Bogue Island at the outlet of Pamlico Sound and across the sound from Beaufort, which is two miles north, and Morehead City, the terminus of the Atlantic and North Carolina Railroad about the same distance west.[3] We arrived at the latter place about sunset, stayed at the one hotel overnight, and crossed the next morning to the Fort in a sailboat manned by two [N]egroes with whom we had many a sail afterward. The island is a sand bar about twenty-six miles long upon which high dunes had been cast up by the action of wind and water on the ocean side, on which coarse grass and a few bushes grew. Back of the dunes, there was a thick growth of pine trees, except near the Fort. Jetties of large rocks protected the Fort from the encroachment of the sea, which in connection with the winds constantly changed the outline of the coast.

Our quarters were at the foot of the glacis of the Fort, back from the beach on the sound side. A gallery ran the length of the front, and one in the rear separated the main part of the house from the kitchen and servant's room. Besides the latter, we had two bedrooms, a living room, and a dining room, all of good size. Two colored women were our servants: Aunt Rene, a good old soul, did the cooking; Eliza, the housework and looked after the children. The outside work was done by a soldier striker.[4]

Fish of many varieties were to be had for very little. White fish, sea trout, croakers, and sheephead could be caught at the wharf, and we spent much time taking them with hook and line. When the mullet were running, a long seine belonging to the artillery was hauled by some fishermen on shares, and we often went to the beach on the ocean side to see the beautiful fish that were ensnared in this manner. My childhood days came back in my mind when I saw the seine hauled in the Bay of Biloxi on the Gulf Coast of Mississippi. Officers and soldiers caught huge drum from the ends of the jetties and blue fish from sail boats. I started out once after blue fish but had to be landed, as the rough water made me seasick, but I was usually a very good sailor. . . .

Large flounders, or plaice, were speared along the shore; a large cresset filled with burning fat pine in the bow of a canoe lighted up the fish so that they could be seen. Rock crabs were thick at certain seasons under the wharf and around the piles, and Negro boys brought us soft shell crabs from the marshes nearby. We bought oysters by the canoe-load and had them dumped into a little inlet where we could get them fresh from the water. Diamond-back terrapins could be bought for twenty-five cents a piece. Conchs were to be had for the digging, and we sometimes made soup of them for a change.

All of our food that was taken from the water was very fine and Aunt Rene cooked it to perfection, but we didn't relish the flavor of fish in the native beef that was furnished us, so when we felt like having a good roast or a steak we sent to Fulton Market in New York, and a steamer that made one trip a week to Morehead [City] brought it to us.[5]

Chickens, eggs, and sweet potatoes were to be had in Beaufort, and in season, peaches, cantaloupes, and watermelons were plentiful. The latter cost about three cents a piece, so we would buy a canoe load and pile them up in the fireplaces, where they would keep cool, for we rarely could procure ice. The water barrels, to which we had become accustomed by this time, stood on the back gallery and were filled daily from a well, the water in which when low was pronouncedly brackish.

During some seasons of the year we had raw oysters on the half shell before nearly every meal, sitting or standing on the back gallery and taking them from Eliza as fast as she opened them, and I could play that I was a girl again at home. Winter evenings we frequently had oysters roasted in the dining-room fireplace on a grate over the coals and would eat until there would be quite a pile of shells in front of us. The rule is to eat until you cannot see over the top of the pile in front of you.

There was much to interest us in the sea and on land. We fished, sailed, rowed, bathed in the sea, gathered seashells, [and] strolled along the beach and among the dunes. Some of the beautiful seashells were washed up by the waves, and others we dug out of the clean, white sand. Sometimes we would find a nautilus or Portuguese man-of-war in a small pool left by the receding waves, and I would carefully sink a tin pail under it so as to take it home. When there, I changed it to a basin and told the children about its habits. One of the latter Claude touched, and I can yet see his surprise when the water turned purple from the fluid it threw out to hide within.[6] We frequently kept sea anemones in glass jars of sea water for the children to watch and see them throw out the fringe-like tentacles, when they resembled beautiful flowers. Much of our time was spent on the beach in the sand of which the three boys loved to play. They would dig holes and I would cover their feet and legs, greatly to their delight. They liked to bury a fiddler crab and watch him dig his way out. They called the sea cucumbers "doughnuts."

We had no bathtubs, so the children were tubbed, except during the warm season, when we took them to the ocean, back of the hospital, or the inlet at the end of the line of officers' quarters. Claude loved the still bathing, but when there was surf, he was afraid of it. Father tried to induce him to go into it with him, but he screamed and ran away along the beach like a sand piper. Where the water swept around the jetties, the current was very swift, and the young boy of one of the soldiers

who jumped from the end of one of them was carried out to sea and not
seen again.

Little green and black frogs were numerous in the marshes, and one of
the men killed and dried enough to form a gun squad. He placed them in
their proper positions at a small cannon and gave the group to Father. We
seldom heard a songbird and there were not many ducks, gulls, snipe, or
curlew. In the winter Father killed rabbits, and once he went on a hunt
toward the west end of the island but saw no deer. The glacis was covered with white clover in which there were many wild flowers. The children loved to roll down the slope, and it was here that Phil, under Eliza's
encouragement, while we all watched him, tried to drop salt on a bird's
tail. Claude and Hal had tried to do so elsewhere some time before that.

During the summer months, the winds from the southwest came
laden with mo[i]sture, which would take the starch out of dresses, etc.,
and our shoes sometimes became covered with mould over night. There
were a few days and nights that we would feel wilted. We experienced
one furious storm, the like of which we have not seen since. It carried
away the wind gauge when it registered seventy-five miles an hour. The
water was lashed so that the air was filled with spray, and it was driven
under our houses to the glacis of the Post. [It] float[ed] the boardwalk,
upon which Father fell, striking the back of his head, when he went out
to try to anchor it. The hospital was cut off from the Fort, the wharf was
torn to pieces, and most of the boats [were] carried away. It rose so rapidly that a laundress and her children had to climb on a table in their little
house, and the men who pushed a boat to their rescue waded to their
armpits before they reached them.[7]

The wind was so strong that men crawled along the ground and held on
to the rails of the tramway to get to the wharf to save some of the boats.
The roof of a large hotel in Beaufort was carried away, and a large schooner
[was] tossed over the sea wall into one of the streets. Several times I
thought of old Fort Hamilton [Hampton], which once stood on what was
now only a sand bar a few feet under water on the opposite side of the inlet
and over which we had sailed many times.[8] We were very much relieved
when the tide began to run out and the wind abated, but we had no com-
munication with the mainland for several days. Our carpets, curtains, and
some of our bedding were soaked through and could be dried only with
difficulty, as the salt crystallized on them for some time afterward.

The Fourth of July, 1876, was celebrated in Beaufort, and we went over in a large boat rowed by a crew of soldiers who sometimes took us to town. When the tide was low, the water was quite shallow over one of the bars and the men had to wade, pushing the boat until they came to deeper water. Many of the artillerymen went over and took part in the parade, which was one to be long remembered by the inhabitants. First along the street came a few cows, some pigs, and numerous squawking geese. These were followed by a crowd of ragged, barefooted Negroes cheering, talking, laughing, and marching to the time of the music of drums and bugles. Then came the artillerymen in their full dress uniforms with red trappings, looking very gay. The whole population gathered at the stand from which patriotic speeches were made, and we heard the history of the Mecklingburg [Mecklenberg] Declaration.[9]

There was not much to be seen in Beaufort except the great heaps of oyster shells. It was a summer resort for people from the interior who came over to our island for the bathing. The other sand bars were inhabited by poor, illiterate fishermen called "bankers," who wore very little clothing and lived mostly on fish that they caught and the few sweet potatoes that they raised.

Just before we went to the Post they had captured a whale sixty feet long, and with the proceeds of the sale of the baleen and oil each family was able to buy some clothes, a couple of chairs, and a few boards with which to erect a school house. They depended upon Father for medical and surgical treatment. The government had authorized the giving to them of medicines, dressings, etc. After they had been to the hospital, they would come to our quarters for old clothes, tea, sugar, etc., sometimes bringing a curious fish, a seashell or two as a present.

The first one that came was announced to us by Eliza as a "banker," and we were surprised to see, instead of a well-groomed, successful looking man, a poor old ragged fisherman. He had come to ask Father to go to see his youngest son, who had not slept throughout a night for weeks on account of the great pain in one of his thighs. Father went and found that the thighbone was diseased, and he afterwards operated — 75 — upon the boy. Some weeks later the old man presented Father with some tough, dried, and smoked mullet roes, saying as tears rolled down his cheeks that he brought them in gratitude for what had been done for his son. . . .

Along the island were kitchen middens in the form of high hills of seashells, indicating that a large, prehistoric population had opened oysters, clams, and other shellfish here for generations. Some stone and other implements and a few skeletons of human beings had been exhumed.

The Fort was garrisoned by two batteries of the Second Artillery, commanded by Captain John I. Ro[d]gers.[10] The other officers were Captain Frank B. Hamilton; First Lieutenants Medora Crawford Jr., Eli L. Huggins, William Stanton; Second Lieutenants Charles A. Tingle and later Eli D. Hoyle. The women were Mrs. Rodgers, Mrs. Crawford, and her mother. Some of the officers and all of the men were quartered in the casemates of the Fort, which in summer were very damp and not fit for habitation. . . .

On Thursday, March 15, 1877, our fourth son, Francis Addison Corbusier, was born at 11 A.M. He was quite a fat baby and had soft down on his arms and shoulders and very light colored hair of a reddish tinge on his head. He was always bright and well and had a very happy disposition, which he had [has] retained to the present day. Eliza was his nurse, and she was a gentle, capable girl.

The garrison was withdrawn in April 1877, and Second Lieutenant William A. Simpson was detained to take charge of the property, except that of the Medical Department, and he and Father shipped the serviceable stores mostly to Charleston, South Carolina. A few men were left behind to do the packing, and while doing this Mr. Simpson messed with us. The children were very fond of him, and Phil called him "Impshy."

The house was over-run with mice, and the great amusement after supper was to close the doors and then go mouse hunting. Father, Mr. Simpson, and the boys on all fours would look under the furniture and poke around with sticks. When one was found, a shout went up and all scrambled to catch it.

We left Fort Macon April 29 and arrived at Charleston, May 1, 1877, where Father was assigned quarters in the Arsenal grounds on the Ashley river. We occupied one side of a brick house, and First Lieutenant Thomas R. Adams, Fifth Artillery, and his wife, the other side. Major David H. Kinzie, Captain, Fifth Artillery, was in command, and First Lieutenant Frank Thorp was the quartermaster. About the center of the city was the Citadel, under the command of Captain Henry F. Brewerton, under whom were First Lieutenants Selden A. Day, Anthony W. Vogdes,

Elbridge R. Hills, Estcourt J. [James Estcourt] Sawyer; Second Lieutenants William B. Homer and Granger Adams, all of the Fifth Artillery.[11] Captain Samuel S. Jessup [Jessop], Assistant Surgeon, had charge of the hospital, and the sick of the Arsenal needing treatment in hospital were sent over there, Father going over every morning to do his share of the work.

We did not unpack our messing outfit but took our meals just outside the grounds with a Mrs. Black and family, whose cooking was done in the best southern style. Officers and soldiers were charged no fare on the streetcars. The men we met were very cordial, but few of their wives called upon us, as they were the last to forget that the war was over.[12]

After we had been in Charleston only five weeks, Father was ordered to proceed without delay to Chattanooga. We packed very hurriedly and were ready to leave when another telegram was received which re[a]d, "For without delay, read: without *unnecessary* delay." We arrived at our new station, June 9, 1877, where there were two companies of the Eighteenth Infantry, Captain Edgar R. Kellogg in command. The other officers were First Lieutenant George S. Hoyt and Second Lieutenant Daniel H. Floyd. The quarters were small houses that had been built for the workmen at the National Cemetery, upon which few repairs had been made to render them habitable.[13] Mrs. Kellogg and Mrs. Hoyt were very companionable and we spent many happy hours together.

We had no difficulty in securing a fine cook. She liked to surprise us with some dainty dish. Often she would say, "Miss Fanny Hoyt will smell this and be here pretty quick." I would tell Mrs. Hoyt, who lived next door, what our cook had said, so she would just drop in, much to the delight of Jane. Mrs. Hoyt's cook was an old colored woman, who while sitting on our back gallery after dark would relate wonderful stories about ghosts and strange people she had known. . . .

Chickens and eggs were cheap, as were peaches, pears, apples, strawberries, and blackberries. A Mrs. Blackberry supplied us with many of these as well as with milk and vegetables. Her flower garden was my delight, and I loved to visit it and gather its flowers. Our cook and she were great friends, and in the afternoons they would often pack Frank off with them to show him with pride to their neighbors.

Phil was now pretty independent of his nurse and could usually take care of himself, but one day I was on the Kellogg's gallery when Phil ran back to our house alone, and one of the goats, which the Kellogg children owned and drove, followed him full of play. Phil wasn't used to goats, so tried to avoid him by getting close into a corner of the gallery. The goat reared and then, with his head down, made several passes at Phil as if to butt him, so Captain Kellogg had to run to his rescue.

We looked from our front gallery up to Lookout Mountain in front and Mission[ary] Ridge on our left, where great battles were fought during our Civil War. Our drives often took us to the foot of them through groves of oaks, hickory, chestnut, and pines, and once we went up to the summit of Lookout itself on a picnic. From here we could see a portion of four states, and the Tennessee River, which seemed a mere thread of silver, winding about the mountains.[14] Down a deep gorge were the bones and part of the trappings of a mule that had fallen into it.

In the mountain, which is a limestone formation, are great caves called "The Mountain City." A narrow passage way leading from one of the caves was a short way down to our carriages, so we followed it and all except Mrs. Kellogg negotiated it without difficulty, but she got caught and had to be turned sidewise and pulled through. She lost one of her slippers during her struggle, which she never recovered.[15]

We were not at Chattanooga long before the great strike of railroad employees occurred and Father was ordered to accompany troops to the Quartermaster's Depot at Jeffersonville, Indiana, and he left with a company of Infantry on July 25.[16]

Congress had not appropriated money for the payment of the Army that year, so Father had to pay a discount of 10%, $13.33, at the bank to get his pay accounts for July cashed, but only this one month, as Jay Cook[e] & Co., of New York advanced the pay of officers for an interest of 6% a year until Congress appropriated the money.[17]

While Father was away, Lieutenant Floyd loaned Mrs. Hoyt and me a basket phaeton and a small mule, which he needed only a part of the day. It was great fun to drive this little mule to town and to hear the comments of the people about his size. Dr. Van Deman visited the sick at the Post and one night gave a "fate sham peter," as the townspeople called it.[18] His lawn was lighted by means of numerous Chinese lanterns, and the affair was quite a brilliant one. President Rutherford B. Hayes visited the city, but none of us were invited to the reception given to him at night. Even Mrs. Hoyt, whose silver, etc., was borrowed for the occasion and was a cousin of the President, was not invited.

CHAPTER ELEVEN

"We Could Improvise Anything Necessary for Living the Simple Life"

CAMP SHERIDAN, NEBRASKA, NOVEMBER 1877–APRIL 1880

FATHER RECEIVED AN ORDER TO proceed to Camp Sheridan, Nebraska, while he was still at Jeffersonville but accompanied the troops back to Chattanooga. It didn't take us long to get ready, and we went to Sidney, Nebraska, by rail via the Union Pacific Railroad, where at Fort Sidney, which was on the west bank of the north fork of the Platte River, we were furnished an ambulance and four mules. The Fort was at an elevation of 6,700 feet above the sea level, and Brevet Lieutenant Colonel Charles Winne, First Lieutenant and Assistant Surgeon, was Post Surgeon.[1]

From here we made the drive of 120 miles to Fort Robinson in three days, stopping one night at a house on the north fork of the Platte, and another on the Niobrara River. When about half way to Fort Robinson, we met Captain Curtis B. Munn, Assistant Surgeon, and family on their way to the railroad, and we exchanged ambulances so as to return them to the Posts where they belonged.

At the north fork [of the Platte] after a very good supper, at which we had delicious antelope meat, I examined the beds which we were to occupy that night. They were bunks of rough boards supporting bed ticks of hay and some dirty ragged comforts. When I asked one of the two daughters of the house for some sheets, she called her sister to bring her the sheets that were on the sick man's bed. It is needless to say that we didn't use the sheets, but tossed the dirty covers from the bed ticks and slept on our wraps.

We were at Fort Robinson one night.[2] Two or three troops of the Third Cavalry were stationed there, and I think that Brevet Lieutenant Colonel Frederick Van Vliet, Captain, Third Cavalry, was in command. It [If] not then, he was soon afterward. Captains Peter D. Vroom and Joseph Lawson, and First Lieutenant Albert D. King were among the other officers. The next day, November 23, 1877, we were given a fresh team and we drove east forty miles to Camp Sheridan, our destination. After passing the old Red Cloud Agency, not far from the Post, there wasn't a habitation on the road or within sight, and we met no one.[3] Cattle and cowboys had not yet entered that country, but they began to come in within a few months, and about a year later longhorn steers could be seen grazing along this road.

Our new station, 162 miles from Sidney, was located a mile below the old Spotted-Tail Indian Agency on the east side of Beaver Creek, which empties into White River a few miles north.[4] The buildings were on a terrace, which, flat at first, gently sloped eastward up to the foot of the hills a few hundred yards away. In the opposite direction and across the creek was a high bluff, which obstructed our view of the country beyond. On this bluff and on the hills back of us were several scaffolds on which the Sioux Indians had placed their dead. The Agency had been removed to the Rosebud not long before, and half a mile below, a Frenchman, who was the beef contractor (who on occasions acted as a guide), and his Indian woman and half-breed children, were the only inhabitants within forty miles.[5]

Father relieved Captain Egon A. Koerper, Assistant Surgeon, who shortly afterward left for another station. Deane Monahan, Captain of Troop G, Third Cavalry, that garrisoned the Post, was in command, and under him were First Lieutenant Emmet Crawford, Third Cavalry, and Second Lieutenant William P. Goodwin, Fourteenth Infantry. Later, Second Lieutenant Halverson F. French joined the troop.

Our quarters, which were a one-story frame building of battened upright boards, were quite comfortable. A gallery ran along the front and a vestibule gave entrance to three rooms, one of which was on each side and one at the back. The latter opened into the dining room, and back again of this were the kitchen and servant's room. A cellar beneath the kitchen was surrounded by sawdust held in place by boards.[6] Against the fence of the back yard were the stable and chicken house, and near the back gate stood the water barrels which were to be seen at every frontier Post. I think that there were five sets of officers' quarters, and in front of them all were wild cucumber vines trailed up the galleries.

Across the parade were the hospital and the men's quarters, and at the north end the sutler store, not far from which was a quartermaster and commissary storehouse of stone. We had to camp out in our quarters for the three coldest months of the year, as our household effects did not come until we had written several times about them and a tracer was sent out, which at length found them under a great pile of sacked grain in a warehouse at Sidney. This experience taught us to always send out a tracer to follow our effects as soon as we arrived at a new station.

Father and I had become by this time quite expert in devising ways and means of making ourselves comfortable, and we could improvise any-thing necessary for living the simple life. The quartermaster furnished us with stoves, tables, and a few barrack charis [chairs], and beds were bor-rowed from the hospital. We made dressers, bureaus, washstands, a lounge, and shelves out of boards and covered them with calico bought at the sut-ler store. Fortunately for us there was a sawmill at the Post, but we were greatly rejoiced when at length our things came.

We had only the most necessary pieces of furniture [such] as six fold-ing dining room chairs, two folding rockers, a folding high chair, all of black walnut with woven cane seats and backs, mattresses in sections, sets of bed springs and feather pillows, a spring lounge with detachable legs, and a sewing machine. With such articles as brass curtain poles, carpets, hang-ing draperies, engravings, etc., that were easily packed, we were well pro-vided. Shelves against the wall, hidden by cretonne or other curtains, served for closets, wardrobes, and dressers.

The next spring [1878] I raised geraniums, nasturtiums, and other flow-ers, and although there were no indications that vegetables had ever been raised here, we planted a garden down near the creek. When we were about to reap the fruits of our labor, a cloudburst washed everything away. We heard a peculiar noise and on looking south to the head of the creek saw a great copper-colored cloud, the shape of a scroll, unroll itself and pour down a deluge of water which rushed along with such force that it carried trees and rocks before it. The men hurried with ropes to tie fast the bridge that crossed the creek, but it was tossed upon the crest of the water and carried away before they were half way to it.

The next year [1879], however, we were successful far beyond our expectations in raising as fine vegetables as can be found in the most fertile parts of the country. Father had the fire wood, when delivered by the contractor, piled so that it would nearly enclose an acre or more of ground on the first terrace above the bed of the creek, and on this piece of ground we planted and gathered more lettuce, radishes, peas, beans, leeks, onions, sweet corn, cucumbers, spinach, squash, and tomatoes than we could eat, and a few potatoes. We frequently sent some to our friends at Camp Robinson and the Agency, who had not been so successful as we were. When the cold weather came on we pulled the tomato vines up by the roots and hung them up in the cellar where the green fruit continued to ripen for several weeks.

Captain Crawford, who was then in command of the Post, also met with great success. He had the former agency corral ploughed, and his men raised a variety of vegetables. He also could treat his friends at Fort Robinson with the produce of his garden, and when in the fall the Commissioner of Indian Affairs, Carl Schurz, accompanied by Count Donhoff [Dernhoff], Mr. Webb Hayes, and a gentleman connected with the *New York Times*, on their way to the Pine Ridge Agency, took luncheon with us, we had on exhibition a table full of the finest specimens of each of our gardens.[7]

At the luncheon, we had a roasted hindquarter of antelope, a kind of meat none of them had ever eaten before, and I remember that the Count said in his German accent, "Antelope meat is a very fine meat, Mr. Schurz," and in his enthusiasm he gave his nose a peculiar twist and off shot his *pince nez* and flew almost a foot and then sprang back to fall against his chest. . . .

Spike-tail grouse, which were very numerous, were delicious when young, but in winter tasted of the sage, which they fed upon. If drawn as soon as shot, however, and laid in salt and water a few hours before cooking, the sage flavor is not so noticeable. Father and Captain Crawford hunted them as soon as they were large enough, and in winter we always had a row of them hanging on the north side of the house.

There were also great flocks of blackbirds, and more than once we had four and twenty baked in a pie, the first ones shot by Captain Crawford to please the children, who were devoted to him. Frank called him "Campo," and he called Frank, "Franko." He messed by himself for some weeks, but one day his soldier cook was taken sick and Father asked him to come to us until his man was well, and he seemed so happy that I insisted that he should remain with us, and he did. He was gentle, kind, chivalrous, and ever ready to undertake any perilous duty for which he might be detailed.[8]

Years afterward, one mile north of the Arras river, 50 miles southwest of Nacori, Mexico, and about two hundred miles from the border, he lost his life while on very hazardous duty in charge of Indian scouts chasing the Indian chief Gerinomo [Geronimo], who had fled into Mexico. A force of Mexican soldiers on January 11 were firing at his Indian scouts when, to save them, he stood upon a rock and called out that they were Americans. For answer they fired a volley and wounded him. He died January 18, 1886.[9]

At the end of a year Eliza wanted to return to her mother, who had written that she was dying. [B]ut [she] was found to be in a good state of health, and Eliza wanted to return to us. Mother had in the meantime sent us a woman from Elmira. Louie was a fine cook and never tired of work but about once a month had paroxysms of rage, and then she would fling saucepans, flat irons, or anything else at hand at our soldier striker, Lewis. He would rush down the steps into the yard to get away from her and at length said he couldn't stand such treatment any longer. He wished to return to his troop but was too good a man to lose, as he took excellent care of the horses, chickens, cow, etc., and I prevailed upon him to stay with us.

Louie said he didn't know how to milk, and she did that for herself, saying that at a dairy in Elmira she had milked forty [cows] a day. She came in her bare feet one meal to wait upon the table, and Captain Crawford, happening to look down, was very much surprised when an explosive, "Well!" came from her, and she seemed ready to spring upon him. Another time she brought in a platter which was so hot that the steak upon it was sizzling and placed it so far away from Father that he had to draw it toward him. She then waited to watch him burn his fingers, and as he shook them and looked at her she snapped out, "Well, couldn't you see it was hot?" We couldn't help laughing, and she stamped out of the room.

Her spells always ended with a flood of tears, and she would be very
repentant and beg to stay with us.[10]

Toward the latter part of the first summer [1878], we had a terrific hail-
storm. The hailstones were very large, many of them seven inches in cir-
cumference and weighing an ounce and a half when gathered after the
storm. These were made up of smaller ones frozen together and came
first from the west and then from the north, shattering all the panes of
window glass, some hundreds in number, on those sides of the quarters.
Young chickens were knocked down and killed, and horses and cattle considerably bruised. The next summer there was another great fall of hailstones, but none were so large as these.

Coyotes were numerous and sneaked about at night uttering their
plaintive yelps. They would sometimes get on the roof of our chicken
house looking for a place to get in, and skunks would sometimes manage
to find an entrance. Father more than once got out of bed and, lightly
clad, would go out to shoot one of them. Among the hills back of us a few
hundred yards we saw every morning in mid-winter great grey wolves
prowling about. The men poisoned many of them for their skins with
which to make carriage robes. Holes were bored in a log and these were
filled with lard or suet in which strychnine was placed. The wolves would
lick at these holes and die nearby.

. . . In the fall of the year the grass would dry up, and several times we
saw fires nearby. They were much to be feared, and on the approach of
the first one all of the soldiers were turned out with gunnysacks to burn
a space around the Post as a guard. . . . The men were left to see that the
fire did not jump it and reach the buildings.

The boys enjoyed hunting for fossil remains in the many bluffs and
learned a great deal about geology. Father taught them botany in the
creek bottoms and on the hills, geography at the creek-side, and zoology
wherever a skeleton of an animal lay. One lesson every day was to write
about what they had seen the day before. Their pony, a very dark bay
mare called Jen, seemed to appreciate a joke, as whenever she came to a
nice sandy spot she would buck Claude and Harold off her back and then
turn with erect ears to look down at them.

As Phil grew larger, he wanted a pony. He had ridden, as had the
other boys, at first in Father's arms and afterward behind him, so we
caught a white colt that hung about the Post, having been left behind

by the Indians. The boys called him "Ghost," and Phil tried to mount him by himself while the colt was tied to the fence and no one else was around. He put a box at the colt's heels and stood upon it, when up went the heels, away went the box, and Phil very suddenly sat down on the ground. I happened to look up from my machine at which I sat sewing and, looking out of the window, saw what had happened. I ran out very quickly, but Phil wasn't hurt and had rather enjoyed the encounter with "Ghost."

Father had two horses that he bought of the Indians, one of which he afterward traded for a black cowpony that had been ridden from Texas by a cowboy, one of a party that were delivering longhorns at the Agency. He was black, having one walleye, a white face, and two white hind feet. He was afraid to enter the stable but was so tired and thin that two men managed to push him in. The next day he wouldn't come out, so he was left for a couple of days to get used to his quarters. But it was a long time before he would enter or come out without a snort and a plunge, and a stranger couldn't induce him to come out. That fear was what saved him from being stolen after he was fat and well-groomed, . . . [as was attempted] while Father was presiding at a literary and debating club which he and Captain Crawford had assisted the men to organize.

That night there were many cowboys present and people from the Pine Ridge Agency to hear the question debated whether the Indians would be better off if they were transferred to the care of the Army.[11] Louie, who was sitting in her room, heard a noise and on looking out of the window, saw one of our horses outside the stable and saddles on the ground. Two men were trying to get Baldy out, and he stood bracing himself with his forefeet set, pulling back as if he were holding a steer. Louie ran to the door and called to Father that someone was stealing his horses. The sergeant of the guard in the guardhouse nearby heard her and was soon in the yard, but the would-be thieves got away in the dark. Father tried to break Baldy to harness and hitched him to a heavy cart, which he carried far out on the prairie at a break neck speed, the man who was holding the reins dropping out of the back of the cart as the horse dashed through the corral gate.

CHAPTER TWELVE

"It's an Army Wagon, and Painted Blue!"

CAMP SHERIDAN, NEBRASKA, AND PINE RIDGE AGENCY, DAKOTA TERRITORY, 1878–1880

THE OGLALA INDIANS, WHO HAD BEEN removed from the Red Cloud Agency the year before to the Missouri River, where the Indian Bureau wished to establish them, would not remain there. [They] returned in the fall of 1878 to their old country and located themselves about twenty miles by wagon road northeast from Camp Sheridan, and here the Pine Ridge Agency buildings were erected. Dr. V. T. McGillycuddy, a former Acting Assistant Surgeon, United States Army, was sent to them as their agent.[1]

He proved himself well fitted for the position, managing them and their affairs in such a manner that he soon gained their confidence, and as long as they were under his charge, [they] remained peaceful and contented.[2] He procured wagons for them and had them haul their own supplies, furnished by the Government, from the Missouri River. They built houses, dug wells, began to cook on stoves and adopt other ways of the white man. He enforced the laws by means of police of their own people. All white men living with Indian women—squaw men, as they were called—that wished to remain on the reservation were required to marry them according to our customs. [A]nd be it said to the credit of these men that with few exceptions they complied with his order without any demur, and the very few that went away soon returned to marry their faithful companions and give their children a legal status. These women were gentle, industrious, and made these men good wives.[3]

The tepee belongs to the woman, and if her husband misbehaves, she can and does turn him out. Even American Horse, a chief, was once disciplined in this manner by his squaw.[4] They did not whip their children, and the boys were treated with great consideration. A boy would consider it an indignity to be struck by a woman. I knew a Piute boy to take poison parsnip because his mother whipped him, and Father had great difficulty in saving his life. The boys were taught very early to ride horseback, to use the bow and arrow, and the girls to perform the simple duties that would later be required of them. They carried their babies strapped in a hoo-pa on their backs, suspended from a strap that is passed around the forehead. Jugs of water were carried by them in the same manner.

Four missionaries established themselves at the Agency, three of them Episcopalians and one Roman Catholic.[5] Two of the former, [the] Reverend John Robinson and the Reverend ___ Wolcott, frequently came over to hold services for us, and a French Jesuit to minister to the men. The latter was cultured and very agreeable and we always entertained him, as we did the clergymen of our own denomination, but one day a rough, red-faced man came to our door instead of our gentle friend, who told us that the latter had been sent to France for discipline, as he was too liberal in his ideas and associated too intimately with Protestants. We did not entertain the new man, and the work that the other had been carrying on very successfully at the Agency was annulled by him, much to the advantage of the men of the other denomination.

Many of the supplies sent by the Government to Indians had never reached them, so Army officers were detailed as inspectors to witness the issue of all of their annuities and report upon their quality. Father was selected for that duty at Pine Ridge Agency. Every ten days he would get up before four A.M., eat his breakfast, and drive the twenty miles so as to arrive at the Agency by seven A.M., at which hour he would begin to receive the cattle.

Formerly the cattle would frequently be let out at night, and in the morning the Indians would find the corral empty. Then to pacify them, the contractor would present them with a few head, or a herd of scrawny steers would be delivered in which were three or four fat ones, and one of the latter would be slaughtered, weighed on steelyards, and its weight taken as the average for the whole bunch. The Indians would fare very well if they received even two-thirds of the beef to which they were entitled.

To prevent any further fraud, Father saw that the corrals were so well constructed that the palisades could not be pulled up by the cowboys with their lariats. The cattle were kept over night without water and in the morning weighed on platform scales, run into a chute, and there cross arrows branded on each one, so that if any did escape they could be identified. They were then run into another corral from which the head of each family received all that belonged to him.[6] When a steer was released from the corral, they would chase him about as if he were a buffalo before killing him, and we heard that formerly Indians were sometimes accidentally shot while engaged at their customary sport. It was a long time before this steer-baiting could be stopped.

After the issue, Father would return to the Post, except when he had to receive a winter's supply of cattle or the yearly supply of clothing and other annuities, and then he would be gone for ten days or two weeks. He also received their first herd of stock cows and bulls.[7] There was rarely any sickness at the Post. If there was an emergency case, a courier took a short cut to the Agency to recall him.

Once when he was away I had canvas stretched tightly on the floor of the vestibule and the dining room, nailed down, and diamond-shaped figures painted in black and grey. These colors were a departure from the time honored Army blue. "It's an Army wagon, and painted blue!" exclaimed an Army woman, with an emphasis on the word *blue*, who had hurried to the corral expecting to have a drive in a new ambulance.

One Christmas Eve we expected Father home, as he had been gone nearly two weeks, and we worked fast to have everything ready for the commemoration before he arrived. Captain Crawford and the boys strung popcorn and cranberries. Louie and I made mince pie, fruitcake, crullers, and other good things. The pine tree for which the Captain had sent to the hills the day before was brought in and pine branches hung on the walls. The weather was very cold, and as the sun sank westward grew steadily colder. I began to fear that Father would not come and half hop[ed] that he was not out in the cold, but shortly after sunset he came. Both he and the driver had run alongside the ambulance nearly half the way to keep from freezing, the intense cold having come on just after they left the Agency.

After the boys had gone to bed, we decorated the tree. Mother had sent us tinsels and bright ornaments, candles, candies, and many presents. The Captain was as much in sympathy with the occasion as if he were with his own family.[8]

Christmas morning was, as usual, greatly enjoyed by the children, as well as the rest of us. We had sent a wagon to the railroad, one hundred sixty-two miles, as we did about once a month, for supplies that we had ordered from Grand Isle [Island], Nebraska, where such articles were quite reasonable in price: eggs, ten cents a dozen; butter, fifteen cents a pound; chickens, ten cents a pound; turkeys, twelve cents; and ducks about the same price. We sent to Chicago for Booth's oysters, which came in flat tin cans packed in ice, so that the dinner we sat down to was a sumptuous one. But before eating our own, we went over with Captain Crawford to inspect the men's dinner, which was equally as good as ours, for the Captain was a good provider. The boys always liked to go over on such occasions, as they were always treated to some plum duff, which they pronounced a delicious dish.[9]

In September 1878, three hundred Cheyenne Indians under Lone Wolf, Wild Hog, and Dull Knife set out from the Cheyenne and Arapaho Reservation near Camp Reno, in the Indian Territory, to return north to their old home in Dakota.[10] Troops were sent after them, but they moved so rapidly that before they could be intercepted they were well up in Nebraska, had committed many depredations on the way, and killed forty or more men, women, and children.[11] When they reached the Union Pacific Railroad, nearly one half of them, mostly young men, headed by Lone Wolf, left the older people and later surrendered. The others, under Wild Hog and Dull Knife, continued on their way to the old Red Cloud Agency.

The Twenty-Third Infantry under Major Alexander J. Dallas pursued them from the south up through the Sand Hills across the Niobrara River until they were headed off on the north by troops from the Third and Seventh Cavalry when they entrenched themselves on Chadron Creek, about eighteen miles west from Camp Sheridan. A mountain howitzer sent from our Post soon dislodged them, and they were induced, October 24, to give up their arms and were taken over to Fort Robinson, where the

49 men and 100 women and children were confined in an old building. They, however, managed to get ten rifles and five pistols into the prison by taking them apart and having their women and children hide the pieces and ammunition in their clothing.

An attempt was made to separate Wild Hog from his people, when they barricaded the windows and doors, and at night, on January 9, 1879, made a dash for freedom. Some of them were shot down while crossing the parade ground. Dull Knife was wounded in the leg and escaped to Pine Ridge, and the others fortified themselves among the rocks and did not surrender to troops A, C, B, F, H, and L, Third Cavalry, until not a man was left alive and very few women and children were not wounded. Of the 150 confined, 64 were killed, 58 were taken to the Pine Ridge Agency, 21 were sent back to the Indian Territory, and 7 supposed killed, as they could not be otherwise accounted for.[12]

Probably 100 soldiers were engaged, and 11 of them were killed or died of their wounds. Captain Henry W. Wessels [Wessells] Jr., Third Cavalry, and nine enlisted men were wounded. The prisoners passed through our Post on their way to Pine Ridge and remained over the night of March 15, 1879. The oldest male among them could not have been fourteen years of age, and he was wounded. They were a pitiable sight. Father dressed their wounds and we took them cakes, sweets, and such food as their captors did not have to give to them.

The troops that came to the Post during the Cheyenne affair were entertained by us, and at every meal we sat down with five or six of the officers at the table. In about two weeks' time we had the pleasure of having forty or more officers of different regiments. Besides Major Dallas, there were Brevet Lieutenant Colonel Caleb H. Carlton, Major, Third Cavalry; First Lieutenants John C. Thompson and [George W.] Baxter, Third Cavalry; Brevet Lieutenant Colonel Joseph G. Tilford, Major, Seventh Cavalry; Brevet Colonel Frederick W. Benteen, Captain, Twenty-first [Seventh Cavalry]; Captain Myles Moylan, [Seventh Cavalry]; First Lieutenants Ezra B. Fuller, Charles C. DeRudio, Winfield S. Edgerly, George D. Wallace, Charles A. Varnum, Luther R. Hare, Ernest A. Garlington; and Second Lieutenant Herbert J. Slocum [all of the Seventh Cavalry]; Second Lieutenant George A. Dodd, Third Cavalry; Second Lieutenant Lea Febiger, Twenty-third Infantry. First Lieutenant Victor Biart, Assistant Surgeon, was with the Infantry, and the night before he arrived, having only his saddle blanket to sleep under, [he] crawled into an ambulance to share the blanket covering the corpse of a soldier who had been accidentally killed by a comrade.

Major Dallas one day was using some profane language, and Father told Claude to play farther away. The Major said, "You sent the little fellow away so that he wouldn't hear me swear," and apologizing said that he used such language only when in the field, but that in the Post he was a very good Catholic and even kept a priest as his personal chaplain.

Woman's Dress, an Oglala Sioux, was one of the scouts during the Cheyenne affair at Fort Robinson and was wounded at the rifle pits. For his services he was retained afterward on the pay roll, and Father examined him for reenlistment every six months. He gave Father his "Coups," which were pictures in colors of all of the great feats of his life, beginning when he was a boy and stole a horse from another tribe and ending with the wound he received near Fort Robinson.[13] This record was lost with all the rest of Father's valuable pictures and notes of the Sioux in the great fire in San Francisco.

Once we had Lieutenant General Philip Sheridan with us, [and] when he took our Phil upon his knee, he looked up questioningly, so I told him that I was on the other side during the Civil War and our boy was not named after him.

With the Agency so near we were not so isolated as we had been before it was established, as a daily buckboard carrying the mail kept us in touch with the people over there. For a time it was driven by a man who had gone East about a year before with his pockets full of money, got married, went on his wedding trip in a private railroad car, came back west, soon went broke, and was glad to carry the mail from Robinson to the Agency. He wore a high white hat and had gay ribbons on his whip. . . .

After the Indians located at Pine Ridge, some cattlemen drove in their cattle and assumed control of the rangers [ranges] with a pretty tough lot of men, some of whom came into the country to hide away from justice. There were several shooting scrapes after which Father's services were needed. Horse thieves became numerous, and the Indians had to keep a pretty close watch over their horses.

Road agents were not uncommon, and one of them, "Lame Johnny," who had robbed a stage, was arrested for stealing Indian horses. The sheriff and a posse were en route with him from Sheridan to Deadwood when a crowd from the latter place took him from them and lynched him on what is now known as "Lame Johnny's Creek."[14] We learned that his mother in the east offered a large reward for the arrest of the men who murdered her boy, probably not knowing that he was a desperate character.

Another man—the son of a judge, and who went by the name of King, had been well brought up, but after leaving his home in Texas had killed a man—was shot in self-defense by one of the sons of Irwin, his employer, in the bunk house about twelve miles from Sheridan on the road to Robinson. Father had treated him for a wound once before, but this one was fatal.

We celebrated the Fourth of July, 1879, as had never been done in that country before. We invited the officers and soldiers at Fort Robinson, the Agent at Pine Ridge and his employees, the Indians, and the men on all the cattle ranges about us. Great roasts of beef, loaves of bread, and pots of coffee were prepared for the Indians, and we had at our table the Agent, the Surgeon, the Missionaries, and as many of the employees from the Agency as we could accommodate.

After our dinner, finding the chiefs on the gallery, we had them come in for ice cream and cake. Among them were old Red Cloud, Young-Man-Afraid-of-His-Horses, and American Horse, who all thought very much of Father.[15] When asked if they wished anything more, they pointed at the chicken and beef. These were given to them, and then they asked for soup, with which they finished their meal. They had already partaken of a bountiful repast, but it would not have been good form for them to leave until they had eaten everything in sight.

After dinner the program for the day was continued. A three mile hurdle race came next, and Long Dog, who came in first, as he sank down on the grass said, "No run good today, heap eat dinner doctor's house." He came in far ahead of all of the others but had not understood that he must jump the hurdles. Indians are not good jumpers, and high jumps are out of the question.

Besides foot races and horse races, we had wheelbarrow races and sack races, climbing a greased pole, catching a greased pig. Then there was a tug of war, the cowboys against the soldiers, who could not move the former after they dug the big rowels of their spurs in the ground, and finally [the soldiers] gave in. We had prizes for the winners and had to make up a special purse for Red Dog.[16]

At night we had fireworks followed by minstrels given by the enlisted men. Then they had a dance, in which the squaws did the best they knew how, but the supper afterward was to them a grand success, and after eating all they could, they gathered and carried away in their skirts and blankets every scrap that was left. Some of the cowboys were heard the next day to say that they had ridden eighty miles to celebrate the Fourth and it was the best day of their lives, as they had never seen such sports before.

The Indians frequently came to the Post, and among the occasional visitors was "Three Bears," whom Captain Crawford always received very cordially and never permitted to go away empty-handed, as the Indian [had] saved his life when he was ordered by the commanding officer of Fort Robinson to go with thirty cavalrymen to the relief of the Indian Agent at Red Cloud Agency, who had declared his intention to raise a flag pole. And the Indians, saying he should not fly a flag over them, had cut into pieces the pole he had brought from the hills and were making threatening demonstrations.[17]

On the approach of the soldiers, the Oglalas drew up in front of the gate of the palisades, probably a thousand in number. The Captain informed them through an interpreter that he had been ordered to go inside of the enclosure and requested them to stand aside that he might obey the order. Then could be heard the noise made by the cocking of their guns, when Three Bears called to his band, and separating from the others, they followed him and rode through to the gate, making a passageway for the troops to enter.[18] Whenever the Captain went over to the Agency, which he often did with Father, he would take jams, jellies, candies, and cakes and go himself to give them to the family of Three Bears.

There was one Indian, however, that was an insistent beggar. "Two Lance" would come in his spring wagon holding an umbrella over himself with one hand and a palm leaf fan in summer in the other hand, while his wife drove the team of ponies. Two Lance, Mrs. Two Lance, and three children would begin a search for the Captain, who after many of their visits, once tried to hide from them, so came into our quarters and sat for a long time before going back to his own. But when he did return there, they were on his gallery waiting. So they received what they came after: coffee, sugar, tobacco, baker's bread, and sweets. He laughed very heartily at himself when he told us how they trapped him.[19]

CHAPTER THIRTEEN

"To Worship in Their Own Fashion"

AN OGLALA DANCE IN THE SUN, DAKOTA TERRITORY, JUNE 1879

IN JUNE 1879, ABOUT THE TIME OF the year that the sun was farthest north, the Oglalas held their customary yearly ceremony known as the Sun Dance, and we all went over to Pine Ridge to witness it.[1] Efforts had been made to have the Indians discontinue it, but the whites had given them no better method of communing with the spirit world and the sun, the source of all life, so they continued to worship in their own fashion.

We arrived early on the plain east of the Agency and saw the great tribal circle of tepees, each band in its proper place. Several mounted men in their war bonnets of eagle feathers reaching nearly to the ground seemed to be delivering messages as they passed from the south around the circle west, thence north, and afterward east. After watching the people preparing to leave their camp to attend the commemorations, we drove to a large circular enclosure of poles, branches of trees, and canvas, having only one opening, and that on the east. Then seeing many Indians moving south, we followed them to the hills and seated ourselves near the summit of one that overlooked a grove of trees not far away.

Very soon we heard the chanting of many voices, and a long line of mounted Indian warriors in their war bonnets, war shirts, blue leggings trimmed in various colors came into view, and behind them or to their right came other lines of mounted men until there were at least one thousand all told. They dismounted and after them followed their women and children, some on horseback, some in wagons, and others leading ponies hauling travois which held their babes. Large drums were brought forward, placed on the ground, and each one was surrounded by five or six men and women. We were on the east and extreme left of the line and only a few feet from one of the bands.

After the men had seated themselves the chanting was resumed, accompanied by the beating of the drums, the high-pitched voices of the women mingling with the deep tones of the men. Occasionally the drumming and singing would stop and a man would arise and count a "coup," which when ended would be followed by the triumphant yells of the people and quick beating of the drum. A "coup" is a deed of prowess of which a warrior boasts; it may be of a horse stealing trip or the killing of an enemy, and to strike an armed foe with a bow is considered a grand "coup." There was a tall, spare Indian named "No-Flesh," whom we had frequently seen before. . . . [W]hen he counted a "coup" and yelled, [he] showed his teeth between his thin lips, and the expression on his thin face was as if he was relating some horrible act of barbarity, but I did not learn what it was.[2]

A tree was selected at the foot of a hill on the far side of the valley and women approached to lay their hands upon it, a declaration that they had lead irreproachful lives during the last year.[3] It was afterward cut by men and women, and when it had fallen it was cleared of its branches except near the top, where a few were allowed to remain. It was then taken to the enclosure accompanied by the horsemen, who when nearby, dashed ahead yelling as if elated at the success of some great undertaking. The tree was erected in the centre, and a bundle of some sort in a bunch of sage was fastened high up, and just beneath it the figure of a man about a foot long.[4] After we had seated ourselves in the shade of brush and canvas, not far from the south of the entrance, a large drum was placed in position nearer the entrance and surrounded by some six or eight men and women who began to chant, beating time on the drum.

The eight or ten penitents who were to undergo the ordeal entered in single file soon afterward, the head one carrying in front of him the skull of a buffalo bull. They passed us, went to the west side where they seated themselves in a row, placing some sticks and the buffalo skull in front of them to form a sort of alter [altar]. Then Red Cloud arose and, facing the pole, looked upward while supplicating the sun that their women might bear many boys, that the grass might be abundant, buffalo plentiful, and [that] they should have a great increase in the number of their horses.[5]

The dancing then began and was to continue four days and four nights, during which time the men were to fast, neither eating nor drinking, but they could smoke tobacco. It actually didn't last more than three days. Always facing the east and looking up at the pole and into the sun until it had passed the meridian, the dancers, each with a whistle made from a leg bone of a turkey between his lips to blow short blasts while keeping time with his feet, moved forward and back hour after hour, until too exhausted to stand up. When one would fall, a great yelling took place and the drums were beaten the harder and faster.[6]

One man after a while was approached by a medicine man, who raised a fold of the skin from the upper part of his chest, ran the blade of his knife through, pushed in a wooden skewer and fastened it to a rope, and the other end of which was attached to the pole high up. As the man danced again he threw himself backward in his efforts to tear out the piece of wood. He fainted several times and lay still for a while, to rise again and dance. The medicine man at length examined the wound, and when the man made the next attempt to free himself, he broke loose.[7] We suspected that the medicine man cut enough of the skin to make the task easier. A fire was kept up the whole time on the east of the pole, and when it needed replenishing a man would come in with wood, count a "coup," and lay it on the fire.

About noon food was brought in for the onlookers. We partook of some of it, and when the god [dog] meat came around, Lieutenant Charles G. Starr, First Infantry, said he would eat some of it if I would, so I ate a small piece. The boys ate it without any demur.

In the interval between the dancing, horses were given away by the dancers and others. Sometimes the horses were brought in, but oftener sticks as pledges for horses were given to be reclaimed afterward. When a poor old woman received a horse, she would cry out praises for the donor and say that he was a brave man. A man is not considered brave by them unless he is good to the poor, no matter what feats of daring he may have performed. The dancers underwent this sort of penance to fulfill a vow made to the sun in return for some favor or mercy they had asked and received.

The children and I did not stay longer than one day, but Father remained over. At the end of the dance the men were given sips of water from a buffalo horn to break their fast. Afterward, Father procured from a medicine man, who officiated at the dance, several pictures, one of which was a teepee upon which there was painted a rainbow. Entering the doorway was a creature, the fore part of which was buffalo and the hind part man from his waist down. Another picture was a tatanka [buffalo] teepee and about it were figures of spiders, swallows, and other birds, and surrounding the whole were the busts of many women.[8] He also managed to procure the buffalo horn from which they slaked their thirst after the dance. This had a buffalo carved upon it in relief in the best Indian style. But these were lost as were many Indian pictures and valuable notes on the Sun Dance in the great San Francisco fire.

CHAPTER FOURTEEN

"Thirty Miles from Water and Ten Feet to Hell"

EN ROUTE FROM CAMP SHERIDAN TO FORT WASHAKIE, WYOMING TERRITORY, APRIL 27–JUNE 1, 1880

ATHER WAS ORDERED TO Fort Washakie, Wyoming, in April 1880 and was relieved by Acting Assistant Surgeon Grimes. We hurriedly packed, as he had to accompany Troops H and K of the Third Cavalry from Fort Laramie to his new station, and we started early on the morning of the 27th so as to make a drive of forty miles to Fort Robinson. Here we remained over one day with Assistant Surgeon William B. Brewster, while our baggage wagon continued on to make in two days the distance we would drive in one day.[1] Several troops of the Third Cavalry garrisoned the Post, the commanding officer of which was Brevet Lieutenant Colonel Frederick Van Vliet, Captain, Third Cavalry. Some of the other officers were Captains Peter D. Vroom and Joseph Lawson, and First Lieutenant Albert D. King, who had two sweet and very bright little girls, Flora and Mary.

We passed them while we were looking about the Post, and Flora said in an awed voice to her sister Mary while pointing at Claude, "He's a pirate." The latter, who was about her age, didn't act the part but walked on very indignant that he had been mistaken for a pirate. Flora was at Fort Sam Houston, Texas, in 1914–1915, the wife of Major Jessie McIlvaine

Carter, Third Cavalry, and had two just such daughters of her own. The Major commanded the Second Squadron of the regiment, and the one in which Philip's troop E was one of the units.[2]

We left Robinson in a large new ambulance drawn by six fine horses. It was upholstered in leather and had pockets in which to place small articles that one might need on a long drive. We crossed White River some eighteen or twenty times and were enjoying the rugged scenery on both its sides when, on going down the cut through which the road again led to the river, our driver ran the wheels of the near side up on to the bank and upset us into the water. He was thrown under the heavy leather curtains of the vehicle and Frank, who sat next to him, along with him. Father, who was also on the front seat, was hurled forward, and the front wheel was dragging over his legs when he felt the reins in the water and, grabbing them up, was able to stop the horses and pull himself free.

Father told Louie to run to the horses' heads, and he then went to rescue Frank. As he raised the top of the ambulance, the driver called out, "The boy is all right," and helped to extricate Frank and himself from the water by getting his shoulders between the top and a small log upon which the uprights had been broken. He had held Frank's head above water against the leather curtain, which I had tried in vain to unfasten.

I climbed out as fast as I could and helped the children to the far bank. The river was narrow and not over a foot and a half deep but was made a little deeper by the ambulance damming it back. We were all wet from head to foot. I undressed the children as fast as I could and wrapped them in a buffalo robe that escaped much wetting. Fortunately the sun was shining and we were sheltered from the wind by the hills, which were close by on each side. We were sixteen or eighteen miles from Camp Robinson, and our baggage wagon was nearly as far ahead of us. Our driver was badly bruised and lay in a half-drunken stupor. He hadn't shown any signs of intoxication until he came to the last and worst crossing—the twenty-second, I believe.

One of Father's ankles was swelling rapidly and becoming painful, so Louie was the only one that could go for relief. . . . Father mounted her bareback astride of what he thought the best horse and gave her a note to Colonel Van Vliet explaining our predicament. On reaching the Post, she stopped long enough at the cavalry stables to call out that Frank was drowned and Father had broken a leg.

Colonel Van Vliet came to our assistance, bringing the Post surgeon, eight enlisted men, and another ambulance. By the time the party reached us, our clothes were dry and the driver had sobered up considerably. Father's leg was put in splints, the ambulance was hauled out of the water to be taken back, and we changed to the one that had been brought out and continued on, but with only four mules for our driver to manage. It was long after dark before we came to the camp that our wagon and escort had made in compliance with orders to await us. We were all glad to get into our tent and go to sleep.

The next day we drove on to Fort Laramie, which was located on the bluffs of the west side of the Laramie River, a mile and a half above its junction with the Platte, at an elevation above the sea level of 4,516 feet and eighty-nine miles from Cheyenne, a station on the Union Pacific Railroad. Troops of the Fifth Cavalry formed the garrison, and among other officers stationed here was Captain John B. Babcock, whom Father first met at the San Carlos Indian Agency in Arizona some eight years before.[3] About ten miles east of the Post on August 19, 1854, Lieutenant Grattan of the Sixth United States Infantry and thirty men were killed by Sioux Indians under Mat-o-way-whi, or Startling Bear.[4]

We learned that the two troops H and K had left for Fort Washakie a day or two before Father had received the order to join them here. Their whereabouts was not known, but it was thought that we might overtake them, so after a delay of one day, a plaster cast had been put on Father's ankle and he had a pair of crutches made. We were furnished an ambulance, a wagon, and an escort of Corporal Boyd and a few men to proceed to Fort Fetterman, Wyoming Territory, where we arrived the third day, having had a very enjoyable drive of eighty miles northwest of Laramie, except when coming around a mountain where the road was narrow, the wind was strong, and we were so afraid that we would blow over into the canyon [that] we all moved to the side of the ambulance nearest the mountain. The Fort was about fourteen miles west from the Black Hills on a plateau one hundred thirty feet above the North Platte River, at an elevation of about 8,500 feet.[5] The views were fine, the whole country green and covered with wild flowers.

Major Isaac D. De Russy, Fourth Infantry, was in command, and we met, besides him, Captain William H. Powell and family, Lieutenant Horace Neide, Fourth Infantry, and Captain Robert W. Shufeldt, Assistant Surgeon.

We were kept waiting a long time after Father reported to the commanding officer before we could learn where we might stay for the night. After a time we were shown to a set of vacant quarters, which we occupied, and Louie prepared our luncheon. For a time, I could not walk across the room without having vertigo, as the altitude affected me. We dined with the Shufeldts.

Having learned that the troops were too far ahead of us to try to catch up with them, we had to go to Rock Springs, on the railroad eighty-three miles distant, and wait there until we could telegraph for transportation from Fort Washakie to meet us at the nearest railroad station to the Post. We left Fort Fetterman with a spike team of three horses and a mule, but the mule gave out very soon and our driver had to return for another animal when he managed to get a horse in exchange.

The road was mostly down grade, which in many places was quite steep, and at the worst part of it the boxing of one of the front wheels broke and a large piece fell out. Louie, who was a pessimist and since our upset had been constantly watching for something else to happen, was over the wheel and on the ground in a jiffy. She walked ahead looking for something with which to make repairs and hadn't gone far before she found an old shoe, the sole of which the driver forced into the hub of the wheel and then drove slowly on.

The boys enjoyed the rock[s] and trees, the badgers and chipmunks, which were numerous, but the rest of us had to watch the wheel, and we were very glad to arrive at Rock Creek in safety.[6] We remained there two days and then heard that an ambulance and wagon would meet us at Green River. We were glad to get away from the house in which we had been staying, as Louie, still looking for trouble, found body lice in the blankets that had been loaned us.

At Green River, as Father stepped on to the platform which was covered with a light fall of snow, one of his crutches went through a knothole and broke off, but the plaster cast was strong and saved his ankle from further injury. There was an adobe hotel here, and close to its front wall on the platform was a cage holding a large African lion. Our beds were in the room next to the lion's cage, and the head of one was within two feet of the cage, but we soon became accustomed to the roars of the animal and they didn't keep any of us awake.[7]

Our wagons came that afternoon and we started on a one hundred forty-seven-mile drive. For some distance we followed upwards the windings of

Green River close to the immense vari-colored rocks on its east side, chromolithograph pictures of which I had seen and admired, but the rocks themselves, lighted up by the rising or setting sun or when partly covered with clouds, were beautiful in coloring beyond all description by pen or painting. After a time the road led us among the great gashes made in the rocks by wind and water and between the high bluffs. Sometimes we crossed great washes, and again we followed them for many miles. After we had driven a long way, we passed a home station of the mail route. On one of the doors of the stable was painted, "Ten miles from wood, Twenty miles from grass, Thirty miles from water and Ten feet to Hell."

We passed through South Pass and Miner's Delight, both deserted places.[8] As we descended the mountain at South Pass we saw what one would believe to be a prosperous town, but as we drove into the principal street and stopped in front of a hotel, not a soul could be seen. Down the street which ran parallel with a creek were signs reading, "Wholesale Groceries, Liquors, Jewelry, Boots and Shoes, etc.," and the names of the proprietors in some instances. . . . The gold that was supposed to be in the mountains, which were filled with prospect holes, had not been found, or else was not in paying quantities. South Pass was on the old emigrant road over which thousands of seekers of the treasures at the end of the rainbow in the golden west had passed.

That night we spent at the old deserted Camp Stambaugh, Wyoming, well up in the mountains where there was a telegraph station. We went into an empty set of quarters which were in a fair condition of repair and, judging from the papers on the floor, had been occupied by Captain [Charles] Porter of the Eighth Infantry.[9] A broken cook stove, an old table, and a couple of broken chairs were the only furnishings, and we made the most of them. There were no bedsteads, so our beds were made on the floor. This was the 30th of May, and that night there was a deep fall of snow and it drifted into the men's vacant quarters, to which the officers, we were told, had sometimes been forced to tunnel after a great snowstorm. We remained here May 31 to wait for the snow to melt. The mail carrier that came along told us that the snow was three feet deep beyond us but was melting fast in the bright, warm sun.

We took to the road again on June first, a warm, bright day, and soon began to descend the mountains. There were places where in winter the snow would lie forty feet deep and over which the tri-weekly mail carried on a buckboard would pass toward morning, when there was such a crust that the horses would not break through. . . . When we came to a steepest part of the road, it could not always be seen, so all of us, except Father and Frank, jumped into the snow and walked.

I had on Father's long canvas leggings, which reached to my waist, and I waded through the wet snow at first nearly to my waist, and often a stone would slip from under my feet and down I would go. [B]ut as we descended rapidly, [the snow] became in an hour or so shallower, and at length we walked on bare ground and came to the foot of the mountain. Here we dried our clothes in a pretty little house. We then drove down the creek to camp near where it ran into a broad valley, pitching our tent for the night in a warm, sheltered spot among wild flowers and green grass which was nearly a foot high.

CHAPTER FIFTEEN

"Heap Papoose Pretty Soon"

FORT WASHAKIE, WYOMING TERRITORY, JUNE 1880–OCTOBER 1881

W E ARRIVED AT FORT WASHAKIE on June 2 and were welcomed by Captain and Mrs. Gerald Russell, who had told the drivers to bring us to their quarters.[1] The two troops of the Third Cavalry had been at the Post some days before we came. Brevet Lieutenant Colonel Julius W. Mason, Major, Third Cavalry, the commanding officer, had but recently arrived. Captain Henry W. Wessells Jr. had Troop H, and Captain Gerald Russell, Troop K. Oscar Elting was a First Lieutenant, and the Second Lieutenants were Joseph F. Cummings, George W. Baxter, Allen R. Jordan, and later, George H. Morgan.

We remained with the Russells over night and the next day selected quarters, an adobe house, next to theirs, which was at the north end of the line. A hallway ran the length of the building and had two rooms on each side. Back of these was an *L*, in which was the kitchen. In front was a gallery, and back, a small porch. A high board fence enclosed a yard of fair size, and along the back fence were a stable and a chicken house.

The Post was one hundred and forty-seven miles from Green River and not quite so far from Rawlins, both stations on the railroad. It was well out from the foot of the Wind River Mountains, on the south side of the north fork of Little Wind River, a tributary of Wind River, which in its turn is a tributary of the Big Horn. The elevation above the sea is about [5,462 feet]. The mountains west held some peaks that were nearly 14,000 feet high. Its buildings were in a compact form, and the parade was not large. Water was conducted by means of a ditch from the river, and the parade was flooded every day to keep the grass green. Ditches also ran between the houses, and the gravelly soil was always saturated with water.

In our dining room floor was a trap door, which on raising we found beneath a pit nearly full of potatoes and other rotted vegetables that had sprouted. Father at once recommended that the ditches between the houses be discontinued and the parade be wet less often.[2] We were soon settled, as we had brought our household effects with us. At first we had Louie to do our housework and a soldier striker to look after the horses, cows, etc. We secured cows from the range very soon, but the first one kicked our man over and pulled loose from the fence. I heard a great noise, and on looking out into the yard, I saw the man on the fence and the cow making passes at him with her horns. We tried others, however, and at length found one that was quite docile.

After a time, Louie became troublesome, and we sent her home to Elmira. Later she died in an insane asylum. We then had for a time to depend upon a soldier to cook for us. His name was Fry and he would have mean spells, becoming surly. Always after one of them he would say that he had from boyhood been treated like a dog, so ought to be treated as one now.

The Masons couldn't get a cook from the troops so asked the Sutler's Chinaman to get one for them. [He] . . . sent for another Chinaman, [who] . . . turned out so well that we asked him to send away for one for us, and ours proved to be the best one of all. We paid him $25.00 a month. Beng was very economical, neat, clean. He didn't like to have me come into the kitchen, and if I started to show him how to make a new dish, he would follow me about with a cloth in each hand. If I dropped a little flour or anything else on the table he would quickly wipe it up with one cloth; and if on the stove, out would go the other cloth to rub it clean.

The boys didn't eat much for breakfast, and Beng would put their plates away and when they came in later would bring them out and say, "You no eaty your blekfast, you eaty now." We had breakfast about 7 A.M., dinner about 1 P.M., and supper [at] 7 P.M., and Beng was always very punctual and wanted others to be so. The boys taught him to ride horseback, and he was very proud to learn. When the boys left him alone, at first the pony would go and bang his head over a fence, and Beng would remain seated on the pony until someone came along and led the latter out to the road again. But after awhile he managed very well and would ride regularly to take his baths at the hot spring. He was always offering us presents and wanted to give me a heavy gold ring, but we compromised on some artificial flowers to wear in my hair. . . .

We [had] started from Sheridan with Baldy, the boys' pony, and her colt. Father had leather boots made for the colt, as it was thought we would have a long march before us. At Fetterman a man made a good offer for the mare and her colt, so we sold her, and at Rock Creek we sold Baldy for a good price. We knew that horses could be bought of the individuals at Fort Washakie. Father very soon had horses for which he paid $15.00 to $20.00 each, but good buffalo ponies or racers were valued at $50.00 to $100.00. A two-year old stallion could be had for $10.00. The pony Father bought for the boys was a frisky sorrel, which would often follow me and pull my sunbonnet off and run away with it when I was not on my guard.

Father and the older boys rode every day and often went hunting. When he went after duskey [dusky] grouse, which were very numerous in the low hills at the foot of the mountains, he would take Claude and Harold on one horse, and when he reached the hills he would dismount and let one of them mount his horse. And the two would ride among the bushes to flush the birds, as at that time he had no dog. He often went out for deer, and he fished a great deal.

Bull Lake, some fourteen miles north, was full of salmon trout, and its outlet, with smaller trout. He and other officers would drive over there in the afternoon to fish until dark and have a fish supper. The next morning they would start in early, fish until near nightfall, and then come home, bringing trout enough for all of the families. While they were fishing, the soldier cook would watch, and when he saw them coming toward camp would make up fresh biscuit, fresh coffee, and put fish on to broil. They usually ate four meals a day on such occasions. We went over there once in winter and heard the sound something like the roaring of a bull, made by the water under the ice, from which the lake derived its name.[3]

The boys had their lessons every day, and Father taught them geography at the riverside, zoology, botany, and geology on their rides. The river was a very attractive stream, as it ran swiftly and tumbled over its rocky bottom, and flowers were thick on its bank. The rocks were filled with fossil shells where the river leaped out of the mountains about five miles up, and the skeletons of horses, cattle, coyotes, wolves, deer, antelope, beaver, badgers, buffalo, bear, and other animals lay about the country. Father collected many of the skulls and other bones on their rides and hunts for the boys to study. The day after a ride they would write about what they had seen the day before.

At one time there were five pet cubs in the Post, grizzly, cinnamon, and silver tip bear. Mr. Cummings had one that he would sometimes let run loose. The little scamp would roll in the ditch and run the whole length of the line over all of the front galleries, turning over flower pots and anything else he could reach, and when he arrived at the upper end he would make a dash for Mrs. Russell's pet lamb, which she often staked in the corner of the parade ground. Out would come the Russells and off would lope the cub to look up further mischief. One day he ran into our house, and, hearing his chain rattling, I went into our bedroom, and there the little rascal was drying himself after his bath and a roll in the dust by rolling on our bed. As I started for him with a whip in my upraised hand he whined and held up his little paws begging for mercy. He grew very fast and Mr. Cummings was getting afraid of him when one day he escaped to the mountains.

The lamb, after he grew large, was about as mischievous as the cub, for he would try to butt us over when we were not looking. He would often get tangled in his rope and then bleat for help, and once Mrs. Russell was caught in his rope and thrown to the ground.

There were many bears in the mountains, and once when Corporal Boyd of Captain Russell's Troop, whom we had brought with us from Fort Laramie, was out with his troop he tried to capture a cub but did not see the mother, who happened to be near by. She started for him, so he climbed a tree, which she watched for a long time and then, as he supposed, went away. He descended from the tree to go after his carbine, which he had laid on the ground at the time he was going to pick up the cub, but she had simply hidden and was watching him. Before he knew it she was upon him, so he threw himself upon the ground and kept perfectly still while she clawed him. He lay still a long time and then, thinking she had gone, raised his head, but she was near by and came for him again tearing his flesh badly. He was a long time recovering from his many ragged wounds.

One of our calves was badly torn one night as we thought by a bear, but it might have been a lynx or wildcat. Several times a bear was reported in the willows along the creek, but by the time armed men could reach the place, the bear was a long way off; and several times beef that was hanging at the slaughter pen, near the river, was carried off at night, so the butcher got a gun, and one morning there lay a large silver tip bear dead. We had bear meat that day for dinner but didn't care much for it, on account of the strong flavor, and everyone who wanted bear's oil for his hair or other purposes could get it. It was thought to promote the growth of hair on the head, but I think, judging from what the old trappers said, it was of more value used internally for a bad cough. The country was full of large and small game, and Father and the boys one day counted seventeen big-horns (mountain sheep) high up on the rocks in the mountains about eight miles from the Post.

In the winter of 1880 Father, Mr. Morgan, and ten enlisted men went on a hunt east of the Big Horn River to procure game for our Christmas dinner. The mountains and country around Washakie were covered with snow, but twenty miles or so east there was scarcely any, so the game had gone there. The party wanted to get to a herd of several thousand buffalo which Father had seen some Crow Indians tell the Shoshones and Arapahos about by means of signs. But a soldier who had come through there and said he could guide them took the wrong trail and led them up Poison Creek, the water of which was in holes and was bitter with Epsom salts.

There was no wood here, and they couldn't find enough snow with which to make coffee for the whole party so used the bitter water. They had some wood in their wagons and could for a time have a fire in their tents, but in the night the temperature fell very low and only their buffalo robes prevented them from suffering. The temperature at the Post that night was –37°F. During the night the salts took effect, and by morning they were too weak to hunt.

Father had killed an antelope the day before, and the men, another one, but by the time they reached camp the meat froze and it crumbled under the knife when they tried to cut it. So after that they did not draw their game until they reached camp, and then they took out the liver and cut it into slices before it could freeze. He [Father] had ridden out from the camp the afternoon before and found the carcasses of many buffalo and this morning wanted to cut across the country to look for the herd, but the rest of the party had lost their enthusiasm and wanted to return to the Post. So the men were told to load the wagons and prepare to return.

He went to the top of a hill and south from it saw a broad valley in which were grazing hundreds of antelope. They were so curious that they came within rifle shot, and he killed one and, hitching his lariat around its horns, dragged it up over the hill and down into camp. His horse felt too good to permit him to carry it. The wagons were ready to start, but the men had heard Father's shot and were watching for him. As soon as they saw what he had and he told them that the valley was full of antelope, they forgot their tummies and went over the hills on a lope.

It did not take them long to fill the two wagons with enough meat for the whole Post. That night they camped on the Big Horn, where they built rousing fires and had excellent water, although they had to cut through the ice at least three feet to reach it. It was a sight to see the frozen carcasses of the antelope stood on their feet as they were unloaded, and both wagon tailgates were covered with pieces of frozen livers. The Indians found the buffalo and brought in some two thousand hides. Father had his pick of the lot and bought two fine large ones and one silky calfskin which had been skillfully tanned by the Indians.

We had no bathtubs and no bathroom so we had to tub the children, or we drove to the hot spring, about two and a half miles east, twice a week. It [was] a small pond and the water boil[ed] up in the centre, not boiling hot, but hot enough at 115°F. We had a bathhouse divided into two rooms over the water on the west and near the outlet, where the temperature sometimes was 110° but usually 100° to 105°, and we looked like boiled lobsters when we came forth from it, usually after only a dip. The Indians bathed in the outlet, which was about six feet or so wide and a foot or more deep in the middle. Officers that came on court martial duty would sometimes remain at the Post to bathe in the water and invariably were benefited if not cured of their rheumatism.[4] There were tar springs north of the river from which bitumen slowly came up and spread out over the gravelly soil to dry and form a hard crust.

We had many delightful drives and rides, some short and some long ones. The "sink" of the Popoagie [Popo Agie] River was a favorite picnic resort for us, and all of the officers and their families, except the officer of the day, would sometimes spend the day there. We went to Lander, a small group of houses about fifteen miles south, and then drove up the south fork of the Little Wind Rover [River] to the "sink," the place where it runs underground for a quarter of a mile or more. It disappears roaring into a great cavern and comes out quietly among broken rocks, where it spreads out into a pool. Claude caught his first trout above the sink, and he was very proud of it.[5]

Once Father, Lieutenant and Mrs. Baxter, and I went well up into the mountains. We drove about eight miles and then took to our saddle horses to make the ascent, which was very steep. Father insisted that Mrs. Baxter and I should ride astride, but I had always ridden a side-saddle before that and so had Mrs. Baxter, and we both objected strongly for a time to the new method.[6] However, we felt safer in men's saddles, and I am sure that it was easier for the horse. A couple of thousand feet up we had a grand view and could see numerous peaks, Frémont's among them, the top of which is 13,790 feet above the sea level. We could see broad swathes of trees which had been torn out of the mountainsides by cyclones and great patches where the trees were dead from forest fires. In these spaces raspberries had sprung up, and I used to give the Indians glass jars in which to gather the fruit so that we might make shortcake and jam of it.

We didn't have many visitors from the outside world, but one of them was Mr. Jacob L. Wortman, who went north into the badlands to collect paleontological specimens for Professor Edward D. Cope of Philadelphia, and he found many rare specimens, among them a four-toed horse.[7] His brother, who had always lived in Oregon, came to join him and stopped at a station, Eureka Springs, I think, about half way from Green River. . . . Among other visitors were the Governor Hoyt of Wyoming on his way to the Yellowstone Park and two Frenchmen, viscounts, on a hunting trip.[8]

The sutler was J. K. Moore, and his wife was a very pleasant woman. They had a little boy who played with our children. Miss Daisy Bronson was one of the visitors at the Sutler's, and Lieutenant George Morgan soon fell in love with her.[9] Later they were married. She was accomplished in many lines and was well adapted to army life on the frontier.

Frank had what was called mountain fever for two weeks, and we once
had an epidemic of scarlet fever and dip[h]theria, when Captain Wessells
lost two children. Claude and Hal had the membrane form on their tonsils and the nose, but with them the disease pursued a mild course. It had
been very fortunate that Father had found and cleared out the pit under
the dining room and had insisted that the water in the ditches between
the quarters be cut off.[10]

The Shoshone and Bannock Indian Agency was about two miles from
the Post and was in [the] charge of Agent Charles Hatton, who had with
him three of the Ballou family, a nephew of Senator Ferry, a head farmer
with his wife and daughter, an issuing clerk, and a blacksmith, nearly all
of whom were from Ypsilanti, Michigan.[11] What they were all doing no
one could see. A sawmill stood idle, some fifty wagons and a lot of harness was half way between Green River and the Agency, exposed to the
sun and rain. A former agent had built houses for many of the Indians,
who had lived in them for a time and then abandoned them to return to
their teepees.

There were over one thousand Shoshone[s] here and more than nine
hundred Northern Arapahos. The sick used to come to Father for treatment until a physician was sent out by the Indian Bureau. There was no
house for the new man, and he was allowed to occupy the quarters at
the Post of the hospital steward, who was not married and lived in the
hospital.

This man came from Kansas and said he was a graduate of a Chicago
college and also of Bellevue in New York. He was uneducated, and
Father wrote to the colleges making inquiries about him. Just after he
received replies saying no man of the name had graduated at either one,
this man stepped out of the billiard room kept by the sutler and whipped
his wife, who had gone there to call him to dinner, so Father requested
him to leave.

The Indian Bureau, after his appointment, had asked for his diploma
and other information concerning him, but he could not furnish what
they required, so now the Indian Agent discharged him. Off he went,
leaving his wife behind. In Lander he offered to remain there if the people would guarantee him $1,000.00 a year, but none responded and Mr.
Amoretti, a merchant, said he would pay his stage fare to Green River if
he would leave the country. [S]o he took the money and left. It turned out

that he was one of the saloon druggists that sprang up in Kansas to dodge the prohibition law, and when the law was more strictly enforced he found himself out of a job. [B]ut having some influence, [he] secured the appointment as surgeon of the Agency.[12]

He was followed by a graduate of a college in New York who took a great interest in his work and who fell in love with the head farmer's daughter. He came over to the Post Adjutant to marry them but was referred to Father, who was Judge Advocate of the Garrison Court Martial as well as of a General Court. There was no minister of the Gospel in that part of the country, but Father thought that the Agent could marry them. I think that they, at last, found a justice of the peace to perform the ceremony; anyhow, one was performed. Father might have officiated, as a couple can get up in the presence of witnesses and declare their intention, which was enough in Wyoming to make them man and wife. It is related of an army officer on duty in Texas that he married a couple and they did not live happily together, so they came to him a year or so afterward and he divorced them, saying if he could marry them, he could divorce them.

The Shoshones were camped up the river from us, and the Arapahos, below. Washakie and Black Coal and one other were the chiefs of [the] former, and "Friday" of the latter.[13] Friday, when a boy, had been to school for a time in St. Louis, and Father made notes as he related his early history. These were destroyed in the fire in San Francisco. Friday died May 13, 1881, of disease of the kidney.

In October 1880, Father inspected their annuities and witnessed their issue. We saw the Shoshone Sun-dance in 1881 and it was similar to that of the Sioux, but I did not see any Indians trussed to a pole to tear through the flesh and break loose. The dance was a long one, and the Indian who was the most persistent dancer had a large goitre, a disease not uncommon up in this country and thought to be due to the snow water, which dissolves the limestone rock in its descent from the mountains. Father procured the buffalo horn, which had a buffalo carved in relief upon it, out of which they drank and broke their fast after the dance.[14]

A large party of Oglala Indians under American Horse from Pine Ridge paid a visit to the Shoshones one time. They had lost many of their horses the winter before and came over to beg some from the other tribe. We drove out to meet them, and American Horse was so delighted to see

Father that he hugged him. When the visitors were near a group of teepees they dismounted and approached, dancing. American Horse took
Father's hand and urged him to come along, so the latter danced with the
Oglalas, keeping time with their singing.[15] Dogs were brought out of the
teepees, grabbed by the hind legs, their heads broken on the ground, and
then taken away to be cooked for a feast. We didn't wait for the dog feast.

The Oglalas made presents of beaded bags and other articles for personal adornment to the occupants of the teepees. American Horse spent
much of his time on our gallery and conversed with the Shoshones by
means of signs, and at our request his people gave a dance on the parade
ground for the garrison. Colonel Mason had quite a paunch, which
amused the Indians very much, and American Horse said, pointing at it,
"Heap papoose pretty soon."[16]

When they left to return to their agency they were well provided with
horses. If, at any time the Shoshones should be short of horses, they
would go to the Oglalas, just as the latter had come to them. The Crows
also visited our Indians and had days of feasting. They danced on the
parade for us. They communicated with our Indians, as did the Sioux, by
means of signs.

There were frequent horse races among the Indians on our track.
Many buffalo robes, blankets, and all sorts of Indian possessions frequently changed hands. Dick, a son of Washakie, was of a sporting disposition and always had fast horses. Old Washakie was a quiet and rather
reserved man and had a very sweet, kindly smile. Nearly everyone who
came to the Post noticed his resemblance to the picture of Washington.

Father became a captain August 5, 1881, and he received $2,000.00 a
year and a fogy, making his pay $183.55 a month.

CHAPTER SIXTEEN

~~~

"The Woods Here Were a Delight to Us"

BACK EAST TO ELMIRA AND FORT MACKINAC, MICHIGAN, OCTOBER 1881–SEPTEMBER 1884

EARLY IN THE FALL OF 1881, . . . having been informed that he would soon be relieved from duty at Fort Washakie and ordered East, [Father] deemed it wise to send the children and me ahead of him, so as to get us away before the bad weather set in. [S]o we left Washakie early in October. Lieutenant Morgan's sister went with us, and her brother accompanied us to the railroad. Father drove with us to our first camp to see that we started right. He had our beds made on the ground, but the Morgans had theirs on cots, which they soon found too cold, and they too slept on the ground, which was far warmer.

Instead of going to Green River we took the road to Rawlins, so that if we were caught in a storm, the snow was not likely to be so deep as it would be on the other road. The first storm of the season did catch us, and the wind howled about us for a time but soon blew itself out. We were well provided with buffalo robes and warm wraps, and I had woolen stockings to pull over the children's shoes to keep their feet warm.

The streams were full of ducks, and our soldier cook hunted them and feasted us upon them. At the Sweetwater, one of our camps, the boys were throwing stones at what I supposed to be domestic ducks and I called them to stop, when the ranchman said, "They are not my ducks, mam, but wild ones, so let the boys throw stones at them as long as they wish."

One of our camps was at "Old Soldier," where there was a man living alone with only a shepherd dog as a companion. About sunset he said to the dog, "It is time the cattle were here," and off the dog went to bring in the small herd. In the morning the dog drove it out to the grazing ground. This man killed mostly big game of all descriptions and in a large room of rough boards he had the carcasses of deer, antelope, buffalo, bear, grouse, and ducks ready for shipping to the East.

When we arrived at Rawlins, the quartermaster there invited us to his house.[1] This contained a bedroom, a living room, and a room that he used as his office. His wife had gone home, so we remained with him overnight and boarded the eastbound passenger train the next morning. Many troops were on it en route to Yorktown to celebrate the centennial of the surrender of Cornwallis, October 19, 1781.[2]

When we stopped at Cheyenne for dinner, Mr. George Jones, who was running the Railroad Hotel, and Mrs. Jones with several waiters following came to escort us to the dining room, as Father had telegraphed that we were coming. Here a delicious dinner was ready for us. The great dining room was decorated with the mounted heads of buffalo, deer, big horns, antelope, and other animals, and we had various kinds of game to eat.

As we were seating ourselves at the table, in came Captain Emmet Crawford, who was stationed at Fort D. A. Russell near town.[3] He had taken into our sleeper a great basket of lunch that had been cooked by our old striker, Lewis, who was now the Captain's cook. When we returned to our car, there stood Lewis, and the boys all rushed to greet him. We found that Mr. Jones had also provided us with a large basket of the very best that the hotel afforded.

There were no dining cars in those days and sometimes the eating stations were a long way off at meal time, so experienced travelers always carried a basket of lunch and a spirit lamp with which to make hot coffee or tea. We had enough food to treat some of the passengers who were not so well provided as we were. In Captain Crawford's basket we also found a five-pound box of candy.

Miss Morgan was in my charge as far as Omaha, and there she took a different road from ours. She said she had never traveled with anyone who had more friends and received more attention and courtesies than we did, and she hoped . . . one day to travel with us again. We never met her again, however, much to my regret, as we had taken a great liking for each other. Her brother and his family we have met several times since, in our many army changes.

The children and I went again to grandmother's house in Elmira, and Claude and Hal entered the Sullivan Street public school. There was a Negro girl in Hal's grade who delighted him when she would hold up her hand and while holding on to her clothes say, "Please, teacher, let me go out, I am coming to pieces." Phil and Frank were sent to a kindergarten for two hours a day.

Father remained at Fort Washakie until November 9, 1881, when he was relieved by Lieutenant William H. Arthur, Assistant Surgeon, and then left by stage to take the train East at Green River. He had a very cold drive day and night, although he wore a buffalo overcoat over his other overcoat. He was on a leave of absence from November 27, 1881, to March 27, 1882, most of which he spent in New York taking special courses in surgery and other professional study, working under Professor Austin Flint Sr., Dr. William H. Welch, and Professor Joseph D. Bryant.[4] The next spring, after he had gone before the army medical board and passed his examination for promotion, he was ordered to Fort Mackinac, Michigan.

Our fifth son, William Tremaine Corbusier, was born at 154 Washington Street, Elmira, New York, at 10:40 A.M. Tuesday January 31, 1882.[5] Dr. John Flood attended me, as Father could not leave New York. This was the first time he had not been with me at the birth of our children. My nurse was the best one I ever had. When not waiting upon me, she read to the boys or told them stories about England, where she was born. . . .

Theresa, still with Mother, also helped to look after the children. Mother was very happy to have a grandson born in her house and was very loving and good to us all. She was good to everyone and more especially to the old people that lived in her neighborhood, some of whom looked to her for their daily bread. And her neighbors, when sick, came to depend upon her to look after them and their families. She had no fear of contagious diseases and would be the first to give aid in such cases. Jew and Gentile, Roman Catholic and Protestant alike blessed her. A Roman

Catholic priest even mentioned her in his prayers in church after she had taken into her home a poor boy, who occasionally worked for her, and cared for him during a long siege of typhoid.[6]

Before leaving Fort Washakie, we [had] sold our furniture, china, bedding, and most of our hangings, so we had to replace them before going to our new station. Father purchased glassware and a complete set of English china having a reddish pattern stenciled upon it and some furniture in New York. Mother and I chose the bed and table linen in Elmira. We had much sewing to do, as readymade underclothing could not be had in the shops then as now.

As we were not going into the Indian country, we had no difficulty in finding a nurse for the children, and Carrie Greatsinger, who lived with her stepmother on her deceased father's farm, . . . consented to go with us. The children were soon devoted to her, and Will in particular. We were very sorry when she became engaged to be married to a corporal who was not a good enough man for her. She left us February 4, 1884, and married him after his term of enlistment had expired. He spent her money, treated her badly, and then reenlisted, leaving her with two children to support. She procured a divorce and sometime later he died. She married again, making a happy match. Many other of our nurses and maids married soldiers, but all the others did well.

We traveled by rail to Detroit, Michigan, and thence by boat to Mackinac, where we arrived April 23, 1882. The Fort stood on a bluff on the south side of the island, and the parade ground, about which the buildings were grouped, was about one hundred and fifty feet above the straits on a terrace that one could reach by driving up a steep road along the south side of the bluff or one [road] still steeper that led up the west side to the back of the Fort.[7]

People on foot usually climbed the long flights of steps that were the shortest way up to the quarters, and a cow once chose this route, climbing until she reached the parade, some one hundred and twenty steps up. An old stone building on the south side of the parade, used as officers' quarters, and two stone block houses with superstructures of hewn logs, built about 1780, still remained of the old Fort. The stockade that formerly surrounded it had disappeared, but occasionally the base of a palisade would be found, and Frank, when a portion of the stonewall along the old road fell, found one of the three pronged spikes that topped each palisade. The boys made quite a collection of old French, English, and American Army buttons that they found back of the Fort.

On the crest of the hill, a few feet above the parade ground and west of it, were one single and one double set of officers' frame quarters. We occupied the west side of the double set, which contained three rooms having very high ceilings on the first floor and three rooms with low ceilings above. A gallery ran across the front of the house, and from it and our front windows we had an extended view of the Straits of Mackinac, to the west into Lake Michigan and to the east and south into Lake Huron, Round Island, Bois Blanc Island, and the southern peninsula of Michigan. On the highest point of the island, which is two hundred feet above the straits, were the remains of old Fort Holmes, so named after Major Andrew Hunter Holmes, Thirty-second Infantry, United States Army, who was killed here August 4, 1814, when the United States forces made an attack upon the British.[8]

There were still a few patches of snow in sheltered spots in the woods, and the quarters were chilly enough to require low fires in the large base burners, one of which was in each room downstairs, one in the hallway, and one upstairs. We burned coal for the first time at a military post and still used kerosene for illuminating purposes. All the water we used we pumped from a spring at the foot of the hill to a tank back of the quarters and thence distributed by means of a wagon and kept in barrels. We had no bathroom or bathtubs, and there was not one on the island, so we used washtubs and had regular tubbing nights. Our furniture had been shipped ahead of us, and it arrived a day or two after we did. This time we had enough without having to devise means of making ourselves comfortable, as we had so often heretofore done.

Captain George W. Adair, Assistant Surgeon, had been the Post Surgeon but had left before we arrived, and Dr. John Bailey of the island was looking after the sick at the Fort. Brevet Major Edwin E. Sellers, Captain of Company C, Tenth Infantry, was in command, and the other officers of companies of the Tenth Infantry stationed here were: Brevet Major Charles L. Davis, Captain of Company C; First Lieutenants Walter T. Duggan and Dwight H. Kelton, who was the quartermaster and subsistence officer; and Second Lieutenant Edward H. Plummer. Later, they were relieved by two companies of the Twenty-third Infantry under Brevet Lieutenant Colonel George K. Brady, Captain of one company, and Captain

Greenleaf A. Goodale; First Lieutenants Edward B. Pratt and Calvin D. Cowles and Second Lieutenant Rozier J. Clagett were the other officers.

In summer throughout August there were probably two thousand people on the island, but in winter few remained, and these were mostly of mixed breeds, descendants of French voyageurs, fur traders, Indians, English and American soldiers. The visitors came from Detroit, Chicago, New Orleans, and other cities, and when they arrived most of the inhabitants rented their dwellings and removed to their out houses. The hotels were the Mackinac House, near the landing and noted for its fried whitefish; the John Jacob Astor House, kept by Mr. [James Franklin] Cable, on the street back, famed as the old headquarters of the Astor Trading Company; the Island House, kept by Mrs. [Henry] Van Allen, on the street east of the others; and the Mission House on the point at the east end of the street or shore road. Near the latter was the cottage of Brooks, Clark, and Sheely, at which the young people frequently met to play bowles, act charades, and have other entertainment.[9]

The first year we were on the island three or four cottages were built at the Annex; Mr. [Gurdon] Hubbard's [was] the first one on the west side beyond the Devil's Kitchen, and one of them was occupied by Mr. and Mrs. Charles Fletcher and their children, Blanche and Theodore, and Mrs. and Miss Sheldon, mother and sister of Mrs. Fletcher; and one by Senator [Francis Brown] Stockbridge and wife.[10] Mr. and Mrs. David Carter and daughter, Josey, and Miss Hattie Leonard, Mrs. Carter's sister, came to the Mission House, and Mrs. John Bagley, her children, and grandchildren to the Island House. We came to know them all very well.

When stationed in Detroit from 1890 to 1893, we renewed our friendship with them and our children with theirs, and in 1914 we met Mr. and Mrs. Fletcher and Miss Sheldon in Smith's Parish, Bermuda, where they lived in Monticello, a house belonging to Miss Anna M. Outerbridge.[11] Bishop Samuel S. Harris of the Protestant Episcopal Church was one of the visitors to the island in August 1883, and we enjoyed conversing with a man so well versed in subjects outside as well as in his profession. The Rev. ___ Williams, nephew of Dr. John Bailey, and his sister, Miss Williams, were also welcomed visitors.

Our old friend Colonel Roger Jones surprised us one morning by dropping in upon us. He had eaten breakfast at a hotel but had dinner with us. He inspected the Post and left the next day. Dr. Holliday and family of

New Orleans came one summer and occupied a cottage. He was an intimate friend of my father's and attended the sick of the two thousand men that the latter had working to stop the great Sauvé Crevasse in 1849.[12] Nearly all of the visitors left early in September to return to their homes in time to enter their children in the schools.

We had been so much at stations where there were only a few trees that the woods here were a great delight to us. When we arrived, the greens of the maple, beech, poplar, oak, etc., were beginning to brighten the darker shades of the hemlock, cedar, spruce, pine, and juniper among which they were interspersed. Wild flowers were beginning to bloom, and soon we found them wherever we strolled—trailing arbutus, moccasin flower, Indian pipe, blue gentian, and anemone or wind flower. At the base of Fort Holmes, hill ferns and brakes luxuriated and the maidenhair was the daintiest of them all.[13]

On the side of the hills we found the pure white flowers of the bloodroot. In midsummer the slope of the hill along the flight of steps was thickly covered with large white daisies, having rich golden centres, and the passengers from the steamers stopping at the landing would gather them by the armful. I filled our one bay window with hanging baskets of vines and potted plants, which we had to carefully cover on winter nights to keep from freezing. There were so many of them that it looked like a luxuriant garden. The soil was very rocky, yet we raised the finest of Irish potatoes, lettuce, cucumbers, etc., which grew fast during the long daylight and short nights. The potatoes seemed to vie with the stones to become larger than them.

We enjoyed long walks and frequent drives about the island. One drive was three miles north across to British Landing, where the road ended in a gravelly beach. Rocky bluffs arose from the shore of the rest of the island, and on the east side there was a large arch cut out by the action of frost and water. It was still broad enough for people to walk over, and one of the attractive sights was to go there to watch the moon rising under it. One night we saw a couple arm in arm silhouetted on the large red moon beneath it. There were also Lovers Leap, Devil's Kitchen, and Sugar Loaf. The latter was a high rock at the junction of two roads and was a beautiful cone until the quartermaster of the Post stripped it of its trees and left it bare.

We often visited St. Ignace, where we saw the monument and grave to [of] Père Marquette,[14] and once [we] had a picnic on the southern peninsula, where after an early morning sail—we started at 4 A.M.—we broiled whitefish just out of the net on hot coals and served it on a large shingle as part of our breakfast. Old Gerome, who spoke a mixture of very broken English and broken French, was a favorite with all, and his sailboat was the one we always hired.

We made fishing excursions to the Schneaux [Cheneaux] Islands in a small, chartered steamer, which towed numerous rowboats for the use of these [those] that wished to troll for pickerel or pike. The women would usually remain on the steamer and catch tubs full of perch. Some who had never caught a fish before and had to be taught how to bait a hook caught so many that they tired of the sport. Father often went for trout in the streams of the peninsula north of the Cheneaux.[15]

At other times we would fish for lake trout, and Father caught many very large ones but nothing weighing twenty pounds, as did the one he bought from the fishermen one day to send to Uncle James Corbusier in Toledo by the steamer, *Flora*, which came up from there once a week with vegetables, fruits, butter, eggs, etc. But the whitefish caught in nets is the kind we probably enjoyed the most. The islanders, however, thought that the head of the lake trout was the best part of the best fish and in consequence of this preference were dubbed, "Fish-heads."

. . . The islanders fished through holes that they cut through the ice, some with hooks and other times with nets, so we had fresh fish throughout the winter. Dogs hauled their nets and sometimes there would be as many as four dogs hitched to one sled.[16]

The first summer—July and August 1882—we were at Mackinac, Mother came to visit us and Uncle George Myers, who was crippled from rheumatism, came with her. Before long he could walk up all the steps from the road below to our quarters on top of the hill, although when he came he had to walk up to the stairs to his bedroom on hands and feet and come down backward.

Mother enjoyed herself, and we all loved to have her with us and wished she could have stayed always. She loved to go after berries and one day came back from Bois Blanc Island so badly bitten by mosquitoes that she was sick the rest of the day. There was a sandy beach on Round Island to which we sometimes went to bathe, the only good bathing place we had. Uncle James and cousins Ada and Etta Corbusier and cousin Henrietta Rowsey lived in Toledo, and we were glad they were so near that they could visit us.[17]

. . . There was a small new Episcopal Church at the foot of our bluff, which was supported mostly by the garrison, and Father was soon made a vestryman and later a warden.[18] He assumed charge of the Sunday school and organized a class of adults for the study of the Bible. In summer he drew a large class, as his many years among the Indians and his study of ethnology gave him an insight into the teachings of the Old Testament that few men have. He selected many books for the Sunday school library which contained stories of the mountains and woods, trapping and canoeing, habits of wild animals, and histories, such books as the children of the village had never seen before and which interested them more than the stories of good and bad little boys, which it had formerly contained.

The Reverend [Moses] Stanley was the rector. He also served the church at St. Ignace, where he remained much of the time in winter but frequently crossing the ice, sometimes walking eight miles to hold service on Sunday on the island. The next summer a house was built for him south of the church. He gave magic lantern exhibitions in Truscott's Hall, much to the delight of the children. Every summer we had a fair for the benefit of the church. There was much musical talent among the visitors, and we gave fine vocal and instrumental concerts. At the one in August 1883, Mrs. Louis Brechemin from Fort Brady and Mr. David Carter of Detroit were among the singers. Fancy articles were sold and refreshments served.

The first summer I went up to Fort Brady at the Sault St. Marie—"The Soo"—to visit Assistant Surgeon Louis Brechemin, the Post Surgeon, and his wife. I saw the wonderful locks and the great rocks deep down in the clear water from the upper deck of the boat and had the working of the locks explained to me by the Captain.[19] I did not care to shoot the rapids, although with an Indian to guide the canoe the undertaking was not a dangerous one.

. . . Ojibwa Indians came from the mainland with baskets woven of sweet grass, birch bark curios, raspberries, maple syrup and sugar in large birch bark baskets. Once Father secured some beaver tails, and we again had them with our buckwheat cakes in winter. . . .

Our eldest three boys went to the Post School, as did three of the Sellers boys, Edwin F., David F., and Paulding F., who lived in the quarters west of us. Two boys of an enlisted man also attended. The first teacher was Sergeant J. Fred Grant, Company C, Tenth Infantry, who delighted in telling the boys all the mischievous tricks he did when a boy. They would then do as he had done, and once they locked him in the schoolroom to see him crawl out of a window and drop to the ground as his teacher had done.

He marched them down to the commanding officer and entered a complaint. The latter dismissed them with a reprimand, and the sergeant would march them back to the school again later to tell them about some other mischievous act. The march to the Adjutant's office and the formal complaint and reprimand delighted the boys, and they looked forward to such occasions as a game of some sort. They had a few minutes' drill every day, when they were treated as soldiers, and the Sergeant for a short time was a very strict disciplinarian in talk, and this the boys all liked. On Monday, May 18, 1883, Private Anderson Crawford relieved him. The boys had a vacation in summer and started in school again September 10th.

The fall of the year saw the island in its best array. The woods were gorgeous in the vari-colored trees and shrubbery, and then the aurora borealis in all its splendor would sometimes be seen. Great quivering needles of long, gorgeous colored light would shoot up to the zenith, and a loud buzzing sound could be heard.[20]

As winter came on and the ice began to form, we anticipated the closing of navigation and ordered our winter supplies in time to come up from Detroit by the last boat, the *City of Mackinac*, *City of Detroit*, and another time the *City of Cleveland*. We stored them in our cellar under the kitchen, closed the door, packed in straw, and then set in place a second door. From that time on we entered the cellar by means of a trap door in the kitchen floor. We laid in a hind quarter of beef, a whole sheep, half a barrel of corned beef, a large keg of pickled pigs' feet, salted fish, cabbages, potatoes, turnips, carrots, parsnips, sweet potatoes, onions, celery with roots in sand, apples, and a barrel of cider.

Just before Christmas we sent an order to Detroit for chickens, ducks, and turkeys and had them brought over the bridge of ice from the terminus of the railroad at Old Mackinac on a one-horse sled. We procured venison and other game from the northern peninsula and fish caught by the islanders through holes in the ice. We had our Christmas tree at home, although there was also one at the church.[21]

Snow began to fall in September, more in October, and [began]to collect in November. By spring it would cover all the fences and be piled up higher than our heads at the sides of the paths that were made throughout the Post and down to the village for us. It would fall and pack, and then more would fall. The straits were soon frozen far out, and the skating season set in. Father and the larger boys spent much of their time on the ice, as did the people from the Fort and village. I would go out on the ice too, to be pushed about on a sled.

After the snow rendered the ice rough, Father made sails to carry. One kind was on a bamboo pole bent as a bow and carried on one shoulder, and another was a square sail to carry on the back, often with a topsail to raise above the head. Later still, iceboats were built and old ones repaired, and we would fly over the ice. The Straits at the southwest point of the island, where the water is very swift, was the last to freeze over and the first to open—March 23, 1884. It was called "Dead Man's Hole."[22]

After the ice bridge was formed, our mail was brought from St. Ignace on the north peninsula about nine miles on a sled hauled by a horse, and for a good part of the winter it was carried across from the railroad at old Mackinac on the south peninsula to St. Ignace by the steamer, *Algomah*. [B]ut one winter this strong and powerful steamer broke all the flanges from her screw and was two months getting across to St. Ignace, as she could be moved only as the ice was cut out in front of her and pushed back. Father and the boys went out to see her, February 9, 1884, and had to climb over hummocks of rough ice the great part of the distance of five miles to reach her. From the middle of January to the middle of April, after the ice broke up, the mail sometimes had to be brought by row-boat around the east side of the island.

The winters were very cold, but the air was dry and we spent the greater part of the day out of doors and the early part of the night during the superb moonlight nights. The coldest weather was ten degrees below zero, January 23, and February 5, 1883. The ice cut in January 29th and February 2, 1883, to be stored in our ice-house, was 17 inches thick and in places, 24 inches. Father and I drove across the ice to St. Ignace several times, once on March 5, 1883.

Coasting on the steep hill west of us was a favorite amusement, and the hill was frequently full of men, women, and children in the afternoon. All sorts of sleds were flying down or slowly coming up. Many would carry away out on the ice of the lake. Once, Mrs. Sellers and Mrs. Plummer were at the top of the hill and as none of the boys were around to take them down, Mrs. Sellers said, "Oh, I know how to guide the sled," so down they went, but they did not see a hole in the ice on the lake and into it they plunged. They were hauled out immediately, but before they could reach a small house nearby their clothes froze stiff. Fortunately they were none the worse for their cold bath.

The hole into which they fell was the one from which most of the water for the people in that part of the village was dipped. The villagers hauled it in barrels on dog-sleds. One dog, with a little assistance, would drag a sled having a twenty or thirty gallon barrel of water on it. Dogs also hauled their wood, which was cut mostly on Bois Blanc and Round Islands. In summer they were turned loose to forage for their food, and they found it mostly in our garbage barrels. They were so patient and faithful at their work that I loved them and didn't mind the trouble they gave us when prowling about in our yards in search of a meal.

We spent much time in reading and sent for all of the histories and romances of Mackinac that were ever published. It was here that Dr. Beaumont, while Post Surgeon, performed the experiments upon Alexis St. Martin, who had a fistula into his stomach left by a gunshot wound, and here John Tanner related his life history.[23] Miss Martha Tanner, aged seventy years or more, told Father how she interpreted the story to Dr. James, as she could speak better English than her father. She had cancer of the breast and was a patient of Father. There were other cases of cancer and several of tuberculosis near by her house. In the same neighborhood were several habitual morphine users, and the villagers generally had some preparation of opium in the house, which they gave to their children or took themselves for any slight ailment.

Crows began to appear March 14, 1883, and swallows, May 16. The crows came in March 17 in 1884. Toward the spring of 1883 in the latter part of April (28th), when the sap began to rise in the trees, Father instructed the boys how to tap the sugar maple in the woods, collect the sap, boil it down over an open fire, and test it to learn when it was ready to crystalize into sugar. The pleasure derived by father and sons was very great. One day they tapped eleven trees and caught four gallons of the sap.

April 21, 1883, the *Algomah*, the railroad steamboat that plied between the railroad terminus on the southern peninsula at Old Mackinac and the other in the northern peninsula at St. Ignace, thence to the island, reached the latter for the first time since February 5th, the day the ice bridge had formed in the winter. She came in here at 10:30 A.M., and the steamer *City of Cleveland* from Detroit at 4:30 P.M., April 20th, 1884; the steamer *Flora* steamed in from Toledo through a thick fog April 27, 1883; and the *Champlain* from Chicago, April 30, 1883; but the little *Lady May*, our ferryboat to St. Ignace, could not begin to run until April 29, 1883. The *Saint Mary* was the first steamboat down from the Sault Saint Marie, and she arrived May 2.

July 4, 1883, was celebrated with many kinds of amusements, [such] as walking, running, hurdle, pony, row-boat and tub races, climbing a greased pole, jumping, and go as you please, and at night, fireworks. A salute of 38 guns was fired at noon from the brass field pieces.

During the fall of 1883 our boys had the whooping cough, as well as the rest of the children in the Post and the village. Father and I were both affected and he treated himself, our boys, and the Sellers boys every night in a small room, which he filled with an antiseptic spray so that all would be free from cough during the night.[24]

Toward spring of 1884 we were looking forward to the breaking up of the ice and the coming of the boats, when early in April the weather suddenly turned warm. The snow melted and water flooded the parade ground and coursing [coursed] down all the hills, [but] in a few days disappeared except in some protected spots in the woods. During those few days, colds were very prevalent, and while the snow was still melting and the air saturated with moisture, Major Sellers opened his cellar to look over his remaining winter's supplies, took off his coat while in a perspiration, contracted pneumonia, and after only a short illness, died April 8, 1884. He was buried on the 12th and nearly the whole population of the island followed his body to the grave. We were very sorry when the Tenth Infantry left, May 13, 1884. Our boys missed their playmates, the Sellers boys, to whom they were much attached.[25]

Only once did Ned Sellers and Claude have a falling out, and then Ned went home and said, "What am I to do, my best friend and I have quarreled," and Claude coming in said, "I want to leave this place. I can have no more pleasure here, Ned and I have disagreed about a miserable little matter." Their rooms faced and their windows were open. Both boys worked with their scroll-saws in a disheartened sort of way for a short time, and then Claude sang out, "Oh, Ned, here is the piece of black walnut I promised you," and downstairs ran both boys to meet again and continue their play.

But Jerry Ryan, who played with the boys at school, was a pretty tough boy. He was in many a fight with the boys in the village, in which he was usually a winner. He tried to awe the other boys at the Post, but fear was something I never saw Claude exhibit, so he and Jerry clashed one day and had a setto. Father heard that they were fighting, and looking through the latticed shutters of a back room, [he] heard Claude say, "Jerry, that's a foul. If you want to fight, fight like a gentleman," and at it they went again. They kept at it until both were worn out and some blood had been spilled from their noses. Lieutenant Duggan also watched them from a back window and thought, as Father did, that it would be better for them to fight it out. They were so well matched that neither was much hurt, and the fight was a draw.

Lieutenant Colonel George K. Brady, who succeeded Major Seller in command, had a young calf that he sometimes staked on the lawn between our grounds and his.[26] This lonely animal and a rabbit that was one left of a pair that had been given to Phil became playmates. The rabbit, with ears thrown back, would jump upon and look at the calf as it lay on the grass. The calf leaped to its feet to throw up its tail and cavort about the rabbit, which would dodge first one-way and then another to avoid the threatened butts of the calf.

Early in April 1884, Phil went to the hospital garden to get some horseradish roots that he heard the men were going to dig, and, getting his feet wet, wore his shoes all the morning. That night he began to cough and pleurisy developed in his left side. He had to be very carefully nursed, and to give us a rest Lieutenant Duggan often sat with him at night and insisted that I go to bed. When convalescing, Phil didn't improve fast enough so I took him to see Dr. Austin Flint of New York, who advised that we take him to a dry climate.

Claude and Harold remained with Father while I was gone, but I took Frank and Will with me to leave them with Mother in Elmira and bring them back with me on my return. Shortly afterward, Brigadier General Robert Murray, then Surgeon General, United States Army, who had inspected the hospital the year before, while he was the Medical Director, Department of the East, informed Father that he would have him ordered to Arizona, so that he might go to Fort Whipple, Prescott, Arizona.[27]

CHAPTER SEVENTEEN

჻

"But of the Ice We Had None"

FORTS BOWIE AND GRANT,
ARIZONA TERRITORY,
OCTOBER 1884–OCTOBER 1888

THE ORDER SOON CAME AND on September 30, 1884, we—except Claude who had gone to Lawrenceville, New Jersey, September 3—left Mackinac.[1] We spent the night of October 2 with the Bagleys, went on to Elmira through Canada, and arrived 6 P.M. October 3. [We] remained with Mother until October 18 and then at 5:50 A.M. took a train on the Erie Railroad to Buffalo. [We] changed to the Michigan Central Railroad, went through Detroit, and arrived in Chicago 1 P.M., October 19. [We] left there on the Alton Railroad, arrived in Kansas City 8:25 A.M., October 20, [and] left there 10:10 P.M. [We] passed through the Raton Pass 4 A.M., October 22nd, arrived at Deming, New Mexico, 7 A.M., October 23.

At Albuquerque, 6 P.M., October 22, a telegram, directing him to go to Fort Bowie, Arizona, was brought to Father on the train. So we detrained at Bowie Station on October 23, 1884, to take an ambulance to the Fort.[2]

On our arrival there, we learned the reason for stopping us. Captain J. De B. W. Gard[i]ner, Assistant Surgeon, had jumped from a buckboard and broke[n] one of his thighbones. Father happened to be within calling distance and was sent to look after him as well as the rest of the garrison and, more especially, Mrs. Wilber E. Wilder. The Beaumonts very kindly took Father, Will, and me into their quarters and entertained us very hospitably. Captain [William A.] Thompson took Harold, Philip, and Francis.

The boys were very popular, Will in particular, whose expressions were frequently repeated. He called a mule, a "mulloo," and in two or three days the whole garrison adopted that word.

The Fort was at an elevation of about 4,820 feet above the sea level, on the side of a hill in Apache Pass of the Chiricahua range of mountains in Cochise County, about one hundred miles east of Tucson and thirteen miles from Bowie Station on the Southern Pacific Railroad. There were high, steep hills north and south. Bear Spring, three-quarters of a mile distant, furnished the water. The quarters were of adobe and quite comfortable.

Brevet Lieutenant Colonel Eugene B. Beaumont, Captain, Fourth Cavalry, was in command, and with him were his wife and Miss Natalie S., his daughter. Commanding Troop K was First Lieutenant James Parker, and one of the Second Lieutenants was Wilber E. Wilder, Troop G. We remained here until November 10, 1884, and after the birth of a son, Throop, to the Wilders. When the little fellow was two or three weeks old, Father was relieved by another surgeon.

We drove to Fort Grant by a very good road starting at 8:15 A.M., November 10, via "Dos Cabezas," passing there at 11 A.M. to reach Wil[l]cox, where an ambulance from Fort Grant met us. We left Willcox at 1 P.M. and arrived at Fort Grant at 6 P.M. Here we remained until October 23, 1888, very nearly four years. Our new station was on the east side of the Sulfur Spring Valley at the foot of Mount Graham in the Pineleño Range and twenty-seven miles north of Willcox, the station on the Southern Pacific Railroad.

The view to the south was one of great extent. We could see "Dos Cabezas" near Fort Bowie and the mountains in Mexico. Back and east the mountains rose to the height of 10,650 feet, or over 5,000 feet higher than the Post. At sunset these and the Santa Catalina range on the west of the valley were lighted up with tints of purple, pink, and lilac, and the soft shades of the afterglow lasted for a long time, making a lovely picture never to be forgotten. Old Camp Grant had been at the junction of the Aravaipa and San Pedro Rivers, where malarial fevers were so prevalent that the present location, at about 4,000 feet elevation, had been selected as a more healthful one.[3]

Father had expected to go to Fort Whipple and the Surgeon General intended that he should go there, but the Medical Director of the Department, Brevet Colonel Bernard J. D. Irwin, Lieutenant Colonel Surgeon, wrote to him that he thought that Fort Grant was a more desirable Post, so had him ordered there.[4] Phil was now so well that we were content to remain here.

It was the headquarters of the First United States Infantry, with Colonel William R. Shafter in command. Serving under him were William E. Dougherty, Captain of Company B, and Robert G. Heiner, Captain of Company A; First Lieutenants Louis Wilhelmi, the Adjutant, Frank H. Edmunds; Second Lieutenants Thomas H. Barry, the Quartermaster, Hampton M. Roach, and James S. Petit. Later came Lieutenant Colonel Charles G. Bartlett, who was in command for a time, and Major Edward Collins.

Some troops of the Fourth Cavalry were part of the garrison, and among the officers were Captain Allen Smith, Troop A; First Lieutenant Otho W. Budd, Troop C; Second Lieutenants Guy E. Huse, James Lockett, Troop A; and James Brailsford Erwin. We had an excellent band, and the Adjutant, who was himself an excellent musician, selected the music. It gave frequent open-air concerts, and when an officer and family arrived at the Post, it would serenade them.

Father chose the best quarters available. They were next to those of the Commanding Officer on the north and large enough to house us very comfortably, as they had three good bedrooms, a large sitting room, a dining room, a good kitchen, and at the back, a bedroom for the servants. A wide gallery that ran across the front and one at the back were connected by a hall, which ran through the middle of the house. We had worked very hard and were settled when Captain William A. Thompson, with Troop G, Fourth Cavalry, took station at the Post and we were ranked out, January 15, 1885. This was our first experience of having an officer of higher rank turn us out of quarters.[5]

We then moved into "Brown's Folly," which was a large, ugly stone structure and the first one built at the Post. Brevet Major William K. Brown, Captain, Fifth Cavalry, who was in command at that time, designed it, intending that all of the officers should live there and mess together.

Originally it was surmounted by a cupola, which could be seen for miles away. Father had slept in it in May 1874, while he was on a scout after hostile Apache Indians under Eskiminzin.[6] We occupied the rooms on the north side of the long hallway. Our kitchen was detached from the house by a covered driveway.

The boys once found a bumblebee nest under the kitchen, pulled up a plank or two, and sent Frank under to get some honey. He went in but soon came out with mad bees clinging to him and inflicting their stings. He was always ready to undertake any such risk. A burro, one morning, found its way into the hallway and serenaded us, much to the delight of the boys.

We didn't remain in the "Folly" very long, but as soon as a captain vacated a set of adobe quarters at the extreme south end of the line, we moved into them, March 1885. We were not in them long before we were ranked out again and took other quarters, in which we did not remain longer than a couple of weeks when we returned to them and remained undisturbed during the rest of our tour at the Post.

The walls were very thick, which made the rooms cool in summer and warm in winter. A wide hall ran from front to rear, through which there was almost always a good draught of air and the front part of which was my sitting room on very warm days. The summers, however, were not uncomfortably warm, as the thermometer rarely rose above 100°F and not often that high.

We hung portiers [portieres] across about midway to make a room for a bed, in which two of the boys slept when they did not sleep on the front veranda, in front of which we planted wild hop vines, cucumbers, and Virginia creepers which were not long in covering the green trellis. On the right of the hallway was a sitting room and a bedroom, and on the left, two bedrooms. Passing through it, we came upon the back gallery, which ran the entire south side of the ell, in which were the dining room, kitchen, pantries, and servant's room.

We hung our ollas on this gallery to cool all of our drinking water, for we had no ice. Once Father sent to Los Angeles for one hundred pounds, so as to have ice cream on a Fourth of July. It was packed in a barrel of sawdust, but only about five pounds came and for once we had a pitcher of ice water.

The drinking water was not above suspicion when low in the wells or creek, so we often strained and boiled it well before pouring it into the ollas. The percolation of some of the water and evaporation cooled that within to a very palatable temperature.

Our butter came in two-pound glass jars and in summer was simply an oil, so to preserve it and our milk, I improvised a refrigerator. I selected the most porous bricks I could get and, placing a square of them in a broad windowsill of the dining room, built up sides and back. Across the top I laid narrow strips of wood, upon which I rested another square of bricks. The lower sash of the window was then pulled down so as to touch the top layer, and the bricks were kept wet with water, many quarts of which evaporated every day.

The rains came very late in 1884, and there was some snow in December, four inches on the 25th, but it soon melted. The water-pipes froze on the 31st.

In a large back yard we had a chicken house, a small stable for the burros, and an out-of-doors cellar, which was about three feet deep and had a dirt roof, but it wasn't of much use, as it was too warm in summer. The high board fence that enclosed the yard was usually decorated with old horseshoes and other junk brought by the boys from the dump piles where all condemned property was thrown to be destroyed. The boys were always glad for an inspector to come so that they could add to their collection. Once Colonel Shafter gave each one a condemned bugle or cornet, and before long they could blow the calls as well as most of the buglers.

They also collected stone hatchets, slicking stones, metates, pottery, and other relics from the mounds and sites of prehistoric villages of the locality, and in July 1888, on the very tiptop of Mount Graham, Phil found a turtle-shaped vessel of red-clay a little over three inches in diameter. Turned on its back, a hole about three-quarters of an inch in diameter led to the hollow interior. Fragments of pottery were lying all about it. They cut through a mound in October 1886, near the north bank of the creek below the Post, and another, August 1887, and found many stone implements.

We at first had no servant. Sometimes we could get a soldier to wash dishes and clean the kitchen, but it was not at all certain that he would be on hand in the morning to make the fire, as he had his military duties to perform as well. Harold and Philip were my willing helpers, and when he didn't come, Hal would rise early, make the kitchen fire, put the cereal on to cook, grind the coffee, set the table, and then go to the butcher's for the meat. He would look at the chimneys of the other quarters and find that ours was the only one out of which smoke was coming at that hour.

We were the earliest risers, as Father attended sick-call. No work could go on at the Post until the men had a chance to go to the hospital. Those that didn't wish to work would sometimes play sick so as to be excused from duty. Any that really were sick were admitted into the hospital at that hour—not that they could not be taken in at any other time of the day or night. Those that were marked "duty" had a delay in getting to work, and that respite the soldier thought worth going to the hospital for.

Besides the cooking, there was sweeping and other cleaning, wood fires to make and replenish in cold weather, water to be heated for the baths, tubs carried in, filled, and after use to be taken out and emptied, beds to make, stockings to darn, and various other duties to be performed, but the only one I wanted to shirk was the dish washing, and I did not like that. By evening I was glad to lie down on a buffalo robe in front of a big bright fire in the fireplace, and here the boys would join me to chat until study hour.

When we first went into these quarters a Mojave boy named Peter, whose Indian name was Waskebika, came to us. He had been with Captain Heiner and was quite capable to do general housework. Kind and gentle he was, and very ambitious to learn the white man's way of doing things so as to be competent to return to his people to teach them. He would take his study hour in the dining room with the boys and learn his spelling and reading lessons, and he soon began to study arithmetic.

He was doing so well and was so anxious to go to school that Father procured transportation for him and Frank, another Mojave boy, to Lawrence, Kansas, where they entered the school for Indians.[7] Pete had found a twenty dollar gold piece in the bushes near which there had been a circus a few days before, and this, with what money Father gave him, was enough to spend for little things for some time. I put them up enough bread, meat, etc. to last them through and told them that when they heard a man call out, "Twenty minutes for breakfast," to go to a lunch counter with their tin cups and buy some coffee or milk.

They left with great expectations, but, poor boys, we afterward felt sorry that we had sent them away. The indoor life they led did not agree with them. Peter Silver, as he was called by the school authorities, died the next winter, and Frank was sent back to Arizona to die of tuberculosis. We knew several other Indians that came back gaunt and with bad coughs.

If Miss Teed had been with us, we would have educated the two boys along with our boys.[8] Pete had been of great use to Father, who had some knowledge of the Apache Yuma and Apache Mojave dialects of the Yuman language and began to study the Mojave.

For some months, the only children on the officers' line were the two little Thompson girls and our four boys, but after awhile we had more women and children than we had yet seen at an army post.

The Tenth United States Cavalry, composed of colored men with white officers, came from Texas May 2, 1885. The headquarters, band, and four troops relieved the troops of the Third Cavalry, which left for Texas April 11, 1885, eight troops concentrating at Grant. With the Tenth Cavalry or later came Major Frederick Van Vliet, Captains Charles D. Viele, William B. Kennedy, Alexander S. B. Keyes, Joseph M. Kelley, Thomas C. Lebo, Robert G. Smither, and Charles L. Cooper; First Lieutenants William Davis, Mason M. Maxon, Levi P. Hunt, Charles R. Ward; and Second Lieutenants George H. Evans, John Bigelow Jr., Robert D. Reed, Millard F. Eggleston, Charles H. Grierson, Carter P. Johnson, Powhatan H. Clarke, Robert G. Paxton, William E. Shipp, John B. McDonald; and Chapl[a]in Francis H. Weaver.

Colonel Shafter still remained in command of the Post. He was familiarly called "Pecos Bill," a sobriquet he had received on account of a successful campaign against Indians on the Pecos River, and Lieutenant Davis was dubbed "Whispering Bill" for the reason that he had a far-carrying voice and very rarely lowered its tone.[9] The officers from West Point had nick-names, but I can recall only one of them and that is "Oucks Bijoucks," which was Lieutenant Mason's [Maxon's] pronunciation of the words "aux bijoux" in his first French lesson.

With the Tenth Cavalry came a crowd of women and children, and we had no difficulty in procuring servants. For a cook we secured a very large and very black woman, Julia, who was a fine cook. I told her she might have one beau at a time, and one she always had. He came regularly just as we arose from the dinner table to be on hand for some of the dessert. They would sing Moody and Sankey hymns at night and pray together.[10]

She remained with us for some months and until I had saved her enough money to buy a full outfit of clothing and a trunk. Then she began to neglect her work so we had to send her away. One blue silk dress, trimmed with deep white lace I had asked Mother to have made, she wore the first time at a hop. Some of the boys went to the hop-room and looked into a window, and as she entered, the Negro soldier usher announced, "Ladies and gentlemen, let me introduce the 'Blue Bird,'" and she soon had a crowd of admirers surrounding her. She was always good-natured, and once when I scolded her for neglecting her work on account of the attentions of the men, she picked me up and carried me from the kitchen into the dining room.

We had for a time a mulatto man named Duell to take care of the horses and work about house, but we learned that he abused the horses so we let him go, and, vacation coming on, Claude and Harold took charge of them. For some months we had a very excellent mulatto woman cooking for us. Maria was soon joined by Abe, her husband, who was always volunteering to do work about the house. He took a great fancy to Will and played with him a great deal. On Christmas day Will came in with a twenty dollar gold piece that Abe had given him, but which we would not let him keep, as Father learned that Abe was a gambler and was using Will as a mascot, letting him play with his money to give him good luck. Maria came to us so that Abe might gamble with the soldiers. We couldn't countenance anything of that kind so had to send her away.

We at last secured Jackson of the Hospital Corps as a striker. The organization of the Hospital Corps began about this time, and Father transferred colored men from the Cavalry and instructed them in their various duties. For some months I had one of them in our kitchen, teaching him how to cook while he assisted our cook, and it wasn't long before I had trained for him four or five of the best cooks in the garrison.[11]

. . . Father was in the field with a squadron of the Tenth Cavalry, 13 officers and 170 enlisted men under command of Major Frederick Van Vliet, from May 19 to June 19, and July 26 to August 1, 1885, against hostile Chiricahua Indians under Chief Geronimo. When in the field, he always carried a diary in a saddle pocket in which he noted the events of the day, and whenever he passed a post office, stage line, or a courier was sent to a telegraph station, he would tear out the leaves, enclose them in an envelope and send them to me, so I heard from him very frequently and received the latest news of what was going on.[12]

Colonel Shafter often came to me to learn more than he had received officially. He was very kind to the families of the officers that were in the field, walking along the whole line of quarters on his way to his office to inquire if he could be of service to them in any way. "Mrs. D., you should take the children out driving. I will send the ambulance to take you this afternoon," he would say to one of the wives, or "I just had a telegram and the troops are at such a point, all well."

The third day out, while at San Simon station, Father saw Claude, who was on a train en route to Willcox, Arizona, where an ambulance met him to bring him to the Post that evening, May 21, 1885. We were all very happy to be together again. At the time I took Phil to New York to see Dr. Flint, I [had] visited the Lawrenceville, New Jersey, school on the recommendation of Major Charles L. Davis, who had gone there as a boy and whose uncle at that time carried it on.[13] Now Mr. Mackenzie was the head master, and I made arrangements to enter Claude as a pupil.

After I returned to Mackinac, we sent Claude, September 3, 1884, by himself to Mrs. Elizabeth Myers Morgan, a cousin of Father, who met him and took him to her house in Brooklyn, where he remained a few days in order that she might provide him with some articles that he would need. He was much pleased with his surroundings, the teachers, and the boys and was progressing very well in his studies when the holiday season arrived and he went to Libbie's again.

Early in the New Year he returned to the school and shortly afterward contracted the measles from some of the boys who had not been properly isolated at the time they had the disease. He had a very mild case, but his tonsils gave him trouble afterward. The grounds were torn up for the new buildings that were contemplated and the sanitary conditions were not good, so Father sent for him to come out to us, and we could have all of our children until they were old enough to take care of themselves properly.

Father had only one horse when he went out, a beautiful buckskin colored mare with a dark mane and tail that he had bought for $75.00 of a Mexican who had brought her up as the family pet. She was very gentle, bridle wise, easy under the saddle, and easy to drive. The boys named her "Fan." There was one thing that she did not like, and that was a piece of paper flying about. She would watch it and dance up and down until it was out of sight.

While he was over in New Mexico Father bought an iron-grey horse that was stouter than "Fan" and that the boys named "Prince." This horse had many gaits and could out walk any of the other horses, officers or troop. We sent for a buckboard, which we received May 14, 1885, and drove nearly every day. Prince was a scamp and knew who had the reins, as when I drove, down would go his head, or he would put it over on Fan's neck and seemed to say to her, "Don't mind her, she doesn't know how to drive."

When Father returned, he also brought a burra, bought of a prospector, which the boys called "Jen."[14] The packers gave her some bacon every night, and she followed the pack train to get it. She was small and of a light grey color. Soon afterward, the boys found three estrays near the foot of the mountains and brought them in. Two of them were full grown and large, and the other one was a large colt. One was brown and the other two were a handsome grey. We tried to find the owner, but for some time without success, until a sergeant said he thought they might belong to Colonel [Charles Gratiot] Bartlett. Father wrote to him and described the brands they bore, and finding they were his, bought them, paying I think six or seven dollars for each one. We soon afterward procured another one and then each boy had a mount.[15]

They at first rode bare back, sometimes on pads and at length had condemned saddles. They put them in harness and drove them, or they packed one and went camping. The care of them occupied much of their time. The burros often chose dinnertime, just as the boys were sitting down, to start off for a frolic. We would hear the cry, "The burros have gone," and up the boys would jump to bring them back. Jen would sometimes take a notion to return to New Mexico and get away several miles on the road she had come before she would be caught. Jen belonged to Will and did just as she pleased about going anywhere. Sometimes she would not move, but if Will became tired and would jump off and say to her, "Well, go," off she would trot.

Often the whole family would go off for the day, Father, Will, and I in the buckboard, the other boys on their burros. Shep, our darling black and brown collie with a white shirt and white collar, would trot alongside until a playful burro would lay back its ears and nip at him when he came close enough, and then he would fall behind or run under the buckboard. There were some Mexican adobe houses out in the valley, and often when we passed them, their cur dogs would be fighting. Shep liked a scrap of the kind and would jump in, bite right and left, scatter the group, and then walk or trot quietly away.

Within the Post, whenever a dog from the soldiers' quarters crossed a rocky walk that ran the length of the parade and Shep was in sight, off he would go for the intruder and back would run the other dog, sometimes yelping as if hurt. Shep would not cross to the other side of that line unless he was with the boys, and then he would keep close to heel, with eyes alert, realizing that he was on the other dogs' land. For a time we had a fine Gordon setter, "Don," and an Irish setter, "Di," but an epidemic of a distemper carried them off as well as many of the other dogs.

Father hunted small game some, but it wasn't plentiful and the air was so dry that the dogs would run over the "fool Quail" that would lie close to the ground early in the morning; when there was some moisture in the air, the dogs could scent them.[16] The boys made bean-shooters from small forks of a mesquite bush and India rubber elastic bands, with the use of which they became expert marksmen, Frank in particular, and they would kill many birds, rats, etc. with them. After a time they had air guns in which they used BB shot.

Father taught Claude how to handle a shotgun and afterward a rifle, and told him which was the end to turn from him. Claude laughed and said he knew, but one day Father saw him looking down the barrel and took the rifle from him, telling him he didn't know the right from the wrong end, although he thought he did. After a few days further instruction he let Claude have the rifle again.

There was an ex-soldier named Montgomery who hunted and brought game, as deer, antelope, and peccary, to the Post for sale. He took a great liking for Claude and offered to give him lessons in deer hunting. An appointment was made, and Claude joined him a few miles out, where after a little instruction how to hunt the black-tailed or mule deer, he went ahead of Montgomery the next morning, December 27, 1887, and killed his first deer, a doe. Back he came to the Post with it strapped behind his saddle.[17] Not long afterward the mountains were covered with snow early one morning when Father arose from his bed, and awakening Claude, he pointed to a grove of black oaks on a slope near the foot of the mountains and told him that probably a fine fat buck was feeding there, to go afoot and keep a good lookout, or else the animal would see him first. In less than two hours time the other boys, who were watching, shouted, "Claude has shot a deer," as they saw him on a great boulder waving his hat. They jumped upon their burros and went up to pack the carcass home. It was that of a large black-tailed buck, and Claude was pronounced a skilled hunter.

The Post was a very healthful one and usually Father could easily do all of the medical, surgical, and sanitary work, but sometimes the men would return from service in the field with diarrhea and dysentery, and once the recruits from Jefferson Barracks, Missouri, brought typhoid fever with them, which they spread along the railroad and at different posts en route to their stations. At such times Father needed an assistant, and assistants were sent to him, among which were Acting Assistant Surgeons James Carroll and Abraham P. Frick [and] Assistant Surgeon Rudolph G. Ebert, but they were soon sent away on some detached service.[18]

How to educate our children became a problem. Father and I gave them instruction right along, but we now were not able to spend so much time with them as we had heretofore done. Before we left Mackinac, Father had requested President James B. Angell of the University of Michigan to send us a teacher from among his students, but none of them wanted to come. After our arrival here, he applied to an agency in New York without success, yet about that time a teacher committed suicide by drowning because she couldn't secure a position. We at length concluded that the fear of Indians prevented any applicants, so after Claude joined us Father wrote to the State Normal School, San Jose, California, and we received two applications and selected Miss Ida Teed. We never regretted our choice, for she was well equipped for her work and soon adapted herself to the army life. At first she was quite critical, as she had secured the knowledge she had of the army second hand from books and magazines.[19]

Claude met her on the road between Willcox and Grant. When she arrived in November 1885, a great fire blazed in the fireplace, and some officers and their wives were calling when she entered the house. She was surprised at their very courteous manners and refinement. She rather expected to meet men made rough by their employment of fighting Indians and frontier life.

She received a great deal of attention, and all the youngsters were ready to take her out horseback or driving, but she was rather reserved in her manner and preferred the family life, of which she had seen very little while teaching school. She loved the mountains, the trees, and wild flowers, and she and I wandered everywhere collecting all sorts of plants to press. Her collection of ferns was increased by gold back and silver back maidenhair, which we found under the rocks in the dry arroyos, but there were many other varieties. Mine were burned in San Francisco's great fire. She was always ready for a climb among the rocks, oaks, and pines in the mountains with the boys, who when out of school, treated her as if she were a girl of their own age.

Until the Tenth Cavalry came there were very few women at the post—Mrs. Shafter and her daughter, Mary, for a while, [and] Mrs. Thompson, Mrs. Wilhelmi, Mrs. Barry—but afterward there were Mesdames Cooper, Davis, Ward, Van Valzah, Bigelow, Eggleston, Keyes, Misses Sue and Kate Murphy, and at one time there were several young lady visitors, among them Misses Davis, Locke, and a Miss Winter from Honolulu. Mr. William Holmes McKittrick, who afterward married Mary Shafter, was also a visitor. Other visitors were Miss Nugent, who was shortly married to Colonel Van Vliet, and Miss Van Doran, married to John Norton, the Sutler.[20]

Brevet Major General Benjamin H. Grierson, Colonel of the Tenth Cavalry, relieved Colonel Shafter and was in command of the Post until his retirement, and then Brevet Colonel Anson Mills, Major, Tenth Cavalry, succeeded him.[21] Mrs. Mills and their two children, Anson and Constance, came with them. Will now had playmates about his age, and our other boys also found boys of their own age. Maxwell Keyes, who lived in the next quarters to ours, was one of them, and the boys thought very much of him.

Mrs. Mills and I formed a lasting friendship, although during the last years of her life we did not meet. She died in Washington, D.C., May 14, 1917. We had many tastes in common, and read history, novels, French, etc. together, and when Mrs. Charles Porter, formerly Miss Carrie Wilkins, came, we three, with others, took up a regular course of reading. Often we would have quite a roomful of officers and their wives, but after awhile the others dropped out and we three were usually left to pursue our own course. After Mrs. Porter left, Mrs. Viele was one of the trio.[22]

. . . Often Mrs. Mills and I would take our children away for a picnic, Miss Teed always with us, and occasionally others of the garrison. The creek that ran past the Post, when filled with water, was always very attractive, and we sought out the many beautiful spots nearby and high up. Our table would be a large flat rock near deep holes in which the children could bathe or paddle. There were yellow and purple columbines, lobelias, primroses, wild currants, and wild grapes. The black oaks added much to the picturesqueness of the sides and afforded a delightful shade from the hot sun.

Sometimes after school on Friday we would go over to Stockton's Pass, six or seven miles southeast, take tents, bedding, and cooking utensils and camp there until Sunday afternoon. The boys baked potatoes in the hot ashes of our campfire, broiled bacon, fried eggs, [and] made coffee, learning how to cook for themselves. From here we would climb up among the pines and rocks and lie on the rocks, talking, while the children were exploring the many beautiful spots about us.

On descending, we would have to toboggan when we came to some very steep places that were covered with pine needles. Mrs. Mills and I [went], wrapping our skirts closely about us; she would take Constance, and I, Will, and down we would slide, all shouting and laughing. It brought back to me the trip in 1869 when Father and I went from McDermit to Camp C. F. Smith, and returning by a short trail that led down a very steep mountain, we descended in this manner. It was to these pines that we would go for our Christmas trees, making a day of it and returning in the evening with a wagon load of greens.

There was a rough trail up the mountains by which we could reach the top of Graham Mountains by a shorter route than by an old logging wagon road which ran up a cañon some distance north, and this we usually climbed to get up to a beautiful grassy flat bordering a small stream of cold water and surrounded by pines, aspen, and other trees. We sometimes went up the old road to spend a day and night among the pines. Once a copper-colored rattlesnake made its appearance among our rolls of bedding before we had unpacked them, and once a skunk crawled over the boys as they lay asleep at night and licked their dishes and frying pan.

When we went by trail, I would drive in an ambulance about a mile to the foot of the mountains and there mount Fan or one of the burros to make the climb of three miles, which took at least three hours. There were some good resting places on the way, from which we had grand views of the country, each succeeding one more extended as we climbed

higher and higher, until we came to the pines when the trail was an easy one and led through small grassy parks. Our tents were pitched near the water, and we gathered twigs of balsam pine upon which to lay our mattresses. The fires were made, and the air, already of a balsamic odor, would soon be replete with the fragrance of the burning pine.

From September 5, 1887, to the 9th was one of these trips. We had five
pack mules and two packers, John Moulder and Charles Mimmet. Our
cook was a soldier named Charles Jones. I rode a small black mule named
"Monk"; Claude, a small mouse-colored mule, "Blue"; Hal, his burra,
"Fanny"; Phil, his burra, "Julie"; Frank on "Jake," Julie's colt; Willie, behind
Jones on "Bush." Colonel Mills and his son Anson were with us, and on
the 8th Father, Miss Gheisling, and Miss Kate Murphy came up. It rained
on the 9th, making the trail down the mountain very slippery.

The boys wore out their riding breeches so fast, even corduroy, that we
asked Captain Crawford to send us some buckskins from the San Carlos
Agency. He had them smoked by the Indians, and then I made breeches
for all that lasted for months. Mother did most of our shopping and sent
many things by mail, but in the fall we would receive a box by freight
which usually contained from seven to ten pairs of shoes, seven of over-
shoes, six suits of children's clothes, and underclothes for the whole family, besides maple sugar, cherries dried by Mother, canned fruit, etc.

In May 1888, the month in which people often lose all energy, become
listless, and go to bed, Father sent many patients up to our favorite resort,
and Colonel Mills gave him ten soldiers to build log houses for them, and
later, to expedite the work, he had fifteen soldiers on the job. After the
end of the school year we also went up, July 17th, and Chaplain Weaver
with us to take charge, as Colonel Mills and Father could come up only at
the weekend.

At one time there were thirty people in our camp besides our fifteen
workmen. The tired and sick ones were not long in recuperating in the
invigorating air. The pack train made regular trips and brought us whatever was necessary to make us comfortable, even to a cook stove. Every
night campfires were lighted, around which men, women, and children
gathered to talk and sing, but we all retired to our beds early and were
soon lulled to sleep by the murmurings of the little brook. Mrs. Mills and
her children, Mrs. Viele and her sister, Edith Miner, and our family messed
together, and we had a very good colored cook. The families of Commissary Sergeant Burrows and Moyer, the blacksmith, were on the opposite
side of the brook. Montgomery one day appeared and became a member
of the camp. The boys were delighted, as he had a fund of stories, most of
them about bear, deer, peccaries, rattle snakes, etc., all of which animals he
had killed, and of escapes from the Indians. We were there two weeks.

The summit of Mount Graham was several hundred feet above us and we would ascend to it for the grand view, which included range after range of mountains, long broad valleys that extended into Mexico many miles south. On the east the mountains were much steeper than on the west, and in places there were sheer descents of many hundred feet. San Simon Valley lay at the foot, and beyond it loomed the Mogollon Mountains.

One day in midsummer we saw from here a thunderstorm below us, and it was a sight worth climbing up to witness. Flashes of lightning darted through the great bank of cumuli clouds spread out roll against roll and moving steadily along, and we could hear the waffled peals of thunder now and then. We not infrequently saw lunar rainbows.[23]

Mother came out to visit us from January 15, 1887, to March 10, and we were very sorry when she had to leave, but a dear friend of hers, Mrs. Anna Bell, who was in Pasadena, California, with Florence, her daughter, was urging her to join them. Florence had tuberculosis and Mrs. Bell needed Mother, so she went. Father secured a leave from April 5 to May 5, 1887, and also went to Pasadena to see Florence, but nothing could be done except to prolong her life a little longer. . . .

Miss Teed left us July 3, 1887, after we had engaged Mr. William B. Cairns, a student in the University of Wisconsin, whom she had recommended to replace her. She thought that the boys should now have a man to instruct them, Claude especially, but she had become such a necessary part of our household and the boys had done so well under her conscientious guidance that we were very sorry to lose her. As well as other branches, she had taught them to read music and draw.

She went to Los Angles and several years afterward to New York, where she is now, 1918, one of the inspectors of art in the public schools. She has learned several languages and [has] taken two degrees in Columbia College, New York, has executed some very fine watercolors, and her pictures in oil have won mention in art exhibits. She not only taught our children, but also the children of some of the other officers and one or two civilians for a time. We have met her many times, as she frequently visits Harold and his family in Plainfield, New Jersey. She has told me many times that the two years spent with us were the happiest of her life, and I hope that all of her remaining years will be as happy.

Mr. Cairns arrived September 25, 1887, and remained with us until July 1888. He was a clean, decent, well-appearing young fellow and hard student, tall, rather loose-jointed and with a nose that was somewhat flat at the end, the kind that literary people not infrequently have, but he hadn't the training to impart his knowledge to others as Miss Teed had, so although the boys did well under him, they didn't improve so rapidly as they had done.[24]

Our boys were far ahead of others of their age among civilians, except in mathematics, as they were taught zoology, botany, geology, [and] ethnology by Father and knew what was going on in the world. They were close observers and made collections of all sorts of objects, and especially of stone implements, pottery, etc.

The Sergeant [J. Fred Grant] at Mackinac had taught them how to tease a teacher, and they read how boys hazed their tutors, so they were not long in testing Mr. Cairns. He, however, usually took all very patiently, even when they led him close to a hornet's nest, and the furious bees that they had excited by shooting stones into their nest swarmed after him and inflict[ed] the mule he was riding with such stings that it dashed into the bushes. [O]ne leg of his trousers was ripped its whole length and he was pretty badly scratched. They then rode ahead to reach the Post before he did and tell several young ladies to be on the lookout for him, but they saw him only afar, for he dashed into his room to change his clothes and treat his scratches and bruises.[25]

He never told us whether he knew that the rascals had set the hornets at him but did say that his mule became unmanageable. The girls tried to tease him, and they taught him to dance just to have a good laugh at his expense, but he practiced the steps and persevered until he became an acceptable partner in a waltz, etc. He returned to Wisconsin, and some years later we heard that he was a professor there of literature, I think, and had written a book.[26]

Chaplain [Francis Heyer] Weaver was a very good man and carried on the school for the enlisted men and their children to the satisfaction of all, but he couldn't preach a good sermon, so we frequently requested him to omit his sermon and have a service of song. The room in the old hospital building that had been a ward would then be crowded, mostly with colored women and soldiers, to its utmost capacity. We had a small organ, and Moody and Sankey hymnbooks had been sent out by an organization of ladies in the East. Mrs. Mills acted as organist, and Mrs. Viele, Edith Miner, Father, and I formed a sort of choir to be joined by the melodious voices of the Negroes, which carried far out into the beautiful night and upward toward the stars. . . .

I had carried on a Sunday school before the Chaplain came and continued the work after he assumed charge. There was so much in Arizona to liken to Palestine, and the children could understand many allusions in the Bible that children in the Eastern and Southern states could only partially comprehend.

Captain Emmet Crawford stayed with us March 11th and 12th and again October 26 and 27, 1885, while on his way with his command of Indian Scouts to follow Geronimo into Mexico, where in January 1886 he was killed by Mexican soldiers while he was trying to prevent them from firing upon his Indians. Lieutenants Marion P. Maus and William E. Shipp were with him on this ill-fated expedition. Lieutenant Maus was taken prisoner by the Mexicans, and it was said in jest that he was swapped for a mule, but he did surrender some mules and the Mexicans released him. He, however, received a Medal of Honor for his achievements.[27]

We had many visitors at the Post; usually officers and their families passed frequently en route to or from other stations, Brevet Major General George Crook, Brigadier General; Brevet Major General Nelson A. Miles, Brigadier General; Captain Henry Ware Lawton, afterward Colonel and Major General of Volunteers, [who] was killed in the Philippines, December 19, 1899; and Assistant Surgeon Leonard Wood, among them.[28] Miss Hattie Leonard, sister of Mrs. David Carter of Detroit, paid us a visit and painted some exquisite watercolors. While she was with us, we gave a progressive whist party and she decorated a book as the booby prize, entitled on its cover, "What I Know About Whist." Colonel Shafter was the recipient, and a shout arose when he opened the book and found every page blank. We met her frequently afterward, and Harold took lessons in watercolors from her while we were stationed in Detroit.

A Miss Giesling of Kentucky was with the Davises for a while. She had been at the San Carlos Agency as a teacher of the Indians, but she whipped an Indian boy and tried to push him into a big wood stove, or pretended she wanted to do so. Her usefulness as a teacher of Indians ceased right then, and she came away in haste.

Frederick [Frederic] Remington at one time carried on his work at Grant, staying with Lieutenant Powhatan Clarke. He made many of his watercolors in the shade of our quarters, and Claude rode Fan and other horses for him while he took snap shots. He frequently sat on our front gallery at sunset to absorb the surpassing colors of earth and sky at that hour.[29]

After the rains fell in August the country would be quite green for a short time, and those in the late winter would cause grass to spring up and wild flowers to appear in immense patches and our creek to fill up. Then the cattle would fatten, but they would soon exhaust the scanty grass and most of the water, too. The soil was decomposed granite and so porous that it did not hold water long. Wells had to be dug very deep to find any. Our water supply came from the creek that had its source in the mountains, and it flowed past the Post except during the dry season.

It was piped to our quarters from a small concrete dam about a mile up and was of an excellent quality, but every summer the time came when the water in the creek didn't reach the dam and there was no road to permit wagons to go high up where there was running water or where it lay in pools among the rocks in the creek bottom. Then resort was had to a rill some five or six miles south, from which a water wagon full could be procured once a day. One morning, October 10, 1885, after I had taken enough for our coffee I had a cupful left with which to bathe our faces, and the dishes could not be washed that day. As to laundry work, none could be done for two weeks.

After Colonel Mills came in command, he had boards hauled up the creek as far as possible and then carried by hand higher up in order to make **V**-shaped troughs by means of which to conduct water down to the small reservoir. He then cut a road over which iron pipes could be transported, and these were laid to replace the wooden troughs. He had a large pond dug on the parade ground in December 1887 and which he named Lake Constance, after his daughter, and several large sprinklers installed.[30]

More cottonwood trees were planted, which were irrigated every day. Sewer pipes were laid, bathrooms [were] installed in the quarters and water closets outside. The sewage was led to the dumping ground, on which all the refuse from the stables had been deposited for years. After this was ploughed in, we planted gardens which grasshoppers ate up so often that most of the officers and companies gave up in despair, but Colonel Mills and Father planted the fifth time and succeeded beyond all their expectations in raising vegetables from all the varieties of seeds they put into the ground. We had muskmelons until late in the season, watermelons, some of which Father had sunken in the ground to eat on Thanksgiving Day, and tomatoes until Christmas that ripened on vines that Father pulled by their roots and hung in our out-of-doors cellar.

The last year we were here some Mormons from the valley of the Gila River brought watermelons to sell. The largest weighed seventy pounds, and the smallest, forty pounds. We had many watermelon parties, as one family couldn't finish a whole one at a sitting. Virginia creepers, wild hops, and wild cucumber vines soon covered thickly the trellis on our front gallery.

I had often heard that corn was planted with a crow bar when one day, well out in the valley, we saw one of the new settlers at work, and on driving close to him, we saw him remove a shovel full of soil, drive a crow bar down a foot to make a hole into which he dropped a few grains of corn (maize). He said that there was moisture enough at that depth to germinate the seed, and when the rains came they would spring out of the ground and grow very rapidly. We saw the field when the corn was eight to ten feet high.

We always planted something wherever we were stationed, and here Father started a little orchard at the hospital the first year and demonstrated to the settlers around us what fruits they could raise. He sent to Rochester, New York, for apple, pear, cherry, plum, peach, and fig trees, grape, blackberry, and raspberry vines, and red currant bushes, all of which, except the raspberries, flourished. There were grapes on the vines and a few delicious peaches on the trees before we left. . . .

One of the bushes back of our quarters was called "the butcher birds' Christmas Tree" by the boys, as upon its numerous thorns there were grasshopper, bits of lizard, mice, and small birds which the birds had placed there. As the trees in the Post grew larger they attracted many birds, such as Arizona canaries, mocking birds, humming birds, doves, meadowlark, quail, and crows. The boys nearly always had some pet birds. The butcher birds that they had for awhile in a large cage hung bits of meat on nails, and when they were free hung scraps of meat on nails along the fence, but they fell into disrepute after they cruelly scalped a caged canary that belonged to one of our neighbors. . . .

The only animals they did not attempt to pet were the skunks, although very beautiful in their stripes of black and white, which frequently came out from under our kitchen where they had been littered and had the back gallery to themselves, as they resented our approach by unfair means. We often heard the kitten-like cries of the young ones at night. After they were fully-grown and began to frequent our chicken house, Father shot several.

There were rattlesnakes and many kinds of lizards and the so-called horned toads. The Gila monster was quite common in the San Simon Valley, but I think Grant was too cold for them. Father brought one home from the San Simon Valley and placed it in a box that had slats very close together, but the animal must have been able to flatten itself out very thin to get out, as while I was lying on my bed and Will by my side, he called out, "The monster, the monster!" I looked in the direction he was pointing, and there lazily approaching the bed was the creature. Father then put it in a large coal oil can with plenty of sand, but it didn't live long, and we think the cold killed it or possibly some of the mineral oil remained in the can.

While in the box it had been fed on raw eggs. It was nearly twenty inches long and looked as if made of black and orange colored beads. Its head was very broad, and its teeth, which are grooved, had at their bases minute poison sacks [sacs]. When angry, it would swell up and blow at you. The Mexicans told us to keep away from it at such times, as it cast a poison which if it fell upon the skin would cause bad sores and that the bite was venomous.[31]

We had one shock of earthquake that I remember, and it threw some vases from the mantel. The children ran from their schoolroom to watch the yuccas waving as the tremor passed down the valley. Some people across the valley said that they saw smoke and flames issuing from an old crater. . . .

Before leaving Grant, Father bought a lot of range cows and young steers and left them in Paddy's charge for one third of the increase.[32] At the end of ten years, there was no increase for Father and he sold what remained, receiving about the amount that he had invested. Father grub-staked an old prospector named Lighter, who went about leading his packed burro. The old fellow brought in some ore which essayed very high in silver and gold, but just then the Indians at San Carlos became troublesome again and Father couldn't go to verify his discovery and Lighter didn't return after the Indians quieted down.[33]

On August 23, 1888, Miss Kate Murphy and Second Lieutenant John B. McDonald, Tenth Cavalry, were married in the new hall. We draped the room with flags, curtains, and evergreens and covered the floor with rugs, so that it had a very festal look and especially so when the officers in their uniforms and the ladies in their handsome gowns had assembled.

In the summer of 1888, the troops of the Tenth Cavalry were relieved by companies of the Twenty-Fourth Infantry, and Lieutenant Colonel Edward P. Pearson was placed in command the latter part of September. He was satisfied to let all matters rest in status quo, except that he ordered us down from the mountains as he feared the Indians would massacre us, but they were not the resort of any and none were nearer than ninety miles. Colonel Mills left the Post October 1st.[34]

Father had been trying to get an ice plant for the Post and had forwarded recommendation upon recommendation for nearly four years when he received a letter from the Surgeon General that one was on the way. The new commanding officer, who was slow to see the benefits we would derive from having ice, required some urging before he would consent to let the plant be erected in a two story adobe building that was really built for the purpose when Colonel Mills was in command, but was used as a carpenter and paint shop. The Tenth Cavalry had called it "Mills' Folly" because it had two stories, and what was the use of such a house in a military post.[35] The day that we left Fort Grant, the ice-making machine was started, and Father let a little ammonia escape from one of the drums, just enough to cool one finger, and we had a whiff of the ammonia as we drove away; but of the ice we had none.

There were a few cattle ranches in the valley when we first went to Grant, but other settlers came in and fenced in the land to raise crops of various kinds, and the old time cowboys, or vaqueros, began to disappear. There were very few left when we came away. Some took wives and went to farming, some sought other vocations, and a few left for the cattle ranges further north.

There were no civilian physicians in this part of the country. One came to Willcox but didn't remain long, and he was replaced by a farrier who took up the practice of medicine. But the people depended upon the Surgeon at the Post for skilled treatment. Father had usually to drive long distances, and once he was driven thirty miles in about two hours to see a patient, having relays of horses on the road. The people were not able to pay him what his services were worth, so he only averaged about $1,000.00 a year. . . .

CHAPTER EIGHTEEN

"He Was Not Wicked but Only Unfortunate"

FORTS HAYS, LEWIS, AND LEAVENWORTH, KANSAS AND COLORADO, OCTOBER 1888–JULY 1890

W E ALL LEFT FORT GRANT ON October 23, 1888, four years to the day since we entered the Territory, and Willcox [at] 8 A.M. October 24, arrived at Deming, New Mexico, about 1 P.M. There Father and the oldest four boys changed trains, while Will and I went on to New Orleans, where we changed trains to go to Amite, sixty-eight miles north on the Illinois Central Railroad, to visit my sister, May Addison, and her family, who lived in our old home, Dunbarton, where we arrived October 28. After spending a delightful month with them, we joined Father December 13th at Fort Hays, Kansas, where he and the four boys had arrived October 29, 1888, and where we remained until November 12, 1889.

The Post was three-quarters of a mile south of Hays City, a small town on the Kansas Pacific Railroad, near the central part of the state, and located on a terrace one-fourth of a mile south of Big Creek, a tributary of the Smoky Hill Fork of the Kansas River, at an elevation above the sea level of 2,107 feet.[1]

A few elm and cedar trees grew along the creek, in which there were a few carp and from which ice was procured for the garrison and the town.

Away from the creek, the country was treeless, and the monotony of the landscape was relieved by limestone bluffs only. The climate, always dry, was hot in summer and cold in winter. High winds tempered the heat but intensified the cold, and they whistled through our frame quarters and shook them until I was afraid they would be blown away. Prairie fires were common, and fire-guards had to be burned around the Post to protect us from them.[2]

Our quarters were built of rough lumber, hard to keep clean, had none of the modern conveniences, and were much in need of repairs. Father had relieved Major Henry M. Cronkhite as Post Surgeon and had gone into his quarters, which were next to the hospital on the east. All the water we used was hauled in a wagon up from a well near the creek and kept in barrels, from which we dipped it when required.

Our garrison was a very pleasant one. Colonel John E. Yard, Eighteenth Infantry, was in command until February 17, 1889, when he died of pneumonia, and he was succeeded by Brevet Lieutenant Colonel George K. Brady, Major of the regiment. The captains were William H. McLaughlin, George N. Bomford, and Charles B. Hinton; the Lieutenants, William B. Wheeler, George T. Turner, William T. Wood, Edson A. Lewis, and Charles McClure, all married except Lieutenant Turner, and, excepting Major Brady and Captain McLaughlin, [all] had children.[3]

Sally and Harry Wheeler, who lived at the west end of the line, were pretty lively youngsters and never lacking in the initiative. Sally took our boys to some raised beds made in an attempt at a flower garden back of her home and pointed them out as the graves of her mother's four deceased husbands. Her mother had actually lost but one husband.

Harry would be on his knees praying when his stepfather entered to admonish or punish him for some prank, and his prayers would be so long that the stepfather would quietly leave the room. He once told his mother that he was not wicked but only unfortunate. Once when put to bed and locked in so that his father and mother might have a quiet time at the minstrel show in town, he let himself out of a window and went over to the soldiers' quarters in his nightshirt and shoes, procured an overcoat, and drove with some of the men to town. His mother was enjoying the show, when, happening to look over toward some of the soldiers, she saw Harry's head among them. He was never locked in again.

. . . Hays City had been at one time the resort of many tough charac-
ters that congregated here during the building of the railroad, and many
were the stories we heard of their evil actions. One of the reminders of
those days was "Boot Hill," upon which those that died in their boots
were buried, and very few men died in their beds. But now the inhabitants
were of a different type, quiet, industrious, and acquiring the culture of
older towns. They had the best of schools and good churches. Saloons for
the sale of alcoholic beverages were unknown. Captain C. G. Gordon, a
retired Army officer, owned considerable land and lived here.[4]

Nearly all of the early towns in the West grew up at or near army
posts, to which the settlers looked for employment, support, and protection from the Indians. Many discharged soldiers took up land, and some
officers invested their savings and resigned or when retired, remained
near their old stations. The posts were centres of refinement, and some of
them are still resorts of the people of the cities that have sprung up within
my recollection.[5]

Our boys attended the public school in Hays, L. H. Gehman the Principal. [They] made excellent progress in all of their studies and were promoted to higher grades. The methods of teaching fitted in better with the
training they had already received than those pursued at the schools they
subsequently entered. Willie entered his first school in September and for
a day or two had a pain in his stomach about school time, so I put him to
bed and the pain soon left. In a few days he was as eager to go as the other
boys. The boys continued their music lessons on the violin, except
Harold, who had them on the banjo, and they also had dancing lessons.

Claude graduated from the High School May 23, 1889, in a class of five,
the first that had taken the course, writing his essay on the Mound
Builders, and entered the University of Kansas at Lawrence, Professor
[Francis Huntington] Snow, President, in September 1889.[6] The others of
the graduating class were John G. Huntington, Mary B. Thomas, Elsie
McIntosh, and Katherine D. Courtney. The commencement exercises
were held in the Lutheran Church (Reverend J. B. Killinger, the pastor),
which was tastefully decorated with flowers and plants. The Eighteenth
Infantry band played some choice music. The Reverend C. Thomas pronounced the invocation; Reverend D. B. Whimster, the benediction; Hon-
orable James H. Reeder presented the diplomas. The Board of Education
was J. M. Yost, President, M. G. Huntington, Treasurer, and F. Havemann,

Secretary. The exercises passed off very well until toward the last, when a terrific thunderstorm hurried most of us home.

Mr. J. M. Yost, who owned a flourmill in town, had several children, and his two girls, Jennie and Rosie, became warm friends of Phil and Frank. Another boy claimed that the girl he walked home from school with was prettier than Rosie, which Frank disputed, and the wager of battle was to decide the question. Frank came home with both ears swollen, one eye blacked and closed, and face well scratched, but exultant. "Anyhow, I licked him," he said, and when we went to Fort Lewis he named his pet goat Rosie.

There was in 1889 an abundance of rain for the first time in three years, and the grain fields, which extended for miles, promised an unusually large yield, which was badly needed by the farmers, who were nearly all in debt owing to the bad years. The creek was bordered by beautiful box elders, elms, and banks of grass. Wild flowers made a garden of the prairies, and the yards in town were full of cultivated plants and flowers.

Claude went to work in Mr. Yost's flourmill on August 1, 1889, so as to establish a residence in Hays City, as he was very anxious to go to the United States Military Academy. Father had tried to get an appointment at large from the President, but failed owing to lack of political influence. Then he tried to get one through Mr. F. J. Turner, United States Representative from this District, but didn't have enough influence to secure it, and Orrin R. Wolfe, the son of a deceased army officer, received the appointment.[7]

We were very glad that we were at Hays at a time that Mother had to go to Fort Collins, Colorado, on business connected with a hotel, the Tedmon House, they owned there and rented, as she visited us ten days in February [1890] on her way back home. The boys hung about her and listened to her witty talk and her quaint aphorisms. She brought a prairie dog which she tried to pet, but he didn't take well to confinement in a box and would frequently escape to make himself cozy elsewhere. Once he dragged a shawl that Father's father had brought from England before the war and cut holes in it. When Mother reached home, Grandpa Jones said he should have a mate and bought one; but the pair cut the curtains, dug up the lawn, and not long afterward one of them disappeared, when the other was given to a man who kept a bird store.

We had weekly hops, and during the winter, dinners and oyster suppers. Five o'clock teas were not in vogue at that time and were looked upon as a very cheap and poor way of entertaining one's friends, and we lived so close together that we met frequently, especially at guard mounting, when we would assemble on the veranda of the quarters nearest the music. Occasionally there was a play in the hall in town or a circus.

Our boys, with the others, sometimes gave a minstrel show. On one occasion Frank appeared with a lynx skin over one shoulder, one around his waist, and a spear in one hand, looking very fierce. He was the Zulu that killed the Prince Napoleon, but Hal introduced him as the Prince, and we all shouted with laughter.[8] Back behind the curtain fled Frank as fast as his long legs could carry him, Hal following at his heels. They reappeared shortly and the show went on, but the second appearance was not encored in such a hearty manner as was the first.

Father usually cut the boys' hair, and when five had to undergo the ordeal, it was quite a task. Frank was the most restless one and afraid of his ears, and one day his ear was accidentally nipped a little. He didn't dare to move then for fear of further nippings, but the tears ran down his cheeks, catching and holding the hairs until Father completed his work.

There was a settlement of Russians a few miles northeast of the town. They were descendants of Germans that had been induced to emigrate to Russia in the time of Peter the Great by the promise of exemption from military duty. This generation was called upon for this duty and they did not like it, so came to Kansas.[9] They were a quiet, sober, industrious, law-abiding people and succeeded in raising fine crops of wheat in this dry country, where most other settlers failed. Their houses were of magnesium limestone sawed into blocks and were furnished with furnaces that had very long smoke flues built of the same kind of stone. For a fuel they used the refuse from the stables and corrals made into blocks and dried, just as the early emigrants when crossing the plains used "buffalo chips" in a treeless country. . . .

Assistant Surgeon General Charles Page, Medical Director of the Department, inspected the hospital on September 13 and had lunch with us. Companies B and H left on September 19, 1889, to go to a camp of instruction near Arkansas City, Kansas, and later went to Fort Clarke [Clark], Texas. Orders came to abandon the post. Taps was sounded as the last company of the Eighteenth Infantry marched out of the Post, November 1, 1889.

A large amount of government property not worth transporting was sold at auction. People from the surrounding country came in to bid, and many returned home with their farm wagons piled up. The day was a very cold one, and just enough snow had fallen to make the ground wet and muddy and a strong wind was blowing. Father sold nearly everything in the hospital, but before he could complete his papers [he] received a telegraphic order to hasten to Fort Lewis, Colorado. The abandonment of the Post was a great loss to the town, as the greater part of the pay received by the officers and men was spent there and hay, grain, wood, etc. were purchased.

Father was sorry to have to leave, as he had a good consulting practice and did nearly all of the surgical work in the town and for some distance east and west along the railroad. Claude wrote that he had seen Margaret Mather in *Romeo and Juliet*, his first Shakespearian play.[10]

We left Fort Hays on November 11th and stayed until the next evening at the Brunswick Hotel kept by Harvey Penney. A crowd of friends whom we were sorry to leave bid us goodbye at the train. We arrived at Denver 8 A.M., November 12th, and went to the Markham Hotel to stay until 10 P.M., when we took a train on the Denver and Rio Grande narrow gauge road for Cucharas, where we changed early the next morning to a day car for Durango, Colorado. The scenery, especially through Vita [La Veta] Pass, [was] grand. Our engine could be seen much of the time, and often we were on a ledge close to the mountains on one side and steep cliffs on the other. At the summit was a shaft erected to the memory of ex-president Garfield by a party that were passing through on the first train while his funeral was taking place in Ohio. Arriving at Durango, on the Las Animas River and terminal of the roads, about 9 P.M. of the 14th, we stayed at the Strater House.[11]

An ambulance met us, and the next morning, November 15th, we ascended the mountains twelve miles to the Post, which was located at Pagosa Springs in the gravelly bed of the San Juan river, at an elevation above the sea of ___ feet.[12] The drive was through a cañon along which there were several very productive soft-coal mines. Pine groves covered the sides of the mountains. On arriving we selected the frame quarters at the west end of the officers' line, which were very comfortable ones, although there was water among the stones under the house all winter. The lower floor was up at least six feet so the rooms were not damp. We borrowed bedding and took our meals at mess for two weeks, at the end of which our baggage arrived and we started housekeeping. We burned soft coal, which we bought for $2.50 a ton from a mine nearby, as the mountains were full of it.

The necessity for Father to hurry to the Post had passed, and First Lieutenant Nathan S. Jarvis could have performed the duties very well, but he was a nervous, discontented man and wanted to get away. He soon asked for a leave of absence, and Father approved his application. Brevet Major Tullius C. Tupper, Captain, Sixth Cavalry, was in command, and the officers of the other two troops were: Captains Adam Kramer, William M. Wallace; First Lieutenants Francis H. Beach, William Stanton, William H. Carter; Second Lieutenants John N. Glass and Augustus P. Blocksom, George McK. Williamson, Sixth Cavalry; and three companies of the Sixth Infantry: Captain Stephen Baker, First Lieutenant Stephen W. Groesbeck, Second Lieutenant Zerah Watkins Torrey of the companies of the Sixth Infantry, and Chaplain William J. Larkin. Also Lieutenants Amos B. Shattuck and Frank D. Webster [were at Fort Lewis].

The air was dry and crisp, but Father and I were affected by the altitude, our hearts beating faster on exerting ourselves. The boys, except Claude, who was at the University of Kansas, were very well. Phil and Frank each had a goat to drive, which they named Jennie and Rosie after the two Yost girls in Hays. Navajo Indians frequently came to the Post with blankets and pottery for sale, and we bought four very handsome blankets at about $12.50 each to add to those we already had.

Father had some practice, and he took Hal with him on a trip down the southwest side of the mountains to a valley thirty miles distant. By the time his patient could be left the sun was pretty well down, but the air was clear. As they ascended the mountain on their return, snow began to fall and the road became more and more obstructed and after the sun went down was hard to follow.

There were no houses to stop at, so they had to keep right on. The snow packed between the spokes of the wheels, and although they had a buckboard and a team of two strong horses, both had to get out and plough their way through the snow, now up to their knees. Hal most of the time went ahead with a lantern to pick out the road, but sometimes he drove the horses. For fifteen miles and all night they slowly toiled and climbed.

Toward morning the snow ceased to fall, the road could be seen better, and they made better time. They reached the Post about 7 A.M., just as a mounted rescue party was ready to start down the road to look for them, although Major Tupper did not believe that Father had started back. I, however, was sure that he had, as he never missed sick call.[13]

. . . On the day before Christmas Chaplain Larkin had a turkey shooting and asked Frank to help him, promising him a shot. He didn't know Frank very well, or he would not have given him the first shot. Frank put a bullet through the turkey's head, ran to the box, grabbed the turkey, and came home as fast as his legs could carry him, not heeding the chaplain's call that it was a mistake.

The boys went to the Post School for a time, but the soldier teacher usually had a drink with the Chaplain on his way to school every morning and had a bottle in his desk in the schoolroom until the boys found it and threw it out. Chaplain Larkin didn't remain in the service very long. I think he was wholly retired.[14] Claude and Harold had [G]erman under Private Bromstead of the Sixth Cavalry, Phil, violin lessons from Private Stewart, and Latin and Literature from me.

The epidemic of influenza of 1889 and 1890 reached the Post on January 5, 1890, when the first cases occurred in the quarters at the east end of the officers' line. It soon spread and Father had a mild attack. He put everyone to bed except Major Tupper, who said it was absurd to go to bed for such a slight ailment, but it caused the Major's retirement from active service not long afterward.[15] Father couldn't rest, as he had so many cases to treat and no one to assist him. I was in bed two weeks and confined to my room four weeks. One of my ears troubled me for some days. The children had the disease in a mild form and were not long in bed.

After the epidemic had passed, Father's stomach would hold only the simplest of food, but he felt well and went to Durango on March 8th, where he engaged to do several surgical operations with Dr. W. R. Winters. After that, he made a report on the epidemic and sat up late one night to finish it. Toward morning of the 9th he vomited his dinner and in the morning wasn't able to raise his head from his pillow, but when time for sick-call came he had the hospital steward come over with the books, and he prescribed for the different cases of sickness. This went on for two or three days more, when he said he could do so no more.

Lieutenant William H. Carter, who lived next door, was very kind and came in to sooth[e] Father, who was very nervous, worrying about his work. He said it was time for Father to give up, so Major Tupper telegraphed to headquarters and Lieutenant C. N. Berkeley Macauley, Assistant Surgeon, was ordered to Lewis. Forty feet of snow on the railroad delayed him, and he had to make a detour of many miles in a stage to reach the Post. We had been snowbound twice before, and each time was without a mail for a week.

Later Major Henry M. Cronkhite, Surgeon, was sent as Post Surgeon. Father was in bed over a month before we could take him to a lower altitude. His entry to sick report was March 14, 1890, for chronic gastro-intestinal catarrh due to malarial poisoning. I had written to the Surgeon General, who on my request had him ordered to Fort Leavenworth for treatment and informed Father that he would be ordered to Fort Wayne, Detroit, Michigan, when well enough.[16] He smiled for the first time since he took to his bed when I showed him the telegram.

One day he asked, "How are you going to pack without my help?" I told him that Mr. Carter and I already had everything ready to ship, except the few things in his room. We had removed things to vacant quarters next to ours and worked so quietly that Father couldn't hear a sound. His hearing was very acute, and he could hear the voices downstairs, and footsteps on the floor and stairs were very distressing to him. Harold was of great help in nursing Father, so faithful, quiet, and tender.

So 3 P.M. on April 9, 1890, we started, Father in an iron cot, which was lashed in the ambulance. The snow had begun to melt early in March, and there was very little left on the road. As we descended the mountains he felt better, and we had him carried in a chair up to the second story of the Hotel Strater in Durango. In the morning at 7 A.M., April 10th, he was carried to the railroad train. It had no sleeper, but fortunately the superintendent of the road, Mr. Cole Leyden [Lydon], was there in his car, and he turned it over to us, which kind action set our anxieties as to the trip at rest.[17]

There were still probably twenty feet of snow along the track where the blockade had been. As we descended we could see Holy Cross Mountain and had other views grand to behold. There were flocks of blue birds near the snow, and below many wild flowers were in bloom. We changed cars at Cucharas and took a sleeper. We were at the Windsor Hotel in Denver on the night of April 10th.[18] Father remained in bed the next day, while the boys and I went to the Highlands and Berkely, two beautiful suburbs. At the latter there was a lovely little lake having on it a small steamer and many rowboats. Captain Lafayette E. Campbell, Quartermaster, had procured half-rate tickets for the children and me.

He met us at the station and saw us again when we left at 8 P.M. of the 11th, and the boys and I went as far as Lawrence, Kansas, where Claude, who was a student in the University of Kansas, met us at 4 P.M. of the 12th. As we stopped a few minutes at Hays City, a crowd of our friends stood at the station to greet us, and we were laden with roses and bouquets of other flowers. Father changed cars at Lawrence and was taken thirty-four miles fa[r]ther on by Mr. Macauley to enter the Fort Leavenworth Hospital, which was in [the] charge of Major Alfred A. Woodhull, Surgeon and Brevet Lieutenant Colonel, where he remained from April 12 until July 7, 1890.

Claude had boarded with Mrs. Frazer, 813 Rhode Island Street, but he and Harold took a room at 1000 Kentucky Street, Mr. Andrews. The other three boys and I had rooms at Mr. Greenamyer's, 1033 Vermont Street, paying $18.00 a month rent. We all took our meals at a restaurant, $2.75 each a week, but the meals were so poor that we soon left it and went to Miss Cora Gill's, where we had excellent fare. Her house was farther away, and at first it was too long a walk for me, as my care of Father and the great heat of the season had almost prostrated me.[19]

It was so late in the school year that they could not advantageously enter the classes, so April 14th Harold began to take Latin at the high school, arithmetic at the grammar school, and algebra from a senior class student. Phil, Frank, and Willie went to the Quincy Street Grammar School a block away, and after it closed, to a private school, May 15th, kept by Mrs. Wood and Miss Welsh.

Claude had to collect and describe forty different wild flowers, and he found at least one flower that was not known by the Professor of Botany to be in Kansas. Harold had a congenial friend in George E. Little, with whom he studied and collected birds and their eggs and nests. They walked many miles every day, some days as many as fifteen. Philip and Francis played baseball during their leisure hours. Willie had the measles from May 17th and had to witness from a window a lawn party next door to which he had been invited.

The streets were lined with trees, mostly maples and elms, the lawns covered with a thick sod of beautiful grass, and the yards filled with fruit trees. Roses were abundant, peonies in profusion, and we soon had strawberries galore. On hot nights the yards were lively with children and some grownups taking a shower bath from the rubber hose attached to the faucets.

The University is located on a hill, Mount Oread, overlooking the city, and there were three churches within two blocks of us. Although the influences were usually good I was glad to be with the boys, as Kansas was a prohibition state, and alcoholic liquors were smuggled in original packages and the students tempted to drink. They could get credit at the stores and were not discouraged to contract debts. After the University closed Claude went to Ann Arbor, Michigan. He then went to Toledo.

Father improved very slowly and about the middle of May could be wheeled about in a chair. One day, Colonel Carle A. Woodruff of the Artillery, whom we had entertained at Camp McDermit in 1871, and his wife had a dinner cooked expressly for him of hominy, corn bread, chicken, etc., and he spent a good part of the day at their quarters.[20]

He left Leavenworth on July 7th and proceeded to Fort Wayne, Detroit, Michigan, where he remained, staying with the Tiltons until he procured a sick leave of four months from July 21. The four boys and I went to Toledo to visit Uncle James Corbusier and the Rowseys from August 12th to the 25th and then took the steamer *Greyhound* to Detroit and went out to Fort Wayne. . . .

Caroline Eliza Robinson Dunbar,
Fanny Dunbar Corbusier's
mother

George Towers Dunbar Jr.,
Fanny Dunbar Corbusier's father

Fanny Dunbar and her sister, May, in 1846

Fanny Dunbar in 1861 at age 23

William Henry Corbusier in 1865 at age 21

Fanny Dunbar Corbusier, April 1869, shortly after her
March 22 wedding at Dunbarton in Amite, Louisiana.
The photograph was probably taken in New York City.

The Corbusier children, Elmira, New York, 1882
Left to right: Francis A., Claude R., Harold D., and Philip W. Corbusier

The Corbusier family on the porch of their quarters at Fort Grant, Arizona, 1885
Mounted, left to right: Harold D., Philip W., Francis A., William T., and
Claude R. Corbusier; *top, left to right*: Mrs. Fanny Dunbar Corbusier,
Miss Ida Teed, and Dr. William Henry Corbusier

Photo courtesy Arizona Historical Society/Tucson

Constance Mills and Claude Corbusier, Fort Grant, Arizona

The Corbusier family, Fort Wayne, Michigan, 1893
Top row, from left: Harold D., William T., Philip W. Corbusier;
bottom row, from left: Francis A., Fanny Dunbar, William H., and Claude R. Corbusier

Photo courtesy Arizona Historical Society/Tucson

William Henry Corbusier and Fanny Dunbar Corbusier on the *Arizona*,
on which Dr. Corbusier would sail to Manila, August 1898

Fanny Dunbar Corbusier, September 1899
Photo courtesy Arizona Historical Society/Tucson

Fanny Dunbar Corbusier with Harold's daughter,
Barbara Corbusier, Plainfield, New Jersey, July 20, 1909

Left to right: Philip W., Fanny Dunbar, and Harold D. Corbusier
at 612 Park Avenue, Plainfield, New Jersey, August 19, 1909

Left: Claude, Belle, and Frances Corbusier; *center*: Fanny Corbusier;
right: Philip, Ida, Phyllis, and William H. Corbusier II;
Winship Park, Marin County, California, March 8, 1914

Colonel Philip Worthington Corbusier in uniform, date unknown

Photo courtesy Pierson Kerig Collection

Fanny Dunbar Corbusier, May 4, 1916

William Henry and Fanny Dunbar Corbusier in front of
the Keystone Hotel, Saint Augustine, Florida, March 26, 1917

Photo courtesy Pierson Kerig Collection

William T., daughter Ellen, wife Mabel, and infant Mary Haller Corbusier, with Fanny Dunbar Corbusier (*center*) at 154 Washington Street, Elmira, New York, November 5, 1917

Philip W., William H., and Harold D. Corbusier
in Plainfield, New Jersey

Left to right: Major, Medical Corps, Harold D. Corbusier;
Lieutenant Colonel, Medical Corps, William H. Corbusier;
Captain, First Antiaircraft Battery, Claude R. Corbusier;
July or August 1919

Photo courtesy Arizona Historical Society/Tucson

William Henry Corbusier, Colonel, United States Army, Retired, November 1924

Photo courtesy Arizona Historical Society / Tucson

William Henry and Fanny Dunbar Corbusier's monument,
Arlington National Cemetery

CHAPTER NINETEEN

"All of My Darling Boys"

FORT WAYNE AND MACKINAC, MICHIGAN, JULY 1890–JULY 1893

WE STAYED WITH THE TILTONS over night and then took possession of our quarters to begin housekeeping with a few articles of furniture we bought, awaiting the arrival of our freight.[1] That soon arrived, and we worked hard to get everything in place, the boys helping until the schools opened. Before I could find a good cook, Uncle James and Cousin Ada Corbusier and Cousin Gertrude Rowsey came to visit us and go to an exposition, but on the frontier I had learned how to provide for a house full of visitors. The boys slept on pallets on the floor. I did the cooking, and the soup was so good that Uncle James partook of two platefuls and requested my receipt for making it. They didn't stay long, but April 9, 1891, Ada and her sister Etta came to pay us a longer visit.

Father spent a few days of his leave with Uncle James in Toledo and then started East August 5th, via Detroit, thence by boat to Buffalo and from there by rail to Elmira, New York, where he remained from August 8th to the 11th. On the latter date Mother and he started to visit his Uncle John and Aunt Susan Myers, resting two days in New York. At the end of this visit, Father went to New York and remained from September 9th with Cousin Alice and Gilson Whitson, 487 Lexington Avenue, who were very kind and administered in every way to his comfort.[2] While there his weight increased from 128 to 142 pounds. He returned to Fort Wayne November 21, 1890, where he remained until July 18, 1893, except from June 13th to July 14th 1891, when he was at Fort Mackinac, Michigan, with a battalion of the Nineteenth Infantry for target practice; July 15 to 21, 1891, at the encampment of the Michigan State Troops at Whitmore Lake; May 30th to July 18th, 1892, again at Fort Mackinac; at Island Lake, Michigan, August 15th to 23rd, 1892, as Instructor and Inspector of the Medical Department and Hospital Corps, Michigan State Troops; and at Columbus Barracks, Ohio, April 4th to June 3rd, 1893.[3]

The Fort, built about 1863, was four miles from the City Hall, which was in the centre of the shopping district. The officers' quarters were outside, and ours were a double set near the middle of the line on the west side of the parade, from which the view across Detroit River, about a mile to a short canal bordered by willows, was a very picturesque one. The trees bordering the parade and an Indian mound near the north end added very much to the beauty of the foreground.

Great cigar-shaped iron freight boats carrying mostly copper ore from Lake Superior were then a novelty, and we watched them and other craft pass the Post with interest. The quarters were large enough and comfortable, but ugly and old looking. After I had them painted to my taste and the poor imitation of oak on the doors had been covered by another color they presented a better appearance.[4]

The garrison was composed of the Headquarters, band, and four companies—A, E, G, and H, I think, of the Nineteenth Infantry with Brevet Major General Charles H. Smith, the Colonel, in command. After he retired in October 1891, Lieutenant Colonel Charles A. Wikoff was in command, and he was succeeded by Colonel George M. Brayton, June 1892, who, when retired, was succeeded by Colonel Simon Snyder. The Captains were James E. Bradford, Emerson H. Liscum, Jacob H. Smith, Charles A. Vernou, and Charles. B. Hall; the First Lieutenants, Alexander McC. Guard, Cornelius Gard[e]ner, Alexander H. M. Taylor; Second Lieutenants, Christian C. Hewitt, William P. Evans, Francis H. Franch, William T. Wilder, Zebulon B. Vance, and Cyrus S. Roberts, and later Truman C. Murphy and Jasper Brady. The Surgeon was Henry R. Tilton and later Justus M. Brown. First Lieutenant James Lockett, Fourth Cavalry, was recruiting officer in Detroit.

We felt very much at home in Detroit, as we had met many of the people while at Mackinac and had some warm friends among them. So many army officers had married here that the city was called "The mother-in-law of the Army." We again met the Fletchers, Carters, Bagleys, Poes, Algers, and others. Mrs. John Bagley's children were Mrs. Sherman, John, who was married, Frances (Mrs. Brown), Olive, Margaret (Mrs. Hosmer), Helen, and Paul.

There were a number of retired army officers living in the city, among them Captain Charles Wheaton, who had a wife and two daughters, Anna and Gertrude. Our garrison was a very pleasant one and most of the officers were married and had children, among which were the Bradfords, who lived next door to us, Mary Tilton, Gertrude and May Hall, Mary Smith, Lily Snyder, Belle and Walter Vernou.[5] The Halls left for Maine in July 1892.

The boys soon had a large circle of friends in the city. Phil and Frank formed a baseball team which they called "The Greyhounds" and played such excellent games that the whole Post turned out to see them. The fishing was very good, and we could get frogs' legs from the other side of the river. We had a hop every Friday night throughout the year, which drew many young people from the city, and in the winter many girls and boys came to skate on the river.

The eight o'clock horse car carried quite a crowd of children to the city schools and the 2 P.M. and 4 P.M. cars returned them. The public schools in Detroit were not so good as those in Hays, Kansas. Harold and Philip entered the high school in the tenth and ninth grade, respectively; Frank, the eighth grade, and Will, the first grade in the Webster Grammar School, September 1, 1890.

Claude was transferred, October 2, 1890, as a sophomore from the University of Kansas to the University of Michigan, where he joined the Delta Tau Delta fraternity. He remained only a year and then said he didn't care to complete the course so left and tried to find a position of some sort.

At length he went to Cincinnati for a firm, which he supposed to be a reliable one, but was cheated out of his salary and left stranded, so Father sent him money to pay his expenses home. He arrived March 18th, very happy to get back after his rough experiences, and on April 12, 1892, [he] secured a position with Frederick Ste[a]rns & Company for $5.00 a week, having charge of the filling of orders in the different departments and out of this had to settle some debts he owed. He left home at 6:15 A.M. and returned at 6:30 P.M., except on Saturday, when he came at 4:30 P.M. In October 1894 he went to Park[e], Davis & Company.[6]

On December 19, 1890, my sister May's daughter Maud came to visit us and stayed over a year. She was a beautiful girl and was much admired by both girls and boys. She had never been North before, and the life here was new to her. She was full of fun and took such a part in the boys' amusements that they were devoted to her. She enjoyed the weekly hops at the Post, the parties in town, the skating, walks in the woods, rowing on the river, fishing, etc. The first winter she was with us she was one evening dressed for her first large party when she broke out with the measles and could not go. She said it was hard luck to have "a kid's disease" at such a time.

Her father, Henry Sands Addison, died in New Orleans on June 14, 1891, and she returned to her mother in Amite, Louisiana, where she afterward was married to Robert S. Ellis of Amite, later Judge of the District Court. She is a noble woman, and it has been a great pleasure to visit her and see her as a wife and mother of six bright children in the midst of her family. Before she left us, I went to Amite, November 16, 1891, to visit my sister May at our old home, Dunbarton, and returned to Fort Wayne, January 19, 1892, the day after Maud had left.

On Christmas Day 1890, we had all of our dear boys at home. At the hop the night before Claude had several of his fraternity friends, who were attentive to Maud. Mother's letter received in the morning was read. She said:

> I can look back to my childhood days and recollect what a gala day it was on Christmas. We were a large family and each one tried to get to his or her stocking first early in the morning. They were hung at a large open fireplace so that Santa Claus might see them as he came down the chimney and into the room to fill them from his big bag that was so full of good things. Thirteen children hustled to get there to peep in and see what they had. After breakfast the big sled was hitched up, the bottom covered with straw, blankets and robes

thrown in, and the children piled in back of Mother, with a baby in her lap, and Father who sat in chairs. Then we were off for Granny Myers', three miles away near Rockland Lake. When we reached the old brown stone house there was a scampering to get out of the blankets and into the house, where we each was received with an old fashioned hug and many kisses.

Then for a high old time. Great basketfuls of walnuts, hickory nuts, and chestnuts, some of the latter from the old tree where my grandfather Joris (George) hid when his father, Garret Myers, was taken by the British during the Revolutionary War. The big cellar was full of apples and all sorts of country good things, which we were free to take on Christmas and we were not slow to get among them. When we returned home at night Granny Myers gave us each a doughnut and a big copper penny, which made us just as happy as children are in these days with all the beautiful toys that money can buy. The doughnuts were cut in the shape of a boy; at least they had a body, head, legs, and arms. If we happened to break one we could eat it, but you boys cannot eat your toys when you break them. Times have changed in the sixty years since then.[7]

Frank broke out with the measles January 1, 1891, Phil, on the 10th, and Maud, on the 14th. The skating on the river was fine on the 20th and they could not go out, but in February they enjoyed it the more. Claude came home April 10, and was with us until the 20th during the spring vacation. Etta Corbusier and Gertrude Rowsey came from Toledo on the 9th. Gertie was taken sick in a few days and went home. Etta was in bed a week quite ill with the grippe, but she remained with us until the 20th, when Uncle James came and took her home. We heard that Mother had a very severe attack of the grippe.

May 1, 1891: we spent most of the day in the woods down the river near the Exposition grounds, gathering buttercups, violets, dogtooth violets, anemones, star of Bethlehem, chickweed, and many ferns. August 5, 1891: the great Grand Army of the Republic Parade took place and the old soldiers were received with great demonstrations. They were several hours passing the reviewing stand. Beautiful arches with suitable decorations and inscriptions had been erected in many places. Their encampment was called Camp Sheridan, and many were lodged in the Exposition and other buildings.[8] Henrietta Rowsey and her daughter Henrietta and Etta Corbusier came, and we were all invited to view the parade by Mrs. John Bagley at her home, corner of Park Street and Washington Avenue. We were there from 9 A.M. until after 4 P.M. Among those assembled were Mrs. Adams, a brilliant woman, Mrs. Bagley's sister; Mr. and Mrs. John Bagley Jr.; Mr. and Mrs. Charles Ducharme; the wife of Senator Julius Caesar Burrows; Mrs. and Dr. Frank Brown; Helen and Olive Bagley; Major Hopkins; Collector of the Port, Colonel Cooper; and Mrs. Holden.[9] At the appointed time, John Bagley telephoned to the USS *Michigan*, and the first gun of the national salute was fired, which was the signal for the procession to move. The Revenue Cutters *Fessenden*, *Johnson*, and *Perry* also fired salutes. One of the nights we were invited aboard the *Michigan* and *Fessenden* to witness the display of fireworks at the foot of the City Park, Belle Isle, an island in the Detroit River. Perry's fight on Lake Erie was reproduced, and an officer, whose name was Perry, a descendant of the Commodore, from the Cutter *Perry* impersonated his ancestor.[10]

Among the visitors in the city were Dr. [Josephus R.] Corbus from Chicago, who in January 1865 relieved father as surgeon of the Sixth Illinois Cavalry at Eastport, Mississippi, and [his] brother, [who] dined with us.[11] Dr. [C. M.] Woodward of the Michigan National Guard, his wife and daughter, and many veterans from Bridgeport, Connecticut, etc., called upon us. . . .

Claude was home during vacation and returned to Ann Arbor September 26th. The other boys started in school again on September 7. Helen Bagley frequently spent the night with Maud. Colonel B. J. D. Irwin, the Medical Director, was at the Post in September to inspect the Medical Department. Dr. Tilton was away for two months, and Father had all of the work to do and he was not yet strong. October 6: Mrs. Alice Whitson, Father's cousin, and her son Charles came to visit us for a month, but the illness of her husband Gil cut their visit short.

In October 1891, there was a new call added to the others, "Call to quarters," fifteen minutes before taps, and on the last day of October the flagstaff, which was very old, blew down, and in May 1892 a new one was erected in front of our quarters and near the river bank.[12] It was 102 feet high above the parade and 125 feet above the level of the river. A salute of twenty-one guns was fired, and the troops saluted the colors as they were run up and unfurled.

May Addison, my sister's other daughter, came to us November 16, 1891, and entered the high school. She took music lessons, so we had a piano in the house for the first time since our marriage.

On Christmas 1891 we had the usual large package from mother and in it, a plum pudding. Each of the boys received a handsome silver teaspoon from their grandmother; Father, a slumber robe and a pillow; and I, from Father and the boys, a dozen handsome fruit knives, a tea cup and saucer from Hal, one from Maud, and a beautiful paper ball from my sister May.

The river was frozen over and the young people all enjoyed the skating. In January 1892, while I was in Amite, Father and all of the children had the grippe again. Dr. Tilton was also sick and Father had much work to attend, and he, not well.

Frank graduated from the grammar school January 27, 1892, and entered the high school. He played a violin solo at the graduating exercises and also at the Conservatory of Music. He and Phil have kept up their music and are progressing very well. Willie has been promoted to A grade 3.[13]

May 30, 1892: Father left this afternoon on the steamer *City of Alpena* for Mackinac Island with the battalion of the Nineteenth Infantry, where they go into camp for target practice. We had had rain nearly every day this month, and it was so rainy and cold at Mackinac that Father stayed the first night there with Major Edwin M. Coates, Nineteenth Infantry, commanding officer at the Fort. He afterward went into camp in the government field and messed with three other officers.

On June 20, 1892, the boys, except Claude, May and I left for Mackinac on the *City of Alpena* and arrived 7 A.M. of the 22nd. The band and headquarters arrived on the 25th and remained until July 2. May and I visited Mrs. Coates until the 29th and then spent a week with the wife of Dr. John Bailey in the village. The boys went into camp.

We found that many changes had taken place in the years since we left the island. Cottages had been built along the front and sides of the island and a huge hotel, The Grand, just beyond the government field. There were many carriages and saddle horses in the streets and yachts in the straits. The so-called "Smart Set" was there, and the women wore fine gowns, but we felt at home in the woods, which were the same although drier, and we enjoyed the lovely drives and walks as we did formerly.[14] Claude, Alvin and Whelan Stearns, and Mr. Rankin came up on the *City of Mackinac* July 18th, spent most of their vacation canoeing among the Cheneaux Islands, and on the 31st returned to Detroit.

There were three hops a week at the Grand Hotel and two at the Astor House, so the children could dance to their hearts' content. The music at the Grand was excellent, but the Casino was badly ventilated and there were only narrow boards against the walls to sit upon. At the Astor the room was a fine one, but the music was not so good.[15]

When Father left, July 18, we took possession of two large tents and one smaller one, which were framed and floored, connected by tent flies, and pitched in a field of daisies. Here we enjoyed ourselves in the open in camp once more. The boys took turns making the fire in our cook stove and put the hominy or oatmeal to cook and, when May and I appeared, helped to get the rest of the breakfast. We enjoyed whitefish, lake trout, and other fish, which we cooked to our own taste. During the day we roamed the beautiful roads and at nights usually attended the dances at the hotels. May received much attention, as she had very gentle and charming ways. Steward Edward White and James Murfin were among her admirers. We saw much of [the] Hamiltons and Wendels and Mrs. N. P. Harrison of Chicago, whose children Bartlett, Mamie and ___ were Willie's playmates and had their own picnics in the woods. Captain Frank D. Baldwin, Fifth Infantry, and Major General Nelson A. Miles were visitors on July 9, 1892.[16] On the night of July 14, 1892, we saw a most magnificent display of the aurora borealis I have ever seen.

We left Mackinac August 6 on the *City of Alpena*, very sorry to go. On our arrival home I found that my maid, Pauline, had taken good care of our quarters. On August 15 Father left with the troops for Island Lake, Michigan, as Acting General Inspector of the Medical Department of Michigan State Troops on the Governor's staff to organize the Medical Department and Hospital Corps of the State.

He had already drilled men of the Light Guard and Light Infantry in their armories in Detroit. The state sent him a horse which had not been broken to the saddle, and when Father mounted him, we were afraid he would be bucked off. [B]ut he had ridden such horses before and at length made the horse understand what he was to do.[17] Claude and Hal spent the day of the 21st at the lake and had such a good time riding horseback that they didn't reach home until late at night.

Mother came from Elmira on August 18, 1892, and remained until the latter part of September. At first she had a sick spell of a few days, but soon [she] began to enjoy her visit. We would spend hours at Belle Isle, sitting under the beautiful trees, feeding the squirrels, watching the passing ships, and talking. She was very sweet and kind and full of gentle humor, and our days passed very happily. On September 1, she weighed 166 pounds and her height was 64 3/4 inches, and I weighed 106 pounds and was 62 5/16 inches tall. On September 1, May weighed 106 pounds and her height was 63 5/8 inches. In October she left for her home, as her mother could no longer afford to keep her here at school. Poor child, we hated to have her go, and we all missed her very much.[18]

The winter was a very gay one, and we attended many delightful receptions and one wedding. At Christmas [1892] we had our tree as usual and decorated it mostly with the beautiful ornaments that we had kept from past years. My presents were mostly of cut-glass from Father and the boys. The day wasn't as noisy a one as in the past, as the boys were too large for toys and they all knew who Santa Claus was. Hal was laid up with a sprained knee, having been thrown from our horse, and had it in plaster-of-Paris about a month. On the last night of the year all the young people of the Post came in to be with Hal and see the New Year come in.

We had a heavy snowstorm January 1, 1893, but it did not keep Willie and me from going to the services at Grace Church. We had the coldest weather that had been experienced here in years, the snow lay on the ground for months, but we were all well, as the air was dry. In April 1893, the horse that threw Hal crowded Frank against a post in the stable and injured one of his knees so that it had to be put in plaster-of-Paris, and we had two boys on crutches. On April 2 the wife of Captain Charles Vernou, who had been ill for a long time, died in a hospital.[19]

On April 4, Father went to Columbus Barracks, Ohio, to relieve Dr. [Augustus Andrew] De Loffre and remained there until June 3, when he returned here.[20] I loved to look around the table and see all of my darling boys at home, and it makes my heart ache to know that soon we will be separated, we know not for how long.

CHAPTER TWENTY

"No Way for Husband and Wife to Live"

ANN ARBOR, MICHIGAN, AND FORT SUPPLY, INDIAN TERRITORY, JULY 1893–SEPTEMBER 1894

O N JULY 8TH, WE WERE SHOCKED by an order that Father received to report for duty at Fort Supply, Indian Territory. He expected a change, but not to such an isolated post. As there were no schools there we could not go with him. Our precious darling Papa left us on July 18th, 1893, at 7 A.M., all of us accompanying him to the train, and we were separated from him for a year. It almost broke his dear heart to leave us, and the house was desolate without him. We feel that we may never be all together again.[1]

Before he left, Major Smith, Captains Gard[e]ner and Hall, Lieutenants Evans, French, Murphy, and Roberts presented Father with a beautiful umbrella and walking stick of Italian grapevine, the handles of which were buckhorn mounted with silver, accompanied by a very complimentary letter expressing their appreciation of his prompt and kind attentions and their great esteem of him as an officer. He had a number of letters from grateful patients given to him at various posts.

He wrote in Chicago, where he remained three days and a-half to visit the Exposition.[2] He reached his Post on the 24th, where he was very lonely in his large quarters. The weather there was intensely hot. He has been promised an eastern city after his tour there.

On August 1, 1893, I went to Ann Arbor with Mrs. [Jacob H.] Smith, and her sister-in-law, Mrs. Murfin, drove us all about the city. The next day I had my first experience in house hunting. I signed a lease on the 4th and then learned that the window shades, etc., did not go with the house so paid $5.00 to be released and I engaged rooms.

August 10, 1893: Mother and Aunt Louise MacRae arrived from Elmira. We went to Belle Isle, the Red Inn on the Canadian side for frog's legs, Grosse Isle, Sugar Island, Port Huron, and once Aunt Louise and Frank had a sail to Put-in-Bay. On the 28th Aunt Louise and Phil left for the World's Fair in Chicago. They engaged rooms, and Mother and Hal and Frank followed on the 29th. I gave Hal $20.00, Phil and Frank each $7.50, and Aunt Louise gave each of the latter $12.00. Claude, Willie, and I were very lonely in the quiet house. Alvin and Whelan Stearns dined with us for the last time. They were earnest young men, just the kind for Claude to associate with.[3]

On the 31st I went to the city to pay my bills and felt very sad at the thoughts of leaving. We had enjoyed our tour here and had many warm friends whom we were to leave. It had been a good place in which to educate our boys, and they made many friends. It was the only really fine station that we ever had. We spent September 1st, the last day at the Post, with Major and Mrs. Smith, who were unusually kind to us. I shipped all of our household effects, except a few articles I sent to Father and some to Claude's room in Vinewood Avenue. He will pay $7.00 a month for his room and $3.50 a week for table board. He is now receiving $10.00 a week. I was very tired, homesick, and almost crazy.[4]

We had a warm invitation from Mrs. [John] Bagley to visit her, and the same from Mrs. Poe, wife of Brigadier General Orlando Poe, Engineer Corps.[5] Willie spent two days with Harold Sherman at Mrs. Bagley's, who gave him as a parting gift a beautiful little steam engine. He and Harold had formed a Society to bring about eternal peace among the people of the world. Harold was President, and Willie, Secretary and Treasurer. When they parted they had $3.45 in the treasury. Harold brought me a box of beautiful flowers from his mother, Florence, when he came to see us leave. Claude bid us goodbye at the train and we arrived in Ann Arbor at 5:30 P.M., where we went to Mrs. Murfin's home, and she did all in her power to cheer me up.

September 2, 1893: Willie entered the fifth grade of the Tappan School, one block from our rooms on College Street, opposite the University campus.[6] Our freight arrived, and I had it sent to 49 Washtenaw Avenue, Mrs. Alletta Steadman's. I missed Father, the bugle calls, the gathering on the veranda at guard mounting in the morning, and everything seemed strange and unnatural. Phil and Frank returned from Chicago on the third and had much to tell about what they had seen.

On the fourth we took possession of our four bright sunny rooms, bathroom, storeroom, and large garret and worked hard to get our furniture unpacked and set in order. We paid $20.00 a month rent and $15.00 a week for table board. Mrs. Murfin loaned me a mineral oil stove so that I might cook extras. The house was heated by a furnace, and we found it comfortable. Phil, twelfth grade, and Frank, eleventh grade, entered the High School. I paid $23.00 school tax for three months but was not charged except that once.

Hal returned from the Fair on the seventh, having profited very much in the nine and a-half days he was there. Phil and Frank were rushed for the ATO Society and joined.[7] It met once a week at one of the boy's houses, [where they] had a simple supper, sang, and told stories. When they met at our house they had winnewurst, ice cream, biscuit, ginger ale, etc.

On the 15th I introduced Hal to President [James B.] Angell of the University, and he had his examinations for entrance from the 25th to the 30th, which he passed except Literature and Physics, and in these he was conditional. [B]ut was admitted Oct. 3, 1893.[8] His matriculation fee was $10.00; annual fee, $20.00; laboratory materials, $5.00. He is a dear earnest boy and studies hard, having 21 hours a week, but it is all work that he loves and he is happy. Claude comes up nearly every week on Saturday to remain until Monday.

October 7th, I hired a horse and wagon for the afternoon for $1.50, and Mrs. Murfin, Alice Brown, our four boys, and three smaller ones from the neighborhood drove out Washtenaw Avenue two miles and gathered nine bushels of black walnuts and one of hickory nuts. This was the first nut hunting our boys had ever done, and they were wild with delight as the nuts came down in showers from the heavily laden trees when they danced upon the branches. We ate our lunch under one of the trees and then went to work or play again. Once while Will and Clay Murfin were on the same branch, they slipped and, grabbing the branch, hung to it while abusing each other for the mishap. This was so absurd that Mrs. Murfin and I shouted with laughter until tears rolled down our cheeks. . . .

Once a month Hal, Phil, and Frank went to a Social of the Hobart Guild in Harris Hall of the Episcopal Church, where there was a library, gymnasium, baths, and dancing room.[9] There were many friends of the boys here from Detroit in the High School and University. October 31st: after studying their lessons, the three oldest boys changed to their oldest clothes and about 10 P.M. left for the campus. Here a huge bonfire was started, and a crowd of students gathered to roar like lions and rush one class against another.

After a time some of them began to tear palings from the fences to add to the fire, and policemen arrested one of the crowd and started away with him in a horse car. The crowd shouted at the top of their lungs, followed and tried to rescue the boy. They broke some of the windows of the car, and two other boys were arrested. One escaped, and a policeman, not able to catch him, seized Frank, who was the tallest one in the crowd nearby. The boys didn't get home until 3 A.M. the next morning, as they were a long time in bailing him out of jail. Although no offence could be proved I had to pay charges amounting to $8.20 and back hire for the Sheriff, $2.50. The young man was badly frightened and very careful how he mingled in a crowd doing a "rush." Willie limited his fun to pulling doorbells and tapping on windows. . . .[10]

December 11, 1893: Claude saved the chemical laboratory of Frederick Stearns & Company from fire. He was warned by a boy who heard two men talking, and he offered to watch the lower story. About 2 A.M. he saw a bright light and two men coming from a shed in the yard as he passed a window. He fired his revolver at them, but they escaped through a ventilating shaft. He then turned on the alarm, and the Fire Department soon put out the fire. The firm was much pleased with his courage and faithfulness and the newspapers gave an account of the affair.[11]

Willie sings in the choir of Saint Andrew's Episcopal Church on Division Street and has a very good voice, which has recently improved very much. He often sings song after song to me in the evenings. He takes lessons on the violin but doesn't care to practice. Father sent a fine steel engraving of Gilbert Stuart's portrait of Washington to the Tappan School, and Willie presented it with appropriate words.

December 25th: I have been in bed with the grippe for four days, but today we all had dinner at Mrs. Wallace's and it was a very poor one. Dear Mother, with her usual thoughtfulness, sent us a large basket containing plum pudding, fruit cake, nut cake, doughnuts, preserves, etc., so we ate our dessert in our room. Father wrote that he had been invited to dine at Captain [John Soast] Bishop's. He sent $25.00 to be divided among us. We sent him a fine hairbrush and a comb. Hal received a pair of cuff buttons from Mamie Tilton, and a silver hat marker; Phil and Frank, ties and money; Willie, four books, a scarf pin, and money; and I, a cut-glass ink-stand and toilet bottles, handkerchief from Frank and Bishop Brooks' *Year Book* from Mrs. John Bagley.[12] On 26th, Hal and Phil went to Detroit to stay with Claude, and Frank [went] to visit Whelan Stearns.

Willie and I were alone, and New Year's Day was the strangest one I ever passed. On January 2, 1894, Willie and I went to Mrs. John J. Bagley's in Detroit and remained until the 13th. The whole family gave us a warm welcome, and we occupied a suite of rooms that had held Lincoln, Emerson, Edwin Arnold, Dean Stanley, and many other eminent men.[13] I went to the theatre, The Bohemian Club, and heard many lectures, attended afternoon teas, visited two days at the post [with] Mrs. Jacob Smith, attended one hop, had luncheon with Mrs. [William P.] Evans, made many calls, and saw Claude play in "Zulu" for a benefit to raise money for the poor. The Archeological Society held a meeting at Mrs. Bagley's at which Mr. Fred Stearns read a paper on Ancient Japan.

We changed our boarding place to Miss Decker's Forest Inn on Forest Avenue, January 16th, a clean bright house. The meals were excellent. There were a number of bright students here and I loved to hear their talk, all so happy and interested in their studies. In February, I had a severe attack of bronchitis, and the three boys, sore throats, owing to the severe weather with heavy snowstorms and the difficulty in keeping our rooms warm. The mails have been delayed. We hear that Maud is teaching school in Napoleon, Louisiana, and May, near Amite.

March 2nd: Dr. Vaughn has prescribed for Frank, who is quite nervous, constantly twitching the muscles about his eyes.[14] Mrs. [Florence] Sherman visited Mrs. [James B.] Angell and she told us much about Kananda, the Hindoo who has been staying at the Bagley's and giving lectures on his religious beliefs, which are almost identical with those of the Unitarians. He is a very learned man, his manners most courteous and gentle, [and] and his voice and personality charming.[15]

March 22, 1894: Father and I have been married twenty-five years and it is hard for us to be so far apart, but much worse for him, dear fellow. It is no way for husband and wife to live, and only the welfare of the children reconciles us in the least.[16] The boys have studied hard during the last semester so as to pass their exams. Frank lost some time on account of not being well; Phil could do better but he would rather play foot-ball than study. Hal has done much laboratory work in which he is greatly interested. He joined the Delta Upsilon fraternity, the boys of which are a fine lot.[17]

While I was at Mrs. Jacob Smith's at Fort Wayne in April, Claude had the German measles. Major Justus M. Brown, Post Surgeon, sent for him and cared for him in his own quarters. He and his family were very kind to both of us.[18] I had Phil come to appear before a board to examine candidates for appointment to the Military Academy at West Point, and he was physically the best of the many applicants, but we had no political influence and he did not get the appointment. Phil was very much disappointed.

The freshmen had two banquets on May 21, as college politics divided the classes into the fraternities on one side and the independents on the other. The sophomores succeeded in carrying off one of the toastmasters. Hal was manager of the Freshman Banjo Club, and he practiced as much as he could. He was also running every day to take part in the exercises on Field Day. I was the chaperon for the girls at the Delta U party in the fraternity house. It was a lovely gathering, and the boys were delightful hosts. I was also a chaperon at the Senior hop at the Waterman gymnasium on the campus. The dancing lasted until the "birds began to sing." It was a queer sensation to come home in the early dawn from the brilliantly lighted hall.

The schools closed in June, and the students scattered to the four points of the compass. They vanished in a night and the streets were almost empty, houses closed, and all places were quiet and lonely. About July 1, 1894, I rented Forest Inn, 18 Forest Avenue, fully furnished even to table linen, china, and silver, and the rent was $20.00 a month. The heat was intense, but we had the whole house in which to spread ourselves, and we enjoyed ourselves thoroughly, but how lonely the house was in the afternoons when the boys were away. I am like Claude, poor boy. I want my home again.[19]

Hal left on July 5th to go with Claude to Topinabee, Michigan, on a two weeks canoeing trip with the Minnehaha Canoe Club, of which Claude was the Commodore—he taking his Racine, and Hal, his birch bark canoe.[20] I was in bed two days with a severe attack of rheumatism. Hal returned and Claude with him to spend a few days, both looking very well from their delightful trip. We are counting the days when Father can come home. It will not be long we hope.

September 1: we have moved into 41 Forest Avenue and have a house to ourselves, paying $20.00 a month, and [we] like housekeeping much better than boarding. On the 10th, Phil, Frank, and Willie began school again. Phil takes Physics, Geometry, and French; Frank, Physics, Chemistry, and German; and Willie is in the Sixth grade. Hal gives the other boys drawing.

CHAPTER TWENTY-ONE

"The Day Was One Never
to Be Forgotten"

MICHIGAN SCHOOLS, NEW YORK CITY,
AND FORT MONROE, VIRGINIA,
SEPTEMBER 1894–SEPTEMBER 1897

ARLY IN SEPTEMBER FREIGHT CAME from Father, and I was made homesick to see the familiar objects. He arrived about the twentieth, having a month's leave, most of which he spent working in the Bacteriological Laboratory nearly very hour of daylight.[1] Before he left Fort Supply, the Cherokee Strip was opened to settlers, and he saw the first man to arrive at Woodward, the railroad station, jump from his horse, and drive a stake on 160 acres of government land.[2] Claude came to see us while Father was here, and it was very good to be all together once more. He is now with Parke-Davis and Company, having a better position.[3]

Father left us October 17, and I went with him as far as Detroit. He visited Mother and on the 20th reported in New York, to which city he had been ordered on his own request, as Attending Surgeon and Examiner of Recruits. He was there to October 22, 1895, and then was granted a leave to November 11.[4] While he was ill at Fort Lewis he invested $500.00, March 28, 1890, in the Bangkok Cora Bell Silver Mining Co., through Major and Paymaster D. N. Bash; and in Denver, April 11th, $75.00 more.[5] He sold this stock in December 1895, at a profit of $750.00, more than enough to counterbalance his loss in the Washington Bank of Tacoma, which was wrecked through the dishonesty of the directors. This money was a god-send, as Father had no private practice after leaving Fort Lewis.

He sent me $100.00 for myself alone, and I felt like a Rothschild, or at least as I suppose one feels at times, and didn't I give some nice presents on Christmas. Will also sent gifts of money to Mother and the boys. Hal was given a Delta U pin by Father, Mother, and me; Frank, an ATO pin. I sent my sister May a barrel of fruit, nuts, some dress goods, and other useful articles. Claude came home, and we had as happy a day as we could with precious Papa away. How time flies; if it would only wait just a few years.[6]

In January 1895, I went to Detroit twice on shopping trips. In February we had some bitter cold weather, and I was confined to the house most of the time for fear of rheumatism. We all had the grippe again. Claude [was] also in Detroit. March was cold and windy, snow and ice every-where, making the sidewalks so slippery that walking was dangerous. I fell on the ice and badly bruised one side and a leg. I suffered such great pain that I had to remain in bed several days. My heart has troubled me very much.[7] In April the weather turned pleasant and base and football came the rage. Phil was wrapped up in football.

July 5th, we left Ann Arbor this A.M. for New York and stopped in Toledo several hours to see Father's Uncle James. Thence we went to Fos-toria [Ohio] and there changed to the Baltimore and Ohio Railroad. On the evening of the 6th Father met us at the ferry on the Jersey City side, and we all went to cousin Alice Whitson's home, 487 Lexington Avenue, New York, where we were very cordially received and everything was done for our pleasure and comfort. Six boys in the house, as Alice had two sons, Charles and Frank. The two families were taken by Gil, her husband, to Manhattan Beach, where we had a delicious dinner, heard Sousa's band, saw "1492" in the vaudeville theatre, and saw the great pyrotechnic display "The War between China and Japan." One night we went to the Madison Square Roof-Garden, a delightfully cool place, heard fine music and saw a celebrated Spanish dancer, Otero, I think. Every motion was grace and modesty, and her face bewitching in its brightness.[8]

We spent one day—the 11th—at and near Nyack-on-the-Hudson. The day was one never to be forgotten, and the weather was perfect. Father hired a team and a large carriage, which one of the boys drove, and we visited all the places of interest connected with the history of the Myers family. The house on the Stephen Myers farm still stood in which Father's mother and all her sisters and brothers were born. We walked about the lawn and pictured them as they all looked in those days, saw the fence corners in which Father played when he visited his grandmother. On the road there he showed us an impression in a rock, which he used to think had been made by a man's foot when the stone was soft. Everyone we asked about the roads was a distant relative or intimate friend of the Myers family. We passed the site of the old red schoolhouse on "Casper Barrack" (Hill) where Mother went to school, and the site of the school house near Rockland Lake, now Valley Cottage, in which Joris Myers and Samuel De Baun, both great-grandfathers of Father, were trustees away back in 1812 and which their children attended.[9]

We stood under the old chestnut tree, then only a shell, behind which Garret Myers tried to hide when the British and Tories captured him during the War of the Revolution.[10] The old brown stone house had been replaced by a wooden frame one, many of the timbers of which had been taken from the old one, but the cellar was there unchanged, the same stone sill, steps, and floor on which the British had thrown butter, milk, and other food. On shelves were great pans of milk, earthen crocks of butter, and we would not have been surprised if a red-coat walked in and began smashing things. We returned to the City feeling that we had lived a long time ago.

Father and Gil made several trips out on Long Island looking for a desirable place for a summer outing and selected Amityville. Gil, Alice, and their boys went to the New Point Hotel, but our boys and I took board July 13 at the Van Nostrand Cottage kept by Mr. Ward Smith, which was beautifully located near the water, an inlet from the bay. What a rest for me, and I hope[d] to get a little fat on my bones. Our rooms were neat and clean and free from musty smells; the table was only fair. The boys had a large catboat that held some fifteen persons, which they manned themselves and sailed up and down the Great South Bay, often going to Oak Beach to bathe in the surf. [B]ut when Father and Gil came for the weekend we had a large schooner in which we would go out on the ocean.

Mother, Grandpa Jones, and Aunt Louise spent a few days with us and had a delightful time. They added very much to our enjoyment and happiness. Grandpa took the boys blue fishing twice. The hotel was dull by day but bright at night, when our boys, who were all fine dancers, were very popular with the girls. Miss Snieder of Newark, New Jersey, sometimes played for us on her violin. Colonel Edgar Buffington and wife of Brooklyn, Mr. and Mrs. Robert Sayer and her sister Miss Mahr of New York, and Miss Wason were at our cottage, and many nights we had musical and vaudeville performances.[11] I was usually the audience, as all of the others took part. . . .

The meals at length became very poor, and one night after Mother left we found a bag of ship biscuit that she had left and the whole party marched around while one of them handed the biscuit out and another, with a pitcher and a glass, served water. After that we went to the Bay View Hotel, where the surroundings were not so attractive but the meals were far better. For three days in August, I visited Miranda Hall and Libbie Morgan, cousins of Father, in Brooklyn. On August 27, Father and Hal witnessed the unveiling of the monument in Prospect Park, Brooklyn, in memory of the Maryland 400, who so distinguished themselves at the Battle of Long Island.[12]

We left Amityville September 3, 1895, and visited cousin Alice again. Phil and Frank remained a week and then went to their grandmother's for a visit. Hal remained in New York until it was nearly time for the schools to open, and the three returned to Ann Arbor to open the house, which we had locked and left. Willie and I went to Baltimore and spent a week with my Aunt Mary Robinson and a few days with my Aunt (Trottie) Mary E. Dunbar. While there we went by electric cars to the Hannah More Academy. There had been many changes but enough of the buildings and dear old trees were there to make all to look like home to me.[13]

September 28th: Willie and I went to visit Mother, and I heard from Father in Washington, where he had successfully passed his examination for promotion. He will be ordered to Fort Monroe, Virginia. The weather was very hot and he felt the heat very much. He received his majority October 17, 1895, and his pay was $270.83 a month; the next August, after twenty years service, [he] received four fogies i.e., [a] 40% increase, making his pay $291.67 a month.[14]

He was granted a leave of absence from October 22 to November 11, which he spent partly in New York but mostly with Mother in Elmira. While en route to his new station, [he] visited my Aunt Mary Eliza Dunbar in Baltimore, afterward taking a steamer of the Old Dominion Line to

Fort Monroe, where he remained on duty from November 12, 1895, to October 12, 1897.[15] He stayed with Doctor Vickery a few days and then occupied his own quarters.

We thought it would be better for the boys to continue their studies in Ann Arbor, so Willie and I returned there October 2. We had our house repapered, painted, and other improvements made so that it looked very pretty and homelike. I had rheumatism and swelling of the thyroid gland in November and was obliged to remain in the house while Doctors Vaughn and Dock treated me, and I felt the intense cold of the winter.[16] Claude came up for Christmas, and we had two of Hal's Delta U friends with us. All we wanted to make us perfectly happy was to have Father with us.[17] The boys remained well all winter.

Father thought that the climate near the seashore would help me, so Willie and I left on February 6th to go to him. The other three boys remained in the house, as I had rented it for a year and had our cook Katy Tims to look after it, but they took their meals at Mrs. Barr's and I left them very comfortable.[18] Willie and I stopped in Elmira to see Mother from the 7th and then spent a week with my Aunt Mary E. Dunbar . . . at 14 West Hamilton Street, Baltimore. . . .

We arrived here, Fort Monroe, Virginia, by boat on February 28th, and I already felt much better and hoped to get well here. Father was looking much better than he did in New York, where he worked very hard. The house had been nicely cleaned, and we felt at home but took our meals until May at the Hygeia, which filled up during Lent.[19]

The Post is located on Old Point Comfort at the east end of a peninsula, which during great storms is converted into an island.[20] This peninsula is west of Chesapeake Bay, north of Hampton Roads, and separated from the mainland on the north by Mill Creek. On the bay side there is a fine, hard, sandy beach on which we collected many beautiful shells. Hampton is three miles away. Newport News is seven miles from here on the James River.

The quarters Father selected were on the far side of the second frame house, just south of the sallyport inside the Fort and not far from the hospital. The Kobbés were in the other side of the house.[21] Downstairs we had two large rooms, and a hallway along one side led back to the dining room and kitchen. A gallery ran across the front of the house, and another along the side of the back. Upstairs we had five bedrooms and a bathroom, etc. A large back yard was enclosed by a fence, which was hidden by white honeysuckle vines, and we had beds of roses and violets and many elephant's ears, which bore beautiful lemon-colored flowers. The parade ground was large, covered with white clover and dotted with numerous magnolia, holly, and live oak trees. Three of the latter were near our quarters.

There were several brick and stone houses inside the Fort, one of which, a brick, was occupied by young married officers and was called "The Incubator." [A]nd a few officers lived in casemates. There were also quarters outside along the street leading to Phoebus and Hampton. These were occupied by the instructors and student officers of the Artillery School.

Artillery garrisoned the Fort with Colonel Royal T. Frank, First Artillery, in command. Major Richard S. Vickery was Post Surgeon until his retirement December 7, 1895, when he was succeeded by Major Edward B. Mosely, who was ill much of the time when Father was in charge and had all of the work to do. Later came Major Calvin De Witt. Among the other officers of Artillery were: Captains John L. Tiernon, John P. Story, William A. Kobbé, Brevet Lieutenant Colonel, George G. Greenough, John M. K. Davis, William T. Stewart, Henry C. Hasbrouck; First Lieutenants William P. Dufall, Edward Davis, the Adjutant, John D. C. Hoskins, John P. Wisser, Edward A. Millar, Samuel E. Allen, John W. Ruckman, Elmer Hubbard, Willoughby Walke, Charles D. Parkhurst, George O. Squier; and Second Lieutenants Peyton C. March, Tieman N. Horn, Andrew Hero Jr., and Edward J. Timberlake. Captain John W. Pullman was the Quartermaster, and Colonel William A. Marye [was] in command of the Ordinance Depot.

We began housekeeping on May 14th, having engaged good servants: faithful old Jane, an old time Virginia cook from Charles County, and her granddaughter Susan, who was our housemaid. The more guests we had in the house, the better they were pleased. There was an excellent market in Norfolk, across Hampton Roads, and prices were very reasonable. The country people, mostly colored, brought us chickens and eggs and we had "branch meal," i.e., white corn meal ground by waterpower.

During the season we had delicious figs, cantaloupes, watermelons, peaches, and grapes. Fish of many varieties were plentiful, the best of which was the silvery pompano. After that came the red snapper, and we never had better oysters, clams, shrimp, hard and soft shell crabs. In vacation the boys caught so many crabs that they contemplated shipping a barrel of them to New York, but then the markets wcrc glutted, so they sold them to the Chamberlain Hotel for twenty-five cents and then went out of business.

Young Will attended the Misses Tilestons' school in Hampton, Virginia, and we paid $50.00 for the school year. He went over on the streetcars daily with Virginia Evans and the other children. Rear Admiral Robley D. Evans was then on lighthouse duty and had a bungalow near the beach south of the Fort.[22]

In May 1896, young Will and I went to Baltimore and Washington to do some shopping and were three weeks with my Aunt Trottie, who went with us by water on our return to the Fort and stayed ten days.

Trottie was delighted to again visit Old Point Comfort, which for many summers was the resort of the Dunbars where they always stayed at the Hygeia. She had seen very little of Army life since she was a young woman, when many officers were frequenters of her home, among which were Colonel William Whistler of the Fourth Infantry; Captain Samuel Ringgold of the Flying Artillery, who died of wounds received at Palo Alto, Texas, May 8, 1846; First Lieutenant Jacob Edmund Blake of the Topographical Engineers, who was on General Worth's staff in the Mexican War and who, while in Mexico on returning from a recognizance [reconnaissance] May 9, 1846, threw his revolver on his bed when it accidentally discharged and killed him.

His brother, George Blake, First Lieutenant of the First Dragoons in 1836 and later a Brigadier General, and their sister Elizabeth were very intimate with the family, and on his return from the Mexican War he visited us in New Orleans. We children were very fond of him, as he entered into our sports as if he were of our age. He would permit us to tie his hair up in colored ribbons—men wore their hair long in those days—and would play the part of any animal we wished him to be. . . .

My mother and his highly accomplished sister corresponded for many years, and I had some of her interesting letters written when she was eighty years of age. They were beautiful specimens of handwriting and were all illustrated to give point to her witty sayings. Major General William Jenkins Worth and General Zachary Taylor were among my father's friends, and he presented to the latter a medal struck off in honor of the General's victories in Mexico.[23]

Mother and Grandpa Jones came to us the latter part of May and remained until early in September. The beach charmed Mother, and she was on it most of the time. It was so beautiful, and she enjoyed catching crabs and meeting the carts as they brought fish from the nets. I, too, enjoyed it all thoroughly. The weather was delightful and the water views charming. On June 27th Harold, Philip, and Francis came, and we were a happy household. If Claude could have been with us, my happiness would have been complete. We had firecrackers and fireworks on July 4th, and there were athletic sports on the parade, so the big and little boys had a good time. Dr. I. Pettus, Marine Hospital Service, his wife, and her two sisters, Rosalie and Florence Caden, took luncheon with us.[24]

At night we used to go to the Hygeia to sit on the esplanade over looking the water and listen to the music, watch the dancers, and enjoy the refreshing breeze. Harold was much in the company of the Caden girls, as they were great friends. The wives of many naval officers came to the hotels to be with their husbands when they came into port. Richmond P. Hobson, who afterward distinguished himself by sinking the collier *Merrimac* in Santiago harbor, often came ashore, and other naval officers too numerous to mention. Mrs. Moses, the wife of Lieutenant L. H. Moses, of the Marines, was at the Hygeia for some time.[25]

Among other visitors that we had that summer were Mary Smith, daughter of General Charles H. Smith, and Lilly Snyder, daughter of Colonel Simon Snyder, who came at the same time.[26] Frank left September 22, 1896, and Hal and Phil on the 29th for Ann Arbor, and the house was desolate again. Phil entered the University of Michigan, taking chemistry, and Frank continued in the high school. Mother sent the three boys a large box of good things for Thanksgiving Day, thoughtful as always of others. They couldn't come home for Christmas, but Claude, whom Father had not seen for two years, was with us for three days. He was traveling for Parke-Davis and Company, with whom he has been two years.[27]

The climate was mild in the fall and winter, damp and chilly in the spring, very warm during the long summers, and rather debilitating in August and September, when the humidity was great. The ramparts cut off much of the breeze.

January 1, 1897, there was a hop at the Hygeia, and we remained to see the old year out. At midnight the naval vessels in the harbor all rang sixteen bells, bands played [with] fifes and drums, making all the noise they could. Mr. Robert Buchanan, a nephew of Senator Zechariah Chamberlain [Chandler] of Michigan, and his wife, niece of Samuel Tilden of New York, sat with us.[28]

. . . Father had a large and lucrative practice among the inmates of the hotels, which during the winter and spring were mostly from the northern states and in the summer from the South. Many of his patients were suffering from nervous prostration following the grippe, and he was eminently successful in treating these cases.[29]

In June 1897, Mother and Grandpa Jones came again. On the 26th Phil arrived, Frank on the 28th, . . . Hal on the 30th, and then came Claude on July 2nd, bringing with him Mildred Hilliard from Louisville, Kentucky. Our cup of happiness was full to overflowing.[30] Mildred's father came up with them. He went to the Hygeia but had dinner with us. His sons, Byron and Ike, came later. Four of our boys slept at Lieutenant Ruckman's, nearby, as we now had ten in the family, and how happy we all were to be together once more. During a convention of dental surgeons, Dr. Charles Grey Edwards of Louisville was at the Hygeia, his daughter Ida and Miss Irene Peter with him, and it was then that Philip met his wife, Ida.[31]

Although the beautifully furnished and attractive Chamberlin was open, the old Hygeia was the favorite hotel, and its pavilion was very popular with the young people.[32] When not bathing, they were dancing, and our boys, Father, and I would sometimes all be on the floor at one time. The naval officers, when the fleet was lying in the Roads, and the artillery officers added very much to the attractiveness of the gatherings. Our young people talked, sang, played their different musical instruments, lounged in the hammocks—all very happy, as we older ones were. We can never forget those days. Life was worth living, having them all with us. The days there can never be forgotten.

The boys were in the water much of the time along with the other boys, the Evans, Pullman, and Booker, and other girls who were excellent swimmers. Often at night the water would be full of phosphorescent jellyfish, and one night, as far as we could see, it was all-aglow. Wherever the waves broke there were flashes of light. Boats moving about created these flashes; ropes hanging in the water became strings of jewels, and moving fish were streaks of light. The children dove and swam about to stir up the jellyfish and cause them to flash oftener. Trails of light followed their course, and as they emerged from the water, they looked like mermaids and mermen covered with jewels for Neptune's ball.

Claude left us the first week in August, and then Mother, who had not been well for some days, and Grandpa went. Phil and Frank started for California the latter part of August to enter Leland Stanford University, Palo Alto, on September 4, Father having been informed that he would be ordered to the Pacific coast. They went via the Southern Pacific Railroad from New Orleans and visited the Hilliards in Louisville on the way, and Phil met Ida again.

We then began to pack our effects, Harold assisting, as he didn't return to Ann Arbor until the middle of September. The latter part of August I went to Baltimore to bid good-bye to my relatives there. After that young Will and I left for Amite, Louisiana, to visit my darling sister May and her children, and in New Orleans I saw some relatives whom I had not seen in more than thirty years. It did me good to meet with such a warm welcome. My sister May and I loved every spot of our sweet old home, "Dunbarton." We lived over again our lives of many years ago. Her two sweet daughters were both married: Maud to Robert S. Ellis, a lawyer, [and they] live[d] nearby on a pretty farm. May was with her mother; her husband Carl Kuster was in New Orleans, sixty-eight miles south, in a drug house. Yellow fever was then epidemic in the city, but there was never a case in Amite. Young Will had a horse to ride or drive and enjoyed himself thoroughly.

Father and Harold remained at Monroe, and then Father had a short leave, which he spent in New York. Harold returned to Ann Arbor, where he lived in the Delta U house, visiting the Hilliards in Louisville en route. He completed his studies and received the degrees of B.S. and M.D. from the University of Michigan, June 22, 1899.[33]

CHAPTER TWENTY-TWO

"Raised beneath the Flag"

ANGEL ISLAND, CALIFORNIA, OCTOBER 1897–AUGUST 1898

FATHER REPORTED HERE FOR DUTY October 18, 1897, and remained until May 17, 1898, on which day he was made the Medical Purveyor and Disbursing Officer of the Medical Department of the Expedition to the Philippines, later called the Department of the Pacific and the Eighth Army Corps. Young Will and I joined Father on October 31, spending a day en route in Saint Louis with my brother "Buck," his wife, and four children.[1] We were blocked by snow at Hugo, Colorado, 100 miles beyond Denver, and were delayed fourteen hours.

We spent the first night in San Francisco at the Occidental Hotel, and Father took us over to the Island the next morning. The island, which is the largest in the bay, is about one mile across and about five miles north from the city, which we reached in half an hour by means of a small government steamer, the *General McDowell*, that made two or three round trips a day, stopping at Alcatraz Island and, on specified days, also ran to the Presidio.[2]

The Post was on the west side of the island, on a long slope in a depression between the hills where there was less fog than in the city, but we would run into it a few minutes after leaving the island. Our quarters were frame ones and the more northern of the two sets at the upper side of the parade, which were in a poor condition and forlorn. We had them re-painted and papered after the troops came back from their summer camp, [and they] were quite comfortable, although the rooms were small. The view from the gallery in front was a grand one with Mount Tamalpais off to the right and the Golden Gate directly opposite, both of which grew upon us the longer we gazed upon them.

The ivy was a foot or more thick, and we had to cut out most of it to let in the sunshine and give us an uninterrupted view. Calla lilies were so thick on the terrace in front that the bulbs were crowded together in great masses. We dug them all out, enriched the soil, and then replanted some, but planting most of them at the base of the stone wall of the terrace. We pruned the rose bushes and had the grounds in fine shape when the Spanish War was forced upon us and our family was scattered far and wide.

Colonel Marcus P. Miller, Third Artillery, was in command and had serving under him Captains James O'Hara, William E. Birkhimer, Benjamin H. Randolph; First Lieutenants Henry C. Danes, Morris K. Barroll; and Second Lieutenant William S. McNair. The chaplain was John H. Macomber; and Captain Paul P. Straub, Assistant Surgeon, was Father's assistant.

Young Will entered the Polytechnic High School in San Francisco, going over on the 8:20 A.M. boat and returning on the 4:30 P.M. Phil and Frank came home every weekend and often brought friends with them. Once when we were watching for the boat to come, our Chinaman cook, Lee, came to the window and I said to him, "You better set the table for five more," and he replied, "Yes, I know, all the same, eight," and sure enough eight came, and among them was Miss Agnes Morley, whom the boys had known in the University of Michigan and had transferred to the Stanford University. The two boys joined the Beta Theta Phi [Pi] fraternity and live[d] at the fraternity house.[3]

. . . We had come to California hoping that we would remain here until Hal, Phil, and Frank had completed their course at college and Will graduate[d] at the Polytechnic School, but in March both Phil and Frank, as soon as there was talk of war with Spain, wrote that they were drilling and asked for permission to be among the first to enlist, as they had been raised beneath the flag and would fight for it and their country.[4] Father gave his consent and on April 20, after 125,000 volunteers were called for by the President, Frank with thirty-one other Stanford students responded to the call and enlisted in Company K, First Regiment, National Guard of California so as to be among the first to the front.

[They] came to San Francisco May 5 and were mustered into the service of the United States on May 6 at the Armory, corner of Gough and Page Streets, as Company K, First Regiment of California Volunteers, Captain Thomas J. Cunningham. The Colonel was James F. Smith; the Lieutenant Colonel, Victor D. Duboce, First Battalion; Charles I. Tilden, Second Battalion; and Major Hugh T. Sime, Third Battalion. Frank was made a corporal May 4.[5]

The regiment marched to the Presidio on May 7 and camped on the large plain fronting the bay. They were drilled five hours a day. Thousands of people visited them daily, taking them flowers, books, and all sorts of eatables. Frank's tent had the Stanford color, scarlet, flying from its peak and was a great centre of attraction. I always had some shopping to do for them and went over every day. They broke camp on the morning of Monday, May 23, and in heavy marching order went to the Pacific Mail dock, foot of Brannan Street, where they embarked on a chartered steamer fitted out as a transport, the *City of Peking*, and sailed at 5 P.M. on May 25, 1898, with the expedition to the Philippines, numbering 49 officers and 973 enlisted men. . . . The *Australia* and *City of Sidney* were the other ships of this, the first fleet, carrying the rest of the troops, Brigadier General Thomas M. Anderson in command of all.[6]

The latter ships followed the *City of Peking* out of the harbor, and all sorts of crafts, steamboats, tugs, launches, etc., accompanied them to the Golden Gate. Whistles blew, bells rang, bands played, horns were blown, flags waved, and great crowds of people cheered. We went along, taking the *McDowell* at Clay Street, and carried the Stanford colors which, when the many students saw, they gave their college yell time and again and cheered heartily. They were all so brave and bright. When the *Australia* came abreast of Alcatraz Island, the Fort fired a salute in honor of General Anderson. Major Thomas H. Barry, the Adjutant General, took mail and packages to the fleet and remained on each ship for some time, so we had a long talk with Frank, took a Kodak picture of him, and then bid the sweet fellow goodbye.

. . . They reached Honolulu on the morning of Wednesday, June 1, 1898, having had a very happy voyage, although Frank had been seasick two days and his berth was so short—only 6 feet long—that he couldn't stretch out in it. The ship was crowded, so he and another soldier about his height—his was 6' 3 1/2"—took possession of a lifeboat at night. They complained that the meals were not properly cooked and the boxes of extras sent them did not show up. The people of Honolulu treated them royally, giving them a $10,000.00 feast.

President and Mrs. Dole visited the ship to see their nephew, Alfred Dole, Frank's chum, and took the two to their home.[7] Here they had horses to ride, and they visited every place of interest. The girls crowned them with flowers and hung leis around their necks, and Mrs. Dole wrote me a kind note, enclosing three Kodak snap-shots of Frank. She provided them with fruits and other luxuries when they left.

Frank wrote to me on June 3rd, but I didn't receive his letter until the 26th. They stopped at Guam, one of the Ladrone Islands, while the cruiser *Charleston* took the island and made the Spanish garrison of six officers and fifty-four enlisted men prisoners, also [capturing] the Governor of the Ladrones. They arrived at Cavite, Philippine Islands, on June 30, according to a cable message sent by Admiral Dewey.[8]

Phil chose the regular army, as he said he would get a commission and remain in it. We knew that he had all of the qualifications to make a fine officer, so he enlisted in Troop C, Fourth United States Cavalry, on May 6, 1898, under Captain George H. G. Gale at the Presidio of San Francisco. John M. Neal [was] the First Lieutenant and Charles T. Boyd, Second Lieutenant of the troop. He worked hard to become proficient in his duties, not only drilling but also learning to make out the company papers. Captain Gale and First Sergeant Beach spoke very highly of him.

He spent Sunday, June 19, with us, and I was very happy to have our dear boy with us. He could come only twice to stay overnight. I am very sad packing away the clothes and other belongings of my sweet dear boys. What a happy day it will be when they come back to me.[9]

On the night of July 13, I was at the Presidio staying with Mrs. Ramey D. Potts, wife of Captain Potts, Third United States Artillery, whose oldest son Douglas was in the troop with Phil. David Anderson, another army boy, was [also] in the troop—all good friends. Phil and Douglas ate their last dinner with us and then had to hasten away. On the morning of July 14, I watched the six troops of the Fourth Cavalry strike their tents at 8 A.M., and Phil was the second in his troop to have his shelter tent struck and his roll tied, showing how his training at home in packing for so many moves had helped him.

The men fell into line at 9 A.M., and fifteen minutes later they marched away to go to the Pacific Mail dock at the foot of Folsom Street, escorted by their mounted band and Troop B of the Fourth Cavalry. It was a beautiful sight to see the well-drilled men, but it made us very sad. We followed them and went on board of the steamer *Peru* to spend an hour with Phil. He had a top berth of three in a tier of iron water pipe and woven wire springs, and the bedding was neat and clean. Major General Elwell S. Otis, who was in command, and his staff were on board and many others that we knew. Drs. Richardson and Quinn were the medical officers.[10]

The chartered steamers, *Peru* and *City of Pueblo*, composing the third fleet to sail, left the dock in the evening and steamed out of the harbor about 3 P.M. of the 15th. We went out on the *McDowell*, which carried the mail, and spent half an hour with Phil and, after returning to our boat, waited an hour while some repairs were made on the *City of Pueblo* so we lay along side and saw Phil that much longer. We followed the steamers to Fort Point and then returned to Angel Island. A strong wind was blowing and the sea outside was quite rough, and many of the men were seasick.

They were in Honolulu for the ceremonies of annexation of the Hawaiian Islands to the United States of America.[11] Phil's letter from there told of the crowding of the men, who were packed so closely together on the *Peru* [that] the air was foul and made the men dizzy. The food was wretchedly cooked and there was very little of it, but after the cargo was shifted, the men were more comfortable. They were in Honolulu 15 days and did not reach Cavite until August 21.

Letters came from Frank, who was in a fight one night when there was a tornado and rain poured down. Only the lightning revealed the struggle. He was at the taking of Manila, August 13.[12] Hal wanted to enter the service, but we advised him to complete his courses of study and secure his degrees before doing so.

Claude was far away, having left Detroit, Michigan, in March 1898 for the Klondike with a party of six others, William Lyster, Prentiss, Sargent, etc. They were well equipped, having a two years' supply of food, warm clothing, etc. They took three boats, one of them a steel launch thirty-six feet long, the others of wood. They went to Edmonton, Alberta, thence to Athabasca River, where they set up their boats and sailed down Great

Slave River and the Mackenzie River to Fort McPhearson [McPherson] and Peel River, where they expected to winter.

Claude knows how to take care of himself, is strong, well, and prudent, yet we are anxious about him. As the winter came on the party broke up and all except him returned south, but he joined some Canadians and proceeded north, wintering at Poverty Bend on Rat River, 1898–99.[13]

I began to pack our belongings, and the dreadful breaking up of our ties made me homesick. From May 17, Father was very busy in San Francisco, fitting out the different fleets with medical and hospital supplies, inspecting ships, clothing, commissaries, etc.[14] He had his office and storeroom at 33 Second Street. The volunteer surgeons knew nothing concerning their duties in connection with the procurement and care of their supplies, so he had to make out their requisitions, filled at 36 New Montgomery Street, the Medical Supply Depot. . . . He made out the invoices and receipts and then had to search for them to get their signatures.[15] He provided them with vaccine virus and urged them to use it at once, and to their failure to fully carry out his instructions were due the cases of small pox among our troops in the Philippines. He devoted all the time he could spare to Red Cross work, which society he helped to organize, and then assisted the ladies with his advice as they consulted him in all matters.[16]

There were many impostors trying to get supplies, so he scanned all demands made upon them. Father had, after the Civil War, seen so many graves marked "unknown" that he saw the necessity of identifying every man by means of a tag of some sort. He wore an aluminum identification disc and recommended its use in the army. It was the size of a silver half-dollar, and the name of the man and the organization to which he belonged was to be stamped upon it. . . . [The soldier wore it] suspended by a buckskin thong from the neck. The California Volunteers were the first of the troops to be furnished with those that he had made, but it was not until 1906 that, in accordance with his recommendation, an order was issued by the War Department requiring every soldier in the army to wear one. And that was not until after he had demonstrated its necessity. Frank's number was sixteen.[17]

Father favored the sending of trained nurses, male and female, to the Philippines and was instrumental in securing for the Red Cross Society permission to send them, and the first twelve or fourteen went over in his charge. Women were not wanted in the islands, but the wife of a volunteer officer of some rank managed to stow away and go with her husband.[18]

Father reported to General Otis and hoped to go with him but could not get supplies fast enough to enable him to go with the third fleet. Medicines, dressings, instruments, hospital stores, bedding, and furniture were not in sufficient quantities in San Francisco to furnish more than the first fleet. And he had to telegraph East for nearly everything he needed, so it was not until August 21 that he could go, and then he had only about a four month's supply for the troops in the islands. He received $10,000.00 in gold from the United States Treasurer to be used for expenses and supplies, but it was only a drop in the bucket and he was sent thousands more.[19] He took with him his hospital steward and privates as clerks. . . .

He left us at 11:50 A.M. on August 21, 1898, on the *Arizona*, formerly an ocean greyhound, a steamer that had fine, large, comfortable staterooms. Will and I spent the evening before with him and some hours the day he sailed. We followed him nearly to Fort Point on the *McDowell* and then returned to our desolate quarters on Angel Island. We were glad when we were through packing and could leave, as the artillery had gone to the Presidio, after having been received [relieved] by companies of the First Washington Volunteer Infantry, who were as yet undisciplined men.[20]

Three of these men were sent to help me pack, and when [they were] through, I gave each one $1.50. They said, "This is the first of Uncle Sam's money we ever received." We turned our effects over to the Quartermaster for storage and spent the night of August 21 with Mrs. Potts at the Presidio. She and I cried together over the war and the departure of our loved ones. In the night I could hear her cry out repeatedly to her younger son, "Jack, I don't like war," and he would answer, "Neither do I, Mother. Go to sleep," until he fell asleep.

CHAPTER TWENTY-THREE

❧❧❧

"All My Dear Ones Are with Me in Spirit"

ELMIRA, NEW YORK, AUGUST 1898–APRIL 1900

WILL AND I LEFT ON THE 26TH on the Union Pacific Railroad and went to Mother in Elmira, New York, and here, 6 A.M. on the 30th, I received a letter from Father sent by the pilot when the latter left the steamer. It was good to receive it, [even] if I did have a good cry. He wrote again in Honolulu, where he arrived August 28 and remained until September 11, 1898, waiting for the steamer, *Scandia*. He arrived at Manila September 28. Brigadier General Henry O. Merriam and Captain Charles King, Brigadier General of Volunteers, were on the *Arizona* as far as Honolulu and remained there, and then Father had the best room on the ship.[1]

On arriving in Manila he found Frank, then a sergeant, feeling badly and soon discovered that he had typhoid fever. He had him sent to the hospital, where the poor boy had a long and tedious illness with pneumonia and phlebitis as complications. He and Orderly Sergeant Chester Thomas were affected at the same time. They were in the same room, which was next to the baths in the Quartel Fortin, just above the Bridge of Spain.[2] All of the wastewater ran under the stone building and had no outlet. It was not until the men began to get ill that the volunteer surgeons learned of all the reeking filth that lay under the floors and had holes cut through the stonewalls to let it out. No wonder so many precious lives were lost. Father watched Frank very carefully, often sleeping near him to see that he was properly nursed. My poor boy had a long and tedious convalescence and was sent to Corregidor Island.

When stronger, he was transferred to the First Reserve Hospital in Manila, February 10, 1899, and the day before he was sent home gave valuable services to Father on March 25, after the battle of Malabon near Manila, March 24, 1899, in caring for the 72 dead and wounded and securing transportation for them to the hospitals.[3] He sailed for home on the United States Transport, *Grant*, March 25, and arrived in San Francisco Harbor April 29, 1899, and went to the hospital at the Presidio, where he hoped to receive a furlough until his regiment was mustered out of the service.[4]

Although still very thin and weak, he was discharged July 1, 1899, from the "service honest and faithful, character excellent, temporary disability one-eight." He returned to the Stanford University in September, after spending a couple of months in southern California, but was unable to study much and in May 1903, after a hopeless struggle, broke down completely and had to give up his college work. He would not ask for a pension, to which he was justly entitled. On September 11, 1903, he was operated upon for appendicitis and since then has slowly improved in health. His sad experience proves how necessary it is to have trained military medical officers to look after our troops in time of war.[5]

On November 8, 1898, Father in his letter of October 1st to the 8th said that the voyage of five weeks was a long rest and he had not felt so well in years. Phil was just over an attack of malaria and then it was I heard that our darling Frank had typhoid fever.[6]

Phil was promoted fast through all the grades to that of First Sergeant of his troop on August 16, 1899, and passed an examination for a commission before Father came home. He was [made] a second lieutenant of cavalry July 25, 1900.

Young Will entered the Cayuga Lake Military Academy, Aurora, New York, September 13, 1898, Colonel Stolbrand, the Superintendent, where he was perfectly contented, but it was very hard to let my last boy leave me.[7] His studies were Algebra, Chemistry, Latin, English, and History. In October, I had letters from Phil, who wrote that he had had an attack of malaria but was getting well. He frequently saw Frank, who had also written.

Also, [I] had letters from Claude, dated July 6 and 16, from Forts Providence and Simpson on the Mackenzie River, Northwest Territories; part of his trip was hard traveling. . . . He was about to join another party, the "Stewart Outfit," and would travel by dog sleds. He had health, endurance, and plenty of good food and was not afraid of the hardships he might have to undergo. God grant he may make his journey in safety. All of my dear ones are with me in spirit every moment, and some days I feel as if I cannot endure their absence any longer.

In December, Will spent the Christmas holidays with us at his grandmother's. We had a fine turkey dinner and tried to be jolly, but it was hard work when we thought of our precious ones so far away, and we hoped that they would all be with us before another Christmas came. Hal dined in Detroit with his friend Kiefer. I received many letters from Father. Frank was sick near unto death but had the good care of a woman nurse, and Father, owing to his great anxiety, was with him every night. One night he had to wade through water to his knees to reach the hospital owing to heavy rains and the consequent rise of the Pasig River. What a providence that Father could be with him, and how I wanted to be there too. Phil was perfectly well again.[8]

January 1899: A new year and the fighting still going on with no prospect of the return of the troops, but I wish that those I love were away from there. Frank was improving slowly and [was] allowed soft starchy food. Father told of the heavy rain in November that flooded many of the streets and saturated the air with moisture so that clothing was damp, shoes mildewed over night, and his surgical instruments rusted. In February he wrote that Frank was still improving, but he had swelling of the abdomen and the veins in one groin.[9]

Phil wrote by every mail. He was then a corporal and had been in several engagements with the Philippine *insurrectos*.[10] Frank was sent to the convalescent hospital on Corregidor Island at the mouth of Manila Bay, where he was to stay until strong enough to return home. Father's letters were in the form of a diary and were full of interesting matter. In March he tells [told] of the fighting and of the many poor Philippinos [Filipinos] wounded or killed, and he sent me many 4 X 5 photos that he took.

In April Frank was ready to leave for home, but some mistake was made so he was staying with Father. More fighting than ever was in progress in spite of the efforts of a Peace Commissioner in Manila.[11]

Will spent his Easter vacation with his grandmother, and I went to Baltimore but spent much of my time in Washington, D.C., with my old friend Mrs. Anson Mills, Number Two Dupont Circle, with whom I had a delightful visit.[12] I went to the Capitol many times to see Senator [George C.] Perkins of California, trying to get Phil a commission. The senator talked well but did nothing. General Mills saw him and Representative [Eugene F.] Loud of California, but neither one did anything for me.[13] There were many vacancies, but we had been on the frontier so long that we had no political influence.

In May I tried to see the President but saw Mr. Cortelyou, his private secretary, only.[14] He gave me a letter from the President to Adjutant General Henry Corbin saying, "I think this young man deserves a commission." So I went to the Adjutant General a second time, feeling sure that this letter was really an order; but General Corbin said, "If he were my boy I would let him work to the end of the two years as then he would surely get it." But I told him that Phil wasn't his son, but mine. He, however, ignored the letter entirely.[15] In the meantime Douglas Potts secured a commission January 1, 1900, but his uncle, Lieutenant Colonel Thomas Barry, was on General Otis' staff and had political influence. Douglas had not been permitted to see much field service.[16]

In May Father wrote that in a long time there had been only a very few light showers. The air was dry and the heat excessive. He had more work than one man could be expected to accomplish, but [he] was trying to hang on. He had two ice plants running, which gave a fair supply of the much-needed ice. Phil had been in the field but had Tiffin with him May 10.[17]

Often my letters were a long time reaching him and one dated April 22 was not received until May 30th. I returned to Elmira May 10. In June, I received a letter telling me that Phil had been north in General Lawton's command and had seen much fighting. Once the heat was so great that a large number of the command were prostrated, Phil among them, but after recovering [he] went into the fight again. Dear sweet boy, how hard he is working to get a commission. General Lawton is so strong himself that he thinks his men are as strong as he, and he doesn't save himself.[18]

In July Phil was sick again after a hard trip and, in August, suffered from Dhobie itch, for which he was so badly treated that in September he had boils when he sent for Father, who went to San Fernando and gave him relief at once.[19]

. . . In August [1899] Will and I were in Gloucester, Massachusetts for three weeks. It is a beautiful place: the rocks, ships, docks, downs covered with wild flowers, and the sea all attracted us. We met many delightful people. Hattie Leonard from Detroit found rooms for us at Mrs. Wilcox's next to Harbor View Hotel, at which we had our meals, which were fine. Trolley cars took one for miles, with the sea in view most of the time. We spent two days in Boston and one in Salem taking in every place of interest. Will returned to school at Cornwall-on-the-Hudson in September, where he had gone in February as the school at Aurora was then consolidated with the New York Military Academy, which I visited and found him well pleased.[20]

Father has had his grounds freed from the dense growth of bamboo, etc., to let in the sunshine and dry his storerooms and had the cesspool back of his house cleaned out. The whole city had been pretty well cleaned up, and health conditions were improving. In October Phil was at Pasig. Letters came from Claude at Tanana on the Yukon River. He had come in from a hard trip and had to do all sorts of work, even carpentering, to raise some money, getting only $100.00 a month and found, but soon did much better.[21] Hal is much interested in his work, and Doctor Wickes, the surgeon in charge, is taking an interest in him. On October 27, I visited Will and in November went to New York for a few days and thence to Washington to visit Mrs. Mills again, remaining until the 29th. We went, among other entertainments, to a charming luncheon given by Mrs. [Martha] Sternberg, the wife of the Surgeon General.[22]

In December letters from Father [said] that he hasn't felt better for years, and the climate and hard work agree with him. He sent me by mail pieces of piña fabric and many curios. Will had a letter from Phil, who was at San Isidro and First Sergeant of his troop, of which he has been at times in command when no commissioned officer was present.[23] I was in Baltimore for a time and then returned to Washington, leaving there and returning to Elmira December 22, so as to be with Mother and Will on Christmas Day, which we enjoyed together and tried to feel jolly. I wanted very much to join Father and be near Phil, as women were now allowed to go to the islands, but I dreaded to go alone and it would hurt me to leave two of my boys behind.[24]

January 5, 1900: Frank has tried to keep up with his college work but could not, so had to stop. It is rumored that the plague has appeared among the Chinese in Manila, but that did not deter me from trying to go there.

On the 10th I went to Baltimore and thence to Washington to try to get transportation on a government transport but did not succeed. The lowest rates by a liner to Hong Kong were $186.00; and from there to Manila, $30.00; fare to Chicago, $15.65; from there to San Francisco, $36.75, army rates; sleeper, $19.00, and then there were the meals, so I felt that I would not be justified in spending so much money unless Father needed me very much. But I felt very badly to have to give up going.

January 17: I received a letter from Claude at Tanana: well, cheerful, and hopeful. He had received letters from Hal and me. There was an Army Post at Tanana and he was delighted to have the society of the officers stationed there; as Dr. [Samuel T.] Weirick, the Post surgeon, had been one of the doctors who attended Frank in Manila, there was a bond of union between them.[25]

On February 9th, I went over to Washington in a snowstorm to help Mrs. Mills receive. The reception was a very beautiful one. The rooms [were] decorated tastefully with flowers and lights, the refreshments delicious, and she had a supper afterward for some of her friends. Among the guests were Brigadier General John M. Wilson, Chief Engineer, a charming man, and his sister, Mrs. and Captain John B. McDonald, Third Cavalry, Mrs. Beach, wife of the Engineer officer, and Mrs. Hall, wife of Doctor Hall of the Army. After conversing for a time with Mr. Wu, the Chinese Minister, I took him to entertain the young ladies, with whom he was very popular.[26] I wore a white waist of jusi from Manila, which was then very rare, trimmed with old Irish point lace given me by my mother, and my skirt was of handsome black crepon.

I received from Father three beautiful tortoise shell combs, a gray canton crepe shawl with long fringe, a lovely satsuma bowl, a silver fork and spoon having black carabao horn handles decorated with silver rosettes, a carabao horn card tray.

. . . February 1900: Colonel, Mrs., and Mamie Tilton are here in Washington. He has had a light stroke of paralysis but is able to move about the house. I received an invitation for the Army and Navy reception at the

White House for the 14th from my cousin Major Charles L. McCauley of the Marines, and went with Mrs. Mills and her niece, Miss Louise Stewart. After our wraps had been taken off, we passed from the vestibule into the state dining rooms, following Surgeon General and Mrs. Sternberg, and we stood where we had a fine view of the President and party as they descended the stairs and entered the Blue Room while the Marine Band played "Hail to the Chief." Then the diplomats passed into the room, and we followed them to be presented by Major McCauley to President McKinley, who shook hands with us all. We bowed to Mrs. McKinley and the wives of the Cabinet officers, who were back of her. She looked so very frail that my heart ached to see the efforts she made to keep up.[27]

We afterward went into the Red Room, the chimney mantles of which were massed with flowers, and took our stand near the door, where we met many people we knew and were introduced to many others. After a time we went into the beautiful conservatory where the Band was playing. I shall never forget the wonderful picture [of] the handsome uniforms of the officers, the red and gold of the band and beautiful gowns of the women amid the gorgeous plants, and I came away delighted with the first reception that I ever attended at the White House.

The 16th and 23rd were Mrs. Mills' days, and I received with [her] and again met many people and among them friends of many years. She had so many guests in her house that on the 22nd I took a pleasantly located room at 1614 K Street, Northwest, with Mrs. Browning and had my meals at Mrs. Mitchell's, 1406 K Street, Northwest at $25.00 a month.

March 1: I have letters from Mother, Father, Claude, Hal, Phil, and Will. Claude enclosed a photo of him and his dogs and sled about to start for Nulato with the United States Mail. He was in good health and spirits. The 9th: I again requested transportation to Manila so as to go with the Philippine Commission and be with good company but was refused, so I could not go to see Father. On the 10th, Mrs. Mills insisted that I should return to her, and as her guests had departed, I went, and on March 14th I assisted Mrs. Sternberg to receive at her home.

March 16, 1900: Orders were issued today relieving Father from duty in the Philippines. Letters from him that Phil was worn out and half-starved, but rest and good food are all that he needs.[28]

March 28: Letter from Claude dated January 27 said he was going to St. Michael's with the mail and might go to Nome. Father's letters come very regularly.[29] March 31: I went to Baltimore and found all sick with the grippe, so I returned to Elmira April 6th, where Will was enjoying his spring vacation until the 12th.

CHAPTER TWENTY-FOUR

"All the Years of Anxiety Have Broken Me Down"

ELMIRA, NEW YORK, APRIL–JULY 1900

A
PRIL 6: I RECEIVED A MEDAL of honor for Father presented him by the Sons of the American Revolution for services during the War with Spain. [April] 19: Claude has a $5,000.00 share in a steamboat, and I sent him a *Seaman's Manual* with which to fit himself for a license to run the boat to Saint Michael's this summer.[1] April 21: Packages came from Father containing mandarin skirts, a beautiful white embroidered cashmere shawl, pieces of piña and an embroidered white linen table cover.

May 1: Letters from Father delayed, [said] he hoped to leave Manila about the middle of the month. I am glad on his account but sorry for darling Phil.[2] May 5: Hal has been to Washington to see General Sternberg, who says there will be no Army Medical Examining Board in the United States, but he will give him a contract and have him ordered to the Philippines, where he can come up before the first board for examination.[3] It will be very hard to part with him as he has been my right hand since Father left. God bless and keep him.

May 10: Another package from Father, and in it were jusi, piña, silver buttons, a diamond and sapphire ring for me, sapphire scarf pins for Hal and Will. May 14: A letter came from Father dated April 8, and packages containing two fans, one for Mother, having beautifully carved tortoise shell ribs, embroidered piña, and a lacquer box lined with very fine Chinese linen. May 15, 1900: My birthday and I am sixty-two years old. How comical it seems. Hal was in Columbus, Ohio, and underwent an examination, which he passed, and his orders will be issued July 1. The loneliness of the last two years has been very hard to bear without Father and now Hal must go to that wretched country.

May 20, 1900: Letters from Father and Phil, the first in a long time. It made my heart light to get it. My precious, precious boy, if I were only with him to help get him ready for his examination, but I know that he will succeed. May 28: A letter from Colonel Thomas H. Barry [told] me that Father is to be ordered to Governors Island, New York Harbor, for duty, and the Surgeon General will approve his application for a leave. Frank has gone to Pacific Grove in California to stay with Mrs. Braden and family for several weeks. She is the fraternity mother of the Beta Theta Pi. The University closed on the 25th. He hasn't done much studying and we didn't expect him to do any, but he wished to keep with the others who had returned from the Philippines.

On May 11, Father wrote that he was going on the steamer *Uranus* of the Compania Maritima for a trip of twenty days to the southern islands. It is a great disappointment that I could not be there to go with him. June 7: Still another package from him enclosing a large piece of blue and white striped jusi for a gown, a sapphire scarf pin for Claude, and one for Frank. Claude's investment in the steamboat *Tanana Chief* has not been a profitable one, as the unprecedented rush to Nome had prevented him from getting a crew.[4] On June 8th, Will came to spend his vacation with us, and how happy I was to see him. He has been practicing in the orchestra at school and plays the violin very well.[5]

Hal is in Battle Creek, Michigan, visiting the Shepards. He is engaged to be married to Louise, their only child, whom I met in Ann Arbor last summer. She graduated the same year that Hal did and is a sweet, intelligent girl, handsome and refined. She and her mother look like sisters. Her father, Freedom G., is [of] the firm of Nichols and Shepard, manufacturers of traction engines and large farming implements.[6] Hal came on June 15th, and how glad I am to have him with us, and we had a great deal to talk about. It nearly kills me to have him go so far away and for so long a time.

[June] 20: Hal and I have been packing such articles as he will leave here and arranging my own things. On the 17th, I had a letter from Claude, who will soon be in Nome. I sent him a full outfit of clothes by express to Seattle to go from there by freight to Tanana, and I took great pleasure in packing them, but he will take more pleasure in unpacking them. Harold left us June 30, and on July 3, his contract and order to proceed to Manila, Philippine Islands, came. I forwarded them to him. We miss him very much. He left Battle Creek July 7 and arrived in San Francisco on the 11th. He left us on June 30th, intending to spend a few days en route with Louise.[7]

. . . On July 5th two letters came from Father in which he described his trip south, also a letter from Phil who was with him on a furlough of twenty days and was to have his examination for a commission [to] begin on June 1st. What a happy boy he will be if he passes, but there is no doubt about that. Father was to be relieved by Major Merritt W. Ireland, Surgeon, and to start home on the *Hancock*, formerly the *Arizona*, on June 15, via Nagasaki. A telegram came from Hal on the 14th of July telling of the arrival of Father in San Francisco Harbor on the 13th, quite well; and on the 21st, I received a letter from Father, who was on the 14th [of July] about to leave the transport. Hal and Frank were on the dock to welcome him, and they went to the Occidental Hotel.[8]

Harold sailed on July 16 on the Transport Steamer *Sumner* with the Expeditionary forces for China, having been assigned to the First Battalion, Fifteenth United States Infantry, Major William Stephenson, the Surgeon, in charge. He felt well, was well equipped, and said I must not worry about him. Darling boy, it will be hard not to do that. He now cannot appear before the board for a commission for a long time.[9] My anxiety about Father and Frank was now relieved, but I had another one to be carried.

July 25: A telegram came from Frank and he arrived at noon. Father went directly to Washington to try to get Phil into the Cavalry, the branch of the service he wished to enter; and on the 20th [25th], I received a telegram from him saying that Phil, our darling boy, had been commissioned on the 25th, a second lieutenant of Cavalry, and would go to the Ninth. How hard I worked to get it for him, but he won it on his own record, having done excellent work. I wrote and congratulated him at once.[10]

July 28: Dear old Papa arrived this afternoon and how strange he looked at first, so brown and thin, wearing spectacles having nickel rims, a small gray felt hat, and a dark blue serge suit instead of his uniform. How good to have him home again from so far away after such a long time and have three of my darlings with me. Poor Mother, too, was happy to see him. She was very sick for over two weeks and at one time feared she would not live to see him again. She was better, but very weak. In August, I was very sick for some days. The intense heat, nursing Mother, and the reaction from the years of anxiety have broken me down.[11]

CHAPTER TWENTY-FIVE

"The Most Beautiful Blue I Had Ever Seen"

FORT COLUMBUS, NEW YORK; FORT CROOK, NEBRASKA; AND THE FAR EAST, AUGUST 1900–AUGUST 1903

O
N THE 15TH [AUGUST 1900], FRANK went to Old Point Comfort for a week, [and] Father, Will, and I left for Hyannisport [Hyannis Port], Massachusetts, on the 16th by a Fall River steamer from New York and part of the way by rail. Mrs. and General [Anson] Mills and children, Mrs. Ollendorf and daughter, Colonel [Charles H.] Alden, Surgeon, and wife, and other old friends were here.[1] We had very comfortable rooms; the meals were good, and the bathing fine. We passed the days sailing and fishing and the evenings on the wide galleries over-looking the water. Frank joined us and he, Father, and Will caught many sharks, one of them about ten feet long which was afterward washed ashore, where a woman found it and had her picture standing by it published in a newspaper as having been captured by her. Father had a leave of absence to September 30, and we spent the latter part of it in Elmira. . . .

On September 30, [he] reported at Fort Columbus, Governors Island, New York Harbor, as surgeon of the fort and Attending Surgeon, Headquarters, Department of the East.[2] He remained here until December 15, 1902, and had for a time charge of the office of the Chief Surgeon of the

Department. Infantry were stationed here for a time and then went to the Philippines. After they left, Major William P. Duvall, Artillery Corps, was in command, and other officers were Captains Louis V. Caziarc, Second Artillery, John D. C. Hoskins, Third Artillery, Eli D. Hoyle, First Artillery, Archibald Campbell and LeRoy S. Lyon, Artillery Corps. The Reverend Edwin Goodwin was the Chaplain under the direction of Grace Church, New York. Father had as assistants First Lieutenants Eugene H. Hartnett and Verge E. Swazey, and afterward, Allie W. Williams.

Some of these officers had just returned from the Philippines, and we could see the depressing effects of a tour in the islands. The change of hours, meals, and sleep also probably affected them. They at first took very little interest in their surroundings and were very listless, but usually recovered their spirits in a couple of weeks or a month.[3]

Major General John R. Brooke was in command of the Department until his retirement July 21, 1902, and was then succeeded by Major General Adna Chaffee. Colonel Henry Lippincott was the Chief Surgeon. Lieutenant Colonel Michael V. Sheridan [was] Adjutant General and later Thomas H. Barry. Lieutenant Colonel George H. Burton [was] Inspector General; Colonel James M. Moore [served as] Chief Quartermaster and later Major Samuel R. Jones; Lieutenant Colonel Edward E. Dravo [was] Chief Commissary of Subsistence.

Louise Shepard visited us for several weeks and then went to Europe. Ida Edwards also paid us a visit, and we became well acquainted with both dear girls.[4]

Young Will graduated at the New York Military Academy June 7, 1901. He was then a lieutenant [and] as an honor graduate could have then entered the army, but he didn't wish to do so. He entered the Polytechnic Institute, Brooklyn, New York, September 23, where he remained until June 1902, and then on the 23rd went to the General Electric Company, Schenectady, New York. He remained there until August 1, 1903, and returned September 28, to the Polytechnic Institute to remain until February 1905.

In April 1902, I went to board at Knight's farm near Sunapee Lake, New Hampshire, where in about a week Father joined me, having a leave from April 21 to May 6.[5] The latter part of April we went to Philip and Ida's wedding, which took place at her home in Louisville, April 30, 1902. Young Will was also present, and the event was a gay and joyous one.

Harold returned from the Philippines and arrived in San Francisco Harbor, August 14, 1902.[6] He came with Company G, Twenty-fifth United States Infantry, as far as Fort Reno, Oklahoma, had a leave of a month, and reported for duty at Governors Island November 1, 1902. . . . He was with us until November 6, on which day he was ordered to Fort Mansfield, Rhode Island, where he was on duty until May 29, 1905, when he left the service. My sister, May, came to visit us and arrived the day after Hal did, November 2, 1902. We were very happy to be together again and hoped that she would pay us a long visit when Father was ordered to another station.

Mrs. Chaffee had returned from the Philippines very nervous, and her condition had enabled a surgeon's wife, while on the transport, to influence her to have her husband replace Father.[7] May and I went to Mother's and afterward to visit Hal. After Father was relieved from duty he had a leave from December 15, 1902, to January 17, 1903, which he spent mostly with us.

In January 1903, I went to Schenectady to visit Will. The house in which he boarded was badly heated, as the baseburner stove in the sitting room would not draw. After a while a swallow's nest was found stopping up the flue. I stayed a night and then was so cold that I went to a hotel but was seized with a severe attack of bronchitis. The next day I spent at Governors Island with Chaplain Edwin Goodwin and family. The next evening I went to Baltimore and the next morning sent for a doctor. Lou Harding came to Trottie's to nurse me, but Trottie was afraid that she would contract the disease.[8]

So I, in spite of the protest of the doctor, went to Mother's the next day, riding in the cars from 7 A.M. to 10 P.M. Mother and May met me at the door and led me to a lounge, where I fell exhausted. Harold came two nights afterward on his way from Mansfield to take me with him to Battle Creek, but I was, to my great disappointment, too ill to go to his wedding, which took place February 4, 1903, at Louise's home. . . .[9] Father received a leave from February 2 to 9 [so] he attended, [and] the next night attended the Junior Hop in Ann Arbor with them before returning to his station.

I joined Father at Fort Crook, Nebraska, in March 1903, and we led a very quiet life.[10] Major John J. Crittenden, Twenty-Second Infantry, was in command, and among the other officers were Major Abner Pickering, Captain Peter W. Davidson, Quartermaster, and Second Lieutenant Dean

Halford. An electric storm one night in early summer was a wonderful sight. The whole sky was light for ten minutes or more, with constant flashes of sheet lightning.

On July 1st, Ida came to stay with us until fall, and Philip, whose squadron of the Fourteenth Cavalry was preparing to go to the Philippines in September, came with her a part of the way and then went to Louisville, Kentucky, to pay her family a visit. On July 8th, Father received a telegraphic order to embark for the Philippines, August 1, and Philip came to visit us just in time to assist us in packing. . . . On the 13th, we shipped our effects with a rush order, 36 packages to be left in San Francisco and 26 to go to Manila, and then telegraphed to keep trace of them. Phil left July 15th to return to Fort Logan, and Ida on the 20th to go to Louisville to stay with her parents.[11]

We left Fort Crook July 24th and arrived in San Francisco, 8 P.M. of the 26th, where we went to the Occidental Hotel and found Frank, who had come down from Crescent City to bid us good bye. Our freight came the afternoon of the 31st, and we stored most of it in the Medical Supply Depot on Mission Street and sent such necessary articles as we had to take with us to the transport.

We steamed away for Manila on August 1, 1903, on the United States Transport *Sheridan* in stateroom Number Ten on the port side, leaving at noon. We arrived at Honolulu, Hawaiian Islands, 2,100 miles from San Francisco, at 7:20 A.M. Sunday, August 9th, and left there on August 11th. While there we had the use of a carriage and colored driver of Mr. Arthur Dillingham, a friend of Phil and Frank, who very thoughtfully sent them to us. After every meal, on looking out, there stood the handsomest outfit of the kind in the islands, ready to drive us wherever we wished to go.

We called upon the Doles, and Mrs. Dole showed us two beautiful trees in blossom that she called the "Golden Shower." The petals were beginning to fall and the ground beneath was the color of gold, they lay so thick. We picked up a long brown pod filled with seeds, which we afterward planted in Zamboanga and raised trees, which were four feet high when we left there. We also called upon the Atkinsons, whose son Robert was a warm friend of Phil and Frank.

We visited every place of interest, as the Pali, the Punch Bowl, Mona Loa, and the wonderful beach at Waikiki.[12] We walked through the markets, in which the fish were of the most beautiful hues and the pineapples

luscious beyond any I had ever eaten before. We lay in a supply of the latter, papayas, figs, and avocados. On one street there was a long stonewall
covered with night blooming cereus, and we went to see them at night
when thousands of the flowers were to be seen in the shade of the trees
or in bright moonlight. We drove to the Pali in a Do[g]herty wagon, taking Miss Houghton, Captain James W. Dawes, Paymaster, and Lieutenant
H. C. Williams, Artillery Corps, with us. The views were grand beyond
description, as there were steep, rugged mountains, great precipices, and
below, cultivated fields and sugar plantations reaching to the ocean in the
distance.

At night we went to the Alexander Young Hotel, where the Twelfth
Cavalry band gave a concert in the roof, which was followed by dancing
to the music of a native band, who often sang as they played their instruments. Quite late one night the Hawaiian sextet serenaded the passengers, playing and singing, and just before we left, came aboard and entertained us for an hour or more, three women among them.

Residents came with leis to decorate their friends. A yellow flower is
the one royalty formerly used, but carnations of various hues were the
most common. The green calyx is pulled off of the stem and the carolla
[corolla] is flattened and strung on some sort of fibre, a great many being
required to form a lei. Native boys, who are wonderful swimmers, followed us as we left the wharf to dive for money until we entered the very
tortuous channel. Father brought some poi on board for me to eat, as he
liked it, but I did not. It is made of the taro root, which is steamed and
then mashed or ground and has somewhat the taste of applesauce. While
we were at the wharf, mosquitoes were rather troublesome at night, but
after we left our electric fan drove them out.

Father had selected as the ones to sit at our table Miss Houghton, Lieutenant Williams, Mrs. and First Lieutenant H. S. Purnell, Medical Department, Captain James W. Dawes, and Mrs. and Lieutenant S. J. Morris,
Medical Department. The bread and coffee were poor; pancakes, tough;
cheese, fair; milk, thin; but we had a good variety of fruits. Among the
passengers were Colonel John B. Kerr; Lieutenant Colonels William A.
Simpson and Henry P. McCain; Major William A. Mann; [and] Captains
W. W. Gibson, W. C. Rivers, and R. E. L. Mitchie of the general staff. Lieutenant Colonel George F. Chase, Third Cavalry, was in command. The
Twelfth Cavalry band gave frequent concerts, and the men, boxing and

wrestling matches. . . . As we passed a string of islands we saw many birds and could hear them at night. Opposite Gardner Island on August 13, several shots were fired from a six pounder and an immense flock of birds arose. The rocks were almost entirely white with guano.

August 16th: At 11:15 A.M., we were startled by the shriek of the siren, which was to notify us that Midway Island, 1,142 miles from Honolulu, was near, and the people on shore that we were coming.[13] The water around the reefs, which are a series of atolls, was the most beautiful blue I had ever seen and on the inside a beautiful vivid green. When a long way off we could see a flagstaff among the sand dunes and bushes.

We anchored on the west side, opposite the entrance to the channel, which lead to the cable relay station, where there were thirteen men and one woman who had been here since April and had one mail since then. They were provisioned for six months and had birds, eggs, fish, and turtle galore. There were some Japanese here who were killing the boatswain and other birds in such great numbers on some of the reefs that the air was filled with the stench from their carcasses.[14] One could go among the nests and handle the young birds while the old ones stood nearby. Afterward, we heard that some United States Marines were sent to the island to stop the slaughter.

We sailed again at 7:15 P.M., and on August 17th, 1903, we crossed the 180° Meridian about 8 A.M. when we dropped a day, so that after that hour instead of being Sunday, it was Monday.[15]

CHAPTER TWENTY-SIX

"No te vayas de Zamboanga"

MINDANAO, AUGUST 1903–AUGUST 1905

W E ANCHORED IN THE HARBOR OF San Luis Depra [d'Apra] at Guam 4:15 P.M. August 24th, where the next morning we were rowed ashore to Piti by two Chammorros [Chamorros] passing over the beautifully colored coral reefs which seemed to be beds of flowers.[1] We could see the cable relay station southwest from the transport and old Fort Santa Cruz south. There was only one carriage drawn by horses at the landing and that was a private vehicle, so we hired a bullock cart provided with a seat for a dollar to take us to Agana about three miles distant.

. . . Miss Meda E. Houghton, who was traveling with us, went ahead on a cart with Mr. John Carrigan of San Francisco, who attempted to make speed and soon heated his bullock so that it started for the water. He sprang to its head and was carried into the bushes and through the mud. His clothes were not of a spotless white when he returned to the road and fell in behind us.

Spider lilies filled the air with their fragrance, but no other flowers were to be seen. Breadfruit, cocoanut, banana, and other trees were numerous. We saw native Chamorros sawing logs of a red wood into boards by hand, as all lumber was sawed until the United States government put up a sawmill. Women were busy shelling corn to dry on mats in the sun.

At Agana, we were received by Doctor [Arthur P.] Crandell at the Service Club, where we were given a luncheon at which Father sat at the end of one table and I at the other, with six ladies on each side. We visited an old church built in 1770 and partly destroyed by an earthquake ten years ago. We mailed letters to go home by the *Solace*, which was to go in a few days, and found a few old postage stamps to send to Will for his collection.[2] There were stationed here 120 or more marines and 138 sailors.

We met the captain of a beautiful sailing yacht, who was looking up the heirs of the so called King of the Caroline Islands, a trader, O'Keiff, I think, who had died leaving much wealth, and wives, and children on many of the islands.[3] The Captain had the air and talk of a pirate, as we see him [the pirate] in pictures, and said he had a fine collection of native arms. When asked how he got them he said, "You shouldn't ask a trader such a question."

Boils, Dhobie itch, and tropical ulcers were very common, and a man at the cable station had fourteen boils opened a few days before. Ten men were sent home a month, six died a year. The last death was due to abscess of the liver. Doctor Young of the Navy, afflicted with boils and abscesses, came aboard to go with us to Manila and thence to Yokohama. This is called "the land of pus and blood." Game abounds as deer, wild hogs, ducks, a small quail, and fish, which are very fine. At night a lot of beef, mutton, and vegetables were unloaded to be taken over to the Navy ship *Supply*. Red ants were pests on the transport, and many people were stung by them.

August 29: We sighted the island of Samar about 5 A.M. [and] Bulusan Mountain later, smoke issuing from its summit; later still, Albay Mountain, 8,000 feet high, an active volcano, both on the island of Luzon. We passed San Bernardino light at 12 noon, [and] Totoog light at 1:30 P.M. Just before this the waters of the tides met between the islands and caused raps as if rushing over reefs. After this we had land quite close on both sides.[4]

Sunday, August 30: We entered Boca Grande into Manila Bay, passing Corregidor and Los Friar Islands. We saw the wreck of the cable-ship *Hooker* on a shoal where she ran aground a year and a-half ago, the officers and crew drunk, it is said.[5] We anchored in Manila Bay about noon Sunday, August 30, 1903, 7,024 miles from San Francisco. A quartermaster steam launch took us to the Quartermaster Depot on the west side of the mouth of the Pasig River.

Here a victoria met us, and we went to 77 Calle Real, Intramurros, a boarding house kept by the Ainles. The Chief Surgeon, Colonel Alfred C. Girard, sent his carriage and beautiful team of large bay horses to drive us wherever we wished to go, and we visited every place of interest. Among other[s], the Jesuit Museum, where we saw the body of a crocodile that was sixteen feet long, and one of a python, thirty-six feet long. In one room Filipinos were carving decorations for the church. They sat on the floor holding a block of wood between the great and second toes of one foot and used both hands at their work. The natives rarely stoop to pick up an article that has fallen but will grasp and lift it between their toes. It may be a handkerchief or even a napkin.

While in Manila we met many people and attended a reception given to Mrs. and Governor William Taft.[6] We left 6 P.M. Tuesday, September 8, on the United States Transport *Seward*, which had a tonnage of 1,296 and accommodations for about fifteen first-class passengers. It was one of the refrigerator boats that carried beef and vegetables to the southern islands, usually making the round trip in twelve days and eight hours. I felt the heat so slept a part of the night on deck in a long bamboo chair. We unloaded beef early the next morning at Batangas. Afterward, [we] sailed between Romblon and Tablas Islands, Masbate and Panay and Negros.

Most of the islands are mountains and have a few flats along the shore on which there are villages. We saw fish jumping out of the water and many fishermen. As we approached Iloilo there were large plains on the island of Negros and foothills, and Panay was flatter. We passed Los Siete Pescados [The Seven Sins] and anchored off Iloilo at 1:45 P.M. Father called upon Colonel John D. Hall, the Chief Surgeon of the Department. After leaving, we passed between Panay and Guimaras. Camp Jossman was on the latter, four miles inland, station of the Twenty-ninth Infantry.[7]

We arrived here, Zamboanga, Mindanao, Philippine Islands, 620 miles from Manila, at 6:15 P.M. on September 11th. Father relieved Lieutenant Colonel George W. Adair as Chief Surgeon of the Department of Mindanao and Medical Supply officer. There were no quarters for us, so we had to take the rooms vacated by Colonel Adair in the lower story of a board[ing] house owned and kept by J. A. Simoes, a Portuguese Malay. Our rooms were on the west side of a large sala which ran from a back to a front veranda, which faced the parade ground and was separated from it by a driveway and a canal twelve feet wide that led the water from the river to the Post. The back veranda hung over the water of the Straits of Basilan, and through its roof passed the trunks of two cocoanut trees. A row of piles prevented the water from washing under the house. The roof of the house was of corrugated iron, which resounded when a cocoanut fell upon it.

The sala was divided by an arch having a heavy rail running to the wall on each side; overhead was latticework. The back half of the sala was our dining room, from which we had a fine view of the Straits through latticed doors, which were never closed. The windows of our two rooms slid from side to side, and the panes in them were of white shell, each check of which was about two and one-half by two inches. Outside of these were heavy sliding shutters having slats, which could be opened by giving a turn to an upright, notched stick. We closed the shell windows only when the rain beat in, and then the rooms would be so dark we couldn't see to read.

The day after we took possession, I had the floors of our rooms scrubbed. "Scrub, scrub what is scrub?" asked Simoes, and when I explained, he brought a pitcher of water and began to pour some into a tumbler and throw it onto the floor. He then told Gabriel, our muchacho (in reality a grown man), to sweep it up, so I had to assume charge. I had Gabriel bring buckets of water from the canal to drench the floor and swab it until it was clean. Simoes' Filippino [Filipina] wife, three children, a dog, a cat, and several chickens came in and perched on the railing to watch the unusual performance.

While we sat on the back veranda, a pipe separated and down came soiled water from a bathtub above, and then down came some into our back room from the upsetting of a washbasin upstairs. The boards of the floor above, which was also the ceiling, had strips like lathing to cover the cracks, and there was nothing to prevent the water from coming down and the sifting of dust on our beds.

Our cook was a Chinaman and our dishwasher a young Filipino muchacho. . . . In the kitchen was a raised shallow box filled with sand to serve as a fireplace for an open fire, in which all the cooking was done, but we substituted an army range. We found the cooking utensils and table thickly covered with grease, which all had to be scraped and scraped again to fit them for our use. A hole in the floor provided with slats was the outlet for kitchen and all other waste, and here I found the boy sitting with a bare leg each side of the opening washing the dishes. As he finished a plate he sat it against a bare leg to drain. When the dishes were dry he arranged them on a shelf outside where the cats ran over and even slept among them. I had many changes to make and had the whole household to teach habits of cleanliness to protect ourselves from disease.

Mr. Simoes was an excellent cook, and his curry and rice could not have been better. Once a week he prepared the dish. The curry was freshly ground, the rice cooked so that the grains fell apart. Bits of salt and smoked fish, bacon, fried eggplant, shredded cocoanut, shredded fried onion, shredded white radishes, red pepper, and chutney, and sometimes as many as twelve different articles, each in its little dish, were set in a large one made for the purpose. A crater was made in a pile of rice and a little of each of these seasonings placed in it. To begin a meal with curry was to end it, as it was very filling. . . .

We had mangosteens—*Garcinia mangostana*—from Jolo, a delicious fruit a little larger than a walnut in its shell, brown outside, which when cut was found to be purple underneath, and in it lay a number of beautiful white seeds thinly covered with pulp which has a delicious flavor. When preserves are made of them the seeds are also eaten. The Moros brought us splendid orchids of many varieties, and great birds' nests, and other ferns, which we hung on cocoanut trees and along the verandas. We also had many potted plants.

The Medical Supply Depot was ordered abandoned August 6, 1904, and Father was relieved of much office work. He was promoted Lieutenant Colonel and Deputy Surgeon [General] April 26, 1904, and his pay and commutation of quarters amounted to $406.33 a month. As a major, his pay, foreign-service pay, and commutation amounted to $360.50 a month.

Phil sailed from San Francisco September 5, 1903, arrived in Manila September 28, and at Camp Overton, Mindanao, October 4, the next post north of us, and a night's sail.[8] On November 17, 1903, Phyllis Edwards Corbusier, our first grandchild, was born in Louisville, and May 15, 1904, she and her mother joined Phil. They came over in Frank's charge, who had his appendix removed in the Letterman Hospital at the Presidio, September 11, 1903, and was not yet strong. They left San Francisco April 1 on the United States Transport *Logan*, arrived in Manila April 28th, and Camp Overton, May 15, and soon came to see us.

. . . Poor little Phyllis, a bottle-fed baby and badly nourished, was reduced almost to a skeleton and no kind of milk or other food gave her any strength, so she had to be taken back to the United States. She and her mother . . . left Manila August 6, 1904, on the *Sherman*, again in Frank's charge. He was much benefited by his trip and saw much of Mindanao and some of the other islands. We were very happy to have him with us, and his music, sometimes the violin and at other times his mandolin, cheered us every night. He learned the Filipino music and surprised the natives with his playing. . . .

On Sunday Major Edward Davis read the Episcopal service at Lantaka Flats, a stone house occupied by officers. Father planned a new thirty-eight-bed hospital, which was completed August 6, 1904, and enlarged to sixty beds December 22.

On the east wall of the fort there was a shrine to Neustra [Nuestra] Señora del Pilar. The legend connected with it was that formerly a portal opened here at which there was posted a Spanish sentry. One night Nuestra Señora del Pilar appeared and informed him that the Moros would attempt to enter the fort at this entrance and surprise the garrison. He told the commandant of her visit, who prepared for the attack, met the Moros, and killed many of them. One morning not long afterward the portal was found closed with this shrine. The Filipinos commemorate the day in October, gather at the shrine by thousands just before sunset, when the sky is of a greenish tint, the same they say that it was on the evening of the Moro attack. After dark, candles were lighted to illuminate, and the ground for a hundred feet was thickly covered with tallow mingled with the soil left from former years.[9]

On Christmas Day groups of children went about taking part in "pastores," in which the participants usually form in two groups, one taking the part of Christians and the other of heathen, or Moros.[10] They recite their parts and engage in mock conflicts in which the Christians always overcome their opponents. Some of them stopped in front of our house to perform, and in one party the always-winning side carried small American flags. One girl, perspiring freely from her exertions, used her flag as a handkerchief [and] started to wipe her face, but I quickly stopped her and explained that it was wrong to put our flag to such a use, so she went to the canal and washed it.

On Good Friday the bells in the churches were not rung, but a sort of wooden clatter called the people to the services. The women were all clad in black, and at sunset there was a long procession from the church bearing various wooden images, mostly of Nuestra Señora del Pilar, and each person [carried] a candle. But on Easter Sunday the bells rang out and the women were in their usual gay colors. . . .

Major General Leonard Wood was in command of the Department, and his aides were Captains George T. Langhorne, Eleventh Cavalry, Halstead Dorey, Fourth Infantry, and later Frank R. McCoy, Third Cavalry. Major Edward Davis of the Artillery was the Adjutant General, and later Majors John V. White and John R. Williams, Artillery, [filled that position]. Major George H. G. Gale [was] the Inspector General, and after him, Lieutenant Colonel Daniel H. Brush. Captain Edward N. Jones Jr. [served as] the Quartermaster, followed by Captain David S. Stanley; Captain Ralph Harrison, the Commissary of Subsistence; and Captain Charles M. Saltzman, Chief Signal Officer; Major Charles E. Stanton, Paymaster; and William G. Gambrill, Postmaster. Colonel James G. Harbord, Captain, Eleventh Cavalry, was the Assistant Chief of Philippine Constabulary.[11] Part of the Seventeenth Infantry garrisoned the post most of the time, Lieutenant Colonel George K. McGunnegle, commanding. The Surgeons were Captain M. A. W. Shockley, [promoted] Major February 17, 1905; Major Edgar A. Mearns, Medical Corps, accompanied expeditions and sometimes First Lieutenant Jesse E. Harris, Assistant Surgeon, and Charles E. Freeman, Acting Assistant Surgeon. Later came Captain Robert W. Patterson [and] Major Francis A. Winter, Medical Corps.

Some of these officers were married and had their families with them. We had frequent hops at the club and many dinners. When the inter-island transport arrived, we gave receptions at the club, and a stringed band of Filipinos played and sang their music. When visitors left, the officers would accompany them to the transport, the Filipino band in the lead . . . playing as the ship left, "No te vayas de Zamboanga." "Do not leave Zamboanga."

On January 2, 1904, Mrs. Jones, wife of the Quartermaster, their boy, and I went to Jolo on the small steamer *Borneo*, where we were entertained by the Romboughs [Rumboughs].[12] Major Hugh L. Scott, Fourteenth Cavalry, was in command. Captain William F. Lewis was the Surgeon. Jolo was a small, quaint, walled town built by the Spaniards many years ago to protect themselves from the Moros. In spite of a guard at the gate, a Moro would sometimes rush inside on a "juramentado" and kill with his kris or campilan all that he met.[13] Several of our soldiers had been killed in this manner. Going and returning we occupied a stateroom which was not furnished with mosquito netting as officers always slept in cots on deck, and we were badly bitten by mosquitoes.

About two weeks later I had malarial fever, which left me with neuralgia, and remedies relieved it only temporarily, so Father thought that I better return to the United States. Accordingly, I started home April 28th, and Father had the Filipino band to serenade me as I left, and the last piece was "No te vayas."

I left the wharf May 5, 1904, on the *Proteus*, I think, a freight boat, which had a few very comfortable staterooms. At Manila I took the transport *Sheridan* to San Francisco. Lieutenant Colonel Edward Davis, Artillery Corps, was also a passenger, [as was] the wife of Captain Walter M. Whitman, Thirteenth Cavalry, with whom I shared my stateroom. Assistant Surgeon William T. Davis was the ship surgeon.[14]

We coaled at Nagasaki, where Mrs. Whitman and I went to a hotel over night. The next day we took rickshaws to Mogi, where we visited a temple, watched the hauling of seines, had a fish luncheon, and then returned to the transport.[15] We stopped at Honolulu one night and part of a day, where we had luncheon at the Royal Hawaiian Hotel and went to a hop on the roof of Young's Hotel. When we were about to start, a Hawaiian who had come from Manila with us and who had entertained us many times by playing Hawaiian and other music on his guitar came aboard, bringing many beautiful leis which he hung about our necks.

Arriving in San Francisco, Mrs. Whitman and I went to the Occidental Hotel for two nights. Major William Stephenson, Medical Corps, called and invited us to go to a theatre, but we hadn't our good heavy clothes yet, so had to decline. She and I left on the Santa Fe Railroad to Kansas City, where we took a room at the Baltimore Hotel, freed ourselves of dust, cooled off in a bath, had luncheon and a siesta. We left the same night, each on a different road, she to go to Akron, Ohio, and I to Mother in Elmira, where I remained for awhile and then went to Fort Mansfield near Watch Hill, Rhode Island, to visit Harold and Louise, . . . [where] our second grandchild, Frances Shepard Corbusier, [was] born on February 22, 1904.[16]

Will had left the Polytechnic Institute in February and was in business in Elmira. In July 1905, he and I went to Louisville and spent a few days with Doctor and Mrs. Edwards. From there we went to Lexington to stay with Mrs. Frances H. DeLong, 3054 North Limestone Street, awaiting Claude's arrival from Alaska. He came two days before the wedding, which took place 9 p.m., Tuesday, July 11, 1905, in Belle's beautiful southern home, the Reverend Edwin Muller of the First Presbyterian Church officiating.[17] Of our family, Harold, Louise, and Ida, besides Will and I, were among the guests present. It was a joyous wedding, and we wished that Father and the rest of our family could have been there. Claude and Belle slipped away at the end of the supper, at which there were many merry, happy toasts. They were gone a week and then returned to start for Tanana, Alaska, in a few days.

The day following the wedding I started for San Francisco, and Will, for Elmira. Harold and Louise paid Ida a visit in Louisville and then returned to Mansfield. I met Claude and Belle in San Francisco and saw them sail for their northern home. . . .

About August 1, 1905, I left there on the transport *Sherman* for Manila. Mrs. Bissett, the wife of a Captain of Marines, was in the stateroom with me. The wife of Major E. R. Cole, United States Marine Corps, was also a passenger.[18] We stopped at Honolulu where the Wite girls, friends of Frank, had me to luncheon at the Royal Hawaiian, as I could not go to their home, not knowing what hour the transport would leave. We also stopped at Guam.

CHAPTER TWENTY-SEVEN

"They Came in Vintas Decorated with Red and White"

ZAMBOANGA, MINDANAO, SEPTEMBER 1905–JANUARY 1906

W E ARRIVED IN MANILA, 8 P.M., September 2nd, where Father met me, and we went to Delmonico Hotel to remain until September 6th, awaiting the sailing of the *Seward* for Zamboanga. Colonel William A. Simpson and Lieutenant Colonel Appel and we were invited to a delicious dinner at Mrs. Gourivitz', an officer's widow and sister of Mrs. Orlando Poe. We met many other old friends while in the city. There were now modern streetcars running in several directions. The walled city and various barrios were clean, and the bad odors formerly so common were no longer noticeable. We left September 6 on the *Seward*, stopped at 2:30 A.M. at Camp Overton, where on September 12th the Fourteenth Cavalry Band gave us a complimentary concert. Phil met us and went with us to Zamboanga, where he remained until the 17th.

On arriving here, Zamboanga, Mindanao, 5:30 A.M., September 14, 1905, we went to our new quarters in which Father had been living since May 1, 1905. In June he [had] invited Mrs. and Colonel Daniel H. Brush to share them with him, and he messed with them until they secured quarters of their own. The house was only a few feet from the stone seawall, beyond which were the Straits of Basilan on the south, and not far from the cocoanut-bordered canal on the north over which was a beautiful rustic bridge. Beyond the canal on the left were tennis courts near an avenue leading to the fort, [bordered by] large Alamendra [almendro] trees—a kind of almond—in which huge bats, having bodies eight to ten inches long and a spread of wings of four or more feet, fed nightly.[1] They came from the direction of Basilan in a long column just after sunset. Our quarters had been built directly in their route, and they were not used to them, so when near [they] would circle about for a while and then fly off to one side.

Our two-story house was built by placing long, large timbers of native wood upright in cement and fastening the rest of the framework to them. The floors were of Oregon pine and the ceiling downstairs of swalley or kissome—strips of bamboo about an inch wide woven together [and] varnished to keep out the insects, but the latter [the insects] bored through, and in the morning piles of fine sawdust would have to be swept up.[2] The rooms were very large and well ventilated. We had large sliding shell windows and outside of them sliding shutters with slats that could be opened by turning a notched upright.

We had rich soil brought and covered the sand to the depth of six inches or more, dug holes in the sand, filled them with soil, rotted wood, and wood ashes, and planted "Golden shower" trees, avocados, many papayas from seed I brought from Honolulu, lemons, oranges, and pineapples, and flowers of various varieties, as the Bandera de España, Corazon de Maria, Corazon de Jesus, and Alfombra de Reina, and roses. Along the veranda we hung orchids and bird's nest ferns. Near the foot of the wharf there was a tree called the "Firefly" because at night it was lighted by myriads of the insects.[3] There was a small plaza in the town in which trees and shrubs were planted and a Filipino employed to water them every evening. He carried out his orders faithfully, even watering all of the wooden lampposts.

Gaspar was our cook, and Santiago, our house muchacho. Both were competent and faithful. The cook did our marketing, and we had him serve all the Filipino vegetables that he could procure. He fattened chickens and ducks to kill, and no one had better ones. General Wood and Major Mearns often brought us jacksnipe and beautifully colored pigeons.[4]

The Moros caught all the saltwater fish, of which the papano was the best, and in their market there were sometimes as many as twenty deep-sea turtles. While at Simoes we had so many turtles that we didn't care for any more. When hen's eggs were scarce, we had the mound bird's eggs, which were brown and twice as large as the eggs of the game chickens which we usually had. Early in the morning we could hear the fishermen blowing conch shells as they came in with their fish to take to their market, which had been established by Captain Finley. When Santiago announced a meal he did it in such a manner that you felt you were going to sit at a banquet, and when he placed a plate before you, you felt that it held the very best thing that you had ever tasted. We were fortunate in having ice, and all of our drinking water was distilled.

The roads leading out of the town to the different barrios had been very much improved by raising their beds and metaling them with finger coral, which soon dried after a rain. We drove frequently in a pony cart and occasionally had a paper hunt up to the gorge, where we would meet to have a supper prepared by our American women, spread on the ground, and lighted by a huge fire. The gorge was a rocky chasm about three miles up the river and was filled with a wild tropical growth through which one would have to cut his way to ascend the stream. Once we had a picnic over to old Port Isabella on Basilan Island, where there was [were] some old stone buildings and the remains of a beautiful garden.

On several occasions (once in September and October 1903), we had sultans, dattos, and other Moros visiting from various parts of Mindanao. They came in vintas decorated with red and white colors, and their gongs could be heard a long way off.[5] They wore tightly-fitted breeches and jackets. The ranking men had umbrella, fan, kris, [and] campilan bearers. A Moro from Magay, the Moro village just across the river, often gave us the "Bee dance," in which he hunted bees, found them, and was at length stung. Captain John P. Finley, Ninth Infantry, the Governor of Zamboanga, did very much to improve the condition of these people, and Datto Mandy seconded him in his efforts.[6] The Bogobos from the east coast of Mindanao, who all looked like pirates, also came. Their tightly-fitted clothes were made of abace [abaca]—Manila hemp—and were heavily ornamented with beads. They also entertained us with their native dances accompanied with their gongs.

— 247 —

While at Zamboanga I made a very large collection of seashells, buying many of them of the Moros, and Father brought me some from every port he visited. When I came home the first time, I brought a barrel full, and by the time we left for home the second time, I had four barrels and two crates of them of all sizes, from minute ones to one pair which was three feet in length. I took great pleasure in the mornings, classifying, arranging, and packing them in cotton, tissue paper, and boxes. Many of them were beautiful and rare.

From January the 14th to the 29th, Father was away. He went to Jolo on the *Borneo* and there changed to the *Gibson*, which took him to Siassi, Bangao, our most southern post, Latitude 5°1'45"N, Longitude 119°47'50"E; Kagayan Sulu; and Puerta Princessa [Puerto Princesa] on Paragua Island, from which latter place he brought back the best oranges we had yet tasted in the islands.[7] The distance from the latter place is 305 miles. While I was away he visited all the other stations in the department in October 1904. He went north to Overton, where he saw Phil, up the mountains to Camp Keithley, across the lake, down the mountains on the other side to Camp Malabang, up the Colorado De Mindanao River as far as Fort Pikit.[8] Brigadier General James A. Buchanan was in command the latter part of 1905 while General Wood was in the United States, and Major J. R. Williams was his Military Secretary. Companies of the Twentieth Infantry arrived about July 1, 1905, and relieved the companies of the Seventeenth Infantry. At one time the wife of Governor Luke Wright was in Zamboanga. I knew her in Mobile during the Civil War when we were both girls, and [we] had not met since.[9]

At 11 A.M. Thursday, December 21, 1905, Father and I left Zamboanga on the little steamer *Sarah*, Captain C. W. B. Maddox, and had a pretty rough trip to Manila. At one time during the night the boat twice apparently went down and struck something. The Captain said it had fallen into the same hole twice; the beds seemed as hard as corrugated iron. We arrived in Manila 6 P.M., December 24, and drove to the Delmonico Hotel opposite the remains of an old church which had been destroyed by an earthquake years before. The accommodations were poor, but they were the best we could get. On Christmas Day we attended the musical services at the Cathedral and enjoyed it to the utmost. Other days we drove about the city or rode on the trolley lines to Caloocan, Malabon, Santa Ana and other places.

We sailed at 1 P.M., January 4, 1906, on the transport *Logan*, formerly the *Manitoba*, Captain W. P. Stimson, and had room 121 on the starboard side. We sat at Retired Brigadier General Butler D. Price's table, and with us were Mrs. Price, Mrs. John C. Clem, Mrs. Harry L. Pettus, and Major Hugh L. Scott. The troops [were] under the command of Colonel F. K. Ward, Second Cavalry, of which regiment there was one squadron, 271 enlisted men. There [were] also fourteen discharged soldiers, eleven sick, four prisoners, two insane, and forty-two indigent civilians.

On the 7th, the passengers began to change their tropic clothes to heavier ones, and on the night of the 8th we needed a double blanket. On Wednesday, January the 10th, we went ashore at Nagasaki, paying twenty sen to be sculled ashore on a sampan and hired a jinrikshaw, paying one yen, about fifty cents of our money, a day. When going up hill we had to have a man behind to push each one.

We visited the temples and in one witnessed a funeral service. The mourners were clad in white, and as we left, each one was given a funeral cake. We saw the bronze horse, many camphor trees, dwarfed cherry and plum trees, camellia, japonicas, azaleas, and many other plants all in bloom. The markets had fresh radishes, turnips, cabbage, lettuce, cress, beans, oranges, apples, pears, persimmons, fish, pork, beef, twigs of cherry and plum blossoms, and lilies everywhere.

The coaling of the ship was done by strings of men and women who passed small basketsful from hand to hand. When emptied, the baskets were thrown back into the barge. There were eight barges each having a gang of about forty men and women. We saw many parol[led] Russian prisoners in the street, army nurses, and recruits, followed by women.[10]

We, of course, purchased beads, kimonos, embroidered waist, cherry lacquer boxes, belts, satsuma ware, buttons, buckles, bags, Kraga cups and saucers, and a round metal mirror, ta-ka sa-go of the year 700. When we opened the package containing the eggshell cup[s] and saucers, which were ornamented with a golden dragon, there were only eleven, so Father had to go ashore again for the twelfth, which had probably been left out intentionally.

We started away from Nagasaki about 7 A.M., Saturday, January 13th. The mountains had a light coat of snow when [and] a cold wind was blowing. The sea was quite choppy. Monday, January 22: We crossed the 180th Meridian and took up a day, so had two Mondays. We had showers of rain every day. On Friday, January 26, we arrived at Honolulu at 11 A.M.

FANNY DUNBAR CORBUSIER   We ate luncheon ashore, drove about the city and made a few calls, among them, one on Mrs. and Brigadier General Davis, Retired, and the daughter.[11] The Hawaiian brass band gave a farewell concert on the wharf and ended with "Auld Lang Syne" as we steamed away at 9 A.M. on the 27th.

CHAPTER TWENTY-EIGHT

"Home, Sweet Home"

UNITED STATES, FEBRUARY 1906–JUNE 1908

ABOUT 6:30 A.M. SUNDAY, FEBRUARY 4, the band awakened us by marching about the transport, playing, "Home Sweet Home," as we entered the Golden Gate. The tug *Slocum* came out for the Second Cavalry and [the] sick, and Frank and Ida, who were up from Monterey, came out to meet us and had luncheon. After that we went to the wharf and waited until our baggage came shore and was examined by the Custom[s] officers. Then we went to the Occidental Hotel, Room 38, which Frank had reserved for us. From Zamboanga to Manila [it was] 591 miles, thence to Nagasaki 1,600, there to Honolulu 4,000, and then to San Francisco 2,100, totaling 8,291 miles.

On Saturday, February the 10, Father and I went to Monterey, leaving [at] 3 P.M., arriving at 8 P.M. Phil met us and took us up to his quarters in the Presidio of Monterey to which Ida returned on the 6th. . . .[1] We remained until the 17th and there was rain nearly every day, but we enjoyed the drives among the beautiful groves of pine and live oaks.

We were at the Occidental in San Francisco until the 19th. Frank was living in the Buchanan apartments, and we dined with him on the 18th. We left on the Atchison, Topeka and Santa Fe Railroad Monday the 19th, reached Williams at noon the 20th, where we changed to a train for the Grand Canyon. Here we had rooms at the Hotel El Tovar. We saw the cañon from different points, at different hours of the day and night, when there was mist and a little snow falling, and when the sun shone brightly, every view too grand for description. We left on the 22nd, arrived in St. Louis on the 24th, and went to the Southern Hotel. We left there 9 P.M. on the 25th and went to Battle Creek, Michigan, via Chicago, where we arrived about noon, Monday, February 26. Harold met us and took us to the Shepard's home, 32 Chestnut Street, where Louise and Frances had been since last June while he was doing special medical and surgical work in New York.

We left Battle Creek March 6th and arrived in Elmira at noon of the 7th, where Will met us and we went to Mother's. She was awaiting our arrival sitting in a chair, as she remained in bed most of the time. Father went to New York on March 26th and met Harold and Louise, who were visiting different towns to decide where to live. They, at length, fixed upon Plainfield, New Jersey, and engaged a house, 921 Watchung Avenue. Father then went to Washington April 15, 1906, and on the night of the 17th wrote to San Francisco to have our household goods shipped to Vancouver Barracks.

Father had received telegraphic orders while in San Francisco, assigning him to duty as Chief Surgeon of the Department of the Columbia at Vancouver Barracks, Washington, and was granted a leave from February 10th until May 8th.

On the morning of April 18th he heard of the earthquake and the great fire following it in San Francisco.[2] We were at first very much concerned about the safety of Frank, from whom we didn't hear for three days, then a telegram came a little after midnight of the 21st, saying that he was safe. Our personal property was still in the Medical Supply Depot, 655 Mission Street, when the fire swept everything before, and in a few minutes after it started, we had lost a collection and accumulations of thirty-seven years. Our beautifully carved Filipino seashells, our collection of Moro brass, Spanish, Filipino and Moro arms, clothes, records, books, among them three old Bibles, oil paintings, daguer[r]eotypes, photographs, and Father's valuable notes that he had made for many years concerning the North American Indians and which he intended to work up after he was retired, all gone. He deposited the little money he received for insurance in the California Safe Deposit and Trust Company, which he lost with other money amounting to at least $2,500.00 more when the company was wrecked.[3]

After Mother had improved very much and was able once a day to walk about the rooms, I visited Harold and Louise at Plainfield on May the 4th. On May the 11th I went to Amite; Father left Elmira May the 3rd for Vancouver Barracks, where he reported on May the 8th, [and] where he stayed with Robert L. Richards, Captain, Assistant Surgeon, for a while.

I joined him at Vancouver Barracks, Washington, about June 23, 1906, and we took our meals with Mrs. A. N. Johnson until we could purchase everything to go to housekeeping with. The Post and headquarters were located east of the town of Vancouver upon a gentle slope on the north side of the Columbia River, 120 miles from its mouth, five miles east of the Willamette River, about ten miles from the city of Portland, Oregon, which we reached by a ferry across the river, then taking a trolley line. Here for many years was the trading station of the old Hudson Bay Company.

Our quarters were a frame building, the third from the east line of headquarters building[s]. A hallway ran from front to rear, on each side of which were two rooms of good size, and a stairway led to a hall above, which divided rooms of the same size of those below. Both hallways led back to an L in which there were on the first floor the kitchen, laundry, and another room; and upstairs, three bedrooms. We had three bathrooms and a fine large cellar in which there was a hot air furnace. We could also heat nearly all the rooms by means of fireplaces.

There was a large lawn in front, and on each side an evergreen hedge. We had beds of jonquils and narcissus at the front and sides of the house and beds of roses on the lawn. We had many cherry and plum trees and some blackberry vines. A driveway separated the front enclosure from a garden in the rear, in which there was an apple tree and more plums. Back of this again was another enclosure in which there was a stable and a cowshed, which were shaded by three very large fir trees.

Brigadier General Stephen P. Jocelyn was in command of the Department and was succeeded by Brigadier General Constant Williams, whose [who] was followed by Major General Adolphus K. Greely.[4] After him came Brigadier General Daniel H. Brush. Major William H. Sage was the Adjutant General; Lieutenant Colonel Samuel R. Jones, Quartermaster; Lieutenant Colonel George B. Davis, Commissary; and Captain J. J.

Bradley, Fourteenth Infantry, Judge Advocate. There were at the Post, Lieutenant Colonel Alexander B. Dyer, Artillery Corps; Lieutenant Colonel James A. Irons, Fourteenth Infantry; Major Harry T. Hawthorne, Artillery Corps; Captain Charles H. Martin, Fourteenth Infantry, Quartermaster; Captain Henry C. Cabell, Fourteenth Infantry; Captains Edward F. McGlachlin, LeRoy S. Lyon, and George L. Irwin of the Field Artillery. Most of these officers were married. The Surgeons were Major William D. Crosby, Major Alex N. Stark; Captains Charles E. B. Flagg, Herbert G. Shaw, Robert L. Richards; Acting Assistant Surgeons W. E. Case and M. A. Hays; Dental Surgeons F. C. Winnery and Alden Carpenter.[5] Major W. P. Burnham was Chief of Staff for a time, and at the Post [were] First Lieutenant Arthur M. Furgeson and Second Lieutenant George W. Cocheau.

My first cook was a Chinaman, Lee Don, and we had a maid, Myrtle Staley, whom Lee called my Jew girl, as she was a Seventh Day Adventist and went to church on Saturday. And later we had Mrs. Rosa Kaake and her boy Charles and a Japanese university student, Misao Mayejima, from March 15, 1907, whom we paid $30.00 a month.

Father was on duty as Chief Surgeon at Camp Tacoma, American Lake, Washington, from August 1 to September 15, 1906, and Phil came up from Monterey to go to the same camp and brought Ida and Phyllis to stay with us while he was there. In 1906, Father planted a fine garden, which produced more vegetables than we could eat, so I had many to give to my neighbors. In the fall we dug sixteen bushels of potatoes, although we had been using them right along. Father went to Alaska June 23rd and returned September 3, 1907. I accompanied him as far as Seattle, where we were at the Hotel Savoy for two days, and then I returned. While gone he visited Liscum, Seward, Egbert, Gilbon [Gibbon], St. Michael, and Davis.[6]

Miss Ida Teed visited me while he was gone. After his return, Mrs. [Frances] DeLong and Daisy, on their way home from visiting Claude and Belle at Tanana, Alaska, where Father had seen them, visited me. In October and November 1906, I had a severe attack of pneumonia and was quite low for some days, and Frank came up from San Francisco to see me. His presence cheered me very much, but I was a long time regaining my strength.

Father had had an attack of the grippe in January 1908, which left him with weak digestion, and at length he had so much pain and burning that the surgeon thought he had cancer of the stomach, but he did not believe this. His weight fell to 128. So on March 9th, he requested to be ordered home to await retirement in order that he might go to Rochester, Minnesota, to consult W. J. and C. H. Mayo.[7] We left March 14th and arrived in St. Paul March 17th, where Major Henry C. Cabell and Captain Eldred D. Warfield met us and drove us to the Major's house and [we] remained until 4:10 P.M. . . . [We] arrived in Rochester 9:25 P.M., where we went to the Cook House. The next day Father was examined by Doctors Gunther and Christopher Graham and, the day after, had a test breakfast at Saint Mary's Hospital. He had been using a lavage tube to wash out his stomach and was already feeling better. It was found that there was an excess of hydrochloric acid, and under the remedies prescribed, he improved very much.

We remained until March 31st, and then went to Lexington, Kentucky, where Phil met us and took us to the State University, where he was Professor of Military Science and Tactics and where Ida and Phyllis were awaiting us.[8] We remained until the 18th and then went to Plainfield, New Jersey, arriving on the 19th, 5:45 P.M., where Hal met us and drove us to his home, where we found they were getting ready to move to 612 Park Avenue. Father was retired from active service April 10th, 1908, having reached the statutory age of sixty-four years.

We remained here until April 23 and then went to Bermuda on the steamer *Bermudian*, Captain P. J. Frazer. We landed at Hamilton and drove four miles to Hotel Frascati at the Flatts, Smith Parish, where we remained until June 10, 1908, and then returned to the United States and Plainfield, New Jersey, both of us in good health.[9]

CHAPTER TWENTY-NINE

"And Looked Out at the Moon and Stars"

ADDENDA BY WILLIAM HENRY CORBUSIER, JUNE 1908–FEBRUARY 1918

I HAD OUR DARLING'S RECOLLECTIONS typewritten in 1914. She then began to amend them and continued to do so from time to time until the exertion of writing became so laborious that she had to stop and reserve her strength to write to her children. She had by this time come to our return from Bermuda the first time and had in effect accomplished what she had set out to do—written her recollections of her life in the Army.

After our return from Bermuda, we visited one son after another, and while en route to the distant ones, and often between times, left the main lines of travel to drive in a buggy, automobile, or sail in a boat to enjoy the beautiful woods, mountains, streams, and to go to the seashore. The climate of Bermuda agreed with us so well, and we made so many warm friends there, that we spent the spring of 1909 and winters and springs of 1910 and 1913 in the beautiful islands. Then too, they had been the home of many of my ancestors on my father's side, from whom the Outerbridges, Trotts, Penistons, Tuckers, and others were descended, and the old records were full of interesting matter concerning them.[1]

We were in Plainfield, New Jersey, a part of the summer of 1908, in which year on August 10th, Barbara Chaffin Corbusier was born.[2] We were there again in the summer and fall of 1909, the winter of 1911, 1912, and 1913 and part of the summer and fall of 1914. Harold gave us frequent drives in his automobile, and often we took our luncheon along and ate it in the woods. While there in November and December 1913, "Little Mother," as the boys all now called her to distinguish her from the mothers of their wives, who were all large, had an attack of bronchitis. We went to Osceola, New York, for trout fishing in July 1908 and thence to Elmira, where my beloved mother had pleurisy and bronchitis and [had] died August 11, 1907, at her home, 154 Washington Street.

In the latter part of August we drove through Yellowstone Park and visited Portland, Oregon, and many other places. We spent the winter 1908 and 1909 in Lexington, Kentucky, with Philip and family. William Henry Corbusier II was born in Louisville, on July 14, 1909.[3] In the summer of 1910 we were at Nirvana Lodge on Indian Lake near Sabael, New York, where Louise and children and Ida and her children also were. We were at the wedding of Frank and Lois in San Francisco, December 15, 1910, as were Claude and Belle, and they had for a month a bungalow at San Anselmo on a southwest slope of a beautiful wooded hill. We were staying with Claude and Belle in Berkeley at this time, and on Christmas morning after the tree was lighted and we had had breakfast, we all went over to Frank's and had dinner with him and Lois. Then their Christmas tree was lighted and presents distributed. This was the first time Frank had entertained any of his family in his own home.

Mother and I remained with Frank and Lois, but Claude and family returned home to come over again on January 1st, and on the 2nd, we all went out for an all-day drive through the Redwoods. Ellen Dunbar Corbusier was born May 16, 1911, at Reading, Pennsylvania.[4]

Phil and family sailed for the Philippines again February 6, 1911, on the transport *Sheridan* and before they left had dinner with us at Claude's home in Berkeley, and it was a very happy reunion, as Frank and Lois were also there. We did not all meet again until Phil and family returned on the *Thomas*, February 12, 1914, when on the 14th of that month we all dined with Frank and Lois. On March 8th, we had a picnic and spent the day at Winship Park, Marin County.

June 19, 1911: We left Berkeley and went to the Yosemite Valley, California, and afterward to Grant's Pass, Oregon, and [in] August 1911 [we] crossed the continent over the Canadian Pacific Railroad, leaving Victoria on the 4th and stopping on the way at Sicamous, Glacier, Field, and Banff. From Toronto [we] went to Montreal by water and there took the steamer *Lake Manitoba* to Liverpool, England. We visited Chester, Conway, Carnovan, Warwick, Stratford-on-Avon, Oxford, London, Liege, Brussels, and at Antwerp on November 4, [we] took the steamer *Lapland* to New York. We were in New Brunswick, New Jersey, with Will and family from June 7, 1912, to January 8, 1913.

"Little Mother" was 75 years old on May 15, 1913, and was at her best. She had her birthday dinner with Harold, Louise, Mr. and Mrs. Shepard, and the children at 612 Park Avenue, Plainfield, New Jersey. Frances called her "Little Gana," and me, "Ganka Kyrnel."

. . . On June 2, 1913, we were in Leonardtown, Maryland, where we found the wills of Joseph, William, and John Dunbar, Mother's first, second, and third great-grandfathers, and afterward in Annapolis, Maryland, we found records of other ancestors of Mother.[5] In October, we began dividing our household effects among the children and sent the last away in January 1914. In December 1913 Mother had another attack of bronchitis. We were with Frank and Lois in Alameda, California, January 15 to April 15, 1914, and on February 12, Phil and family arrived from the Philippines on the transport *Thomas*.

We arrived at the San Ysidro Ranch April 16, 1914, near the Santa Ynez Mountains, overlooking Montecito and having a beautiful outlook. In front of our cottage of three rooms and a bath there were orange, lemon, loquat, guava, and other trees and back of it was the boulder filled creek. Here we drove about in a buggy. On April 30th we started east. We stopped at Fort Sam Houston, San Antonio, Texas, to see Phil and family a few days. We were in Amite, Louisiana, May the 20th to visit Maud and her family until June 5th, and in Laurel, Mississippi, June 8th to the 15th to visit May and her family.

We went west again in 1915 and were with Phil January 18 to May 10, 1915, at Fort Sam Houston, where we met many old friends. From there we went to Los Angeles for six weeks, and from June 15 to the 25th we were at the Exposition in San Diego. Then [we] took in the San Francisco Exposition July 25th to August the 4th, stopping en route at Arrowhead

Springs, California, June 25 to July 6th. We were at the Hunting Tower Inn, near Dingman's Ferry, Pennsylvania, Frances S[hepard] with us, during the summer of 1914, and then visited Will in Elmira, New York.

We were in Alameda again August 4, and here, during an epidemic of the grippe, Mother contracted the disease and from about November 15, 1915 to January 29, 1916, was unable to leave her room. On the latter date we took her in an automobile to Saratoga Inn, Saratoga, California, fifty miles south, where amid the beautiful surroundings she regained her strength. Claude, Belle, Frances, Francis, and Lois made us weekend visits, and we drove out on all of the roads and as far as the big trees near Santa Cruz. In March the fruit trees began to blossom, and we drove for miles among the orchards. On the 14th there was the Poppy Festival and on the 18th, Blossom Day.

On April 30th we went to San Francisco and remained until May 13th, when we left to go to Albuquerque, New Mexico, to visit Mrs. Leoline Clarke and her son Octave Besancon Clarke at Virginia Ranch. Mother and Mrs. Clarke were girls in New Orleans and very old friends but had not met for years. We made many drives with them; had dinner one day at the Pueblo of Isleta, and spent another day at the Coyote Mineral Springs.

From there we proceeded to Fort Riley, Kansas, and arrived June 2, where Phyllis and William Henry II were in [the] charge of a maid—Ida having gone east with a sick friend, and Philip was away purchasing horses and mules for the government. After leaving there we met Ida and Philip in Kansas City June 11, and thence went to Plainfield, New Jersey, to remain until September 28. We attended the meeting of the New York Historical Association in Cooperstown, New York, stopping en route at Newburgh, New York. On October 11, we left to go to Will's in Elmira, where we remained until Dec. 8th, on which date we again went to Plainfield.

I was afraid the winter would be too cold for Mother, so we started for Miami, Florida, January 6, 1917, and arrived there on the 8th. For about six weeks we enjoyed side trips and automobile drives, and then the weather became so hot and Mother began to fail. We therefore left there on March 5th to return north by easy stages.

We were at Hobe Sound until the house closed on the 12th and then went to Daytona. Here the air was too humid and we tried Saint Augustine. As Mother did not improve, we tried Jacksonville, where Father's cousin Henrietta A. Rowsey was living with her daughter Etta, and her son-in-law, James Maurice von Schloenbach, but her heart beat violently, and after resting awhile, we returned to Plainfield, New Jersey, so that Harold might share the responsibility of caring for her. We arrived April 20th and took two rooms and a bathroom on the second floor of 134 Crescent Avenue, where Mother improved slowly.

She was always bright and cheerful but on May 15, 1917, was unusually so. I had congratulated her on reaching the age of 79 years, when at 8 A.M. a night telegraphic letter came from Claude, Belle, [and] Frances De Long in San Francisco with love and congratulations. At 9 A.M., letters came from Will, Mabel, and Ellen in Elmira; and at 10 A.M., letters from Phil, Ida, Phyllis, and Billy at Leon Springs. Letters came from Frank and Lois later. Her nurse, Miss Cornelia van Benschoten, dressed her, and with very little assistance she walked into our front room to sit at the window, through which she could take in the picturesque view.

About 1:30 P.M., Harold entered, bearing a large silk American flag, which he presented to Mother. Nancy followed him carrying a bouquet, which she handed to Mother, curtsied and said, "I wish you many happy returns, Little Gana." Then came Frances and Barbara carrying between them a long-handled basket filled with pink snapdragons, pink roses, and lupines, which after curtsying they presented with their best wishes. Louise came after them with a large bouquet of pink roses and an acrostic. Mrs. and Mr. [Freedom G.] Shepard came last with a bouquet of beautiful salmon-colored roses. There darling Mother sat very happy, surrounded by all of these flowers and the flag overhead while we drank her health in a glass of sherry.

About 6 A.M. on May 30th, her pulse became very rapid, her lips blue, and her breathing labored, but she rallied under treatment. After that one, she had similar attacks, and on June 1st and 2nd Harold remained with us all night. I wired to Will, and he and Ellen came on the 2nd. It made us all happy to see the sweet loving look on Mother's face as she hugged and kissed them. She had another bad attack on the 11th, but under inhalations of oxygen, her distress in breathing was relieved. She began to improve on the 17th, and by July 1 could sit up again. By August 5, she could go out in a rolling chair, but [she] had another setback on August 19; after that she became stronger.

On Monday, September 10, Philip, who had been detailed in the Quartermaster Department and was on his way to France to be in charge of the remount work, came to bid us goodbye. He sailed on the *Cedric*, October 4, and we heard of his safe arrival, probably October 19, in Liverpool.

September 28, 1917: Mother was much stronger and she wished to see our new granddaughter, Mary Haller Corbusier, who was born on July 10, 1917. I thought that a change of scene and climate would benefit her, so we had an automobile take us to Summit, New Jersey, on the Delaware, Lackawana & Western Railroad, where we boarded a train which took us to Elmira, where we arrived that night, Mother none the worse for the trip. She was very happy here with Will, Mabel, Ellen, and Mary and was sorry to leave, but the house was not steam heated and was not warm enough, so on November 12, we returned to Plainfield and came to 120 Crescent Avenue, where we had engaged two rooms, a bath, and a wash room on the first floor.

Saturday, December 8th: Claude came about 10 P.M., en route from San Francisco to France. He was a Captain and Adjutant of the First Anti-Aircraft Battalion, United States Army. He remained with us until 3:15 P.M. Sunday and then returned to Camp Merritt at Tenafly, New Jersey. He probably sailed from Hoboken, New Jersey, December 12, and we were made happy to hear that he had arrived on the other side, probably December 31st.

After he left Mother sat up a little every day until January 2, when her breathing became difficult, her pulse, weak, and her heart beat very rapidly for a time, and then she was quite comfortable again until about 4 P.M., January 6th, [when] she grew worse again and mucus collected in her throat. . . . Under treatment she improved again and slept well. She enjoyed hearing me read over her "Recollections," and we spent many happy hours reviewing the past.

On Friday, January 25th, she felt very tired, and on the 28th at 1:30 P.M. [she] had sharp pain and tenderness in the region of her heart and up the side of her neck. On the morning of the 30th [she] had some cough and nausea. I heard slight ralls [rales] low down in the left side of her chest. Her pulse was weaker and irregular. In the afternoon she was better and slept well. On Friday, February 1, she had slept well and coughed very little. Her mind was clear, but about 9 P.M. many of her words had no meaning. Her hands, feet, and body were cold; her nails, purple; and there was a rattling of mucus in her throat. I could feel no pulse for over an hour.

Oxygen gave no relief, but strychnine, digitalis, and morphia helped her, and she slept quietly from 11:30 P.M.

On Sunday, February 3, she slept much, grew worse, and then better again under morphia, 1/8th grain. The fourth: She slept well last night. We can understand only a few words that she speaks. The violent beating of her heart had probably ruptured some of the small vessels in the speech centre of her brain. She tried to express her wishes with the word, "Campha, campha," which meant, "Give me water, raise my head, wash out my mouth, etc.," but [she] could [only] answer yes or no when asked which she wanted.

Her smile was as sweet as always, and she looked supremely happy as she nestled her head in my hands and placed her arms about my neck. Harold came from Camp Greenleaf, Fort Oglethorpe, Georgia at 7:30 P.M. Mother slept by spells on the night of the 4th and on the night of the 5th until about 3 A.M. of the 6th and then became restless for a time. About 1:30 P.M. she smiled and said, "Darling boys, good wives," "Love to friends," and to Frances and Barbara, "Goodbye, Sweetheart." Once she said, "My world's gone." To Nancy, "Goodbye," and later, "My will is gone out of me." Several times she was heard to say, "Mother, May, Maud, or Claude and Frank." At 6 P.M., her pulse was very irregular, weak, and intermittent; her feet, cold; and her breathing, labored. Two hot water bottles and three pocket stoves warmed her.

At 2 A.M. on the 7th her pulse was very weak, she was perspiring, and she was apparently comatose; at 8 A.M. [she] was sleeping quietly and awoke at 5:30 P.M., spoke to us, and smiled.

Friday, February 8, 1918: Our darling rested fairly well and was conscious at 1 P.M. After that her lips became purple, her body cold, and we could feel no pulse. She passed slowly and quietly away at 8:20 P.M. in the back room on the north side, from the two windows of which she had long enjoyed the trees, shrubs, and green grass and looked out at the moon and stars. All of the family pictures were in her room where she could see them, and we kept flowers on the dresser. She watched some narcissus that Belle sent her grow and bloom. The last book she read was *The Hill-towns of France*, trying to locate Claude and Philip, although we thought they were in or near Paris.[6] The diagnosis made by Dr. Ben Hedges was myo-carditis.

Mrs. Ella Fitzpatrick, the day nurse, and Miss Cornelia van Benschoten, night nurse, couldn't have been more attentive, and Mother had grown very fond of them. On the morning of the 9th, after the embalming of her body, they dressed our darling in the beautiful grey gown that became her so well and that we all admired. The lace was well arranged about her neck, and her hair, so beautiful and white, was dressed as she had always worn it. I placed a pink carnation and some freesia from the last bouquet I brought her behind one ear and pinned a service pin bearing the three stars that I had given her to her gown over her heart.

About 3 P.M. of the 9th, the undertakers came with the casket, which they placed in the front room, and there carried her. She was taken in an auto-hearse to 612 Park Avenue, Harold's residence, where the funeral services were held at 5 P.M.

The Reverend E. Vicars Stevenson, Rector of Grace Church, officiated, and read The Order for the Burial of the Dead from *The Book of Common Prayer*, the Thirty-Ninth Psalm, and seven choir boys sang, "Oh Paradise," "Abide with Me," and "Peace, Perfect Peace," accompanied on the piano by Frederick Smith, the choirmaster. Besides the family and choir, there were twenty-eight people present. The casket rested across the southeast corner of the library and had over it a pall of smilax, white and pink carnations, violets, and orchids from Harold and family, also lavender-colored sweet peas from Claude and Belle, pink roses from Philip and Ida, pink roses and narcissus from Francis and Lois, and Easter lilies from Will and Mabel. Besides these there was a large wreath of calla lilies, white carnations, hyacinths, and violets from Captain Henry H. Scott and Mr. D. E. Victor; a large wreath of galax leaves, white carnations and violets from Mr. and Mrs. L. B. and Mr. and Mrs. M. T. Benton; and also nine or ten bunches of flowers from other friends. On the right of the outer door was a floral piece of four large bunches of violets and two-dozen white roses in smilax and fern leaves.

Our darling lay very beautiful, her head resting on a pillow of soft white chiffon and satin, with which the solid copper lining was lined. A French plate glass, beveled face-panel permitted us to look within. This copper interior was in a solid mahogany square-end casket, having handles of bronze-finished plate. On the cover was a large oval solid bronze plate made by Gorham & Company, on which were inscribed in large script darling Mother's full name and the date of her birth and death. The casket was afterward placed in a chestnut box having copper reinforced corners and handles.

Ida's train was very late, so she did not arrive until after the services. She slept in our front room that night.

We left Plainfield at 10:47 A.M., Sunday, February 10th, on the Baltimore and Ohio Railroad and arrived in Washington, D.C., where Will met us at the station. A Quartermaster hearse and a carriage took us to the Arlington National Cemetery, Fort Myers, Virginia, where we placed our darling's remains in a vault, as no burials are made on Sunday. We remained at the Ebbitt House overnight and the next morning, Monday, February 11th, buried Darling Little Mother, my beloved companion and helpmate of half a century. The Reverend Colwort K. P. Cogswell, Church of the Incarnation, read services at the grave in Lot Number 2009, Southern Division, Officers Section, assigned to me March 30, 1909, by the Quartermaster General, United States Army.

After prolonging her life with tender care and love, we honored her after death as we thought she would wish. She did not wish to be placed in a concrete case, but it hurt me to see the wet red gravel that had to be thrown into the grave. Brigadier General Anson Mills, United States Army, the only one of our friends present, took us to his home, Number Two Dupont Circle, but Harold had to return to his station on the night of the 10th and was not at the grave. Will left for home on the 11th. Louise and I returned to Plainfield on the 13th. General Mills, who lost his wife last year, helped me very much with his sympathy, and we talked about our wives. Mrs. Mills was one of Mother's dearest friends, and I read Mother's recollections of Fort Grant.[7]

I came back to 120 Crescent Avenue, and there I was alone with everything in the rooms as they were when my beloved was carried out. I had her sweet face before me, as I have it now, and the loving happy smile as she cuddled against my hands when I stroked her face. I received loving messages from the boys and their wives, all paying beautiful tributes to the memory of Darling Little Mother, also letters from relatives and a host of friends who all loved her. I wish I could have left everything in the rooms undisturbed, but that could not be, and when Ida returned from Washington on February the 16th, she, Louise, and I carried out our beloved's wishes respecting the disposal of her jewelry, clothing, etc. Emptying shelves, dressers, and bureaus, and opening trunks, packing and sending packages to their destinations was a very sad task to perform. Ida remained with me until the 25th and then returned to Schenectady, New York.

Afterword

"LITTLE MOTHER"

IN THE MONTHS PRIOR TO HER DEATH on February 8, 1918, Fanny Dunbar Corbusier reminisced about her army life. Very few nineteenth-century army officers' wives spent more time in the company of the Indian-fighting army than she. The Corbusiers' army experiences form an almost perfect bridge between the Old Army and the khaki-clad force that would develop early in the twentieth century. Together they participated in many of the momentous events from 1869 to 1908. Their affiliation with the army began with their honeymoon trip West and lasted throughout Dr. Corbusier's military career as a surgeon, for the next thirty-nine years.

Among her peers who have left diaries, memoirs, recollections, or letters, Fanny Dunbar Corbusier is unique in that she was the wife of an army surgeon. First employed as an acting assistant surgeon, or contract doctor, Dr. Corbusier was appointed in 1876 an assistant surgeon, with the rank of first lieutenant in the Medical Department. Because he was a doctor, he was attached to no particular regiment or command, and the Corbusiers interacted with more soldiers and their families than did the average officer and his spouse. Mrs. Corbusier kept meticulous records of the people with whom they served, practically all of whom can be identified using Francis B. Heitman's *Historical Register*.

Mrs. Corbusier also differed from other officers' wives because she was a daughter of the Old South and steeped in Southern sensibilities. Her loyal and gentle nature evolved from a close and loving nuclear family, of which she was the oldest child. Educated first at home and then in female academies, she grew into womanhood steeped in the dominant cultural values of her day. In looking at her behavior throughout her life one realizes that she almost perfectly mirrors the values inculcated in the Cult of True Womanhood: piety, purity, domesticity, and submissiveness.

Throughout Mrs. Corbusier's life, religion occupied a central role in her daily activity and in the lives of her children. In fact, she and the doctor first met at a church social. A lifelong adherent to the Episcopal Church, she had each of her sons baptized in that faith as soon as possible after his birth. Dr. Corbusier joined her in the religious training of their children and in participating in church activities. Much of her reading and social interactions revolved around the church, and she maintained a Christian home for her family.

Although circumstances forced her outside her domestic sphere and into the world at large, she remained chaste and above reproach when she traveled across country without an escort. Her gentle nature and innate kindness attracted true men to her cause, and she and her children always arrived at their destinations safely.

At home she developed her domestic skills into an art and provided her husband with a home appropriate to his place in the military hierarchy. Although she usually had domestic help in the form of a soldier striker or an available civilian, she developed her ability to make-do into such a fine art that she could all but "make soup from a stone." Perhaps her years of reduced circumstances and the scarcity of material goods during the Civil War and Reconstruction gave her an advantage over other officers' wives when it came to entertaining the numerous visiting officers who called at her husband's quarters. Whatever the food on the table, her surroundings were always pleasant because both she and her husband enjoyed improving their physical surroundings by planting flowers and shrubbery.

Of the four cardinal tenets of the Cult of True Womanhood, only submissiveness gave Mrs. Corbusier pause. More than other officer's wives she walked a narrow line because she had been loyal to the South. She realized that the "bloody shirt" could be waved on the domestic front as well as in the nation at large, and she kept her opinions about "the late unpleasantness" to herself. Throughout most of her married life, she acceded to her husband's wishes, submitting to his choice of a career and supporting him in his outside interests. Only when her duty as a wife collided with the needs of her sons did she waiver in her marital loyalty.

By the 1890s, when their sons' educational needs could no longer be met on distant army posts, the Corbusiers faced a dilemma they shared with all other military families: the question of whether to separate so the children could attend school. The doctor's assignment to Fort Supply in 1893 resulted in a division of the family that lasted several years, until the four oldest sons were mature enough to live apart from their parents and younger brother. Remaining behind with her sons created emotional turmoil for Mrs. Corbusier. As a mother, she had made the only choice possible; as a wife, she had deserted her post.

From his personal history, it is clear that Dr. William Henry Corbusier was a precocious youth and an overachiever. He first served as a contract doctor when he was only twenty years old, after teaching himself anatomy and assisting a local doctor. He strove to teach his sons in the same way—being intimately involved in their early childhood learning and exploring with them the natural surroundings wherever they were stationed. He insisted that they keep daily journals and become close observers of nature as well as of the different Indian tribes with which they lived throughout the West.

Dr. Corbusier set high standards of achievement not only for himself but also for every member of his family. In truth, both parents expected their sons to become productive members of society and to take advantage of the educational opportunities they struggled to provide them. However, their eldest son Claude could not accede to the wishes of his parents to follow in his father's footsteps. He left college for a life of adventure, spending time in both the Yukon and Alaska during their gold rushes at the turn of the century. Second son Harold, or Hal, his mother's favorite, fulfilled his parents' dreams by going to medical school and becoming a well-known orthopedic surgeon who rose to colonel in the Medical Reserve Corps. Third son Philip, the one who loved football more than his studies, enlisted in the army during the Spanish-American War and later became an officer with a long, successful career in the Fourteenth Cavalry.

Fourth son Frank, always prone to accidents, left his studies at Stanford along with Philip, and while he was stationed in the Philippines he contracted two severe illnesses, which almost killed him. He was never able to complete his course of study at Stanford but later entered several different careers, finally serving as a vice president of a shipbuilding company. Youngest son William, although educated at a military school, never joined the service. He helped his father with his ethnological studies, and later he honored both parents by using their memoirs in *Verde to San Carlos*.

Regardless of her children's individual strengths and weaknesses, Fanny Dunbar Corbusier did everything she possibly could to help them fulfill their dreams. Because her existence centered on her family, Mrs. Corbusier was much more intimately involved in the lives of her sons than was her husband. It was natural for her to remain with them when his duty called him to remote posts. But she also loved her husband and missed him fiercely when he was away—especially when he went to Indian Territory and later to the Philippines, places whose circumstances prevented her from going. She demonstrated her love for her husband in how she reared his sons. Just as a Spartan mother, she sent her sons off to war, knowing that they would serve honorably. Had she been able, one can imagine that she would have been their camp follower.

Dr. Corbusier left few reminders of the depth of his love for his wife, but from her diary the reader learns that he sent her many presents from his remote posts and always stayed in touch through his daily journal. Although the reader has these glimpses of his feelings for his wife, Dr. Corbusier only displayed the depth of his caring when he wrote about her final illness and death. She had proved her devotion for forty-nine years, first by providing him with a home appropriate to an officer and five sturdy and well-mannered sons, and second by her personal character, which was above reproach. She had a strong foundation in her Christian faith and always strove to be a good neighbor to all she met along the way. Many times during their army life she reached out to those less fortunate and demonstrated her caring heart.

Fanny Dunbar Corbusier lived through the first decade of the twentieth century and saw all eight of her grandchildren. As a mother, she took great pride in the achievements of her sons and encouraged their individualism. So far as financial means and her abilities allowed, she supported all her sons' wants and ambitions. In addition to the successful lives of her children and grandchildren, Mrs. Corbusier's words now stand as her monument.

In her lifetime Mrs. Corbusier saw the desperate and deadly Apaches as well as other tribes conquered and removed to reservations. From her "Recollections," it is obvious that she sympathized with their loss of freedom and supported her husband in his efforts to deal fairly with those Indians in his charge. While stationed in the Philippines, she learned to place her trunk under her bed as protection from the kampilans of the Moros. She also recognized the religious fervor burning in their souls, which prevented any accommodation between them and the U.S. Army.

In sending her husband and sons off to war, Mrs. Corbusier shared the same desire of all wives and mothers—past, present, and future—who see their loved ones sent into harm's way: to do whatever is necessary to bring them home safely. Unlike some wives and mothers who patiently waited at home, she actively sought transportation to the Philippines and fiercely pursued an officer's commission for Philip. These actions, though contrary to the tenets of "true womanhood," came quite naturally to the woman lovingly known as "Little Mother."

NOTES

Introduction

1. Welter articulated this theory to explain the behavior of nineteenth-century middle-class women in "The Cult of True Womanhood," 152.

2. "The Old Army" is a term used by military historians to describe the U.S. Army as an institution throughout the nation's history from 1784 to 1898—especially in peacetime. See Coffman, *The Old Army*, 1986.

3. Cott argues that with the development of a market economy and with men leaving the homestead to work in the mill, office, or factory, work ceased to be home-centered and men moved into the marketplace. Women were left in charge of those domestic chores, such as rearing children and caring for the home, that became known as the woman's sphere. Cott, *The Bonds of Womanhood*, 61–62.

Chapter 1. "Of More than Ordinary Interest"

1. Throughout her "Recollections," Mrs. Corbusier remarked on the keepsakes and "collections of a lifetime" that they lost in San Francisco's earthquake and fires in 1906. For the extent of the devastation see Kurzman, *Diaster!* 248–249.

2. In her "Recollections," Mrs. Corbusier referred to her husband as "father." As editor, I have chosen to capitalize "Father," indicating that she is referring to her husband, Dr. Corbusier. In her diary she also called him Will or Papa.

3. Joseph Robinson worked as a printer and engraver and was proprietor of Baltimore's only circulating library. Knox, "The Longer View," 9–10.

4. George Towers Dunbar Jr. was appointed to this position, which he held for two years, in 1842, not in 1838, as stated by Mrs. Corbusier. Ibid., 22.

5. George and Caroline Robinson Dunbar had a total of five children, three of whom survived to adulthood: Fanny, May, and George III.

6. John Gross Barnard then was a captain in the Corps of Engineers, and in surveying a route across Mexico, the U.S. government was seeking a shorter transcontinental route to California. Heitman, *Historical Register*, 1:191.

7. As a young man, George Dunbar had worked for the Baltimore and Ohio Railroad as an assistant engineer, surveying its route through Maryland and Pennsylvania. Knox, "The Longer View," 7–8.

8. The Hannah More School still exists, serving the needs of emotionally disturbed teenagers. The Hannah More School, "History," website.

The first John Tolley Worthington, son of Samuel and Mary Tolley Worthington, was born September 29, 1760, at "Montmorenci," in Baltimore County, Maryland. Fanny Dunbar was related to the Worthingtons through her mother. Newman, "John Tolley Worthington," website.

9. It is evident that Fanny Dunbar's ability to survive the material scarcity of Civil War and Reconstruction prepared her for similar conditions on the post-war military frontier. Women and children throughout the South mirrored the Dunbars' reduced circumstances. See, for example, Jones, ed., *Heroines of Dixie*, 50–57.

10. Benjamin Franklin Butler "enjoys" one of the most notorious reputations among Union generals for his infamous "Woman Order," issued after his forces had captured New Orleans on May 1, 1862. The order applied a severe penalty to Southern women for "insulting" Union soldiers: "when any female shall, by word, gesture, or movement, insult or show contempt for any officer or soldier of the United States, she shall be regarded and held liable to be treated as a woman of the town plying her vocation." Hern, *When the Devil Came Down to Dixie*, 103.

11. Although Rear Admiral David G. Farragut began his assault on the Confederate forts protecting Mobile and the Confederate fleet guarding Mobile Bay on August 5, 1864, and Fort Morgan, the last major Southern fort at the entrance of Mobile Bay fell on August 22, 1864, Mobile itself did not fall into General Edward R. S. Canby's hands until its surrender on April 12, 1865. Long, *The Civil War Day by Day*, 551–559, 673.

12. Buck Dunbar's artillery battery was with General John Bell Hood's corps on the right at the battle of New Hope Church. Three thousand Confederates were lost in this battle, but General William T. Sherman's progress toward Atlanta was temporarily stalled. Sherman, "The Grand Strategy of the Last Year of the War."

13. Dr. Corbusier had completed his medical education at Bellevue and returned to the U.S. Army Medical Department on a one-year appointment as an acting assistant surgeon. For career highlights of the other officers mentioned, see Heitman, *Historical Register*, 1.

14. Perhaps because of his scientific bent, Doctor Corbusier measured and weighed all members of his family monthly. One would have hoped that love had blinded him to the minor flaw of her "slightly crooked nose."

Chapter 2. "His Pay Was $125.00 a Month and a Ration"

1. Dr. Corbusier and wife are listed among the passengers on the *Henry Chauncey* in the *New York Times*, April 22, 1869, p. 8.

2. The Rodney sisters were daughters of Henry F. Rodney of Lewes, Delaware, and spent their lives as educators.

3. Heitman, *Historical Register*, 1:964. Unless otherwise stated in a footnote, all the officers who are mentioned in the text can be found in Heitman's *Historical Register*.

4. Dr. Corbusier's paternal great-grandmother was Eleanor Catherine Sloat. "William Henry Corbusier," website.

5. For a description of the organization of the Medical Department, see Gillett, *The Army Medical Department*, 12–13.

6. The transcontinental railroad was completed on May 10, 1869.

7. Dr. Corbusier's father, William Morrison Corbusier, had left New York City on January 31, 1849, bound for California along with 157 other gold seekers. His mother, Mahala Myers Corbusier Jones, was descended from the Dutch who had originally settled New York. The couple was divorced sometime before 1854, when his mother married Henry B. Jones. *Twelfth Decennial Census*, vol. 21, sheet 7, line 60; "Ancestry of William Henry Corbusier," p. 7.

8. California is called "the Golden State" not for its gold but for its grassy hills, which have a bright gold color in the summer.

9. Captain McElroy was discharged August 29, 1870, and died December 26, 1870. Dr. George Gwyther is not listed in Heitman's *Historical Register*, so one assumes that he was a contract doctor, a category of service not included in the *Register's* first volume.

10. Frontier merchants discounted greenbacks and preferred payment in gold or silver. Resumption of pay in specie stopped this practice in 1879. Rickey, *Forty Miles a Day*, 128.

11. The word *Piute* is spelled at least three different ways in the literature: See Hopkins, *Life Among the Piutes*, and Canfield, *Sarah Winnemucca of the Northern Paiutes*. Dr. Bernard James Byrne called them Pah-Utes, as did other officers. Byrne, *A Frontier Army Surgeon*, 66.

12. Sarah Winnemucca at that time served as an interpreter for the army at Camp McDermit, later Fort McDermit. Hopkins, *Life Among the Piutes*, 92. She later became a noted leader among her people and an advocate for Indian rights.

Chapter 3. "Pi-u-je Papoosee"

1. This shelter, which the Piutes called a "karnee," was a dome-shaped hut constructed of a light wooden framework covered with sagebrush, grass, tule mats, or strips of rabbit skin. Scott, *Karnee*, 76.

Mrs. Corbusier used the terms "buck," "squaw," "Chinaman," and "negro," which today are seen as pejoratives but were then in common usage.

2. One of the Piutes' favorite foods was "tuuba," or pine nuts, for which they searched the mountains. Hittman, *Corbett Mack*, 52–53.

3. For a portrait of Sarah Winnemucca dressed in her riding habit, see William T. Corbusier, *Verde to San Carlos*, 86–87, 94.

4. William T. Corbusier intimated that his mother was Sarah Winnemucca's amanuensis, although Mrs. Corbusier did not make that claim in her "Recollections." William T. Corbusier, *Verde to San Carlos*, 94.

Sally Zanjani, in her biography of Sarah Winnemucca, accepts Mrs. Corbusier's description of Sarah and her activities while at Camp McDermit. Zanjani, *Sarah Winnemucca*, 106–107.

5. The Piutes knew this game as "natzi'saka," or shinny. Usually only women played, and the object of the game was to get the rag or puck across the opponents' goal. Scott, *Karnee*, 97–98, 153.

6. Bartlett resigned November 15, 1871, and died September 2, 1892. Heitman, *Historical Register*, 1:196.

7. In 1871 the laws in most states forbade the intermarriage of whites and people of color.

8. Bartlett's abuse of alcohol was the reason he left the army. William T. Corbusier stated that his mother taught Bartlett to cook for the officers' mess after he had been cashiered from the army. It is hard to believe, however, that the Corbusiers would have aided someone who was so irresponsible when under the influence of alcohol and had almost caused an Indian uprising. William T. Corbusier, *Verde to San Carlos*, 95.

9. Chief Winnemucca did not approve of Sarah's marriage to Bartlett and was estranged from her for over two years. Canfield, *Sarah Winnemucca*, 76, 79.

10. Winnemucca seems to have been universally liked by members of the army and their families—at least after he had been confined to a reservation. Ibid., 56, 58.

11. Camp Winfield Scott, Camp Three Forks, Owyee River, and Fort McDermit are described in Billings, *Circular Number Four*, 428, 454, 453–454, respectively. For a description of Camp C. F. Smith in Oregon, see Prucha, *Guide to the Military Posts*, 64. Dr. William H. Corbusier and Dr. George Gwyther, both acting assistant surgeons in 1869, co-authored the entry in *Circular Number Four* for Fort McDermit.

12. Sutlers were merchants or traders who had a business arrangement with the commanding officer of a regiment and furnished members of the regiment with articles of food and drink that were not part of their daily ration. General Orders No. 6 of 1867 directed that the army would terminate the warrants of all sutlers on July 1, 1867. For the evolution of the institution from sutler to post trader, see Delo, *Peddlers and Post Traders*, 141.

13. "Grandmother" was Mrs. Mahala Jones, Dr. Corbusier's mother.

14. In the fall of 1868, while marching with troops of the Seventh Cavalry to Washita in Indian Territory, Lieutenant Colonel George Armstrong Custer was amused by the hunting prowess of his staghounds, Maida and Blucher, who chased down and killed a wolf. Custer, *Following the Guidon*, 16.

15. For more information about the military career of Camillo Casatti Cadmus Carr, see Carr, *A Cavalryman in Indian Country*, 15–48. Grant was a native of Canada whose proper name was Alexander Grant Skene. Heitman, *Historical Register*, 1:470.

16. Colonel Roger Jones would come to the assistance of the Corbusiers on several occasions before his death on January 26, 1889. Heitman, *Historical Register*, 1:582.

17. Thomas Thornburg became a major in the Fourth Infantry on May 23, 1878, instead of October 20, 1876, as Mrs. Corbusier stated. Ibid., 959.

18. Captain Horse befriended the Corbusiers and, according to William T., gave infant Claude a lynx skin robe. William T. Corbusier, *Verde to San Carlos*, 105.

19. Mrs. Theller had been previously married to a Mr. Butler and in 1854 had been on the same ship as Dr. Corbusier and his father when they went to California. Mrs. Theller waited for two weeks for First Lieutenant Theller's body to be found and buried, saying, "Oh, my poor Ned, lying there with his face blackening in the sun." William Henry Corbusier (hereafter WHC), "Memoirs," 20; FitzGerald, *An Army Doctor's Wife*, 274.

20. Dr. E. Colmache, another acting assistant surgeon, or contract doctor, wrote the entry for Camp Three Forks in Billings, *Circular Number Four*, 428–429.

21. Fenians were Irish and Irish American militants dedicated to the end of English rule in Ireland.

22. As a "soldier of fortune," Coppinger had served during the Civil War as one of three aides to General Sheridan. The other two were Myles Keogh, who would die at the Battle of the Little Big Horn in 1876, and Major Joseph O'Keeffe, who later died of wounds he received in the Battle of Five Forks, April 1, 1865. Heitman, *Historical Register*, 1;327, 750; Connell, *Son of the Morning Star*, 291–293.

23. Reading between the lines, it seems that Mrs. Corbusier had suffered a miscarriage.

24. I have found no other record of an Indian woman serving as a wet nurse to an officer's child, although young Mary Ellen Marcy was carried on her Oneida Indian nurse's back for several months during her infancy. Hollon, *Beyond the Cross Timbers*, 21.

25. Receiving five to ten dollars extra per month influenced many soldiers to serve their officers' families during their off-duty hours. Stallard, *Glittering Misery*, 29; Rickey, *Forty Miles a Day*, 111–112.

26. "Pi-u-je papoosee" is a Piute phrase meaning "cunning, happy, or sweet baby." William T. Corbusier, *Verde to San Carlos*, 105.

27. A delightful volume devoted to the celebration of Christmas in the frontier army is Cox-Paul and Wengert, *A Frontier Army Christmas*. See especially pages 97–101 for Kate Gibson's description of the impromptu Christmas she prepared for some Indian youngsters at Fort Abraham Lincoln in 1875.

Chapter 4. "Dry Salted Codfish and a Glass of Champagne"

1. A commanding officer could withhold transportation from a subordinate for any number of reasons, as Captain Wagner first attempted to do in this

instance. For a picture of an army ambulance, see Karolevitz, *Doctors of the Old West*, 33. On page 32 of this source, Dr. Corbusier is pictured along with other officers and their dogs at Fort Grant in 1886.

2. Grace and Trinity Churches were the two most prominent Episcopal churches of the day in San Francisco. Reinhardt, *Out West on the Overland Train*, 174.

3. Robert Woodward, proprietor of What Cheer House, had developed Woodward's Gardens on his private estate for his own pleasure, but in the late 1860s he opened them to the public. Cost of admission was twenty-five cents each per day, and the gardens contained a wild animal park as well as food pavilions. Reinhardt, *Out West on the Overland Train*, 174–178, 205.

4. Since Doctors Benjamin and Davis are not mentioned in Heitman, it is assumed that they were both contract surgeons.

5. As will be seen, Mrs. Corbusier was pregnant with her second child.

6. "Mark twain" is a measurement of two fathoms or twelve feet. Samuel L. Clemens adopted the term as his nom de plume in 1863.

7. For another description of how Captain Jack Mellon navigated the Colorado River in the 1870s, see Summerhayes, *Vanished Arizona*, 52.

8. Summerhayes called Captain Mellon, master of the Gila, the most famous pilot on the Colorado, where he sailed until 1907. Summerhayes, *Vanished Arizona*, 52, 308–309.

9. In a humorous entry on Fort Yuma, Assistant Surgeon J. V. Lauderdale wrote, "It is impossible to find a more uninviting spot for a residence than this small promontory of decomposing trachyte." Billings, *Circular Number Four*, 479. The town of Ehrenberg was named for Herman Ehrenberg, who formed a partnership with Charles Poston and began mining silver on a large scale near Tubac, Arizona, in 1856. Hollon, *The Southwest Old and New*, 190; Lamar, *The Far Southwest*, 418–419, 421.

10. Dr. Rose served as an assistant surgeon at Fort Yuma from 1872 to 1874. Quebbeman, *Medicine in Territorial Arizona*, 367.

11. During the 1860s, Polish immigrants Michael and Joseph Goldwater joined Bernard Cohn in operating a store in the gold rush town of La Paz on the Colorado River. In 1867 the Goldwaters bought out Cohn and moved their store six miles downstream to Ehrenberg. Senator Barry M. Goldwater was a grandson of Michael Goldwater. Goldwater and Casserly, *Goldwater*, 53–58.

12. Opuntia is the prickly pear cactus, and cochineal bugs were valued for use in coloring foodstuffs.

13. At that time, Greely was a second lieutenant in the Fifth Cavalry. In the course of a long career, he would become the chief signal officer in the army, introducing the use of radio, automobiles, and airplanes. In 1881 he also led a disastrous Artic expedition from which only six out of twenty-five persons survived. He was in charge of the army's relief efforts after the earthquake and fire in San Francisco in 1906. Heitman, *Historical Register*, 1:473; Kurzman, *Disaster!* 74, 237.

14. Mrs. Corbusier was in the late stages of pregnancy with her second son, Harold Dunbar Corbusier.

Chapter 5. *"Making Soup from a Stone"*

1. The Corbusiers originally had been ordered to Prescott but were diverted with different orders while en route. For the military records of Henton and Trout see Heitman, *Historical Register*, 1:525 and 971, respectively.

2. Mrs. Corbusier had not yet delivered her son, Harold.

3. Dr. Josephus Williams was agent at Camp Verde Reservation, 1871–1873. Quebbeman, *Medicine in Territorial Arizona*, 379.

4. According to the story as told by William T. Corbusier, a tramp appeared at a woman's house begging for cobblestone soup. When she asked what cobblestone soup was, he selected several cobblestones from the backyard and helped her assemble the usual ingredients for making soup. The woman then wanted to know when the cobblestones would be added and he answered that they would not be necessary and threw them back into the yard. William T. Corbusier, *Verde to San Carlos*, 114.

5. The watercress is still growing in the stream at Camp Date Creek, according to Nancy Corbusier Knox, who visited the site with Bill W. Smith in 1997. Bill W. Smith, "Camp Date Creek, Arizona," personal e-mail message to editor (May 1, 2001).

6. Harold Dunbar Corbusier was the only son to follow in his father's profession, becoming a noted orthopedic surgeon.

7. That an officer's wife would ignore social conventions and nurse the child of the laundress who was helping her recover from childbirth runs contrary to the findings of a recent study by Michele Nacy. Nacy, *Members of the Regiment*, 56.

8. Assistant Surgeons O'Reilly and Smart described the climate at Camp Date Creek as hot and dry, with temperature extremes between $21°F$ and $108°F$. Billings, *Circular Number Four*, 475–476.

9. For a description of this phenomenon see Corliss, "Ball Lightning Studies," website.

10. Price compiled *Across the Continent with the Fifth Cavalry*, published in 1883.

11. Dr. Corbusier described the Apache Yumas as Western Yavapais, who along with other Yavapais were forced onto the Camp Verde Reservation in 1871. In 1875 they were removed to San Carlos, but their descendants returned to Camp Verde in 1909. For an account of General George Crook's attempted arrest of Ochicama, see Thrapp, *Al Sieber*, 97–99.

12. The epizootic Mrs. Corbusier referred to was a horse disease that could also be contracted by humans. The disease had spread across the nation, forcing cavalrymen in Arizona Territory to abandon their animals and pack their blankets and rations on their own backs. Bourke, *On the Border with Crook*, 208.

13. Strange as it may seem, the efficacy of this method is confirmed by the fact that chicken eggs require fairly high humidity (55 to 90 percent) to hatch. At Fort Yuma, Assistant Surgeon J. V. Lauderdale wrote that "eggs that have been on hand for a few weeks, lose their watery contents by evaporation; the remainder is thick and tough; this has probably led to the story that our hens lay hardboiled eggs." Billings, *Circular Number Four*, 480; Boyd, *Cavalry Life*, 107. The only explanation I could find for the chickens' walking on their elbows was that they might have been injured by other chickens stepping on them.

14. Mrs. Crook was Mary Tapscott Dailey, married to General George Crook.

15. Carrie Wilkins and her older sister, Ella, were the "daughters" of the Eighth Infantry and beloved by all who met them. Biddle, *Reminiscences of a Soldier's Wife*, 166. *The Colonel's Daughter* was a frontier romance written by Charles King.

16. Brevet Major General George Crook was promoted to the rank of brigadier general on October 29, 1873, and to major general on April 6, 1888. Heitman, *Historical Register*, 1:340. Crook's aide, Lieutenant John Gregory Bourke, would later gain worldwide acclaim for his ethnological studies of various tribes and his works dealing with the military exploits of Crook and his commands. His volume *On the Border with Crook* covers both of Crook's campaigns against the Apaches of Arizona. For a biography of Bourke, see Porter, Paper Medicine Man.

17. Mrs. Hester Dana was the wife of Major James J. Dana, chief quartermaster of the Arizona Department in 1873. Altshuler, *Cavalry Yellow and Infantry Blue*, 92.

18. Captain Porter, after a seven-year courtship, married Carrie Wilkins in 1879. Altshuler, *Cavalry Yellow and Infantry Blue*, 266.

19. A felon is an infection, sometimes serious, that develops on the fingertip.

20. Stephen H. Tyng Jr. had been rector of the Church of the Holy Trinity in New York City. After 1881 he was the manager of an insurance company in Paris. Mrs. Corbusier was probably referring to his father, Stephen H. Tyng Sr., who was rector of St. George's Church in New York from 1844 to 1885. Herringshaw, *Encyclopedia of American Biography*, 951.

Chapter 6. "I Felt Like the Lady in the Circus"

1. Mrs. Corbusier was probably referring to Tiburcio Vasquez, who at that time was the most notorious outlaw in California. Robinson, "Tiburcio Vasquez in Southern California," website.

2. For a description of ranch stage stations available to frontier travelers, for the most part far inferior to the one Mrs. Corbusier describes, see Winther, *The Transportation Frontier*, 68.

3. That Mrs. Corbusier made the trip in that length of time and with so little sleep explains her total exhaustion. Although it is almost impossible to believe that she made the journey from Ehrenberg to Los Angeles in sixty hours, Second

Lieutenant O. L. Hein made a journey of 300 miles in thirty hours during the summer of 1873. Hein, *Memories of Long Ago*, 96.

4. A famous early Los Angeles hotel, the Bella Union was described by Horace Bell in 1852 as a "flat-roofed adobe" with "pigeon-holes" or "dog-kennels" serving as rooms. A steam whistle mounted on the roof called diners to the tables at mealtime. Van Orman, *A Room for the Night*, 33–34.

5. Los Angeles was connected with San Francisco by rail on January 12, 1883, when the Southern Pacific completed its line from San Francisco to New Orleans. Ibid., 102.

6. At that time Wilmington was the seaport for Los Angeles and also the location of Drum Barracks. Today Wilmington is just one of the many smaller cities that have lost their identity to greater Los Angeles. Carr, *A Cavalryman in Indian Country*, 19.

7. Starting in the 1870s, Samuel Clemens spent his summers in Elmira, New York, at Quarry Farm. Paine, Mark Twain, website, ch. 40, par. 12.

Mark M. Pomeroy was one of the most notorious, outspoken newspaper editors of his time, even going so far as calling President Lincoln a "tyrant justly felled by an avenging hand, and who now rots in his tomb while his poisonous soul is consumed by the eternal flames of hell." He became a successful lecturer and a failed railroad promoter during the years after the Civil War. Page Smith, *Trial by Fire*, 798.

Henry Ward Beecher's only daughter to survive to adulthood was Harriet Eliza, who was named for his famous sister, Harriet. Rugoff, *The Beechers*, 507.

Chapter 7. "Sand and Cedar"

1. The military telegraph, built across Arizona, was completed during the summer of 1874 for the cost of approximately forty-six thousand dollars and the hard labor of the frontier regulars under the direction of Major J. J. Dana, Quartermaster. It was another of the unsung contributions of soldiers who were nation-building even then. Bourke, *On the Border with Crook*, 232–233; Tate, *The Frontier Army*, 68–70.

2. The owners of the railroad usually showed their gratitude to the army for all its assistance in building the railroads by allowing families of the officers to ride at half-price. Local Indians usually could ride for free—in boxcars. Biddle, *Reminiscences of a Soldier's Wife*, 210.

3. The eastern division of the Union Pacific Railroad became the Kansas Pacific in 1869, and by 1874 the Kansas Pacific had reached Las Animas, Colorado. Oliva, *Fort Hays*, 9.

4. An extenuating circumstance in this case was that Mrs. Burns had a one-month-old infant. Dr. Corbusier was responsible for getting his patient to a hospital where he could be treated as well as taking care of his family. One member of that family, Hoo-moo-thy-ah, or Mike Burns, had been left behind in the care

of Lieutenant and Mrs. Thomas, Fifth Cavalry. Heitman, *Historical Register*, 1:953. See also WHC, "Memoirs," 89; William T. Corbusier, *Verde to San Carlos*, 49, 124.

5. In the year they had been apart, Dr. Corbusier had been in the field with the Fifth Cavalry against hostile Yavapai-Apaches. Their leader, Eskiminzin, had survived the Camp Grant Massacre on April 30, 1871, and continued to fight for the independence of his people. Thrapp, *The Conquest of Apacheria*, 80–82.

6. For a description of Fort Lyon, see Billings, *Circular Number Four*, 313–316.

7. "Picket Wire" is a corruption of the French term, *le purgatoire*. Biddle, *Reminiscences of a Soldier's Wife*, 121.

8. Raton Pass, 7,765 feet in elevation and one of the most famous passes in the West, lies near the border of southeast Colorado and northeast New Mexico.

9. This is a reference, no doubt, to the mythic Seven Cities of Cibola. See Hollon, *The Southwest Old and New*, 53, 55, 438.

10. Richens Lacy Wootton, a fur trapper, Indian fighter, and Colorado pioneer, built a twenty-seven mile road and an inn at the crest of Raton Pass in 1866. He was known throughout the West as "Uncle Dick," and his inn was one of the landmarks along the Santa Fe Trail.

11. Maxwell's Ranch was a part of the Beaubien-Miranda claim, which became known as the Maxwell Land Grant after Lucien Bonaparte Maxwell, son-in-law of Carlos Beaubien. Lamar, *The Far Southwest*, 141–142.

12. Dr. Corbusier related that new mules were called "shavetails" because their handlers cut their tails short prior to shipping them west on steamers or trains as otherwise they would nibble on one another's tails when confined closely. Emmett Essin has a similar version of the origin of the term and applied it to both junior officers and new mules. William T. Corbusier, *Verde to San Carlos*, 141; Essin, *Shavetails and Bellsharps*, xvi.

13. These springs, known as *ojos calientes*, were valued for their medicinal qualities and used by the army for the relief of "rheumatism and chronic syphilitic complaints." Billings, *Circular Number Four*, 259–260.

14. Dr. Corbusier recalls this somewhat differently, writing that at Los Animas, Colorado, eight civilians joined their party, which until then had consisted of only the Corbusiers and a soldier escort. WHC, "Memoirs," 91.

15. The Pecos Indians abandoned their church in 1838 because of the raids from Plains Indians and joined their linguistic relatives then living in Jemez Pueblo. William T. Corbusier, *Verde to San Carlos*, 144. The area around the ruins is today a national historic site maintained by the National Park Service.

16. The battle, called the "Gettysburg of the West," was fought between Confederate troops from Texas led by General H. H. Sibley and Colorado Volunteers fielded by Colonel J. P. Slough, Lieutenant Colonel S. F. Tappan, and Major John M. Chivington. Because the Texans left the battlefield first, the Coloradans claimed victory. Hollon, *The Southwest Old and New*, 228–229.

17. The Corbusiers visited Fort Marcy while it was deactivated; the army reactivated it in 1875. Frazer, *Forts of the West*, 100–101.

18. San Miguel, rebuilt in 1710 on the site of the older church destroyed during the Pueblo Indian Revolt in 1680, was in a state of disrepair at the time of the Corbusiers' visit.

19. A devout Catholic himself, John Bourke also thought that the paintings at the Cathedral of San Francisco were, "with scarcely an exception, tawdry in execution, loud colors predominating, no doubt with good effect upon the minds of the Indians." Bloom, "Bourke on the Southwest," 10 (July 1935): 307.

20. The Pueblo of Santo Domingo is located between Peña Blanca and San Ysidro, closer to Peña Blanca. The Corbusiers' itinerary more probably was as follows: Peña Blanca, Santa Domingo, Santa Ana, San Ysidro, Baca Ranch, San Mateo, and then to Blue Water (Agua Azul).

21. Baca Ranch, New Mexico, lies northwest of Santa Fe and consists of ninety-five thousand acres of unique topography, the Valles Caldera.

22. This was the second Fort Wingate, established in 1868 on the previous site of Fort Fauntleroy when General William T. Sherman ordered the Navajos returned from Fort Sumner, where they were being held, back to their home country. Billings, *Circular Number Four*, 250–252.

23. The Navajo Church, or Church Rock, a prominent landmark on the Navajo Reservation, is located in the town of Church Rock right outside Gallup, New Mexico.

24. Lieutenant Colonel in the Twenty-third Infantry and grandnephew of the writer Washington Irving, Richard I. Dodge was a prolific writer and meticulous record keeper. He was often assigned such scouting and reconnaissance exercises as the one that produced the itinerary used by Dr. Corbusier. At this time he had served as commander at Forts Lyon, Larned, Dodge, and Whipple and was currently serving at Omaha Barracks, Nebraska. Wayne R. Kime, telephone conversation with editor, August 14, 2001; Dodge, *The Powder River Expedition*, 9n.

25. For a history of the Navajos' return from Bosque Redondo, see Terrell, *The Navajos*, 179–225.

26. Mrs. Corbusier is referring to bayeta, a long-wearing wool yarn used by the Navajo to make bayeta blankets. In Spanish, the term *bayeta* also refers to the red flannel cloth the Navajo unraveled to obtain the red thread used in their weaving.

27. The Hopi call this wafer-like cornbread *piki*. Goddard, *Indians of the Southwest*, 86.

28. Pueblo Indians used these prayer sticks, called *paho*, or *baho*, in supplicating the gods. They might attach a feather or some sacred meal and paint or carve sticks. The Zuni use many prayer sticks in their solstice and harvest ceremonies. Goddard, *Indians of the Southwest*, 106–109, 117.

29. In 1845 the United States Post Office Department established star mail routes to deliver mail to remote areas of the country. During the Indian Wars, danger often outweighed profit along the route. Carriker and Carriker, eds., *An Army Wife*, 74 n.

30. Mrs. Corbusier related previously that they left the miners behind at Fort Wingate, meaning that the family drove ahead of the rest of their caravan through Navajo country and then waited for them to catch up when they entered Apache country.

31. William T. Corbusier wrote that his mother had mistaken Quinriñon Cañon for Queriño Canyon and that she had remembered the itinerary out of sequence. Queriño Canyon is located between present-day Hauck and Sanders, Arizona. They would have passed through the canyon before they crossed the Little Colorado. William T. Corbusier, *Verde to San Carlos*, 150.

32. Sunset Pass, where Captain Charles King was wounded by Tonto-Apaches, is located on the Mogollon Rim where the "Colorado Chiquito goes between two high peaks." King received both arrow and bullet wounds and was rescued by Sergeant Bernard Taylor, who received the Medal of Honor for his heroics. Don Russell, *Campaigning with King*, 48–53.

33. This area is the present-day tourist attraction of Oak Creek Canyon and Sedona, Arizona.

34. This is a Western and Eastern Yavapais phrase meaning "hot water." William T. Corbusier, *Verde to San Carlos*, 244.

Chapter 8. "John Brown Had a Little Indian"

1. Dr. Williams was charged with malfeasance in office and removed. However, Dr. Corbusier and others believed that the cause of his displacement was his strong defense of his Indian clients in opposition to the Indian ring, a group of corrupt politicians, government bureaucrats, and local businessmen who attempted to profit from diverting or adulterating Indian annuities. The officer who accepted or supervised the distribution of Indian annuities could either hold contractors to the terms of their contracts or turn a blind eye to the shortcuts they might take to increase their margin of profit. Captain Bourke wrote that Dr. Williams had refused to receive a sugar annuity because it contained large boulders in each sack. Quebbeman, *Medicine in Territorial Arizona*, 379; William T. Corbusier, *Verde to San Carlos*, 281; Bourke, *On the Border with Crook*, 235.

2. Brigadier General Oliver O. Howard sent Washington Charlie and Pakota or José Coffee from Camp Date Creek to Washington, D.C., to meet President Grant in 1870. William T. Corbusier, *Verde to San Carlos*, 118. Baron Munchausen, 1720–1797, was a German cavalry officer who told outrageous tales of his adventures in Russia.

3. The Southern and Northern Tontos were two divisions of the Western Apaches that combined into one of the seven tribes of Southern Athapascans. Porter, *Paper Medicine Man*, 6–7.

4. The United States Army employed Al Sieber as a soldier and as a scout in the Southwest for twenty-five years. Thrapp, *Al Sieber*.

5. At that time an acting assistant surgeon, or contract doctor, received from twelve hundred to fifteen hundred dollars per year, plus quarters and a daily ration. Gillett, *The Army Medical Department*, 15.

6. Pasemache means "dream man" or "medicine man." William T. Corbusier, *Verde to San Carlos*, 17.

7. William T. Corbusier recalled that when his father returned to San Carlos Reservation in 1921 the Indians again sang, "John Brown Had a Little Indian" for him. William T. Corbusier, *Verde to San Carlos*, 281–282.

8. Major General Crook found great relaxation throughout his life in hunting and pursued that sport whenever he had a chance. Bourke noted that Crook killed thirty-eight wild ducks during a preliminary scout in November 1872. Bloom, "Bourke on the Southwest," 9 (October 1934): 384.

9. L. Edwin Dudley had previously served as Indian Superintendent in New Mexico. The Rio Verde Indians had just started proving that they could become self-sufficient through irrigated agriculture when the government decided to move them off their reservation to San Carlos. Thrapp, *Al Sieber*, 156, 159; Bourke, *On the Border with Crook*, 216–217.

For the Apaches' feelings toward San Carlos, see Ball, *Indeh*, 37–39. Ace Daklugie exploded in disgust at the mention of San Carlos: "San Carlos! That was the worst place in all the great territory stolen from the Apaches." Ibid., 37.

10. For details of the transfer of the Rio Verde Indians to San Carlos see WHC, "Memoirs," 93–97 and Thrapp, *Al Sieber*, 162–169. Reading Dr. Corbusier's "Memoirs," one realizes that this event was one of the significant passages in his life and he was greatly affected by the suffering of his friends.

George O. Eaton was one of the outstanding young officers then assigned to the Fifth Cavalry. It was he who, along with his men, dashed to the rescue of a wounded Charles King at Sunset Pass in November 1874. King later repaid Eaton's heroics by patterning the character of Jack Truscott in *The Colonel's Daughter* and subsequent novels after his friend.

11. Second Lieutenant Carter later wrote a history of the Sixth Cavalry, to which he transferred November 28, 1874. Carter, *From Yorktown to Santiago*.

12. Captain Cronkhite held a regular Medical Department commission as an Assistant Surgeon in 1874. The other three were contract doctors; on their careers in Arizona see Quebbeman, *Medicine in Territorial Arizona*. Dr. Day also was involved in saving the right arm, if not the life, of then First Lieutenant Charles King. King not only kept his arm but also led a long and creative life depicting the trials and triumphs of the Indian-Fighting Army. Ibid., 96–98; Don Russell, *Campaigning with King*, 48–53.

13. Mrs. Corbusier was referring to Montezuma's Castle, located at Camp Verde and built by Sinaguan people. The castle is an ancient "high-rise" cliff dwelling of at least five stories and twenty rooms.

14. Montezuma's Well is situated about fifteen miles north of Montezuma's Castle near Rimrock, Arizona. Modern measurement agrees with that described

by Mrs. Corbusier. One fact that would have interested Dr. Corbusier is that the bottom fifteen feet of the well are filled with brown mud and a "few million leeches." "Montezuma's Well," website.

15. Mrs. Corbusier was partially correct in that Apaches were less dependent upon the horse than the Plains Indians, but they certainly had horses and used them in their raids upon other Indians. After Brigadier General Crook had completed his first "grand offensive" against the Apaches, he had a "band of horses driven down from California, and took the scouts' [Wallapais] pay due them and bought horses for them, so as to get them owners of something, so as to anchor them to some fixed locality." Thrapp, *Al Sieber*, 117–118.

Chapter 9. "The Almighty Made It Last"

1. In April 1875 the Fifth Cavalry was ordered to the Department of the Missouri and Lt. Col. Eugene A. Carr assumed command of the regiment at Fort Hays, Kansas. Over the next several years, the regiment saw duty from the Canadian River in Texas to the Yellowstone River in Montana Territory. Price, *Across the Continent*, 154–155.

2. Located forty miles northwest of Prescott, Camp Wallapai, also called Camp Hualpai, was established by Major William R. Price, Eighth Cavalry, on May 9, 1869, and abandoned July 31, 1873. Frazer, *Forts of the West*, 10.

In 1874 the Hualpais had threatened to leave their agency because their agent was cheating them in their annuities. Attempting to allay their fears about the warring Apaches, General Crook promised that he would send to the Piutes of Nevada and southern Utah and extract a promise that they would send one hundred auxiliaries for service against those Apaches. Many Hualpais joined those Paiutes as scouts in the subsequent campaign. Bourke, *On the Border with Crook*, 161–164; Thrapp, *Al Sieber*, 106–107. For a clearer picture of the Hualpais and their relationship with both the Paiutes and Americans, see Casebier, *Camp Beale's Springs*, 15–24.

3. Camp Mojave, established in 1858 for the protection of the Southern Overland Route to California, was located on the east bank of the Colorado River, near the head of the Mojave Valley. In the summer it was so hot that the whole garrison lay "on the open plain, endeavoring to catch the faintest breeze." Billings, *Circular Number Four*, 467.

4. *Larrea mexicana* is the creosote bush, so it must have made a pungent, if hard bed.

5. General Crook's party had preceded them on this journey in March and April 1875, as Crook departed Arizona Territory for a new command. For a more graphic description of the Marl Springs Station, see Bloom, "Bourke on the Southwest," 10 (January 1935): 20. All these sites are also discussed in Casebier, *Camp Beale's Springs*.

6. The site for Camp Cady was occupied before the Civil War and reclaimed in 1868 but relocated about half a mile from the original site. It set on the north

bank of the Mojave River and was about equidistant between Hardyville and San Bernardino. Billings, *Circular Number Four*, 476–477.

7. Cajon Pass is located in the San Bernardino Mountains, north of the city of San Bernardino. At that time it was on the survey of the railroad from California to Arizona and New Mexico, which was completed in 1881. Bloom, "Bourke on the Southwest," 10 (January 1935): 23.

8. Dr. Corbusier had left the army after his contract expired and was attempting for the second time to set up a private practice in San Francisco. WHC, "Memoirs," 99–100.

9. The Potrero was the common grazing field for horses in San Francisco.

10. Helen Davis, who met Mahala Jones later at Fort Grant, described her as being "a bright old lady full of life and is very fond of all games of cards." Helen Davis to Alice Grierson, February 6, 1887.

Chapter 10. *"Proceed without Delay"*

1. For information concerning Fort Macon, see Billings, *Circular Number Eight*, 153.

Dr. Styer had served as a surgeon in the Ninety-ninth Pennsylvania Infantry and had been dismissed May 1, 1863. He reentered the United States Army in October 1867 and again resigned in 1878. Heitman, *Historical Register*, 1:935.

2. This was Dr. Corbusier's first appointment as an assistant surgeon in the United States Army Medical Department, and he started off his career in the regular army at the bottom of the surgeon's pay scale, without the subsidy he had received from the Indian Bureau for treating reservation Indians. Gillett, *The Army Medical Department*, 81.

3. From the similarity between the two texts, it is obvious that Mrs. Corbusier had access to *Circular Number Eight* when she wrote about Fort Macon. Billings, *Circular Number Eight*, 153.

4. General Orders 92 of 1870 outlawed the use of enlisted personnel as strikers by mandating that "it shall be unlawful for any officer to use any enlisted man as a servant in any case whatsoever." However, this order was not enforced or enforceable because many officers and their families could not obtain other servants at their remote stations. Departmental inspectors usually ignored the soldier servants in the military households they visited while on inspection tours. "General Orders 92," *Index of General Orders*, 1870, 6, Records of the Adjutant General's Office.

5. A weekly steamer also traveled between New Bern, North Carolina, and New York City. Billings, *Circular Number Eight*, 155.

Fulton Market, established as a general market in 1822, was converted late in the nineteenth century to a fish and seafood market. The Fulton Street Market was a victim of the attack on the World Trade Center on September 11, 2001, after which it was moved out of Manhattan to the Hunts Point area of the Bronx. "Markets," website.

6. It seems that Mrs. Corbusier has confused the Portuguese man-of-war with an octopus since the former defends itself with coiled stinging tentacles and does not release a cloud of black ink.

7. This was obviously the Atlantic hurricane of September 13–17, 1876, that hit Puerto Rico and North Carolina. Rappaport and Fernandez-Partagas, "The Deadliest Atlantic Tropical Cyclones," website.

8. Fort Macon was the third fort at this site, the first being Fort Dobbs, erected in 1756, and the second Fort Hampton, built during the early 1800s and washed away. Heitman, *Historical Register*, 2:506.

9. Here Mrs. Corbusier referred to the Mecklenburg Declaration, or Mecklenburg County Resolution, which was reportedly adopted by a convention of citizens in Mecklenburg County, North Carolina, in May 1775 and sent to the Second Continental Congress then meeting in Philadelphia. No original copy of the declaration has ever been found.

10. Captain John Isaac Rodgers was promoted to brigadier general on October 14, 1902. Heitman, *Historical Register*, 1:841.

11. Charleston Arsenal was situated within the corporate limits of the city, near the left bank of the Ashley River, and consisted of eleven and a half acres surrounded by a wall. The Citadel was built as a state military academy with the central portion completed in 1827 and the wings two or three years later. It was first occupied by United States troops in 1865. Billings, *Circular Number Eight*, 123, 124.

12. Other officers' wives felt that same ostracism. One can understand why it would be the strongest in Charleston since South Carolina had been especially punished at the end of the Civil War. Fellman, *Citizen Sherman*, 223–233.

13. The Chattanooga National Cemetery, built after the battles for Chattanooga in 1863, consisted of 125 acres of ground, 75 of which were enclosed by a stone wall to form the cemetery. Barracks for the soldiers were built in 1867, and officers' quarters consisted of small frame cottages. Billings, *Circular Number Eight*, 125.

14. On a clear day, from the top of Lookout Mountain, one can see parts of seven states: Tennessee, Georgia, North Carolina, South Carolina, Virginia, Kentucky, and Alabama.

15. At the time Mrs. Corbusier visited the area, Lookout Mountain Cave had been used for centuries. It housed a hospital during the Civil War. In 1905 the Southern Railway built a railroad tunnel through the edge of Lookout Mountain and closed the natural entrance to the cave. Today the location is the site of the famous Ruby Falls.

16. The economic downturn following the Panic of 1873 created a feeling of unrest among the working classes. In the middle of July 1877, railroad workers went on strike, and miners and other laborers soon followed. Appeals for the intervention of federal troops were answered with at least one-sixth of all federal troops being sent to areas where the violence was greatest; four thousand regulars

plus marines and sailors were on strike duty in six states. President Hayes turned over control of federal troops to the governors of the states in which they were deployed, thereby preventing the army from having power over its troops. Coffman, *The Old Army*, 246–251.

17. A by-product of the disputed election between Hayes and Tilden in 1876 was Congress's failure to adopt a budget before it recessed in the summer of 1877. Financiers such as Jay Cooke and Company advanced the pay of officers until a budget was passed three months later. It is ironic that the failure of Jay Cooke and Company was a major cause of the Panic of 1873.

18. Dr. Van Deman, a local contract surgeon, threw a *fête de champêtre*, which was basically an outdoor picnic and entertainment.

Chapter 11. "We Could Improvise Anything Necessary for Living the Simple Life"

1. Camp Sheridan was located in the northwest corner of the state of Nebraska, 213 miles northeast of Cheyenne, Wyoming, and 43 miles northeast of Camp Robinson. Camp Sheridan was built in 1874 to protect Spotted Tail's band of Brulé Sioux, and in winter the Minneconjous came in from the Black Hills to receive their annuities. Billings, *Circular Number Eight*, 374.

Contrary to Mrs. Corbusier's statement, the elevation of Fort Sidney was 4,326 feet above sea level, and the post was located in the Lodgepole Creek Valley, about twelve feet above the creek. Billings, *Circular Number Eight*, 375–378.

2. Camp Robinson was established at the Red Cloud Agency on March 8, 1874, as the center of control for the Indians at Red Cloud and Pine Ridge agencies. First called Camp Red Cloud Agency, the post became Camp Robinson on March 29, 1874, and was designated Fort Robinson in January 1878. Frazer, *Forts of the West*, 90.

3. The First Red Cloud Agency (1871–1873) was located near the Platte River Road and Fort Laramie. The second Red Cloud Agency (1873–1877) was situated near the confluence of the White River and Soldier Creek, nearby Fort Robinson. The third Red Cloud Agency (1877–1878) was sited on the Missouri River, and the fourth (1872–present) returned the agency to the White River northeast of both Fort Robinson and Camp Sheridan. Mrs. Corbusier was referring to the site of the second Red Cloud Agency. Olson, *Red Cloud*, see map following page 270.

4. The Spotted Tail Agency of the Brulé Sioux had been located at Camp Sheridan from 1874 to 1877. Ibid.

5. The agency had been removed to the Missouri River south of Fort Randall for the winter of 1877–1878 and then to its permanent location on the Rosebud later in 1878. Since the Corbusiers arrived in the area in November 1877, the Brulés would have just arrived at the Missouri River. Ibid.

6. These quarters at Camp Sheridan are significantly larger than those described in Billings, *Circular Number Eight*, 375.

7. Carl Schurz was then Secretary of the Interior, and Webb Hayes, son of President Hayes, was acting as his private secretary. The other members of the party were Mr. Gaullier of the *New York Times* and Count Dernhoff of the German legation. McGillycuddy, *McGillycuddy, Agent*, 144.

8. Captain Emmett Crawford seemed attracted to the children of certain brother officers and remained a steadfast friend to them as long as he lived. He had been one of the three "Guards of Honor" to young Forrestine Cooper at Ship Island, Mississippi, in 1868. Fisher, ed., "Forrestine Cooper Hooker's Notes," 16.

9. For one of several accounts of the death of Captain Crawford, see Thrapp, *Al Sieber*, 313.

10. It would seem that Louie was afflicted with premenstrual syndrome.

11. Army officers often debated this question, especially after some controversial action against Indians had drawn public outrage. For a discussion of the issue, see Utley, *Frontier Regulars*, 408–409.

Chapter 12. "It's an Army Wagon, and Painted Blue!"

1. After this removal and return, the Red Cloud Agency became Pine Ridge Agency and would be the center of the Oglala Reservation from this point onward.

2. Dr. Valentine McGillycuddy remains to this day a controversial figure, with many supporters as well as detractors. The Corbusiers and Captain John Bourke adhered to his policies and to him personally. Bourke concluded, "I could not help saying to myself that this man was carrying on his shoulders the weight of a force equal to one-third the United States Army; were he in the army, McGillycuddy would have been a major-general." Bourke, *On the Border with Crook*, 424–425.

3. During his tenure as agent at Pine Ridge, Dr. McGillycuddy was involved in a vendetta against all those whom he perceived opposed his chosen course for civilizing the Oglalas, He blamed drunkenness among the Indians on white men who lived with Indian women as their desires dictated, tiring of one so-called wife only to take another. Olson, *Red Cloud*, 276. On numerous occasions he banished individuals from the reservation, but I have found no proof that he made the "squaw men" marry their Indian wives according to Western rites.

4. According to Fools Crow, ceremonial chief of the Teton Sioux, the women "were considered owners of the home and made the final decisions regarding it and family affairs." Mails, *Fools Crow*, 16.

5. Only one denomination could be represented at each agency because it was thought that conflicting denominational teachings could confuse the Indians. Red Cloud and McGillycuddy both believed that Catholic priests best served the interests of the Sioux, but Indian Bureau regulations gave the Episcopal Church monopoly control over the souls of the Oglalas, and McGillycuddy enforced the government policy. In May 1879, he told the Catholic priest,

Fr. McCarthy, to withdraw from the reservation. McCarthy moved just south of Camp Sheridan, from whence he could minister to the troops without infringing on McGillycuddy's prerogatives at Pine Ridge. Olson, *Red Cloud,* 267; McGillycuddy, *McGillycuddy, Agent,* 105.

6. All this effort was expended to ensure that the Indians received the annuities guaranteed them by treaty. Captain Bourke remarked that on two or three occasions he had looked into the affairs of Pine Ridge and found that Dr. McGillycuddy had on hand a million pounds of flour and other parts of rations in proportion and had a perfect system of distributing and accounting for them. Bourke, *On the Border with Crook,* 424.

7. In 1879 the Indian Bureau distributed nearly three thousand head of cattle among the Sioux Agencies. The Indians took good care of their herds, rarely killing their seed stock or their increase; however, the dreadful winter of 1886–1887 wiped out most of their gains. Utley, *The Last Days,* 25.

8. Lieutenant Crawford never married and so must have particularly enjoyed joining the Corbusiers' family celebrations.

9. It was part of a captain's responsibility to his company to see that their meals were edible and that holiday fare had some extra touches. Dobak, "Licit Amusements of Enlisted Men," 39–41.

10. Established on the north fork of the Canadian River in August 1874, Camp Reno was located about two miles away from the Cheyenne and Arapaho Indian Agency. On February 21, 1876, the post was designated Fort Reno. Prucha, *Guide to the Military Posts,* 101.

11. On September 9, 1878, some three hundred fifty Northern Cheyennes slipped away from Fort Reno in a desperate attempt to return to their northern home. The number of white civilian casualties of the Cheyenne Outbreak has been disputed, with the Cheyennes being reluctant to accept responsibility for them. Little Wolf, when questioned about those casualties, stated that the Cheyennes killed no civilian until a cowboy killed one of their young men. He also noted that he had harangued his young men, "telling them not to kill citizens, but to let them alone." Grinnell, *The Fighting Cheyennes,* 413; Monnett, *We Are Going Home,* 198–205. For more on this incident, see Buecker, *Fort Robinson,* 135–136.

12. The twenty-one Cheyennes later sent to Indian Territory were first taken to Fort Leavenworth to stand trial for the depredations the Cheyennes had committed in Kansas. The case against Wild Hog and six other tribesmen was thrown out of court in October 1979. Buecker, *Fort Robinson,* 147.

13. Woman's Dress was still a scout at Fort Robinson as late as 1882. He was accused of fabricating the story that Crazy Horse intended to assassinate General Crook on September 3, 1877. The Cheyennes accused Woman's Dress of attempting to betray them and get them killed, just as he had done with Crazy Horse. Buecker, *Fort Robinson,* 145, 112; Sandoz, *Cheyenne Autumn,* 244.

14. Dr. McGillycuddy had turned Lame Johnny (Cornelious Donahue) over to a special agent of the Union Pacific Railroad named Whispering Smith. But

Lame Johnny was taken illegally from Whispering Smith and hanged by the Shotgun Brigade of Deadwood at Buffalo Gap Station on July 1, 1879. McGillycuddy, *McGillycuddy, Agent*, 130–131.

15. These were three chiefs of the Oglalas; the latter two became allies of Agent McGillycuddy in his feud with Red Cloud. Olson, *Red Cloud*, 276–277.

16. Mrs. Corbusier probably meant Long Dog rather than Red Dog, since Long Dog won the race. In 1872 Red Dog was leader of the strongest group of northern Oglalas and an important player in negotiations with the United States through the 1880s. Paul, ed., *Nebraska Indian Wars Reader*, 157; Red Dog is pictured on page 88 in Porter, *Paper Medicine Man*.

17. This incident happened on October 23, 1874, before the Corbusiers arrived at Camp Sheridan. Dr. J. J. Saville, the agent, had decided to erect a flagpole at the agency headquarters. The Indians, who associated the flag with the army, refused to have this symbol of military control flying over their reservation. Red Dog and Old-Man-Afraid-of-His-Horses interceded, helping to avert a disaster. Allen, "Red Cloud and the United States Flag"; Paul, ed., *Nebraska Indian Wars Reader*, 113–121; Buecker, *Fort Robinson*, 3, 36–37.

18. Three Bears had been one of the Sioux delegation that decided to move to the Missouri River in the winter of 1877.

19. In 1874 Two Lance was a guide between Camp Robinson and Sidney, Nebraska, and had been paid fifteen dollars for his services. Buecker, *Fort Robinson*, 74.

Chapter 13. "To Worship in Their Own Fashion"

1. Four years later, in 1883, Red Cloud held the last great Oglala Sun Dance of the nineteenth century; after that date the Sioux conducted their Sun Dance in secret. Porter, *Paper Medicine Man*, 90. Various tribes revived the Sun Dance in the twentieth century as a means of cementing tribal solidarity.

2. No Flesh was described by Captain Anson Mills, commanding officer at Camp Sheridan, as an "eager but not sincere Brulé Sioux" who tried to ingratiate himself with Mrs. Mills by drawing pictures of his heroic deeds, also known as "brag skins." Mills, *My Story*, 155, 158–159.

3. Julia McGillycuddy, whose father attended the Sun Dance in 1881, wrote that four warriors wielded axes on the tree until it trembled and that a maiden selected for her virtue and beauty delivered the final blow. McGillycuddy, *McGillycuddy, Agent*, 170.

4. Mrs. McGillycuddy reported that Edgar Beecher Bronson and Miss Alice Fletcher, an ethnologist from the Peabody Institute in Boston, joined the doctor and Lieutenant Bourke in observing the rites in 1881. (Contrary to Mrs. McGillycuddy's report, Joseph C. Porter wrote that Miss Fletcher attended the Sun Dance in 1882.) They both related that twelve rawhide lariats, along with two rawhide figures about eighteen inches long, were attached to the Sun Pole. The figures

were a male buffalo and an Indian, "naked, his upright penis proclaiming phallic worship." Miss Fletcher secured the Indian effigy for study. McGillycuddy, *McGillycuddy, Agent*, 170–175; Bronson, *Reminiscences of a Ranchman*, 236–241; Porter, *Paper Medicine Man*, 90.

5. The Sioux recognized the central role buffalo played in their existence and paid homage by including the buffalo as an integral part of their worship. For a description of the Buffalo Dance, one aspect of the Sun Dance, see Bronson, *Reminiscences of a Ranchman*, 241–244; Mooney, *The Ghost Dance*, 342–344.

6. Other informants stated that their whistles were made from eagles' wing bones, which makes sense because most Indians would not eat turkeys. McGillycuddy, *McGillycuddy, Agent*, 172; Porter, *Paper Medicine Man*, 92.

7. Mrs. McGillycuddy described the last dancer of the 1881 Sun Dance, who tried valiantly to free himself from the pole. As both the sun and his strength ebbed, a young Indian woman rushed from the crowd and added her weight to that of her champion as he lunged backward. From their combined effort, his flesh yielded and he tore free to the thunderous roar of approval from their watching tribe. McGillycuddy, *McGillycuddy, Agent*, 173.

8. See Powell, *Fourteenth Annual Report*, 1077, for a description of a tatanka, or buffalo bull.

Chapter 14. *"Thirty Miles from Water and Ten Feet to Hell"*

1. Fort Washakie, established in January 1871, was located near the present town of Fort Washakie about fifteen miles northwest of Lander on the Wind River Reservation. The fort was situated at the confluence of the Little Wind and the north fork of the Wind River and designated Fort Washakie in 1878 in honor of Chief Washakie, a Shoshone chief. Frazer, *Forts of the West*, 186–187. Acting Assistant Surgeon Grimes was a contract doctor.

2. Philip Worthington Corbusier entered the army as an enlisted man and was appointed a second lieutenant in the Ninth Cavalry on July 25, 1900. He was promoted first lieutenant on February 2, 1901, and transferred to the Fourteenth Cavalry. Heitman, *Historical Register*, 1:327.

3. Captain Babcock entered the Fifth Cavalry as a second lieutenant on January 22, 1867, and was promoted to first lieutenant on February 14, 1868. He was stationed in Arizona in 1872 at Camps Bowie and Grant and was wounded by the Tontos on June 16, 1873. Altshuler, *Cavalry Yellow and Infantry Blue*, 14–15. For the history of Fort Laramie, see Billings, *Circular Number Four*, 345–350.

4. On August 19, 1854, Brevet Second Lieutenant John L. Grattan and thirty men of Company G of the Sixth United States Infantry, along with two howitzers, went into a Sioux camp to recover a Mormon's cow. The outcome of that encounter was that the soldiers killed Chief Mat-to-i-o-way, or Conquering Bear, and that his Indians killed all the infantrymen except one who died later of his wounds. Billings, *Circular Number Four*, 347; Utley, *Frontiersmen in Blue*, 113–114.

5. Named for Brevet Lieutenant Colonel William J. Fetterman, who was killed by Red Cloud's Sioux in the Fort Phil Kearney massacre on December 21, 1866, Fort Fetterman was established in July 1867. Fort Fetterman's elevation was 5,250 feet above sea level, not 8,500 feet as stated by Mrs. Corbusier. Billings, *Circular Number Four*, 350–351.

6. Rock Creek was established as a freighting station on the Union Pacific Railroad in 1877 and was bypassed in 1900 after the Union Pacific rerouted the main line between Laramie and Medicine Bow. In 1885, scores of Chinese miners working there in the Union Pacific coalmines were massacred in a race riot, and the Chinese government requested that troops be stationed in the area. Reinhardt, *Out West on the Overland Train*, 202; Mattes, *Indians, Infants, and Infantry*, 261.

7. In a 1877 article in *Leslie's Magazine*, the author noted that two magnificent specimens of California mountain lions, tawny yellow like African lions but without manes, "snapped and growled and flung their lithe bodies against the bars with yells of impotent fury" at the Green River Station. Reinhardt, *Out West on the Overland Train*, 83.

8. A party of General William H. Ashley's men, including Jedediah Smith, Thomas Fitzpatrick, William L. Sublette, and James Clyman, "discovered" the South Pass in 1823. In 1861, sixty men located claims along Willow Creek, a northern branch of the Sweetwater about twelve miles northeast of South Pass, in a camp that developed into South Pass City. Miners' Delight grew up several miles east of South Pass City. By the late 1870s both towns were in decline. Hebard, *Washakie*, 38–39, 128, 131, 146–147; Billington, *The Far Western Frontier*, 43.

9. Camp Stambaugh, elevation 7,714 feet, was established near the Sweetwater gold mines as a subpost of Fort Bridger on June 20, 1870. The camp was located midway between Miners' Delight and Atlantic City, which was four miles east of South Pass City. Hebard, *Washakie*, 146–147; Prucha, *Guide to the Military Posts*, 109.

Chapter 15. "Heap Papoose Pretty Soon"

1. Originally named Camp Augur and then Camp Brown, in 1870 this post was moved seventeen miles to the Shoshone Agency on the Wind River Indian Reservation. On December 30, 1878, the name of the post was changed to Fort Washakie in honor of the chief of the Shoshones. When he died in 1900 he was the only full-blooded Indian to be buried with the full military honors of an army captain. Hart, *Old Forts of the Northwest*, 152.

2. As the surgeon assigned to the post, Dr. Corbusier was charged with the responsibility of keeping the commanding officer informed about the sanitary conditions of that post. The ditches brought water to the parade ground, and each officer's quarters had a privy erected at the rear. Billings, *Circular Number Eight*, 327.

3. Located sixteen miles north of Camp Brown, Bull Lake was three miles long and one-half mile wide, possessed clear, cold, sweet water and many large fish, and emptied into the Big Wind River. Billings, *Circular Number Eight*, 325. Today Bull Lake is greatly enlarged by a Bureau of Reclamation dam.

4. In 1874 Acting Assistant Surgeon Thomas G. Maghee wrote in the entry for Camp Brown, later known as Fort Washakie, that the springs were beneficial in treating rheumatic, neuralgic, syphilitic, and skin diseases. Billings, *Circular Number Eight*, 325.

5. The number one outdoor sport at Fort Washakie was big game hunting. One of those who came west in 1889 to partake of that recreation was Owen Wister, author of *The Virginian*. The commanding officer at Fort Washakie offered the tenderfoot the use of an army ambulance and the services of the post's doctor. Mattes, *Indians, Infants, and Infantry*, 260–261.

6. In this instance, both Mrs. Corbusier and Mrs. Baxter were adhering to the tenets of the Cult of True Womanhood by protesting their loss of modesty if they rode astride. On the other hand, Dr. Corbusier was choosing their safety and practicality over any loss of purity on their part.

7. Edward Drinker Cope was one of the two preeminent American vertebrate paleontologists of the late nineteenth century. The other was Othniel Charles Marsh, and between them, they "classified 136 new species of North American dinosaurs." Huntington, "The Great Feud," website.

8. Governor John W. Hoyt had previously visited the Shoshone-Arapaho Agency in 1878, trying to settle the disagreements between the two tribes. Hebard, *Washakie*, 210–214.

9. Called "Jakie" by Chief Washakie, J. K. Moore was a long-time Indian trader and sutler at Fort Washakie. In fact, Washakie thought so much of Moore that he gave the sutler the guns and saddle that President Grant had presented him. Hebard, *Washakie*, 225–226; Delo, *Peddlers and Post Traders*, 177–178.
Second Lieutenant Morgan was stationed at Fort Washakie from October 1880 to May 1882. He was impressed by Chief Washakie and called him a "White Brave," meaning one who would venture where he might be injured. Washakie served on active duty with the army until his death. Hebard, *Washakie*, 266–267.

10. Mountain fever was characterized by a remittent fever, occasionally very severe. Symptoms were headaches, "severe aching through the whole body, insomnia, furred tongue, frequent full pulse, constipation." It was treated with quinine. Billings, *Circular Number Eight*, 385.

11. Here Mrs. Corbusier pointed out once again the graft associated with the Indian Bureau. All of the people involved had ties to Michigan and to Michigan Senator Thomas W. Ferry, who was first elected as a Republican to the House of Representatives in 1865 and then to the Senate in 1871. As president pro tempore of the Senate, Ferry was the presiding officer of the Senate from December 6, 1875, to March 3, 1877, after Vice President Henry Wilson died. He presided over the impeachment of Secretary of War William Belknap and could be called a

"king-maker" in the Tilden-Hayes election crisis. See Page Smith, *Trial by Fire*, 942. It seems ironic that a senator whose own nephew was employed by an Indian agent in a questionable situation would preside at the trial of the secretary of war who was himself being tried for receiving bribes for the sale of trading posts in the Indian Territory. Fisher, ed., "Forrestine Cooper Hooker's Notes and Memoirs," 146–156.

12. The prohibition ballot in Kansas did not pass until 1880, so Mrs. Corbusier may have overstated the case in reference to the agency doctor. She is correct that under prohibition in Kansas, a citizen could obtain medicinal alcohol from a pharmacy if a doctor prescribed it, and by the mid-1880s, one could bypass doctors and get beer directly from a druggist if one had an "ailment." Higgins, "History of Brewing in Kansas," 3, 16.

13. Mrs. Corbusier is mistaken; both Friday and Black Coal were leaders of the Arapaho. Mooney, *The Ghost Dance*, 179, 256, and 318; Olson, *Red Cloud*, 248.

14. The Shoshones also held their fasting dance in June or July annually. For a description of their ritual see the explanation of Dick Washakie contained in Hebard, *Washakie*, 291–295.

15. American Horse, who had known the Corbusiers at Pine Ridge (see chapter 12), was the son of Sitting Bear of the True Oglala Band and son-in-law of Red Cloud. One of the principal chiefs of the Oglalas, he usually could be counted on as a progressive—one who sided with the federal government in its dealings with the Sioux. Hyde, *A Sioux Chronicle*, 214–219.

16. Brevet Lieutenant Colonel Julius W. Mason died two years later, on December 19, 1882. Constance Wynn Altshuler noted that he died from apoplexy, which might explain his enlarged stomach. Altshuler, *Cavalry Yellow and Infantry Blue*, 224.

Chapter 16. "The Woods Here Were a Delight to Us"

1. In 1877, Rawlins was described as having "extremely utilitarian frame houses, devoid of flowers, turf, or shrub" and being home to some six hundred souls, primarily railroad employees. Reinhardt, *Out West on the Overland Train*, 80.

2. For a description of the centennial celebration of Washington's victory at Yorktown, see *Harper's Weekly*, October 22, 1881.

3. Fort D. A. Russell was established on July 21, 1867, three miles west of Cheyenne on the north bank of Crow Creek, a branch of the South Platte, for the purpose of protecting workers on the Union Pacific Railroad and the citizens of Cheyenne. On January 1, 1930, the post was renamed for Francis E. Warren, a Civil War veteran and first governor of Wyoming. Frazer, *Forts of the West*, 184–185.

4. Dr. Austin Flint was a pioneer in clinical medicine and medical education, especially concerned with diseases of the heart. He was an early staff member at the Sisters of Charity Hospital, founded in 1848 in Buffalo, New York. Dr. William H. Welch became pathologist-in-chief at Johns Hopkins Hospital when it

opened in 1889 and dean of its school of medicine in 1893. Dr. Joseph D. Bryant later served as a personal doctor to President Grover Cleveland and was present when the former president died. Sisters Healthcare, "About Sisters Healthcare," par. 13 ("History"), website; "The Association of American Physicians," 1327; *New York Times*, June 25, 1908.

5. William T. Corbusier was the Corbusiers' fifth and youngest son. Late in life he used his father's "Memoirs" in compiling an article for *Nebraska History* and his mother's "Recollections" for the volume, *Verde to San Carlos*—both of which he amended with his own memories.

6. In her obituary, Mrs. Jones was described as "possessing a loveable disposition and being charitable to a fault." *Elmira Daily Advertiser*, August 13, 1907.

7. Fort Mackinac, first a French outpost and then a British fortification, stood on the bluff on the southeast part of Mackinac Island in the straits between Lakes Michigan and Huron. United States troops occupied the fort in October 1796, but British forces recaptured the installation in 1812. The post passed into American hands for the final time in 1815. Prucha, *Guide to the Military Posts*, 89. Harold Dunbar Corbusier provided an intimate family view of the years at Fort Mackinac in the diary he kept throughout 1883 and 1884, published as *A Boy at Fort Mackinac*.

8. Fort Holmes had been located on the highest elevation of the island and about half a mile behind Fort Mackinac. Built by the British and named Fort George during their occupation from 1812 to 1814, the installation was renamed Fort Holmes in honor of Major Andrew Hunter Holmes, who was killed when American forces attempted to retake possession of the post. Billings, *Circular Number Eight*, 43.

9. For the development of the tourist industry on Mackinac, its unique charm and geological features, see McVeigh, *Mackinac Connection*, 91–97, and Kachadurian, *Views of Mackinac Island*, 13–86, passim.

Phil Porter, chief curator of Mackinac State Historic Parks, provided information about various residents of Mackinac Island. Phil Porter, "Re: John Jacob Astor House," personal e-mail message to editor, June 1, 2001.

10. Gurdon Hubbard led a long and eventful life, beginning as a fur trapper and trader on the Illinois and Michigan frontiers and ending as a land developer on Mackinac Island. Senator Francis Brown Stockbridge was a senator from Michigan and served from 1887 until his death on April 30, 1894. McVeigh, *Mackinac Connection*, 96; "Stockbridge, Francis Brown," website, par. 1.

11. Dr. Corbusier was descended from the Outerbridges through members of his paternal line who had immigrated to Bermuda in the 1600s, as explained to me by Linda Foflygen, herself descended from the Penistons and Outerbridges of Bermuda. Linda Foflygen, "The Penistons and Outerbridges," personal e-mail message to editor, July 28, 2001.

12. George Dunbar, Mrs. Corbusier's father, had impaired his health when he struggled to repair this break in the Mississippi River levee. Knox, "The Longer View," 29–36.

13. Over four hundred species of wild flowers are found on Mackinac Island. McVeigh, *Mackinac Connection*, 85.

14. In 1670, Fathers Claude Dublon and Jacques Marquette visited Mackinac Island, and in 1671 Father Marquette began a mission to the Huron and Ottawa tribes at St. Ignace. Keith R. Widder, *Reveille Till Taps*, 2.

15. Les Cheneaux (the eaves) Islands lie northeast of Mackinac Island off the coast of Michigan's Upper Peninsula in Lake Huron.

16. During the 1840s, fishing had succeeded fur trapping as the major industry on Mackinac Island. McVeigh, *Mackinac Connection*, 94–95.

17. George Myers was the brother of Mahala Jones, Dr. Corbusier's mother. Goff, *Modified Register*, 5–6. The other family members mentioned were related through the Corbusiers.

18. The interior of Trinity Church is pictured in Kachadurian, *Views of Mackinac Island*, 86.

19. Situated on the southern bank of the Sault Sainte Marie, Fort Brady goes back to 1750, when the French claimed jurisdiction over all the territory north of the Ohio River and attempted to establish posts at strategic locations throughout the area. The British gained control of the region after the fall of Quebec in 1762. The "Soo" locks connect Lakes Superior and Huron. Billings, *Circular Number Four*, 124; McVeigh, *Mackinac Connection*, 106.

20. According to records, there was a significant showing of the northern lights from November 17–21, 1882. "Frequently Asked Questions about the Aurora," website.

21. Harold Corbusier noted in his diary entry for November 27, 1883, that they had procured their winter supplies, remarking that they could hardly find room enough for storing everything. Harold D. Corbusier, *A Boy at Fort Mackinac*, 60.

22. Dead Man's Hole is located between Mackinac and Round Islands, where the strong current keeps the ice from freezing solidly.

23. Alexis St. Martin's open stomach wound allowed Dr. William Beaumont to study the digestive process in humans for the first time. Dr. Beaumont published his findings, *Experiments and Observations on the Gastric Juices and the Physiology of Digestion*, in 1833. Widder, *Reveille Till Taps*, 70–71. John Tanner was born in Kentucky about 1780 and captured by Indians six years later. He remained a captive for about thirty years, spending his later life around Sault Sainte Marie, Michigan. His life story, *Narrative of the Captivity and Adventures of John Tanner during Thirty Years' Residence among the Indians*, was edited by Dr. Edwin James and published in 1830. Tanner disappeared in 1847.

24. Dr. Corbusier recorded in the *Medical History of Fort Mackinac, Michigan* that twelve children in the garrison had contracted whooping cough in May and June 1883. Happily, he reported in July 1883 that all children had recovered. *Medical History of Fort Mackinac*, Records of the Adjutant General's Office, 75–77.

25. Mrs. Sellers and her children remained at Fort Mackinac for little over a month. As the widow of an officer, she had no legal standing and remained at the garrison through the good offices of the commanding officer. Shirley A. Leckie, *Elizabeth Bacon Custer*, 203.

26. George Brady, one of the captains of the Twenty-third Infantry, was brevetted, as so many officers were, for his service during the Civil War and was, by courtesy, referred to by the title of greater rank. Heitman, *Historical Register*, 1:239.

27. For the career and the administration of Surgeon General Murray, see Gillett, *The Army Medical Department*, 8–9. Fort Whipple was established in 1863 in the Chino Valley near the Verde River. In 1864, the installation was relocated to the north bank of Granite Creek northeast of Prescott. On April 5, 1879, the army combined Fort Whipple and Prescott Barracks into Whipple Barracks. Frazer, *Forts of the West*, 14–15; Billings, *Circular Number Eight*, 554–556.

Chapter 17. *"But of the Ice We Had None"*

1. The Corbusiers had enrolled Claude, aged thirteen, in the Lawrenceville School, a boarding school that still exists today.

2. The Medical Department changed Dr. Corbusier's orders while the family was en route to Whipple Barracks and detailed him to Fort Bowie for temporary duty. Fort Bowie had been established July 28, 1862, by the Fifth California Infantry to protect travelers along the Tucson-Mesilla route and to safeguard an important spring located nearby.

3. Fort Grant, originally known as Fort Aravaipa, underwent five name and four site changes before it was finally situated about two miles from the western base of Mount Graham. Frazer, *Forts of the West*, 9; Billings, *Circular Number Four*, 465–456.

4. Major Bernard John Dowling Irwin, medical director of the Department of Arizona, was famous as the "fighting surgeon" who had won a Medal of Honor for his actions against Chiricahua Apaches near Apache Pass, February 13–14, 1861. Quebbeman, *Medicine in Territorial Arizona*, 34–38.

5. Ranking out of quarters was probably the most difficult social event in the life of an officer's wife because it caused a total disruption of her household and all other households down the line. Though the practice was cruel, a senior officer would not normally choose quarters inferior to those occupied by someone his junior.

6. For Dr. Corbusier's experiences in the field against Eskiminzin, a leader of the Aravaipa Apaches, see WHC, "Memoirs," 81–85.

7. This was the U.S. Indian Industrial School, which opened September 1, 1884, and was designed to assimilate Indian children. In 1890 Congress changed the school's name to Haskell, in honor of the late Dudley C. Haskell, U.S. representative from Kansas. "Haskell's History," website, par. 1–6.

8. Ida Teed was the teacher who tutored the Corbusier boys for two years, 1885–1887.

9. Colonel Shafter gained the nickname "Pecos Bill" after he marched his troops for thirty hours without water in an attempt to reach the Pecos River during his 1875 scout of the Llano Estacado. "Whispering Bill" Davis was Helen Fuller Davis' husband. Carlson, *"Pecos Bill,"* xi, 80; Shirley A. Leckie, *The Colonel's Lady,* 203–204.

10. Moody and Sankey were Dwight L. Moody and Ira David Sankey, two of the nineteenth century's best-known Christian evangelists and authors of many well-loved hymns.

11. Established in 1886, the Hospital Corps was an organization of men who could be "systematically trained to function as hospital attendants." Surgeon General George M. Sternberg set up the Hospital Corps Training School in conjunction with the medical school at Washington Barracks. Gillett, *The Army Medical Department,* 19, 100–101.

12. For Dr. Corbusier's description of these excursions, see WHC, "Memoirs", 107.

13. Davis was promoted to major in the Engineers on April 7, 1888. Heitman, *Historical Register,* 1:357.

14. *Burra* is the feminine form of *burro.*

15. Lieutenant Colonel Bartlett of the First Infantry commanded Fort Grant from April 1883 until the First Infantry left the territory in July 1886. Altshuler, *Cavalry Yellow and Infantry Blue,* 23. The boys' teacher who succeeded Miss Teed in 1887, William B. Cairns, wrote in his diary in September 1887 that while they were on a camping trip some herders accosted Claude and Phil and accused them of not owning the burros. Cairns, "Diary," September 29, 1887, William B. Cairns Collection.

16. Fool's quail are also known as montezuma or mearn's quail.

17. Will Cairns noted in his diary that Claude had returned from his hunt not with a doe, but with a fawn. Cairns, "Diary," Thursday, December 29, 1887, William B. Cairns Collection.

18. Dr. Ebert joined the Medical Department as an assistant surgeon on June 16, 1880. Dr. Frick served as a contract surgeon at Forts Grant, McDowell, Whipple, Verde, and Lowell between 1882 and 1891. No record of Dr. Carroll could be found. Heitman, *Historical Register,* 1:395; Quebbeman, *Medicine in Territorial Arizona,* 342.

19. Eventually Miss Teed so changed her opinion of the members of the frontier army that she wrote an article, "Army Life on the Frontier," in the *Pacific Monthly* magazine.

20. William McKittrick served as one of his father-in-law's aides during the Spanish-American War, which he entered as a captain. Carlson, *"Pecos Bill,"* 193.

21. Mrs. Corbusier is mistaken in her remarks about Colonel Grierson, who was in command of Fort Grant from June to November 1886, when he became

commanding officer of the District of New Mexico with headquarters at Santa
Fe. Grierson gained his long sought star as a brigadier on April 5, 1890, and retired
months later on July 8, 1890. Leckie and Leckie, *Unlikely Warriors*, 289–290,
303–304.

22. Mrs. Porter's companionship was lost when the Eighth Infantry left Arizona in 1886. Mrs. Viele arrived in Arizona in 1885 and went to Fort Grant later, around 1887. She left when her husband was promoted to major in the First Cavalry and transferred in August 1889 to Fort Custer, Montana Territory. Altshuler, *Cavalry Yellow and Infantry Blue*, 266, 343.

23. Mrs. Nanny Mills wrote her mother about this trip in July 1888 and stated that they had eaten bear meat, fawn, and strawberries, as well as having popcorn and "tall tales, taken with a grain of salt" around the campfire. Mills, *My Story*, 193.

24. Will Cairns was a twenty-year-old student at the University of Wisconsin who had temporarily left college to teach school and earn money to further his studies. Having grown up working with horses on a farm in Ellsworth, Wisconsin, he was not quite the tenderfoot Mrs. Corbusier depicted. He wrote of their first trip to the mountains: "I was in the saddle from five to eight hours daily, over places I scarcely could have gone on foot, and of course was a little sore but not as much as I expected." Will Cairns to Rolla Cairns, October 2, 1887, William B. Cairns Collection.

25. Will Cairns told the story a bit differently: "Once 'Old Whitey,' my mule got into a hornet's nest and took me up an almost perpendicular ledge of rock through the thickest underbrush on a keen gallop. I got through all right except that one pants leg was torn completely off a little below the knee. They were an old pair of Dr. Corbusier's." Ibid., 2–3.

26. Dr. Cairns wrote several books; in fact, he influenced the contents of modern American and English college literature courses. In 1979 an endowment provided by his estate created the Cairns Collection of American Women Writers, 1650–1920, which is an "invaluable resource for scholars, teachers, and students of American literature, American history and women's studies." University of Wisconsin-Madison, Memorial Library, "The William B. Cairns Collection," website, par. 1.

27. According to Britton Davis, both Maus and Shipp were with Crawford until his death on January 17, 1886, and Maus then restarted talks with Geronimo, Naiche, and Chihuahua. Davis, *The Truth about Geronimo*, 197–198.

28. Two volumes that depict the career of the "Brave Peacock," then Brigadier General Nelson Miles, are Greene, *Yellowstone Command*, and Wooster, *Nelson A. Miles*. For Captain Lawton's career, see Altshuler, *Cavalry Yellow and Infantry Blue*,
198–199. Dr. Leonard Wood was appointed an assistant surgeon on January 5, 1886, and was later awarded the Medal of Honor for his actions in the field during the Geronimo campaign, an honor Mrs. Altshuler disputed. See Altshuler, *Cavalry Yellow and Infantry Blue*, 376–377, and for a more positive explanation, Lane, *Armed Progressive*, 14–15.

29. Frederic Remington remained a life-long friend of Second Lieutenant Powhatan Clarke, of whom he said, "For personal heroism, none surpass young Lieutenant Clark[e] of the Tenth Colored Cavalry." Remington also wrote an article about a scout he participated in with Clarke and recalled his place of comfort behind the green latticework of the quarters at Fort Grant. McCracken, ed., *Frederic Remington's Own West*, 22–23, 65; Altshuler, *Cavalry Yellow and Infantry Blue*, 70.

30. Major Mills used the labor of Tenth Cavalrymen and hired Mexicans to build Lake Constance. When the fishpond was finished, someone put a shallow, flat-bottomed boat on it, and in one day eight of the post's children, including Claude and Frank, were capsized. Major Mills then declared that he would have a catamaran built for their use. Will Cairns to Rolla Cairns, December 9, 1887, William B. Cairns Collection.

31. The threat posed by the Gila monster was indeed disputed: Dr. H. C. Yarrow of the Smithsonian Institution, writing in August 1885, held that the Gila monster was non-poisonous and that the Arizona whiskey used in treatment of their bites was responsible for the deaths of their human victims. Dr. Edgar Mearns, stationed at Camp Verde in 1886, differed with his colleague, however, stating that the monster had no poison sacs but possessed a deadly breath and poison saliva. Quebbeman, *Medicine in Territorial Arizona*, 212–215; Bigelow, *The Bloody Trail of Geronimo*, 199.

32. Paddy was Patrick Maher, a discharged soldier who lived about ten miles north of Fort Grant.

33. On May 17, 1885, 124 Chiricahua Apaches left San Carlos, led by Geronimo and Nachez. Bigelow, *The Bloody Trail of Geronimo*, xx.

34. The Twenty-fourth Infantry, along with its sister, the Twenty-fifth, were the two "Buffalo Soldier" infantry regiments, composed initially of white officers and black troops. The colonel of the Twenty-fourth in 1888 was Zenas R. Bliss. Heitman, *Historical Register*, 1:123.

Mrs. Mills also noted Pearson's order, writing her mother that the post commander had cut short their vacation at the mountain retreat by sending them a dispatch relating that six Indians had left San Carlos and that he could send pack mules for them to use *only* if they decide to come down the next day. Mills, *My Story*, 195.

35. Major Mills had a personal interest in having ice available to the hospital since his daughter Constance had almost died of a raging fever when they were stationed at Fort Thomas. Colonel Shafter had been able to provide two hundred pounds of ice to bring the child's fever down. Ibid., 186.

Chapter 18. "He Was Not Wicked but Only Unfortunate"

1. The original Fort Hays was established in the fall of 1866 to protect the employees of the Kansas Pacific Railroad from the attacks of Indians. First called

Fort Fletcher for the former governor of Missouri, Thomas C. Fletcher, the fort
was renamed in the winter of 1866–1867 to honor Major General Isaac G. Hays,
killed in the Battle of the Wilderness. In the summer of 1867, the location of the
installation was moved because of the flooding of Big Creek. Billings, *Circular Number Four*, 304; Oliva, *Fort Hays*, 3–15.

2. Officers' quarters at Fort Hays were constructed of unseasoned pine, which shrunk and created gaps that allowed wind, rain, and snow to drive through them. The quarters were plainly finished, weather-boarded frame buildings, painted on the outside. Billings, *Circular Number Four*, 306. A fire-guard, in this case, was a strip of land around the fort from which all vegetation had been removed.

3. Captains Bomford and McLaughlin succeeded Colonel Yard before Major Brady assumed command at Fort Hays. Oliva, *Fort Hays*, 65.

4. Prohibition came to Kansas in 1881. Prior to that, Hays City and other Kansas "cow towns" had their share of saloons, desperate men, and houses of ill repute. James B. Hickok, among others, had once worked as a civilian scout at Fort Hays. Higgins, "History of Brewing in Kansas," 11–13; Olivia, *Fort Hays*, 59.

Captain Charles Garnett Gordon had retired on October 5, 1887. Heitman, *Historical Register*, 1:465.

5. Mrs. Corbusier was astute in her estimation of the influence of the frontier posts upon the settlers and economy surrounding them. For a thorough study of the impact the military had on a frontier economy, see Miller, *Soldiers and Settlers*.

6. Dr. Francis Huntington Snow, a renowned entomologist, became chancellor of the University of Kansas in 1890 and held that position until 1901. Edward B. Kehde III, "President or Chancellor in 1890," personal e-mail message to editor, October 23, 2000.

7. Erastus Johnson Turner served from March 4, 1887, to March 3, 1891, as a Republican member of the House of Representatives. He did not stand for reelection in 1890. "Turner, Erastus Johnson," website.

Orin R. Wolfe entered the Military Academy on September 1, 1889, and remained there until January 17, 1890, when he withdrew. He entered the army as a private on May 28, 1890. Heitman, *Historical Register*, 1:1053.

8. Napoleon Eugène Louis Jean Joseph, Prince Imperial of France, son of Napoleon III and Empress Eugénie, was actually killed by two Zulus, Langalabalele and Zabanga, on June 1, 1879. Morris, *The Washing of the Spears*, 611–612.

9. In 1763 Catherine the Great of Russia invited competing German religious communities to settle in South Russia. In 1871, Russification became governmental policy, and earlier promises to the German settlers, including freedom from military service, were rescinded. This led thousands of Russian Germans to immigrate to America, where many settled on the Great Plains. Sackett, "The Volga Germans in Kansas," 3.

10. Margaret Mather was one of the great Shakespearian actresses in the late 1800s.

11. Cucharas was a small town located on the Denver and Rio Grande Railway, which was completed to that point in 1876. The railroad built southwest from that site, reached La Veta later that year, and arrived in Durango in 1881. Athearn, *The Denver and Rio Grande*, 43–45, 105.

Built for seventy thousand dollars by Henry H. Strater, the Strater House was a first-class hotel with ninety-three rooms. A redbrick Victorian, the hotel remains active today. Caughey and Winstanley, *The Colorado Guide*, 386.

12. Fort Lewis, now the site of Fort Lewis College, is approximately 6,800 feet in elevation. Minna Sellers, "Elevation of Fort Lewis," personal e-mail message to editor, July 17, 2001.

13. William T. Corbusier gave a more detailed account of this house call in *Verde to San Carlos*, 221–237.

14. Chaplain William Larkin was wholly retired on February 16, 1891. Heitman, *Historical Register*, 1:616.

15. Major Tupper retired on July 26, 1893, and died on September 1, 1898. Heitman, *Historical Register*, 1:974.

16. Brigadier General John Moore was Surgeon General in the spring of 1890, but he retired later that summer. Gillett, *The Army Medical Department*, 9.

17. Cole Lydon was Fourth Division superintendent of the Denver and Rio Grande Railroad. Born in Ireland in 1846, Lydon began his career in railroading in 1862. This information was provided by Gordon Chappell of the National Park Service, who is completing his study of the Denver and Rio Grande, *Narrow Gauge to San Juan*. Gordon Chappell to Patricia Y. Stallard, August 7, 2001.

18. Built by a British investment company using the designs of a Chicago architect, the Windsor Hotel resembled Windsor Castle. It had five floors, three hundred rooms, and was opened for business on June 23, 1880. Furnished throughout in Victorian elegance, the hotel featured Haviland china, furniture from Tobey and W. W. Strong, Reed and Barton silverware, and Brussels carpets. Van Orman, *A Room for the Night*, 66.

19. This was another signal that Mrs. Corbusier's health was beginning to fail.

20. Woodruff was then a captain in the Second Artillery. He would be awarded the Medal of Honor in 1893 for his distinguished gallantry earlier in action at Newbys Cross Roads, Virginia, July 24, 1863. Heitman, *Historical Register*, 1:1057.

Chapter 19. "All of My Darling Boys"

1. Dr. Henry Remsen Tilton had joined the Medical Department in 1861 as an assistant surgeon. In 1890 he was a major surgeon. Heitman, *Historical Register*, 1:962.

2. All these relatives can be found in the Corbusier family genealogy. William Henry Corbusier, "Ancestry of William Henry Corbusier."

3. In the 1880s, enthusiasm for target practice and improved marksmanship became the rage in the army. Along with greater emphasis on continuing pro-

fessional training for officers, enlisted men were encouraged to hone their skills as sharpshooters. At the same time army surgeons were requested to help train physicians serving with the National Guard. McChristian, *An Army of Marksmen*, 67–71; Coffman, *The Old Army*, 275–286; Gillett, *The Army Medical Department*, 55.

4. Fort Wayne, located on the right bank of the Detroit River about two and one-half miles from the city of Detroit, was established in 1861. The officers' quarters, two-story frame cottages, were "built somewhat in the cheap tenement style." They were described as "miserably constructed, badly arranged, and unsuitable, owing to a variety of defects." Billings, *Circular Number Four*, 114–115.

5. Captain Wheaton had retired recently, on June 22, 1889. Heitman, *Historical Register*, 1:1022.

6. Frederick Stearns and Company was a pharmaceutical company founded in 1855 by Frederick Stearns, originally a Detroit-area druggist. The company was a major supplier of medication to members of the Union Army. Parke-Davis and Company was one of the most important pharmaceutical companies in America. It introduced new methods for producing drugs, standardized dosages, and discovered medicines such as those first used in treating diphtheria and epilepsy. Worthen, "The Pharmaceutical Industry," website, par. 10; National Register of Historic Places, "Parke-Davis and Company Plant and Research Laboratory," website, par. 1.

7. See Dr. Corbusier's "Memoirs," 3–15, for recollections of time spent on the Myers' family farm in New York during his childhood.

8. On April 6, 1866, Benjamin F. Stephenson founded the Grand Army of the Republic (GAR), whose members came from "honorably discharged veterans of the Union Army, Navy, Marine Corps or Revenue Cutter Service who had served between April 12, 1861 and April 9, 1865." By 1890, the GAR numbered 409,489 members and was a political force in state and national politics. The commander in chief presided over National Encampments such as the one held in Detroit in 1891. Knight, "Brief History of the GAR," website, par. 6–14.

9. Julius Caesar Burrows served in the U.S. House of Representatives periodically from 1873 to 1895, when he was elected to the United States Senate seat previously held by Francis B. Stockbridge. In 1891, he was still a member of the House. "Burrows, Julius Caesar," website.

10. The United States Revenue Cutter Service was the precursor of today's Coast Guard, which was formed in 1915 by combining the Revenue Cutter Service and the Lifesaving Service.

On September 10, 1813, an American squadron under Commodore Oliver Hazard Perry met and defeated the British squadron led by Captain Robert Barclay on Lake Erie, a stunning victory for the young U.S. Navy, which led to General William Henry Harrison's triumph at the Battle of the Thames on October 5, 1813. Perry's report to Harrison of his victory at Lake Erie, "We have met the enemy and they are ours," became part of naval lore. Hagan, *This People's Navy*, 84–87.

11. Dr. Josephus R. Corbus succeeded Dr. Corbusier as an acting assistant surgeon with the Sixth Illinois Cavalry on April 10, 1865. Since he was a contract doctor, there is no record of his service in Heitman's *Historical Register*.

12. The "Call to Quarters" was added to other bugle calls sounded throughout the day to advise soldiers that it was time to be in their quarters and that Taps would sound soon. For a list of the daily bugle calls at an infantry post, see Widder, *Reveille Till Taps*, 13.

13. It is evident from her change to present tense that Mrs. Corbusier was consulting her diary entries from 1892 to 1902 when she wrote her "Recollections."

14. Mrs. Corbusier clearly referred to the island's development; the U.S. Congress had in 1875 made Mackinac Island the nation's second national park. From that point on, locals began encouraging the idea that the island would be a good destination for midwestern tourists—especially the newly rich industrialists and entrepreneurs from such cities as Chicago and Detroit. In 1882 Gurdon Hubbard decided to subdivide his eighty-acre plot, and Charles Caskey started building cottages in Hubbard's Annex. The federal government also expedited the erection of summer cottages by leasing building sites to potential cottagers. In 1887 a consortium of owners of railroad and steamship companies hired Charles Caskey to build the Grand Hotel, the original part of which was completed in four months, to attract the "smart set." Other resorts followed and the tourists came to enjoy a different kind of vacation or summer where today no motorcars are allowed. McVeigh, *Mackinac Connection*, 96–97.

15. Hal Corbusier recorded that on July 11, 1892, he went to a hop but only danced four or five dances because it was so warm. He wrote, "My collar was as limp as a wash-rag when I got to camp. There are a number of people at the Grand now. Most of them come up to show off their silks & sit around where they can be seen by everyone." Harold Dunbar Corbusier, *A Boy at Fort Mackinac*, 91.

16. Captain Frank Baldwin had transferred to the Fifth Infantry on May 19, 1869, and became one of Colonel Miles's most trusted and loyal subordinates. In fact, a friend encouraged Baldwin to cast his fortunes with Miles, implying that promotions would come his way if he "kept a tight hold on Genel. Miles' coattails." (Brigadier General Miles had been promoted to major general on April 5, 1890.) In his long career, Baldwin won two Medals of Honor. Wooster, *Nelson A. Miles*, 58. For an intimate look into the lives of Frank and Alice Baldwin, see Steinbach, *A Long March*.

17. Dr. Corbusier wrote in his "Memoirs" that when he lived in California as a youth, he learned how to handle horses. He noted, "I was soon able to ride the worst broncos on the ranch, which I had to blindfold to saddle, bridle and mount, and I had to learn horse sense to succeed." WHC, "Memoirs," 22.

18. Dr. Corbusier measured and weighed each member of his family every month.

Mrs. Corbusier confided to her diary that May Addison left because she [Mrs. Corbusier] could not help with her expenses. She wrote, "Poor child I hated to see her go. It seemed so cruel but it was best." Fanny Dunbar Corbusier (here-after abbreviated FDC), "Diary," October 1892, p. 35.

19. Mrs. Corbusier recorded in her diary that "Mrs. Capt. Chas. ___ died on the second. She had been ill for some time and was taken to a hospital for the insane and died there." Ibid., April 1893, p. 36.

20. In her diary Mrs. Corbusier took note of this temporary duty by remarking, "Will was ordered to Columbus Barracks, Ohio, on temporary duty. He will probably not return until the middle of May. I hope the change will do him good. He has not been at all well lately." Ibid.

Chapter 20. "No Way For Husband and Wife to Live"

1. Fort Supply, Indian Territory, was established in November 1868 by Captain John H. Page, Third Infantry, on a low sandy bottom between Beaver and Wolf Creeks. The post became Fort Supply in 1878 and was abandoned on February 25, 1895. Frazer, *Forts of the West*, 123–124. Mrs. Corbusier confided to her diary that "It does seem as if some other place might have been found to send him to." FDC, "Diary," July 1893, p. 38.

2. This was the World's Columbian Exposition, or World's Fair, held in Chicago in 1893.

3. Alvin and Whelan Stearns were sons of Frederick Stearns, owner of the pharmaceutical company that Claude worked for.

4. Claude was living on his own in Detroit, working for Stearns and Company. Mrs. Corbusier wrote, "I don't dare say a word to Claude about being lonely for he will miss us so much." FDC, "Diary," February 1892, pp. 29, 40.

5. In 1893, Orlando Poe was a colonel in the Engineers, serving from January 1, 1873, until February 8, 1894, as aide-de-camp to General William T. Sherman. Heitman, *Historical Register*, 1:795–796.

6. Mrs. Corbusier was setting up housekeeping for herself and four sons in Ann Arbor so that Hal could attend the University of Michigan. Philip and Frank were high school students, and Willie was still in elementary school. This was the first time the family had been so fragmented, and all her responsibilities seemed to overwhelm her: "I am so tired, homesick, and lonely I cannot keep from crying. It is all so unnatural." FDC, "Diary," September 2, 1893, p. 42.

7. The ATO Society is Alpha Tau Omega, a fraternity founded in 1865 "to know no North, no South, no East, no West, ... to teach, not politics, but morals, to foster, not partisanship, but the recognition of true merit, wherever found." "The Creed of Alpha Tau Omega," website.

8. Mrs. Corbusier recorded a somewhat different result in her diary: "Hal passed six of eight—Failed in literature and was conditional in Physics." FDC, "Diary," September 25, 1893, p. 25.

9. The Hobart Guild was a social organization in the Episcopal Church named in honor of New York Bishop John Henry Hobart.

10. While Mrs. Corbusier was having such a trying time in Ann Arbor, Dr. Corbusier was not faring much better at Fort Supply. She recorded: "Poor Will has been sick. It is too hard he has to be alone. I wonder how long we will have to live this way. It is such a lonely life, and Will is working beyond his strength." FDC, "Diary," November 1893, p. 47.

11. Two local newspapers included articles about the fire: *Detroit Evening News*, December 11, 1893, p. 1; *Detroit Free Press*, December 11, 1893, p. 5.

12. Frances Bagley was the widow of John Judson Bagley, who had made his fortune in tobacco products and had served as governor of Michigan from 1873 to 1877. He was instrumental in developing the University of Michigan into a true university and in the desegregation of the public schools in that state. The Bagleys had seven children. He died in San Francisco in 1881, and Mrs. Bagley, the daughter of a missionary, carried on his good works. The Corbusiers knew them from Fort Mackinac. Livingstone County, Michigan, GenWeb Project, "John J. Bagley," website, par. 1–4.

Bishop Brooks was Phillips Brooks, rector of Trinity Church in Boston, who is remembered for, among other things, writing the words to the Christmas hymn, "O Little Town of Bethlehem."

13. Edwin Arnold was the editor of the *London Daily Telegraph* and author of several volumes, including *The Great Renunciation*, *India Revisited*, and *East and West*. Dean Stanley was the Very Reverend Arthur P. Stanley, Dean of Westminster.

14. Mrs. Corbusier wrote in her diary that Frank twitched his face all the time and his pupils were dilated. She gave him quinine and iron and urged him to take cod liver oil since he was so thin. In February she noted that she had received a letter from her brother Buck that related his young daughter also had "some nervous trouble." FDC, "Diary," January 18, 1894, p. 50; February 1894, p. 51.

15. Swami Vivekananda, born in 1863, was the Hindu monk who introduced Hinduism to the West.

16. Other army husbands and wives faced the same separation dilemma when their children grew to high school or college age. Parents solved the problem by sending the children to boarding school or to stay with relatives, or the mother took the children to a city where they could finish their schooling. The Corbusiers had tried earlier to send Claude to boarding school, and that had not worked; with such a large family, boarding school was out of the question on the doctor's salary. So, like many others, they divided the family and lived apart for several years.

17. Delta Upsilon fraternity was founded in 1834. "Delta Upsilon," website.

18. The Corbusiers had served at Fort Wayne with Surgeon Brown in 1892.

19. Mrs. Corbusier confided her loneliness to her diary: "But, oh, when the boys all leave in the afternoon how lonely it is. I try so hard not to think of it, but it nearly kills me." She also learned that Dr. Corbusier had received orders to

New York City as Examiner of Recruits, and that they would spend another year apart: "To know I must spend another long, lonely year is dreadful." FDC, "Diary," July 1894, p. 55.

20. A "Racine" was a canoe made by the Racine Boat Company of Racine, Wisconsin.

Chapter 21. "The Day Was One Never to Be Forgotten"

1. The Surgeon General, George Miller Sternberg, said upon his appointment to the post in 1893, "I shall endeavor to promote a truly scientific spirit in the Corps and where I recognize special ability, I will do all I can to aid the respective officer to achieve success." Sternberg, *George Miller Sternberg*, 131. Therefore, Dr. Corbusier knew if he were to be promoted, he had to show achievements in scientific research, and he chose his next assignments with the idea in mind to gain extra medical training while fulfilling his responsibilities as post surgeon. As Mrs. Corbusier noted in her diary, this only extended their separation: "Will is studying these three weeks—studying germs because the Surgeon General [Sternberg] is a bacteriologist. Darling Papa, how we did enjoy the little we saw of him." FDC, "Diary," October 18, 1894, p. 56.

2. The Cherokee Strip, which surrounded Fort Supply, was opened to settlement at noon September 16, 1893. The area was divided into seven counties, with only Indian reservations and the land apportioned to Fort Supply exempted from the opening. Dr. Corbusier had arrived in Indian Territory late in July, just in time for the final preparations for the land rush. Carriker, *Fort Supply, Indian Territory*, 204–215.

3. As Mrs. Corbusier explained in chapter 19, Claude first worked for Frederick Stearns but could not support himself on his pay. Dr. Corbusier interceded and gained him a job with Parke-Davis and Company. FDC, "Diary," October 18, 1894, p. 56.

4. During his year in New York City, Dr. Corbusier wrote that he continued the bacteriological work he had started at the University of Michigan. He also helped to culture anti-diphtheria serum in a horse. WHC, "Memoirs," 112.

5. Daniel Norricks Bash was promoted to major, paymaster on February 11, 1881, and retired on July 2, 1892. Heitman, *Historical Register*, 1:197.

6. On New Year's Day, 1895, she despaired: "Another New Year. This is not living without Will." FDC, "Diary," January 1895, p. 58.

7. In March 1895, Mrs. Corbusier confided to her diary that her heart had troubled her so much it was hard for her to do anything. This was the first time she had mentioned problems with her heart. With all the stress she was experiencing in being separated from her husband, caring for and worrying about five sons, and not having enough money, she was a prime candidate for a heart attack. Ibid., March 1895, p. 58.

8. They attended this performance at the second Madison Square Garden, which was built in 1890 and lasted until 1925. Schoenberg, "Madison Square Garden History," website, par. 4–5.

More than a graceful, modest dancer, Caroline Otero was one of the most notorious courtesans of La Belle Époque, having as lovers five members of royalty and several other of the richest men in the world. However, she was not in New York in 1895, so Mrs. Corbusier may have mistaken her for another Spanish dancer. Lewis, *La Belle Otero*, 97.

9. In his "Memoirs," Dr. Corbusier recorded his vivid memories of his childhood, largely spent on the farm of his maternal grandparents. WHC, "Memoirs," 3–12.

10. Gerret Myers Meyer, born in 1730 and a minuteman in the American Revolution, was Dr. Corbusier's maternal great-great-grandfather. Goff, *Modified Register*, 2.

11. The only Colonel Buffington listed in Heitman is Adelbert Renaldo Buffington, who was promoted to colonel on February 28, 1889. Heitman, *Historical Register*, 1:260.

12. On August 27, 1776, about four hundred troops from Maryland conducted a rearguard action to check the British advance and to allow George Washington's greatly outnumbered Continental Army to escape intact. They launched six desperate counterattacks before they were swept into Gowanus Salt Marsh, where 256 remain. Washington, observing the action from the Brooklyn defenses, mourned, "My God, what brave fellows I must this day lose." On August 27, 1897, General Horace Porter, president general of the Sons of the American Revolution, led a procession of officials, bands, and military units to dedicate a monument to the Four Hundred at Lookout Hill. Carroll, "Maryland's Brave 400," website, par. 1–5.

13. The original Hannah More Academy, where Mrs. Corbusier had resided from 1855 to 1860, was established in 1832 in honor of More, who had started free schools in London for children of the poor. *Hannah More School*, "History," website, par. 2–3.

14. Mrs. Corbusier was somewhat confused in her explanation of the term "fogy," which refers to longevity pay. Every five years, an officer received a ten percent increase in his base pay. So, when Dr. Corbusier reached twenty years of service, he received his fourth ten percent increase in pay, not a forty percent bonus. Using her figures, he was making $3,249.96 a year, and the next year, after his fourth fogy, he would receive $3,500.04 as a major, surgeon. Coffman, *The Old Army*, 266.

15. Fort Monroe is located on Old Point Comfort, site of fortifications in southeastern Virginia since 1609. Fort Monroe remained in Union hands throughout the Civil War and was the site of Jefferson Davis's incarceration afterwards. Billings, *Circular Number Four*, 72.

16. Mrs. Corbusier was manifesting the symptoms of a "thyroid storm," a hyperactive thyroid that can cause metabolic heart disease. Peery and Miller, *Pathology*, 723.

17. In November 1895, Mrs. Corbusier noted in her diary that Dr. Corbusier had complained that Fort Monroe was too quiet after New York City. Mrs. Corbusier commiserated: "Poor fellow, he will be so lonely. It is too bad that we could not all have been with him." FDC, "Diary," November 1895, p. 65.

18. In 1896, Hal, Philip, and Frank, whom Mrs. Corbusier left behind in Ann Arbor, were twenty-three, twenty-one, and nineteen respectively.

19. Named for the Greek goddess of health, the Hygeia was the second resort hotel by that name to be built at the foot of Engineer Pier at Old Point Comfort. "Harrison Phoebus Leaves His Legacy," website, par. 5–7.

20. Originally called Fortress Monroe and completed in 1823, Fort Monroe is a massive structure surrounded by a moat filled with water eight feet deep. The officers and men were originally quartered within the walls of the work. Fort Monroe remains active today. Billings, *Circular Number Eight*, 50–51.

21. William August Kobbé was a captain in the Third Artillery in 1896 and was promoted to major on March 8, 1898. He would rise to brigadier general in the U.S. Army and give valuable service in the Philippines. Heitman, *Historical Register*, 1:607.

22. Robley Dungliston Evans, known as "Fighting Bob," was a captain in 1896, becoming rear admiral in 1901 after his command of the USS *Iowa*, which led the fleet in its victory against the Spanish at the battle of Santiago de Cuba.

23. William Jenkins Worth died a brevet major general on May 7, 1849. He had been presented with a sword by congressional resolution on March 2, 1847, in appreciation of his "gallant and good conduct in storming Monterey, Mexico." Heitman, *Historical Register*, 1:1061.

24. In 1798 Congress established the United States Marine Hospital Service to provide care for sick and injured merchant seamen. In 1870 the Service was reorganized into a national hospital system, with centralized control vested in a medical officer known as the Supervising Surgeon. This position later became that of the United States Surgeon General, and the Marine Hospital Service evolved into the Public Health Service. Virtual Office of the Surgeon General, "History of the Office of the Surgeon General," website, par. 1–2.

25. During the Spanish-American War, Lieutenant Richmond P. Hobson commanded the group of volunteers who intentionally scuttled the USS *Merrimac* in the channel at Santiago de Cuba in an attempt to bottle up the Spanish fleet. The effort failed, but Hobson was awarded the Medal of Honor in 1933 for his actions, and in 1934 he was retroactively made a rear admiral. "Hobson, Richmond Pearson," website, par. 1.

Lawrence H. Moses was commissioned a second lieutenant in the Marine Corps on July 1, 1892. By 1917 he had risen to the rank of colonel and served as the commanding officer of the Eighth Marines until November 3, 1917. Service

Record, United States Marine Corps, Marine Corps Historical Center, Reference Section (Code HDH-2).

26. Colonel [Brevet Major General] Smith had retired on November 1, 1891. Colonel Snyder was in 1896 still the colonel of the Nineteenth Infantry. One wonders if the young women mentioned were potential spouses for two of the young Corbusiers. Heitman, *Historical Register*, 1:895, 907.

27. Claude was still employed by Parke-Davis and Company. Mrs. Corbusier revealed the reason for his visit in her diary, where she confided: "Claude is engaged to Miss Mildred M. Hilliard of Louisville. We have never seen her but hear that she is a very sweet girl." FDC, "Diary," December 1896, p. 70.

28. Zachariah Chandler became mayor of Detroit in 1851. He was one of the founders of the Republican Party and in 1857 was elected to the U.S. Senate, where he served all but one term until his death in 1875. "Chandler, Zachariah," website, par. 1.

Samuel J. Tilden was a crusading politician who helped oust the "Tweed Ring" and was elected governor of New York in 1874. Democratic candidate for president in 1876, he won by a majority of 250,000 votes but lost the election when a partisan electoral commission awarded all the contested electoral votes to Rutherford B. Hayes.

29. Dr. Corbusier's treatment of nervous prostration, or neurasthenia, probably consisted of purging, putting the patient on a liquid diet, and prescribing sulphate of quinine. The disease seems to have been a form of depression. Lenzen, "Diseases of the Ancestors," website, par. 4–5.

30. Mrs. Corbusier wrote in her diary, "Mildred is a dear sweet girl. We love her more every day." FDC, "Diary," July 1897, p. 71.

31. Philip later married Ida Edwards, but Claude and Mildred Hilliard subsequently broke their engagement.

32. The Chamberlain opened in 1896, being the first hotel in the United States to be completely illuminated with electric lights. "When Old Point was a Resort," website, pars. 3–5.

33. Willie was then fifteen. Shortly after graduating, Harold started an internship with the U.S. Marine Hospital in Cleveland, Ohio. FDC, "Diary," July 1899, p. 91.

Chapter 22. "Raised beneath the Flag"

1. Formerly Camp Reynolds, Angel Island is located in San Francisco Bay. The camp faced the Golden Gate, and the officers' quarters were four plain, substantially built frame houses. Billings, *Circular Number Eight*, 497–498.

George Towers Dunbar III, called Buck by family members, was Mrs. Corbusier's younger brother. As a youth, he had fought in the Civil War as a member of Fenner's Louisiana Battery of Light Artillery and had been severely wounded during the battle at New Hope Church on May 28, 1864. He recovered from his wounds but was left in compromised health the rest of his life. When she visited him on her way to California in 1897, Mrs. Corbusier had recorded in her diary his reduced circumstances by remarking, "Poor fellow, if only he had more money to take care of them with." FDC, "Recollections," 3; FDC, "Diary," October 1897, p. 75.

2. The Presidio of San Francisco was activated on June 27, 1776, in the northwest part of the settlement that became San Francisco, overlooking San Francisco Bay, Fort Point, and Alcatraz. American forces took the Presidio from Mexico on July 9, 1846, and established a garrison there on March 7, 1847. No longer a military enclave, the Presidio is now part of the National Park Service. Billings, *Circular Number Eight*, 518–520.

3. When Stanford University opened its doors in 1891, seven fraternities were soon organized. The Stanford chapter of Beta Theta Pi was chartered July 26, 1892, and Frank and Philip were initiated on December 11, 1897, being members twenty-four and twenty-five respectively. Reinhardt, *Out West on the Overland Train*, 205; Ginger Scott-Johnson, "Beta Theta Pi," personal e-mail message to editor, October 10, 2001.

Agnes Morley was born in Datil, New Mexico, in 1874 and attended both the University of Michigan and Stanford with the Corbusiers' sons. In 1941, using her married name, Agnes Morley Cleaveland, she wrote *No Life for a Lady*.

4. In reference to the threats of war with Spain, Mrs. Corbusier confided to her diary, "There is talk of war with Spain to free Cuba and put a stop to the atrocities committed by the Spaniards. Our boys are becoming excited and the whole country is in a state of suspense." FDC, "Diary," March 1898, p. 77.

5. Most of the volunteer officers noted by Mrs. Corbusier are discussed in Linn, *The Philippine War*.

6. The *City of Peking*, built in 1874 and used as a transport on the Pacific during the war, accompanied the USS *Charleston* as it called at Hawaii, captured Guam, and landed the first U.S. Army troops in the Philippines. McSherry, "The Transport Service," website, par. 1. Information about other transports named in this chapter is also available at this site.

7. "President Dole" is Sanford Ballard Dole, who had became president of Hawaii in 1894 and negotiated the islands' annexation by the United States. Dole served as the first governor of the Territory of Hawaii.

8. Launched on July 19, 1888, from San Francisco's Union Iron Works and commissioned on December 26, 1889, the USS *Charleston* was a protected cruiser sent to the Philippines after the outbreak of the war. It convoyed twenty-five hundred troops to strengthen Commodore George Dewey's Asiatic Squadron. On its way to Manila, the ship visited Hawaii and its crew captured Guam. McSherry, "USS Charleston," website, par. 1–2.

George Dewey commanded the Asiatic Squadron and prepared it for war with Spain. His squadron entered Manila Bay on May 1, 1898, and in seven hours his command destroyed the Spanish fleet and guaranteed possession of the Philippines to the United States.

9. Mrs. Corbusier had written in June, "Will expects to go with the last expedition. I am hoping all the time that he will not go at all." FDC, "Diary," June 1898, p. 80.

10. Major General Elwell S. Otis succeeded Major General Wesley Merritt as commander of the Eighth Army Corps in the Philippines. Called "Colonel Blimp" by his own troops, Otis led the United States in its first tropical guerrilla war against the Filipino "Insurrectos." Dr. Richardson was a captain and assistant surgeon with the First California Volunteers. He was appointed an assistant surgeon, U.S. Army, on September 9, 1901. Heitman, *Historical Register*, 1:828; Linn, *Guardians of Empire*, 10–14.

11. Hawaii was officially annexed to the United States as a result of the Spanish-American War by joint resolution of Congress on July 7, 1898.

12. Frank was also present at the battle of Manila that occurred on August 13, 1898, when after a "sham battle," the Spanish defenders surrendered to the combined forces of Dewey and Merritt. Linn, *The Philippine War*, 23–26.

13. Claude and his friends had joined one hundred thousand others in a mad dash to the far north in search of gold.

14. Dr. Corbusier was acting medical purveyor and disbursing officer for Medical Department of the Expedition to the Philippines, later called the Department of the Pacific and the Eighth Army Corps, from May 17, 1898, to April 30, 1900. William T. Corbusier, *Verde to San Carlos*, 290.

15. Volunteer surgeons who knew little of army routine gave Dr. Corbusier a great deal of trouble. His wife observed, "They think what they are pleased to call 'red tape,' in other words system and good management, is all nonsense. They complain when they do not get the supplies that they have made no requisition for." FDC, "Diary," July 1898, p. 83.

16. The American Red Cross was actively involved in screening potential contract nurses, as were the Sisters of Charity, who provided many trained nurses for the war effort. Before the crisis was over more than seventeen hundred contract nurses served. Sternberg, *George Miller Sternberg*, 169–70; Gillett, *The Army Medical Department*, 123–125.

17. In addition to Dr. Corbusier's initiative, Chaplain Charles C. Pierce recommended in 1899 that an "identity disc" be included in the standard combat field kit. The first official tag was produced in December 1906, and the Army Regulations of 1913 made an identification tag standard. Those produced by the Red Cross for the California Volunteers were the first issued to a significant group. WHC, "Memoirs," 113–114; "US Dog Tags," website, par. 3–6.

18. Surgeon General Sternberg had some fear that trained female nurses might be an "encumbrance" on an army in the field preparing for battle. But he and most army surgeons soon realized that an Army Nurse Corps Division of the Surgeon General's Office needed to be established. Nurses were employed under contract and received thirty dollars per month and a daily ration. Gillett, *The Army Medical Department*, 123.

19. Dr. Corbusier was provided cash so that he could buy necessary medical supplies from the local economy since he had left San Francisco without having procured all the needed medical stores. WHC, "Memoirs," 114. See also *Correspondence Relating to the War with Spain*, 2:766, in which General Merritt recommended that if Major Corbusier was not already en route, "the funds in his possession intended for purchase [of] medical supplies be transferred by wire to Captain [Harlan Ellsworth] McVay, assistant surgeon."

20. The First Washington Volunteers had just reached Angel Island, which was a receiving station for new recruits. They would see service in the Philippines also, being involved in the second battle of Manila. Linn, *The Philippine War*, 44.

Chapter 23. "All My Dear Ones Are with Me in Spirit"

1. For Merriam and King's adventures in the Philippines, see Russell, *Campaigning with King*, 115–131. All the transport ships mentioned by Mrs. Corbusier are described at the Spanish American War Centennial Website.

2. The Quartel Fortin (or Cuartel Fortin) was a military barracks located along the Pasig River, which was spanned by the Bridge of Spain in Manila.

3. The Battle of Malabon was part of the campaign to capture Malolos, the revolutionary capital of the Philippines. Linn, *The Philippine War*, 95–97.

4. Mrs. Corbusier used every means at her disposal to gain her son a furlough before he was mustered out of the First California Volunteers. She wrote, "Have been to see General Corbin, Adjutant General. He will not grant Frank a furlough. San Francisco is too cold for him." FDC, "Diary," May 1899, p. 90.

5. This is somewhat of an overstatement in Frank's case, since the level of care he received was extraordinary in comparison to that of other enlisted soldiers. He had the care of three doctors, including his own father, two nurses, and, sometimes, his brother. Even with the extra care he received, Frank suffered a series of health problems that his mother obviously associated with his military service. FDC, "Diary," December 1898, p. 88.

6. The epidemics of typhoid in both Cuba and the Philippines caused Surgeon General Sternberg to appoint a Typhoid Board to study how typhoid spread and to determine a means of prevention. The board, headed by Major Walter Reed, concluded that sanitation was the most effective method of prevention. Gillett, *The Army Medical Department*, 191–193.

7. Young Will was sixteen when he entered Cayuga Lake Military Academy. The academy was begun in 1799 and received a state charter in 1801. The name of the school was changed to Cayuga Lake Military Academy in 1883 and it prospered for a while but was discontinued shortly before 1900. *Auburn Daily Advertiser*, Semi-Centennial Number, 1895, p. 27.

8. Since Frank was a Volunteer, he would be able to return much sooner than Phil, who was in the Regulars. FDC, "Diary," 1–8 October 1898, p. 87.

9. These were complications from his typhoid. Peery and Miller, *Pathology,* 97–98. Frank was at that time in a convalescent hospital on Corregidor Island and had been promoted to sergeant. FDC, "Diary," February 1899, p. 88.

10. After the Treaty of Peace was signed in December 1898, Philippine nationalists, who had hoped for independence and remained entrenched on the outskirts of Manila, organized resistance inside the city. On February 4, 1899, open warfare broke out between forces of the United States, including regular army units like Phil's, and those of the new Philippine Republic. Linn, *The Philippine War,* 42–53.

11. Mrs. Corbusier referred to the First Philippine Commission, appointed by President McKinley to investigate conditions in the islands and make recommendations as circumstances deteriorated in the islands. Linn, *The Philippine War,* 109, 130.

12. Mrs. Hannah (or Nannie) Mills, second of four daughters of Lydia Martin and William Culbertson Cassel, was married to Anson Mills. Mills, *My Story,* 112–117.

13. Senator George Clement Perkins had succeeded Leland Stanford as senator from California. Eugene Francis Loud was a member of the House of Representatives from 1891 to 1903. "Loud, Eugene Francis" and "Perkins, George Clement," websites.

14. George B. Cortelyou was private secretary to President McKinley and later became the first secretary of commerce and labor under President Theodore Roosevelt. In this instance Mrs. Corbusier was certainly acting outside the bounds of the "Cult of True Womanhood."

15. Mrs. Corbusier reported a slightly different version in her diary, where she wrote that her answer to General Henry Clarke Corbin was, "There are many vacancies and I want it now." FDC, "Diary," April 1899, p. 89. For Corbin's military career, see Heitman, *Historical Register,* 1:327.

16. Douglas Potts did receive his commission earlier than Philip Corbusier, but Philip was promoted to first lieutenant sooner than Potts. Heitman, *Historical Register,* 1:802 and 327, respectively.

17. Tiffin is a light mid-day meal to appease one's appetite, or lunch.

18. Henry Lawton became a brigadier general of the Volunteers on May 4, 1898, and a major general of Volunteers on July 8, 1898. He was killed on December 19, 1899, at the Battle of San Mateo, Philippine Islands. Heitman, *Historical Register,* 1:620.

19. Dhobie itch, or *Tinea cruris,* is a superficial fungal infection of the groin and adjacent skin. The infection is spread through use of contaminated towels, sheets, or other personal items.

20. While William T. Corbusier was a student at the New York Military Academy, President Sebastian Jones helped the institution become one of the best-known military schools in the country. The New York Military Academy, "Our History," website, par. 1–4.

21. Claude had settled in a small town lying northwest of Fairbanks on the Tanana River where it joins the Yukon. Gold was discovered in the wide fertile valley of the Tanana in July 1902. Mayer and DeArmond, *Staking Her Claim*, 270–271. "Found" is room and board.

22. The Sternbergs were childless, and Martha assisted her husband in his scientific pursuits as he rose through the grades to surgeon general. She also wrote his biography. Sternberg, *George Miller Sternberg*, 14.

23. In her struggle to obtain a commission for Phil, Mrs. Corbusier contacted every person she thought could help her. She recorded, "Went to see Colonel [W. H.] Carter about Phil's promotion. No enlisted men to be examined until the class at West Point is graduated. But I am determined to see General Corbin and try to get the order." She added later, "I hope I will get his order now there are to be so many appointments made." FDC, "Diary," November, December 1899, p. 93.

24. Mrs. Corbusier had been busy trying to obtain government transportation to the islands. FDC, "Diary," December 25, 1899, p. 94.

25. The army post Mrs. Corbusier referred to is Fort Gibbon, located at the mouth of the Tanana River. Captain Samuel Thomas Weirick was appointed an assistant surgeon in the U.S. Volunteers on April 20, 1901, and was honorably discharged from that position on February 1, 1903. He was a contract doctor when he treated Frank in the Philippines and when he met Claude in Alaska. Heitman, *Historical Register*, 1:1015; 2: 279, 502.

26. Minister Wu Ting Fang was a personal friend of Brigadier General and Mrs. Anson Mills. Mr. Wu entertained Mrs. Mills with stories of his life in China and his adventures abroad. Mills, *My Story*, 229–234.

27. Lieutenant Colonel Henry R. Tilton, who received the Medal of Honor in 1895 for his actions against the Indians at Bear Paw Mountains in Montana in 1877, had retired February 2, 1900. Heitman, *Historical Register*, 1:962.

Mrs. Corbusier's cousin, Major Charles L. McCauley, rose to brigadier general and quartermaster of the Marine Corps on September 8, 1916, and he retired August 24, 1929. Service Record, United States Marine Corps, Marine Corps Historical Center, Reference Section (Code HDH-2).

28. Mrs. Corbusier hoped to go to the Philippines when members of the Second Philippine Commission sailed in June 1900, but she was denied permission. Then her husband received notification that he was to be transferred out of the Philippines, and she lost her justification for going. All her plans for going to the Philippines and helping her son gain a commission seemed for naught. She reached her lowest point emotionally when she confessed, "It was my only chance to go to such a distance and I would have enjoyed it so much. Will having been there so long knows all that there is to be seen. Then to go to Japan, the country of all others I have wished so much to visit. I would have taken Willie by way of Suez—it would have been a delight to us both." FDC, "Diary," March 31, April 1, 1900, pp. 102–103.

29. Claude had become employed carrying the mail between Fairbanks and St. Michael's. In June 1899, news of a gold strike at Nome on the coast of the Seward Peninsula reached the outside world and a new rush began. Claude wrote that he might join it. Mayer and DeArmond, Staking Her Claim, 204; FDC, "Diary," March 28, 1900, p. 102.

Chapter 24. "All the Years of Anxiety Have Broken Me Down"

1. On April 19, 1900, Mrs. Corbusier noted in her diary that Claude had invested one thousand dollars (not five thousand) in a steamer. FDC, "Diary," April 19, 1900, p. 104.

2. Dr. Corbusier was leaving behind Philip, who had not yet taken the examinations required for his selection to the officers' corps. Mrs. Corbusier was heartened, however, by the fact that Philip had received orders to take those examinations. FDC, "Diary," April 26, 1900, p. 104.

3. Hal had interviewed with the Surgeon General concerning an appointment into the Medical Department as an assistant surgeon. In this instance personal associations worked for them; Hal was promised a position as a contract surgeon provided that he passed the necessary tests. Later in the month Mrs. Corbusier recorded, "Hal passed his examinations and will be sent to the Philippines." FDC, "Diary," May 22, 1900, p. 106.

4. Mrs. Corbusier referred to the news of gold being discovered around Nome, which led to a second rush in the summer of 1899 that carried over into 1900.

5. Mrs. Corbusier's depression was lightened by the arrival of her youngest son home from the military school. She recorded, "Everything goes on here in the same dull routine only broken for me by the letters I receive from my dear ones and friends. Will came for his vacation Friday. How glad I was to see him." FDC, "Diary," June 8, 1900, p. 109.

6. Freedom George Shepard was born on July 4, 1844, in Onondaga, New York. His father, David Booth Shepard, was an associate founder of the firm Nichols & Shepard, the makers of heavy steam driven farm equipment. "Nichols & Shepard," website.

7. Mrs. Corbusier remarked at this time, "Summer comes today, but not Will." FDC, "Diary," June 30, 1900, p. 110.

8. Dr. Corbusier had to remain in quarantine for one day before he was allowed to leave San Francisco. FDC, "Diary," July 19, 1900, p. 111.

9. On July 19, 1900, Mrs. Corbusier learned that Harold (Hal) was being sent to China instead of the Philippines to be part of the China Relief Expedition. Hal participated in the China Relief Expedition, which grew out of the Boxer Rebellion. Linn, *The Philippine War*, 207–208.

10. On July 25, 1900, Mrs. Corbusier joyfully noted in her diary, "Our darling boy Phil received his commission—rather was commissioned today second lieu-

tenant, Ninth United States Cavalry. I knew he would get it even when things seemed dark. My own darling, how hard I tried to get it for him." FDC, "Diary," July 25, 1900, p. 113.

11. The years of separation and being on the sidelines as an observer, not a participant, had clearly been trying for Mrs. Corbusier. She had confided to her diary her anguish that her loved ones were in harm's way, and her despair over being a guest in her mother-in-law's home: "I have been so lonely here. No one to talk about the things we all like—no one to discuss a book—never see anyone except those in the house or someone I would rather not see as I have nothing at all in common with them." She ended her diary entries with, "Dear old Papa home. His mother feared she would never see him again." FDC, "Diary," June 3, 1900, p. 107; July 28, 1900, p. 113.

Chapter 25. "The Most Beautiful Blue I Had Ever Seen"

1. General and Mrs. Mills had lost their only son Anson on February 25, 1894, to an attack of appendicitis. Mrs. T. C. Orndorff was Nannie Mills's sister. Mills, *My Story*, 210, 317.

2. The whole of Governors Island, located in the upper bay of New York harbor at the entrance of the East River, was reserved for military purposes. Fort Columbus, which occupied the center of the island, was the headquarters of the Department of the East and the principal recruiting service depot. A permanent stonework, the fort proper consisted of four large brick and stone buildings, with officers' quarters in the building on the left of the parade. Billings, *Circular Number Eight*, 15.

3. Officers as well as enlisted personnel suffered from the pressures of wartime service in a tropical climate. Their malaise probably resulted from the "cumulative and debilitating effects of physical exhaustion, inadequate diet, temperatures well above 100°F, and malaria and various forms of dysentery upon men working under great stress." Gillett, *The Army Medical Department*, 216.

4. Louise and Ida were the fiancées of Harold and Philip, respectively.

5. Lake Sunapee lies about fifty miles northwest of Concord, New Hampshire. At the turn of the nineteenth century, affluent city-dwellers from Boston, New York, and other eastern cities boarded at the lake's large hotels, village inns, and farmhouses. New London–Lake Sunapee Region, "Our History," website, par. 1–2.

6. Harold, now Dr. Corbusier, had been sent to China in July 1900. He then returned to the Philippines and rotated back to the United States in August 1902. Heitman, *Historical Register*, 2:274.

7. Major General Adna R. Chaffee had succeeded Major General Arthur MacArthur as commanding general in the Philippines on July 4, 1901. On February 4, 1901, Chaffee had been promoted to major general in the regular army. He succeeded Brooke as the commanding general of the Department of the East,

and thus had the right to request Dr. Corbusier's transfer. Heitman, *Historical Register*, 1:292.

8. Trottie was Mrs. Corbusier's Aunt Mary Dunbar.

9. Harold Dunbar and Louise Shepard Corbusier would be the parents of three daughters, Frances, Barbara, and Nancy. Harold Dunbar Corbusier, *A Boy at Fort Mackinac*, 97.

10. Fort Crook, established in 1891, was located eight miles south of Omaha. Named in honor of Major General George Crook, Fort Crook is now known as Offutt Air Force Base. Frazer, *Forts of the West*, 86.

11. Fort Logan, near Denver, was established in 1887 as part of a government effort to reduce the number of small western posts and to concentrate soldiers in areas with good rail transportation. Named for Major General John A. Logan, it was a subpost of Lowry Air Force Base. Ibid., 39.

12. The Pali is a majestic three thousand foot cliff located on the windward side of the island of Oahu. The Punch Bowl, which overlooks Honolulu, is a circular tuff cone produced by volcanic activity. Since 1949 it has been the National Cemetery of the Pacific. Mrs. Corbusier was mistaken in her reference to Mauna Loa. The Corbusiers were in Honolulu for only two days (August 9–11), and it took a day and a half to get from Oahu to Hawaii, where the volcano is located. She probably meant either of the two extinct volcanoes that make up the island of Oahu. Winslow, *Fort DeRussy Days*, 93; Pager and Pager, *Hawaii*, 76–85.

13. Midway Atoll is comprised of Sand, Eastern, and Spit islands plus their encircling coral reef. Captain N. C. Middlebrooks discovered Midway on July 5, 1859, and Captain William Reynolds took possession of the islands for the United States on August 28, 1876.

14. Boatswain birds, so named because their shrill calls remind sailors of a boatswain's whistle, are a type of tropicbird widespread over warm tropical and subtropical seas. They are distinguishable by their long central tail feathers. Midway Atoll National Wildlife Refuge, "Quick Reference to Seabirds: Tropicbirds," website.

15. Mrs. Corbusier was right about it being Monday rather than Sunday, but this means they added, rather than dropped, a day.

Chapter 26. "No te vayas de Zamboanga"

1. San Luis d'Apra was the harbor for Agana, the most important city in Guam. At the beginning of the Spanish-American War, Captain Henry Glass of the USS *Charleston* along with the transports *City of Peking*, *City of Sydney*, and *Australia* left Hawaii and diverted to Guam, where they took the island without the Spanish defenders' firing a shot. Francis Addison Corbusier was a corporal in Company K of the First California Volunteers on the *City of Peking* at this time. McSherry, "The Capture of Guam," website.

2. William T. Corbusier pursued this interest in philately throughout his life, even publishing articles on different types of stamps. William T. Corbusier, "The Swastika in Philately."

3. David Dean O'Keefe was a naturalized American citizen from Ireland who in 1871 survived the shipwreck of the *Belvedere* off the coast of Yap (West Carolines). He set up a string of copra trading stations on Yap, Belau, and Mapia and soon dominated that trade, becoming known as the King of the Caroline Islands. He was married at least twice and left behind several children when he was lost as sea in a typhoon in 1901, also leaving behind a fortune of at least half a million dollars or more. "Beachcombers, Traders, and Castaways," website.

4. The lights Mrs. Corbusier mentioned were probably from light houses or buoy markers. Raps are cross currents.

5. The Cable Ship *Hooker* led a very eventful life during its twenty-five years. Originally a Spanish ship, it was captured and sold to the U.S. government for use as a transport. After fulfilling that duty, it was fitted out permanently as a cable ship and went aground on the island of Corregidor during its first mission. Mary Godwin, "Cable Ship Hooker," personal e-mail message to editor, August 13, 2001. See also Haigh, *Cableships and Submarine Cables*, 285–288.

6. William Howard Taft, later U.S. president, had led the Philippine Commission and was the civil governor of those islands from 1901 to 1904.

7. Iloilo is the principal city of the island of Panay, which is located in the Visayas, the second of three major island groups that comprise the Philippines. Linn, *The Philippine War*, 15.

Camp Jossman on Guimaras was named for Second Lieutenant Albert Lee Jossman, who died on July 28, 1902, from wounds he received at the Battle of Bayan on May 2, 1902. Heitman, *Historical Register*, 1:584.

8. Camp Overton was the headquarters of the Fourteenth Cavalry, of which Philip Corbusier was then a lieutenant. Heitman, *Historical Register*, 1:327.

9. The fort, originally named San José, was renamed Real Fuerza de Nuestra Señora del Pilar de Zaragoza in honor of the event Mrs. Corbusier described. The shrine today attracts both Christians and Muslims. "Zamboanga City History," section titled "1700 A.D., Divine Intervention and Expansion," website.

10. *Los Pastores*, or the *Miracle Play of the Shepherds*, commemorate the birth of Jesus Christ.

The Moros are members of any of the various tribes of Muslim Malays living, primarily, in the southern Philippines, centered in Mindanao and Sulu.

11. The Philippine Constabulary was created in July 1901 under Captain Henry T. Allen, who was detached to civil service from the army to establish a civil police force in the Philippines. Linn, *Guardians of Empire*, 19.

12. The Rumboughs were Captain and Mrs. David J. Rumbough. Heitman, *Historical Register*, 1:851.

13. Moro resistance fighters (or pirates, depending on one's perspective) took religious oaths, or *juramentos*, to kill as many Christian invaders as possible and used fierce long knives and swords to do so. Linn, "The Long Twilight," 161–162.

14. Surgeon Davis was assigned to duty on the *Sheridan* to care for those military personnel being transported to and from the Orient. Gillett, *The Army Medical Department*, 208.

15. Mrs. Corbusier's visit to Nagasaki fulfilled a long-held desire to visit Japan. Mogi is a city directly south of Nagasaki.

16. Fort Mansfield was located at Napatree Point near Watch Hill in the extremely southwestern part of Rhode Island. Heitman, *Historical Register*, 2:522.

17. Sometime between December 1896 and July 1905, Claude had broken his engagement to Mildred M. Hilliard of Louisville and had become betrothed to Belle DeLong. Earlier, while still in Alaska carrying the mail, Claude had spent some time in the home of Moravian missionaries, Herman and Ella Romig. Mrs. Romig was favorably impressed by Claude, saying that he was a very nice young man, "in fact I think the nicest one who ever happened along here." FDC, "Diary," December 1896, p. 70; Romig, *When the Geese Come*, 77.

18. Mrs. Corbusier was meeting more Marine Corps officers' wives because the Corps stationed more personnel in the Philippines after their Boxer expedition returned from China in mid-1901. Linn, *The Philippine War*, 207–208.

Henry O. Bissett, from Harrodsburg, Kentucky, attended the Naval Academy, exercised the Marine Corps option, and rose to major before he retired in 1908. E. R. Cole also graduated from the Naval Academy, transferred to the Marine Corps in 1890, and rose to major general in 1924. Service Records, United States Marine Corps, Marine Corps Historical Center, Reference Section (Code HDH-2).

Chapter 27. "They Came in Vintas Decorated with Red and White"

1. The almendro tree is *Prunus dulcis*, a kind of almond.

2. The term "swalley" applied to the bamboo mats that were woven together.

3. The "golden shower" trees have cascades of brilliant yellow flowers that blossom during the dry season in the Pacific islands. The leaves and seedpods are used for medicinal purposes, and green twigs can be used as a fresh vegetable. The Spanish flags (bandera de España), hearts of Mary and Jesus (corazon de Maria and corazon de Jesus)and the Queen's carpet (alfombra de reina) are tropical flowers. Caroline Shunk said that when the fire-tree bloomed, it signaled the time for headhunters to seek their "gruesome trophies." Shunk, *Army Woman in the Philippines*, 86.

4. Major General Wood was the commander of the Department of Mindanao and governor of Moro Province. He was expected to bring the same kind of civil order to Moroland as he had brought to the administration of Cuba. Lane, *Armed Progressive*, 118–119.

5. The sultan of Sulu was the "nominal religious and political leader of the Moros." The dattos were hereditary tribal rulers, but among the Moros then, as now, there was no unit cohesion other than their common religion. Vintas are Moro sailing vessels, equipped with bright sails and outriggers. Lane, *Armed Progressive*, 119–120.

6. Captain Finley had transferred to the Twenty-seventh Infantry on August 18, 1902. He served as military governor of Zamboanga and attempted to administer and enforce the civil codes that Major General Woods had established in Moroland. Lane, *Armed Progressive*, 121–123.

7. Siasi Island lies in the Tapul Group of Islands south of Sulu. Bongao, located on Twai Twai, was the southernmost settlement in American possession at that time. Cagayan Sulu Island lies in the Sulu Sea southeast of Puerto Princesa, a coastal city on Palawan Island. Linn, *The Philippine War*, 4.

8. All these posts were located on the island of Mindanao. Fort Pikit had been a Spanish fort previously. WHC, "Memoirs," 129–130.

9. Luke Wright had served as deputy to William H. Taft and had succeeded him as governor of the Philippines. Linn, *The Philippine War*, 320.

10. In February 1904, the Japanese suddenly attacked and destroyed the Russian fleet at Port Arthur, China. In a move foreshadowing Pearl Harbor thirty-seven years later, the Japanese had transported and disembarked one hundred thousand soldiers in secret. Linn, *Guardians of Empire*, 84.

11. This was probably retired Major General George Whitfield Davis, who understood the difficulty of defeating the Moros. He retired July 26, 1903. Heitman, *Historical Register*, 1:358.

Chapter 28. "Home, Sweet Home"

1. Established on June 3, 1770, by Captain Gaspar de Portolá, the Presidio of San Carlos de Borromeo was situated on Monterey Bay adjacent to the town bearing that name. The United States occupied Monterey on July 7, 1846, and the post was officially designated the Presidio of Monterey in 1904. The installation is still in use, being, among other things, the home of the Defense Language School. Frazer, *Forts of the West*, 27.

2. According to a recent depiction of the calamity, the earthquake and fire resulted in the deaths of at least ten thousand individuals in the San Francisco area. Kurzman, *Disaster!* 248–249. For an eyewitness description of the San Francisco earthquake and fire, see Mahin, *Life in the American Army*, 118–120.

3. In the aftermath of the earthquake and fire, some insurance companies became insolvent because they could not pay out the $300 million claimed as lost. This was only about one-half of the actual value, and often compensation was between five and ten percent of the policy's stated value. Kurzman, *Disaster!* 251.

4. Augustus Greely, who appeared on several occasions throughout Mrs. Corbusier's "Recollections," played a part in the aftermath of the San Francisco earthquake. Kurzman, *Diaster!* 237.

5. In February 1901, Congress provided for one dentist per thousand soldiers up to a maximum number of thirty with the rank of lieutenant, and on March 3, 1911, Congress created the Dental Corps with sixty dental surgeons. Gillett, *The Army Medical Department*, 321, 326–327. Dental surgeons were not included in Heitman's *Historical Register.*

6. Forts Liscum, Seward, Egbert, Gibbon, St. Michael, and Davis, located at strategic points throughout Alaska, were six of the eleven forts established in Alaska during the gold rushes between 1897 and 1904. Heitman, *Historical Register*, 2:494–524.

7. Doctors William and Charles Mayo were the sons of Dr. William Worrall Mayo, who in 1863 went to Rochester, Minnesota, to examine men being inducted into the Union Army. In 1865, he began his private practice, which was joined by his sons in 1883 and 1888. From this combined practice the Mayo Clinic grew. "The Mayos," website, par. 1–3.

8. Philip Corbusier was then teaching in the Reserve Officers' Training Corps program at the University of Kentucky. The act of 1866, which established the organization of the post–Civil War army, authorized the president to detail as many as "twenty officers to teach military science in institutions of higher learning." The Morrill Act of 1862 provided for military instruction in land grant colleges. Matloff, gen. ed., *American Military History*, 290.

9. The Corbusiers went to Bermuda to conduct genealogical research on Dr. Corbusier's family, who had settled in Bermuda before his grandfather James Henry Corbusier relocated in New York City in 1805. Mackenzie, "The Corbusier Family," 108–110.

Chapter 29. *"And Looked Out at the Moon and Stars"*

1. The Corbusiers were conducting the research that would result in "Ancestry of William Henry Corbusier, Lieutenant Colonel, United States Army Retired, and Fanny Dunbar Corbusier, His Wife," of which he made a copy for each of his sons and deposited a copy in the New York Public Library in 1912.

2. This was the second daughter of Harold Dunbar and Louise Shepard Corbusier.

3. This was the only son of Philip Worthington and Ida Edwards Corbusier, and Dr. and Mrs. Corbusier's only grandson.

4. This was the first daughter of William Tremaine and Mabel Haller Corbusier. They would later have a second daughter in 1917 and move to California, where both Frank and Claude had settled. WHC, "Memoirs," 153.

5. The genealogy of the Dunbars and Robinsons is located in the library of the Maryland State Historical Society and also contained in William Henry

Corbusier, "Ancestry of William Henry Corbusier." Also see Knox, "The Longer View," 9–12.

6. Eugénie M. Fryer published *The Hill-Towns of France* in 1917.

7. Fanny Corbusier and Nannie Mills had become fast friends during their time together at Fort Grant and had enjoyed their trips to Hospital Flats, the mountain camp built on the slopes of Mount Graham. Mills, *My Story*, 189–195.

In his tender descriptions of his wife's final illness, death, and burial, Dr. Corbusier revealed a depth of caring not manifested in any other of his writings.

BIBLIOGRAPHY

Manuscripts

Cairns, William B. William B. Cairns Collection. River Fall Manuscripts, Q. University of Wisconsin–River Falls Area Research Center, River Falls, Wisconsin.

Corbusier, Fanny Dunbar. "Diary of Fanny Dunbar Corbusier from January 1892 to August 1900," 29–114. In possession of her granddaughter Nancy Corbusier Knox, Santa Fe, New Mexico.

———. "Recollections of Her Life in the Army, by Fanny Dunbar Corbusier, Wife of William Henry Corbusier, Lieut. Colonel, United States Army, A Retired Deputy Surgeon General, 1918." In possession of the editor.

Corbusier, William Henry. "Ancestry of William Henry Corbusier, Lieutenant Colonel, United States Army Retired, and Fanny Dunbar Corbusier, His Wife." New York Public Library, 1912. Copy courtesy Arlene M. Goff.

———. "Memoirs of William Henry Corbusier, Colonel, U.S. Army Retired," 1926. In possession of the editor.

Davis, Helen. Letters to Alice Grierson, 1887. Available at Fort Davis National Historical Site, Fort Davis, Texas. Also available in Benjamin H. Grierson Papers, 1827–1941. Southwest Collection. Texas Technological University, Lubbock, Texas.

Goff, Arlene M. *Modified Register for Jan Dircksen Myers Meyer, Ancestor of Mahala Myers.* Copy prepared for editor.

Knox, Nancy Corbusier. "The Longer View: George Towers Dunbar, 1812–1848 [1850]." Maryland Historical Society Library, Annapolis, Maryland; also in possession of editor.

Government Documents

Billings, John S. *Circular Number Four: A Report on Barracks and Hospitals with Descriptions of Military Posts.* Washington, D.C.: Government Printing Office, 1870. Surgeon General's Office. Records of the War Department. National Archives, Washington, D.C.

———. *Circular Number Eight: Hygiene of the United States Army.* Washington, D.C.: Government Printing Office, 1875. Surgeon General's Office. Records of the War Department. National Archives, Washington, D.C.

Correspondence Relating to the War with Spain and Conditions Growing Out of the Same, Including the Insurrection in the Philippine Islands and the China Relief Expedition between the Adjutant General of the Army and Military Commanders in the United States, Porto Rico, China and the Philippine Islands: From April 15, 1898 to July 30, 1902. 2 vols. Washington, D.C.: Government Printing Office, 1902.

"General Orders 92." *Index of General Orders, 1870*. Washington, D.C.: Government Printing Office, 1871. Records of the Adjutant General's Office, Record Group 94, National Archives, Washington, D.C.

Heitman, Francis B. *Historical Register and Dictionary of the United States Army, 1789–1903*. 2 vols. Washington, D.C.: Government Printing Office, 1903.

Medical History of Fort Grant, Arizona, Book No. 690 (November 1884–October 1888), 31–193. Records of the Adjutant General's Office, Record Group 94, National Archives, Washington, D.C.

Medical History of Fort Mackinac, Michigan, Book No. 152, (April 1882–September 1884), pp. 53–98. P.I. No. 17, entry 547, book no. 152. Records of the Adjutant General's Office, Record Group 94, National Archives, Washington, D.C.

Powell, J. W., dir. *Fourteenth Annual Report of the Bureau of Ethnology, 1892–1893*. Washington, D.C.: Government Printing Office, 1896.

Twelfth Decennial Census. Chemung County, New York, 1900. Vol. 1. Washington, D.C.: Government Printing Office, 1904.

United States Marine Corps. Marine Corps Historical Center, Reference Section (Code HDH-2), Washington Navy Yard, Washington, D.C. Service Records of Major Henry O. Bissett, Major General E. R. Cole, Brigadier General Charles L. McCauley, and Colonel Lawrence H. Moses.

Books and Articles

Allen, Charles W. "Red Cloud and the United States Flag." In *Nebraska Indian Wars Reader, 1865–1877*, edited by R. Eli Paul, 113–121. Lincoln: University of Nebraska Press, 1998.

Altshuler, Constance Wynn. *Cavalry Yellow and Infantry Blue: Army Officers in Arizona between 1851 and 1886*. Tucson: The Arizona Historical Society, 1991.

"The Association of American Physicians," *Journal of the American Medical Association*, 36 (May 11, 1901): 1–3.

Athearn, Robert G. *The Denver and Rio Grande Western Railroad: Rebel of the Rockies*. Lincoln: University of Nebraska Press, 1977.

Ball, Eva, with Nora Henn and Lynda A. Sánchez. *Indeh: An Apache Odyssey*. Norman: University of Oklahoma Press, 1988.

Biddle, Ellen McGowan. *Reminiscences of a Soldier's Wife*. Philadelphia: J. B. Lippincott and Company, 1907.

Bigelow Jr., Lieutenant John. *On the Bloody Trail of Geronimo*. Los Angeles: WesternLore Press, 1968.

Billington, Ray Allen. *The Far Western Frontier, 1830–1860*. New York: Harper and Row, 1956.

Bloom, Lansing B., ed. "Bourke on the Southwest." *New Mexico Historical Review* 9 (January 1934): 33–77; 9 (July 1934): 159–183; 10 (January 1935): 1–35.

Bourke, John Gregory. *On the Border with Crook*. Glorieta, N.Mex.: Rio Grande Press, 1971.

Boyd, Mrs. Orsemus B. *Cavalry Life in Tent and Field*. New York: J. S. Tait, 1894.

Boyer, Ruth McDonald, and Narcissus Duffy Gayton. *Apache Mothers and Daughters*. Norman: University of Oklahoma Press, 1992.

Bronson, Edgar Beecher. *Reminiscences of a Ranchman*. Lincoln: University of Nebraska Press, 1962.

Brown, Dee. *The Gentle Tamers: Women of the Old Wild West*. New York: G. P. Putnam's Sons, 1958.

Buecker, Thomas R. *Fort Robinson and the American West, 1874–1899*. Lincoln: Nebraska State Historical Society, 1999.

Byrne, Bernard James. *A Frontier Army Surgeon: Life in Colorado in the Eighties*. New York: Exposition Press, 1962.

Canfield, Gae Whitney. *Sarah Winnemucca of the Northern Paiutes*. Norman: University of Oklahoma Press, 1988.

Carlson, Paul H. *"Pecos Bill": A Military Biography of William R. Shafter*. College Station: Texas A&M Press, 1989.

Carr, Captain Camillo C. C. *A Cavalryman in Indian Country*. Dan L. Thrapp, ed. Ashland, Ore.: Lewis Osborne Press, 1974.

Carriker, Robert. *Fort Supply, Indian Territory: Frontier Outpost on the Plains*. Norman: University of Oklahoma Press, 1970.

Carriker, Robert C., and Eleanor R. Carriker, eds. *An Army Wife on the Frontier: The Memoirs of Alice Blackwood Baldwin, 1867–1877*. Salt Lake City: University of Utah, 1975.

Carter, Lieutenant Colonel W. H. *From Yorktown to Santiago with the Sixth U.S. Cavalry*. Austin, Tex.: State House Press, 1989.

Casebier, Dennis G. *Camp Beale's Springs and the Hualpai Indians*. Norco, Calif.: Tales of the Mohave Road Publishing Company, 1980.

Caughey, Bruce, and Dean Winstanley. *The Colorado Guide*. Revised edition. Golden, Colorado: Fulcrum Press, 1991.

Cleaveland, Agnes Morley. *No Life for a Lady*. Lincoln: University of Nebraska Press, 1977.

Coffman, Edward M. *The Old Army: A Portrait of the American Army in Peacetime, 1784–1898*. New York: Oxford University Press, 1986.

Connell, Evan. *Son of the Morning Star: Custer and the Little Big Horn*. San Francisco: North Point Press, 1984.

Corbusier, Harold Dunbar. *A Boy at Fort Mackinac: The Diary of Harold Dunbar Corbusier, 1883–1884, 1892*. Phil Porter, ed. Mackinac, Mich.: Mackinac State Historic Parks, 1994.

Corbusier, William T. "The Swastika in Philately." *The Stamp Specialist: Green Book*, 119–123. New York: H. L. Lindquist, 1943.

———. "Camp Sheridan, Nebraska." *Nebraska History* 42 (January 1961): 29–53.

———. *Verde to San Carlos: Recollections of a Famous Army Surgeon and His Observant Family on the Western Frontier, 1869–1886*. Tucson, Ariz.: Dale Stuart King, 1968.

Cott, Nancy F. *The Bonds of Womanhood: "Woman's Sphere" in New England, 1780–1835*. New Haven: Yale University Press, 1977.

Cox-Paul, Lori A., and James W. Wengert, comps. *A Frontier Army Christmas*. Lincoln: Nebraska State Historical Society, 1996.

Cozzens, Peter. *The Shipwreck of Their Hopes: The Battles for Chattanooga*. Urbana: University of Illinois Press, 1994.

Custer, Elizabeth B. *Following the Guidon*. Norman: University of Oklahoma Press, 1966.

Davis, Britton. *The Truth about Geronimo*. M. M. Quaife, ed. New Haven: Yale University Press, 1963.

Delo, David Michael. *Peddlers and Post Traders: The Army Sutler on the Frontier*. Salt Lake City: University of Utah Press, 1992.

Dobak, William A. "Licit Amusements of the Enlisted Men in the Post–Civil War Army." *Montana, the Magazine of Western History* 45 (Spring 1995): 34–45.

Dodge, Richard Irving. *The Powder River Expedition*. Wayne R. Kime, ed. Norman: University of Oklahoma Press, 1997.

Essin, Emmett M. *Shavetails and Bellsharps: The History of the U.S. Army Mule*. Lincoln: University of Nebraska Press, 1997.

Faulk, Odie B. *Crimson Desert: Indian Wars of the American Southwest*. New York: Oxford University Press, 1974.

Fellman, Michael. *Citizen Sherman: A Life of William Tecumseh Sherman*. New York: Random House, 1995.

Fisher, Barbara E., ed. "Forrestine Cooper Hooker's Notes and Memoirs on Army Life in the West, 1871–1876." M.A. thesis, University of Arizona, 1963.

FitzGerald, Emily McCorkle. *An Army Doctor's Wife on the Frontier: Letters from Alaska and the Far West, 1874–1878*. Abe Laufe, ed. Pittsburgh: University of Pittsburgh Press, 1962.

Frazer, Robert W. *Forts of the West: Military Forts and Presidios and Posts Commonly Called Forts West of the Mississippi River to 1898*. Norman: University of Oklahoma Press, 1965.

Fryer, Eugénie M. *The Hill-Towns of France*. New York: E. P. Dutton and Company, 1917.

Gillett, Mary C. *The Army Medical Department, 1865–1917*. Washington, D.C.: Government Printing office, 1995.

Goddard, Pliny Earle. *Indians of the Southwest*. New York: Cooper Square Publishers, 1975.

Goldwater, Barry M., and Jack Casserly. *Goldwater*. New York: St. Martin's Press, 1990.

Greene, Jerome A. *Yellowstone Command: Colonel Nelson A. Miles and the Great Sioux War, 1876–1877*. Lincoln: University of Nebraska Press, 1994.

Grinnell, George Bird. *The Fighting Cheyennes*. Norman: University of Oklahoma Press, 1955.

Hagan, Kenneth J. *This People's Navy: The Making of American Sea Power*. New
York: The Free Press, 1991.

Haigh, K. R. *Cableships and Submarine Cables*. Worcester and London: Ebenezer Baylis & Son: 1968.

Hart, Herbert M. *Old Forts of the Northwest*. New York: Bonanza Books, 1963.

———. *Old Forts of the Far West*. New York: Bonanza Books, 1965.

Hebard, Grace Raymond. *Washakie: Chief of the Shoshones*. Lincoln: University of Nebraska Press, 1995.

Hein, Lieutenant Colonel O. L. *Memories of Long Ago*. New York: G. P. Putnam's Sons, 1925.

Hern, Chester G. *When the Devil Came Down to Dixie: Ben Butler in New Orleans*. Baton Rouge: Louisiana State University Press, 1997.

Herringshaw, Thomas William. *Herringshaw's Encyclopedia of American Biography of the Nineteenth Century*. Chicago: American Publishers Association, 1902.

Higgins, Cindy. "History of Brewing in Kansas." *Kansas History* 16 (Spring 1993): 2–21.

Hittman, Michael. *Corbett Mack: The Life of a Northern Paiute*. Lincoln: University of Nebraska Press, 1996.

Hollon, W. Eugene. *Beyond the Cross Timbers: The Travels of Randolph B. Marcy, 1812–1887*. Norman: University of Oklahoma Press, 1955.

———. *The Southwest Old and New. The Far Southwest: 1846–1912, A Territorial History*. Lincoln: University of Nebraska Press, 1973.

Hopkins, Sarah Winnemucca. *Life Among the Piutes: Their Wrongs and Claims*. Mrs. Horace Mann, ed. Reno: University of Nevada Press, 1994.

Hutton, Paul Andrew. *Phil Sheridan and His Army*. Lincoln: University of Nebraska Press, 1986.

Hyde, George E. *A Sioux Chronicle*. Norman: University of Oklahoma Press, 1993.

Johnson, Allen, and Dumas Malone, eds. *Dictionary of American Biography*. Vol. 3. New York: Charles Scribner's Sons, 1961.

Johnson, Robert U., and Clarence C. Buels, eds. *The Way to Appomattox*. Vol. 4, *Battles and Leaders of the Civil War*. New York: Castle Books, 1956.

Jones, Katharine M., ed. *Heroines of Dixie: Winter of Desperation*. New York: Ballantine Books, 1975.

Kachadurian, Thomas. *Views of Mackinac Island*. Chelsea, Mich.: Sleeping Bear Press, 2000.

Karolevitz, Robert F. *Doctors of the Old West: A Pictorial History of Medicine on the Frontier*. New York: Bonanza Books, 1967.

Kurzman, Dan. *Disaster! The Great San Francisco Earthquake and Fire of 1906*. New York: HarperCollins, 2001.

Lamar, Howard R. *The Far Southwest: 1846–1912, A Territorial History*. New York: W. W. Norton and Company, 1970.

Lane, Jack C. *Armed Progressive: General Leonard Wood*. San Rafael, Calif.: Presidio Press, 1978.

Leckie, Shirley A. *Elizabeth Bacon Custer and the Making of a Myth*. Norman: University of Oklahoma Press, 1993.

Leckie, Shirley A., ed. *The Colonel's Lady on the Western Frontier: The Correspondence of Alice Kirk Grierson*. Lincoln: University of Nebraska Press, 1989.

Leckie, William H., and Shirley A. Leckie. *Unlikely Warriors: General Benjamin Grierson and His Family*. Norman: University of Oklahoma Press, 1984.

Lewis, Arthur H. *La Belle Otero*. New York: Trident Press, 1967.

Lindquist, H. L., ed. *The Stamp Specialist: Green Book*. New York: H. L. Lindquist, 1943.

Linn, Brian McAllister. "The Long Twilight of the Frontier Army." *The Western Historical Quarterly* 27 (Summer 1996): 140–167.

———. *Guardians of Empire: The U.S. Army and the Pacific, 1902–1940*. Chapel Hill: University of North Carolina Press, 1997.

———. *The Philippine War, 1899–1902*. Lawrence: University of Kansas Press, 2000.

Long, E.B. *The Civil War Day by Day: An Almanac, 1861–1865*. Garden City, NY: Doubleday and Co., 1971.

Mackenzie, George Norbury, ed. "The Corbusier Family." In *Colonial Families of the United States, 1607–1920*, vol. 1. New York: Grafton Press, 1907.

Mahin, Mauree P. *Life in the American Army from the Frontier Days to Army Distaff Hall*. Washington, D.C.: Baker-Webster Printing Company, 1967.

Mails, Thomas E. *Fools Crow*. New York: Avon Books, 1979.

Matloff, Maurice, gen. ed. *American Military History*. Washington, D.C.: Government Printing Office, 1969.

Mattes, Merrill J. *Indians, Infants and Infantry: Andrew and Elizabeth Burt on the Frontier*. Denver: The Old West Publishing Company, 1960.

Mayer, Melanie J., and Robert N. DeArmond. *Staking Her Claim: The Life of Belinda Mulrooney, Klondike and Alaska Entrepreneur*. Athens: Ohio University Press, 2000.

McChristian, Douglas C. *An Army of Marksmen: The Development of the United States Army Marksmanship in the Nineteenth Century*. Fort Collins, Colorado: The Old Army Press, 1981.

McCracken, Harold, ed. *Frederic Remington's Own West*. New York: Promontory Press, 1960.

McGillycuddy, Julia B. *McGillycuddy, Agent: A Biography of Dr. Valentine T. McGillycuddy*. Stanford University, Calif.: Stanford University Press, 1941.

McVeigh, Amy. *Mackinac Connection: The Insider's Guide to Mackinac Island*. Mackinac Island, Mich.: Mackinac Publishing, 1998.

Miller, Darlis. *Soldiers and Settlers: Military Supply in the Southwest, 1861–1885*. Albuquerque: University of New Mexico Press, 1989.

Mills, Anson. *My Story*. C. H. Claudy, ed. 2nd ed. Washington, D.C.: Press of Byron S. Adams, 1921.

Monnett, John H. *Tell Them We Are Going Home: The Odyssey of the Northern Cheyennes*. Norman: University of Oklahoma Press, 2001.

Mooney, James. *The Ghost Dance*. North Dighton, Mass.: JG Press, 1996.

Morris, Donald R. *The Washing of the Spears: A History of the Rise of the Zulu Nation under Shaka and Its Fall in the Zulu War of 1879*. New York: Simon and Schuster, 1965.

Nacy, Michele J. *Members of the Regiment: Army Officers' Wives on the Western Frontier, 1865–1890*. Westport, Conn.: Greenwood Press, 2000.

Oliva, Leo E. *Fort Hays, Frontier Army Post, 1865–1889*. Topeka: Kansas State Historical Society, 1980.

Olson, James C. *Red Cloud and the Sioux Problem*. Lincoln: University of Nebraska Press, 1975.

Pager, Sean, and Sheryl Groden Pager. *Hawaii: Off the Beaten Path*. Guilford, Conn.: The Globe Pequot Press, 2002.

Paul, R. Eli, ed. *The Nebraska Indian Wars Reader, 1865–1877*. Lincoln: University of Nebraska Press, 1998.

Peery, Thomas Martin, and Frank Nelson Miller Jr. *Pathology: A Dynamic Introduction to Medicine and Surgery*. 2nd ed. Boston: Little Brown and Company, 1971.

Porter, Joseph C. *Paper Medicine Man: John Gregory Bourke and His American West*. Norman: University of Oklahoma Press, 1986.

Price, George F. *Across the Continent with the Fifth Cavalry*. New York: Van Nostrand, 1883.

Prucha, Francis Paul. *Guide to the Military Posts of the United States, 1789–1895*. Milwaukee, Wisc.: The North American Press, 1964.

Quebbeman, Frances E. *Medicine in Territorial Arizona*. Phoenix: Arizona Historical Foundation, 1966.

Reinhardt, Richard. *Out West on the Overland Train: Across the Continent Excursion with Leslie's Magazine in 1877 and the Overland Trip in 1967*. Secaucus, N.J.: Castle Books, 1967.

Rickey Jr., Don. *Forty Miles a Day on Beans and Hay: The Enlisted Soldier Fighting the Indian Wars*. Norman: University of Oklahoma Press, 1963.

Romig, Ella Mae Ervin. *When the Geese Come: The Journals of a Moravian Missionary, Ella Mae Ervin Romig, 1898–1905, Southwest Alaska*. Phyllis Demuth Movius, ed. Fairbanks: University of Alaska Press, 1997.

Rugoff, Milton. *The Beechers: An American Family in the Nineteenth Century*. New York: Harper and Row, 1981.

Russell, Don. *Campaigning with King: Charles King, Chronicler of the Old Army*. Paul L. Hedren, ed. Lincoln: University of Nebraska Press, 1991.

Sackett, S. J. "The History of the Volga Germans in Ellis and Rush Counties, Kansas." *Heritage of Kansas* 9 (Spring, Summer 1976): 3–6.

Sandoz, Mari. *Cheyenne Autumn*. New York: Avon Books, 1972.

Scott, Lalla. *Karnee: A Paiute Narrative*. Greenwich, Conn.: Fawcett Publications, 1973.

Sherman, William T. "The Grand Strategy of the Last Year of the War." In *The Way to Appomattox*. Vol. 4, *Battles and Leaders of the Civil War*, eds. Robert U. Johnson and Clarence C. Buel, 247–259. New York: Castle Books, 1956.

Shunk, Caroline S. *An Army Woman in the Philippines and the Far East: Extracts from Letters of an Army Officer's Wife, Describing Her Personal Experiences in the Philippine Islands*. Kansas City, Mo.: Franklin Hudson Publishing, 1914.

Smith, Page. *Trial by Fire: A People's History of the Civil War and Reconstruction*. New York: McGraw Hill Book Company, 1982.

Stallard, Patricia Y. *Glittering Misery: Dependents of the Indian-Fighting Army*. Norman: University of Oklahoma Press, 1992.

Steinbach, Robert H. *A Long March: The Lives of Frank and Alice Baldwin*. Austin: University of Texas Press, 1989.

Sternberg, Martha L. *George Miller Sternberg: A Biography*. Chicago: American Medical Association, 1920.

Tanner, John. *A Narrative of Captivity and Adventures of John Tanner during Thirty Years Residence among the Indians in the Interior of North America*. Edited by Edwin James. 1830. Reprint, with an introduction by Louise Erdrich, New York: Penguin, 1994.

Tate, Michael L. *The Frontier Army in the Settlement of the West*. Norman: University of Oklahoma Press, 1999.

Teed, Ida. "Army Life on the Frontier." *Pacific Monthly* 2 (April 1890): 16–31.

Terrell, John Upton. *The Navajos: The Past and Present of a Great People*. New York: Harper and Row, 1972.

Thrapp, Dan L. *Al Sieber: Chief of Scouts*. Norman: University of Oklahoma Press, 1995.

———. *The Conquest of Apacheria*. Norman: University of Oklahoma Press, 1967.

Utley, Robert M. *The Last Days of the Sioux Nation*. New Haven: Yale University Press, 1969.

———. *Frontier Regulars: The United States Army and the Indian, 1866–1891*. New York; Macmillan Publishing Company, 1973.

———. *Frontiersmen in Blue: The United States Army and the Indian, 1848–1865*. Lincoln: University of Nebraska Press, 1981.

Van Orman, Richard A. *A Room for the Night: Hotels of the Old West*. New York: Bonanza Books, 1964.

Welter, Barbara. "The Cult of True Womanhood: 1820–1860," *American Quarterly*, 18(1966): 151–174.

Widder, Keith R. *Reveille Till Taps: Soldier Life at Fort Mackinac, 1780–1895*. Mackinac, Mich.: Mackinac State Historic Park, 1994.

Winslow, Anne Goodwin. *Fort DeRussy Days: Letters of a Malihini Army Wife, 1908–1911*. M. Winslow Chapman, ed. Honolulu: Folk Press, Kapiolani Community College, 1988.

Winther, Oscar Osburn. *The Transportation Frontier: Trans-Mississippi West, 1865–1890*. Albuquerque: University of New Mexico Press, 1974.

Wooster, Robert. *Nelson A. Miles and the Twilight of the Frontier Army*. Lincoln: University of Nebraska Press, 1993.

Zanjani, Sally. *Sarah Winnemucca*. Lincoln: University of Nebraska Press, 2001.

Newspapers

Auburn (New York) Daily Advertiser, 1895

Detroit Evening News, 1893

Detroit Free Press, 1893

Elmira Daily Advertiser, 1907

Harper's Weekly, 1881

New York Times, 1869, 1908, 1998

New York Herald, 1869, 1881

San Francisco Morning Call, 1880

San Francisco Chronicle, 1927

Online Sources

Ancestry.com. "Corbusier, William Henry." *A National Register of the Society Sons of the American Revolution, 1901.* <http://search.ancestry.com/cgi-bin/sse.dll?srvr=search&Databaseld=3072&db=sevnr&acat>. By subscription only. (April 21, 2001).

"Beachcombers, Traders, and Castaways in Micronesia: Yap." *Micronesia Seminar.* <http://www.micsem.org/pubs/articles/historical/bcomber/yap.htm>. (June 21, 2002).

"Burrows, Julius Caesar." *Biographical Directory of the United States Congress.* 1988. <http://bioguide.congress.gov/scripts/biodisplay.pl?index=B001142>. (October 30, 2002).

Carroll, Charles. "Maryland's Brave 400 at Long Island," *National Society of the Sons of the American Revolution.* <http://www.sar.org/history/MDatLI.htm>. (December 20, 2002).

"Chandler, Zachariah, 1813–1879." *Biographical Directory of the United States Congress.* 1988. <http://bioguide.congress.gov/scripts/biodisplay.pl?index=C000299>. (October 4, 2001).

Corliss, William R. "Ball Lightning Studies." *Science Frontiers Online,* 71, (Sep.– Oct. 1990): 2. <http://www.science-frontiers.com/sf071/sf071g17htm>. (April 9, 2001).

"The Creed of Alpha Tau Omega." *Alpha Tau Omega Online.* <http://www.ato.org/ATO/NATIONAL/HISTORY/ATOCREED.shtml>. (October 2, 2001).

"Delta Upsilon." *Delta Upsilon International Fraternity Online.* <http://www.deltau.org>. (October 2, 2001).

"Frequently Asked Questions about the Aurora: I Seem to Recall Seeing the Aurora a Long Time Ago—Did I?" *Poker Flats Research Range.* <http://www.pfrr.alaska.edu/aurora/INDEX.HTM>. (October 27, 2002).

The Hannah More School. "History." <http://www.hannahmore.org/history.htm>. (May 29, 2001).

"Haskell's History." *Lawrence.com.* <http://www.lawrence.com/visitors/haskell.html>. (December 3, 2002).

"Harrison Phoebus Leaves His Legacy." *Hampton Roads Ticket*. <http://hrticket. com/top/1,1419,N-HRTicket-History-X!ArticleDetail-6605,00.htm>. (May 29, 2001).

"Hobson, Richmond Pearson, 1870–1937." *Biographical Directory of the United States Congress*. 1988. <http://bioguide.congress.gov/scripts/biodisplay.pl? index=H000667>. (October 8, 2001).

Huntington, Tom. "The Great Feud," in *American History: The Magazine of the American Experience*. (August 1998). <http://americanhistory.about.com/ library/prm/blgreatfeud1.htm?terms=tom+huntington>. (October 18, 2002).

Knight, Glenn B. "Brief History of the Grand Army of the Republic." *Sons of Union Veterans of the Civil War*. <http://suvcw.org/gar.htm>. (September 17, 2001).

Lenzen, Connie. "Diseases of the Ancestors." *Diseases and Illnesses*. <http:// www.oregonvos.net/~clenzen/diseases.html>. (October 4, 2001).

Livingstone County, Michigan, GenWeb Project. "John J. Bagley." *Michigan Genealogy on the Web: Portrait and Biographical Album*. <http://www.livgenmi. com/PBjjbagley.htm>. (October 2, 2001).

"Loud, Eugene Francis, 1847–1908." *Biographical Directory of the United States Congress*. 1988. <http://bioguide.congress.gov/scripts/biodisplay.pl?index= L000448>. (June 2, 2001).

"Markets." *NY Food Museum*. <http://www.nyfoodmuseum.org/market.htm>. (August 29, 2001).

"The Mayos." *Rochester, Minnesota History*. <http://www.rochesterusa.com/History.html>. (November 5, 2001).

McSherry, Patrick. "The Capture of Guam," *The Spanish American War Centennial Website*. <http://www.spanamwar.com/Guam.htm>. (October 31, 2001).

———. "The Transport Service," *The Spanish American War Centennial Website*. <http://www.spanamwar.com/transports.htm>. (August 13, 2001).

———. "USS Charleston," *The Spanish American War Centennial Website*. <http:// wwww.spanamwar.com/charleston.htm>. (October 8, 2001).

Midway Atoll National Wildlife Refuge. "Quick Reference to Seabirds and Shorebirds of Midway Atoll NWR: Tropicbirds." <http://www.r1.fws.gov/midway/wildlife/quickref.html#tropicbird>. (January 9, 2003).

"Montezuma's Well." *Road Trip America*. <http://www.roadtripamerica.com/ places/Montezum.htm>. (August 16, 2001).

National Register of Historic Places. "Parke-Davis and Company Plant and Research Laboratory." *Travel Itinerary, Detroit*. <http://www.cr.nps.gov/nr/ travel/Detroit/dethome.htm>. (October 30, 2002).

Newman, Harry Wright. "John Tolley Worthington." *Anne Arundel Gentry; A Genealogical History of Twenty-Two Pioneers of Anne Arundel County, Md. and Their Descendants*. <http://home.att.net/~rWorthington/AA_Gentry/AA_ Gentry_4-John Tolley.htm>. (June 30, 2001).

New London–Lake Sunapee Region. "Our History." <http://www.newlondon-areanh.com/history.htm>. (June 4, 2001).

The New York Military Academy. "Our History." <http://www.nyma.org/
pages/sitepage.cfm?id=6>. (June 2, 2001).

"Nichols & Shepard, Founders and Factory, 1920." *Historical Images of Battle Creek, Michigan.* <http://www2.Willard.lib.mi.us/bcphotos/industries/r05_0483. htm>. (October 26, 2001).

Paine, Albert Bigelow. *Mark Twain: A Biography* (New York: Harper & Brothers, 1912; BoondocksNet Edition, 2001). <http://www.boondocksnet.com/ twaintexts/biography/>. (August 3, 2001).

"Perkins, George Clement, 1839–1923." *Biographical Directory of the United States Congress.* 1988. <http://bioguide.congress.gov/scripts/biodisplay.pl?index= P000232>. (June 1, 2001).

Rappaport, Edward N., and José Fernandez-Partagas. "The Deadliest Atlantic Tropical Cyclones, 1492–Present." *National Centers for Environmental Prediction.* Appendix 2, 16. <http://www.nhc.noaa.gov/pastdeadlya2.html>. (October 3, 2001).

Robinson, John W. "Tiburico Vasquez in Southern California." *Dogtown Territorial Quarterly.* 27 (Fall, 1996): 14. <http://www.californiahistory.com/sample. html>. (September 9, 2000).

Schoenberg, Dan. "Madison Square Garden History," *Radio City Entertainment.* <http://www.radiocity.com/b3d.html>. (December 17, 2002).

Sisters Healthcare. "About Sisters Healthcare." <http://www.sisters-buffalo.org/ home/about/educational/residency>. (October 27, 2002).

"Stockbridge, Francis Brown, 1826–1894." *Biographical Directory of the United States Congress.* 1988. <http://bioguide.congress.gov/scripts/biodisplay.pl?index= S000932>. (June 1, 2001).

"Turner, Erastus Johnson." *Biographical Directory of the United States Congress.* 1988. <http://bioguide.congress.gov/scripts/biodisplay.pl?index=T000419>. (September 23, 2001).

University of Wisconsin-Madison, Memorial Library. "The William B. Cairns Collection of American Women Writers, 1650–1920." <http://www.library. wisc.edu/libraries/Memorial/cairns.htm> (May 26, 2001).

"US Dog Tags: Past, Present and Future." *Military-Dog Tags.* <http://www.military-dogtags.com/id19_m.htm>. (October 10, 2001).

The Virtual Office of the Surgeon General. "History of the Office of the Surgeon General." <http://www.surgeongeneral.gov/library/history/sghist. htm>. (September 29, 2001).

"When Old Point Was a Resort." *Hampton Roads Ticket.* <http://hrticket.com/ top/1,1419,N-HRTicket-History-X!ArticleDetail-6649,00.html>. (October 4, 2001).

Worthen, Dennis B. "The Pharmaceutical Industry, 1852–1902." American Pharmaceutical Association. <http://www.aphanet.org/about/sesquisept00.html>. (December 17, 2002).

"Zamboanga City History." *Zamboanga.com.* <http://www.Zamboanga.com/ html/history_Zamboanga.htm>. (October 17, 2001).

INDEX